"All through my tenure as Music Director of the Los Angeles Philharmonic one name stood out whenever singing in the movies or engaging a soprano of real professional caliber was concerned: Marni Nixon! Any aspiring professional singer reading this book will have tremendous insight into the life of a singer with a deep understanding of musical life in Hollywood."

ZUBIN MEHTA

"What a delicious book! Marni tells her story straight from the heart with great candor and personal courage. It made me laugh and it made me cry. A "must read" for anyone interested in the inner workings of some of Hollywood's most famous musicals."

RUSS TAMBLYN

"As breezy, high-spirited, and candid as a conversation with Marni herself. The 'ghosting' turns out to be only one facet of a sparkling, many-faceted career. What other singer has worked with everyone from Arthur Godfrey to Leonard Bernstein, from Stravinsky to Liberace? An illuminating, funny, touching, and deeply human story."

SHELDON HARNICK

"I was fascinated by this book. You will be, too. Marni Nixon's Hollywood story is unique and, besides all that, she's a nifty lady. Don't miss out on this one."

BARBARA COOK

"This book is the story of an extraordinary woman's life and career, and it provides an intimate look at the often-mysterious workings of the inner world of American film, music, and theater. Marni Nixon has excelled at everything she's ever undertaken and in giving us this book she not only provides an enjoyable read . . . she also produces a valuable documentation of a most colorful period in the history of Hollywood."

JOHN WILLIAMS

"Marni Nixon is a legend in the entertainment business. Now with the publication of *I Could Have Sung All Night* the wonderful person behind the legend appears in full and radiant dimension. A joy to read."

LEONARD NIMOY

"Marni has created a compelling chronicle of her extraordinary musical life, one that is replete with diverse legends from Stravinsky and Bernstein to Audrey Hepburn and Julie Andrews. Her personal story is moving, exciting, and inspirational, and she shares it with wit, candor, and heart."

MICHAEL FEINSTEIN

"*I Could Have Sung All Night* is a great book about a great singer and above all a great lady."

SHIRLEY JONES

"Who would have thought that Marni Nixon, whose prodigious talents for singing, acting, and recording have made an indelible mark in the history of musical theater, would have an equal talent for writing what amounts to a marvelous personal history of the Golden Age of the form? Here, singing in quite a different key, Ms. Nixon gives us a warm, affectionate, and utterly unique perspective on the shows, movies, and personalities who, together with her, created so much of our treasured history. It is a wonderful read."

MAURY YESTON

"Marni Nixon's exquisite voice both behind and in front of the curtain has long been a part of the American consciousness. This wonderful book places Marni herself in the spotlight, where she so rightly belongs."

TREAT WILLIAMS

"The only word to fit Marni Nixon is PHENOMENAL! Has any singer ever had such a command of both serious and popular styles as Marni? How many sopranos illuminate both Arnold Schoenberg and Richard Rodgers with such loving attention to detail and such respect for style? Her underlying honesty makes her compelling as an interpreter, and funny and tough in her recounting of personal tragedies and successes. And it's a wonderful story of a three-dimensional woman, of survival with joy intact. Bravissima!!"

JOAN MORRIS AND WILLIAM BOLCOM

"Marni Nixon is a simply unmissable feature on the map of the musical theater. And her story is typically an insight into sheer musicianship as well as a practical guide to grace. Her book has the same quality as working with her - the feeling that you are being let in on a tremendous secret. And you are. It's a story that ought to give renewed courage to anyone who aspires to work in the theater or film."

DAVID LEVEAUX

"Marni Nixon is one of the most talented musicians ever to have worked in Hollywood. It's hard to imagine so many of the great movie musicals without her."

RANDY NEWMAN

"Marni Nixon, whose magnificent voice dubbed the singing voices of Deborah Kerr, Audrey Hepburn, and Natalie Wood, made them sound great. That's because she's great!

KAYE BALLARD

"Marni Nixon is a legend."

CHRISTOPHER WALKEN

I Could Have Sung All Night

MY STORY

Marni Nixon

WITH STEPHEN COLE

FOREWORD BY
Marilyn Horne

BILLBOARD BOOKS
an imprint of Watson-Guptill Publications
NEW YORK

Executive Editor: Bob Nirkind
Editor: Meryl Greenblatt
Design: Jay Anning, Thumb Print

Copyright © 2006 by Marni Nixon
Paperback edition first published in 2007 by Billboard Books
an imprint of Watson-Guptill Publications, Nielsen Business Media,
a division of The Nielsen Company
770 Broadway, New York, New York 10003
www.watsonguptill.com

Library of Congress Control Number: 2007930409

ISBN-13: 978-0-8230-9968-9
ISBN-10: 0-8230-9968-7
Printed in the United States of America
First printing, 2007

1 2 3 4 5 6 7 8 9 / 14 13 12 11 10 09 08 07

TO MY PARENTS, MY CHILDREN,
AND MY GRANDCHILDREN.

CONTENTS

LIST OF PHOTOGRAPHS

ACKNOWLEDGMENTS

WHEN I FINALLY SAT DOWN to the gigantic task of writing the story of my life, I was tempted to thank everyone from my first-grade teacher to the delivery boy at Fairway Market. They all had a hand in shaping the story of this memoir, but lack of space forces me to concentrate on the people without whom this book would never have come to be. If I left you out, please forgive me.

Family is what life is about and I have been blessed. My forthright, honest, strong, supportive, and hard-working Midwestern parents gave me not only life and the tools to succeed; my prescient mother even left a sheaf of handwritten memories and letters that helped me reconstruct my earliest years. She always knew that I would write this book and wanted to make sure I got it right! My elder sisters Donyll and Adair were incredible at helping me fill in the blanks of my childhood and putting our parents' characters into perspective. My younger sister Ariel (Midge) and my cousin Nelda were also invaluable in offering their recollections as well. My grown children have been endless sources of inspiration and memories. They are, in order of appearance: Andrew Maurice Gold, musician, funnyman, contemporary artist, and insightful record producer; Martha Alice Carr, marvelous psychotherapist and holder of the family's Communication Central Award; and Melani Christine Gold, massage therapist par excellence and certified Hellerwork Practitioner. I am indebted to them and their respective spouses, Dr. Richard Carr and Dr. Howard Friedman.

For helping me plant the seed for this book I must thank the talented J.T. Smith, who lent a hand in the writing and presentation of my one-woman show, *Marni Nixon: The Voice of Hollywood*, at The Little Old School House Theatre in Sanibel Island, Florida. My appreciation also goes to director Alan Bailey and musical director Alex Rybeck. Without them, this book may not have seen the light. And for his help and support and great humor (not to mention great negotiating skills!) over all the years I have known him (too many to count) I humbly thank and give my love to Hal Gefsky, who has never let me stay in a hotel when I am in L.A. and never let me go hungry.

With prescience of my own, I have kept every clipping and program from my long career, but it is thanks to several assistants that these exist in an orderly fashion in what I like to call my archives. These orderly and talented people include Maryann Lopinto, Sarah Wytko, Jeff Hoffman, Laura Koeneman, Jenny Millsap, and most recently Ariane Reinhart. When something needed to be looked up, it's thanks to them that it was where it should be.

I want to thank all the photographers, who are listed with each photo, with a special thanks going to Robert Easterla and Andy Bandit at Twentieth Century Fox for their help in securing a couple of key shots. My gratitude also goes to Nancy Vega, who transcribed hours of interview tapes and actually said she enjoyed listening to them. And, although they had nothing directly to do with the book, I must thank my extended Seattle family, including Andrea and Bruce Lorig, all my *Boomerang* and Cornish cohorts, Geri Sorrentino and Ron Hoefer, and of course all my talented students through the years.

Not to forget the wonderful doctors, surgeons, and staff of the various hospitals who fixed, healed, and attempted to cure me during my cancer treatments and shoulder-replacement operations. Without them I might not be here to write this book at all!

My literary agent Andrea Pedolsky has stood by me during the ups and downs of writing, rewriting, not writing, and everything else that goes with such a project. I am grateful to have found her and grateful that she led me to Bob Nirkind, Executive Editor, whose care and patience and belief in this project have helped sustain it and me for the years it has taken to come to fruition. Bob is fun, funny, and contagiously enthusiastic. His astute comments have helped to shape this book and I am truly grateful. Bob also introduced me to our delightful and smart Editor, Meryl Greenblatt, and she has been every bit as diligent and dear. How lucky that they are also husband and wife! So much easier to get them both on the phone after working hours! My agent Andrea also deserves an extra thank you for finding my ghost writer (or co-author) Stephen Cole, who has managed to merge his voice with mine and has been fun to work with to boot. Stephen has brought his talent as a dramatist to this work and has enriched the telling of my story, without ever once losing my voice. How could I not be grateful?

Finally, I need to thank my patient and sometimes-impatient ("Is this book ever going to be finished?") husband, Albert David Block. He has been there through it all and I hope he thinks it was worth it.

FOREWORD

I WAS TWELVE WHEN MARNI AND I FIRST MET in 1946, and I was so in awe of her, with her pure high soprano voice and her absolute pitch. She was the star of the Los Angeles Concert Youth Chorus, which my sister Gloria and I had just joined. The Youth Chorus was supported by the Los Angeles Bureau of Music (just imagine!), and its conductor was Roger Wagner, who commanded such respect that our name was soon changed to the Roger Wagner Chorale. He was to the West Coast what Robert Shaw was to the East Coast, and with Roger at the helm we toured the world. We were good, and Marni stood out like a beacon!

It's hard to remember all of the musical endeavors in which we were involved around Southern California during the subsequent years, but I remember that at one point Marni, Gloria, and I formed a trio. I think we were pretty fine, but we didn't keep at it very long. Remember, we were all still going to school and doing God knows how many other activities, with music being predominant.

Cut to the dubbing years. We were all involved in it constantly at various movie studios in Hollywood, mostly in choruses, and sometimes as a solo here and there. My sister and I lived in Long Beach, which was a real schlep in those days before the freeways. Still, I suspect we traveled faster than it would take us today with the impossible congestion on those "free" roads. The studio work lasted all day, including the several hours that we were required by law to attend the studio school, where it was lots of fun to meet the child stars from the lot.

I don't know for sure, but I am guessing that Marni was involved in studio work even more than Gloria and I. My zenith came with *Carmen Jones*, which I dubbed for Dorothy Dandridge when I was twenty. At the same time, I remember trying out for *The King and I*. Guess who got it? (I did manage to snag the part of one of the eight ladies who sing "Small House of Uncle Thomas.")

Background music and dubbing were a part of our singing lives, but not of greater importance than the concerts and operas in which we sang as well. My guess is that the legendary films in which Marni provided her dubbing support brought to her a special fame that today is heightened even more. But in addition to her film work, Marni has had a long and distinguished career in classical music that makes her even more amazing. She was on the brink of a career in classical music in those days, and her reputation grew not only as a concert and opera singer, but also as a terrific actress. She sang, among other things, that very difficult role of Zerbinetta in *Ariadne auf Naxos*, by Richard Strauss, with great success.

Whatever her decisions were in her career choices, Marni has had a "great go"! She is still a buddy, after (are you ready for this?) sixty years. We don't see each other nearly enough, but when we do I feel that special connection reserved for old friends who have experienced a bond that is unique—performing together. That tie is so strong. A few months ago I had a vivid dream about Marni. Would you believe she called the next morning to ask me to write this little remembrance? Now that's a real connection!

MARILYN HORNE

OVERTURE

GHOSTS. THEY COME IN ALL FORMS, SHAPES, AND SIZES. SOME PEOPLE believe that ghosts are the spirits of the dead come back to haunt us. There are those who fear them and those who long to see them materialize their entire lives.

I became famous for being one.

Taking a cue from a song from the Irving Berlin musical *Call Me Madam*, a clever writer for *Time* magazine once dubbed me "The Ghostess with the Mostest." This was because my fame was derived from "ghosting," or dubbing, the singing voices of Deborah Kerr, Natalie Wood, and Audrey Hepburn in the film versions of *The King and I*, *West Side Story*, and *My Fair Lady*, respectively. Many, many times this "fame" threatened to turn *me* into a ghost. Being known for only one small aspect of your life can sometimes make the rest of who you are and what you do appear to be invisible. Like a ghost.

But at 2:15 P.M. on August 20, 2004, as United Flight 21 ascended into the sky over New York's JFK Airport, other ghosts decided to make their appearances.

The call from the Academy of Motion Picture Arts and Sciences (better known as the people who give out the Oscars) had come two weeks earlier. The voice on the phone was Ellen Harrington, whose official title is Exhibitions Curator and Special Events Programmer. She told me that the movie version of *The King and I* had been restored to its original "Cinemascope 55" glory and asked whether I would be the guest of honor at the Samuel Goldwyn Theater in Beverly Hills for the first screening in this format in nearly fifty years.

The 1950s was the period when Hollywood was doing the only thing it could do to fight the threat of television's growing popularity: making movie screens bigger, better, and more sumptuous sounding. Everything was in Cinemascope, Technicolor, Stereo, Todd-AO, Cinerama . . . or to top it off (so they thought) . . . Cinemascope 55! Only two films (*The King and I* and *Carousel*, both, coincidentally, adapted from musicals by Rodgers and Hammerstein) had ever been shot in this then-innovative wide-screen process (55 millimeters wide instead of the normal 35), which allowed for greater depth and scope of picture and sound. Neither had ever been shown in its original ratio. Until now.

Although my professional life was hectic as usual (directing students in scenes from operas and musicals that would culminate in performances on Saturday night), after some careful planning and scheduling it was decided I would be plucked from my present-day New York City world Friday afternoon and returned in time to see the fruition of our work on Saturday night. In between I would confront the past.

It was as if fate took my hand and said, "Marni, it's time for some circles to be completed."

Usually I sleep on long plane trips, using the time to wind down from New York's frantic pace. But this Friday afternoon my mind was racing as I anticipated the momentous evening with great joy, while at the same time tried to figure out what on earth I was going to say. I was to be interviewed after the film was screened, as I had been interviewed a hundred times before. But how could I be interesting telling the same old stories? Did anyone really care anymore about how Deborah Kerr and I worked together to achieve the one voice that came out of her lips on the screen? Did anyone even remember who Deborah Kerr was? After mulling over dozens of questions and answers that might be posed, I decided to let go of my anxieties and just enjoy the event. I would not worry about controlling the situation. This was not an easy task, but it was one I had been working on for years.

As I put my head against the pillow I always carried on long flights, the ghosts began to emerge, playing out vignettes from my life. Looking out the window at the white clouds, scenes from my childhood appeared in my mind as if on cue.

There was my mother coming home to 5141 Chesley Avenue in L.A. after pawning her diamond engagement ring so she could pay for my voice lessons. Suddenly she was replaced with my first husband, composer Ernest Gold, playing the piano for me as I sang in the Hollywood Hills house we built together. Then my father and three sisters materialized and we practiced making music as a "family orchestra" on a makeshift stage in our living room at the house near the lima bean fields on Charlene Drive.

There was little Marni at age four, demanding to play the violin. And there she was at sixteen as one of the first soloists in the Roger Wagner Chorale. Then, in a flash, she was driving to Warner Bros. Studios with Audrey Hepburn to work on *My Fair Lady*. Like a film montage underscored with a dramatic score (there was always music), one scene faded as another took its place.

Whenever I return to L.A. (and with my three children living there it is frequently) many emotions hit me, but for some reason, along with my joyful anticipation the feeling that overpowered the others on that smooth flight was one of great, great pain.

Was it the memory of the end of my nineteen-year marriage to Ernest? Was it the loss of continuation of what could have still been out there? Or was it just L.A.? For so many years it had been like a paradise to me. And each time I visited it had changed so much. As Thornton Wilder reminds us in *Our Town*, when you are in paradise, you never seem to know it at the time. Was it the pain, then, of loss? Was it the realization that nothing would ever be the same, that you cannot always have what you want? This was a new concept for the woman who was raised by my mother.

Before I knew it, the announcement was made to stow our trays, put our seatbacks to their upright positions, and fasten our seatbelts. We were landing in L.A. The place I used to call home.

The driver from Empire International Limos had a handwritten sign reading: MARNIE NIXON. Like others before him, he had misspelled my made-up name.

Before I was born Mother was determined and confident she would have a boy to name David. Although my father usually went along with her, he was prepared just in case with her first name (Margaret) and his second (Nixon). So when I surprised my mother by being a girl (she already had two of those), that's what I was named: Margaret Nixon McEathron. But, as usual, mother was prepared, too. She didn't want mother and daughter to get mixed up, so she took the *Mar* of *Mar*garet and combined it with *ni* of *Ni*xon and I was nick-named Marni. She said it came from a poem she would read to my older sisters: "Marni Mitchell. Marni Moo. Marni darling, I love you." Nice and easy, except when it came to others spelling it.

I got into the limo, thoughtfully arranged for me by the Academy, and let myself be embraced by the plush leather of the backseat. The driver, with the euphonious and strangely evocative name of Mark Marcellino, was very talkative and utterly delightful. As we spoke, something about his name was stirring my memory. He avoided the freeway and told me he was going to drive us on a back route so he could get me where I was going on time.

Before I knew it we were in Culver City, driving on Motor Avenue right past what used to be MGM Studios and now belongs to Sony Pictures.

Suddenly there I was in 1947, seventeen years old and entering the gates for the first day of my job as a "messenger girl." I delivered mail and took VIPs on guided tours of the back lot. If I made up enough gossip about the stars (whom I never really met) I would get a $20 tip! Believe me, for $20 I made up plenty of gossip! As a perk, I could watch recording sessions and peek in on films being shot. And during my lunch hours I was given free singing lessons by Jane Powell's voice teacher. Years later Jane and I agreed that he was a lousy coach!

This was the very same MGM where I did my first dubbing job for child star Margaret O'Brien . . . in Hindu no less! This was where I did bit parts playing my violin at eleven years of age. I remember being in the background in films featuring Tony Martin, Deanna Durbin, Mickey Rooney, and Judy Garland. They all appeared as I watched the used-to-be studio that proclaimed they had "more stars than there are in the heavens" go by. How young they all were. How young I was.

As the limo sped along I thought, not only was I coming full circle, but the ghosts were taking me back to where it all really happened.

All during the ride Mark and I were jabbering away about me, *The King and I*, and Hollywood in general, until, out of the blue, he asked me if I had perhaps known his father, Muzzy Marcellino, the world-famous whistler. Did I? Of course I did! Now I knew why the name seemed so familiar.

Chances are, if you hear whistling on a TV or movie soundtrack from the fifties and sixties, it was Muzzy. (Like me, he had also dubbed for stars, most famously whistling for John Wayne in *The High and the Mighty*. And who could forget his poignant whistling of the theme for TV's *Lassie*?)

Thinking about Muzzy brought up the ghost of Ernest, with whom he had worked. Ernest was the father of my children, and out of the blue I found myself remembering our separations throughout the sixties and eventual divorce in 1969. I remembered getting pregnant with my third child and thinking, "He won't leave me now." As quickly as that ghostly memory arrived, it disappeared.

The journey to Beverly Hills continued. As Mark and I talked about the past and how we were connected, he turned onto Pico Boulevard and once again we drove past another piece of my history, Twentieth Century Fox Studios.

I hadn't asked him to take this route. What made him do it? "Well, this is the way," he said, "the secret back way I take when there's traffic on the freeway. We want to get you there on time, don't we?" I could see in the rearview mirror that as he spoke, he had a twinkle in his eye. I began to wonder if this was really an episode of *The Twilight Zone*. I decided to just let the memories all come flooding in. I willingly looked out the window. Into my past.

There was Marni at age twenty-five working with Deborah Kerr and vocal director Ken Darby to make *The King and I* one of the most seamless examples of dubbing in the history of musicals. There's Deborah and me, trading bars of music for "Shall I Tell You What I Think of You?" (filmed, cut, and now lost to the ages), each in our own glass-enclosed recording booth surrounded by that magnificent Fox orchestra. She would point to me and I would sing. I would point to her and she would . . . talk-sing. And suddenly we were making music.

As Twentieth Century Fox receded through the rearview window, the vision faded. But I was ecstatic. It was like everything from my past was flashing before my eyes. And I was coming home like a triumphant warrior.

But then, just before the Fox logo faded into the distance, another memory fell into my head, one from my early childhood. It brought up feelings of vulnerability, fear, and anger and I pushed it away. For now.

The limo approached the restaurant (Kate Mantilini in Beverly Hills) where I was to meet Ellen Harrington of the Academy and Schawn Belston, who worked for Twentieth Century Fox. Schawn actually did the restoration of the film and was going to interview me after it was screened. We had a marvelous time eating and chatting and plotting what we both wanted from the interview. I was told I would have ten minutes in the ladies room at the Academy to change my clothes, put on some makeup, curl my hair, and look glamorous for the photographers. Ten whole minutes! That is, if I didn't have dessert! Ah, the glamour of Hollywood!

When the dinner was over I was surprised that we were piled back into the limo for the two-block journey to the Academy of Motion Picture Arts and Sciences on Wilshire Boulevard. I was a New Yorker now and used to walking. The reason for riding and entering the building from the underground garage became clear when I looked out the tinted windows at masses of people lined up around the block, vying to get in for the screening. As it turned out, many of them couldn't. This evening was much more in demand than I had dreamed it would be.

Wisely, I had reserved a whole row of seats for my children and their guests. I wondered how they would react to this forty-eight-year-old movie that had Mom's voice in it. I wondered how *I* would react.

After Schawn gave an introductory speech and provided some technical details of the film's restoration, the lights went down and Richard Rodgers' brilliant "March of the Siamese Children" came out of the four speakers as the credits rolled across 55 millimeters of carefully restored film and soundtrack. There were the names: Deborah Kerr . . . Yul Brynner . . . Rita Moreno. My name was, of course, nowhere to be seen. This was something that might have been expected to irk me when the film was first released, but it was something I had come to terms with over time.

What I hadn't expected was the excitement of seeing the restoration. Every little detail was as clear and sharp as the day it was shot, from the opening shots of Deborah Kerr on the boat coming into the port of Siam to the presentation of the children on this opulent stage that was a replica of the 1863 Siamese Palace to the Jerome Robbins' exquisite "Small House of Uncle Thomas" ballet. The whole film was just spectacular.

And, of course, the songs, which have been ingrained in my head for so many years (I had done the role onstage several times after dubbing the film) came out of Deborah Kerr's lips as if she were right there before us singing in the best possible sound. You could not tell for an instant it was dubbed. I looked and listened to it all very objectively and wound up saying to myself, "Holy cats, I mean, this is really a good job." I had always known it was good, but in retrospect it really was more impressive than I remembered. And when the music for "Something Wonderful" swelled and the King died and "THE END" appeared on the screen, it was clear that the entire audience had the exact same experience as I had. We were all awash in tears and the film got an ovation that would gladden the heart of any stage performer.

As the lights came up Schawn entered, introduced me, and brought me up to the stage. The audience stood and cheered and as I passed by the row containing my children I realized that, although most of my career was spent on the stage singing both classical and show music, this film, this "secret job," was my legacy. This ghost was alive. Sometimes I resented being remembered for this and the other dubbing jobs, but I realized now that this was something that would outlive me. Something that would last.

Schawn was a wonderful interviewer, and all the stories and memories I feared would bore the audience enraptured them. But in the middle of it all, as I sat there next to a huge replica of "Oscar," I turned and looked at Schawn, who, to me, *was* Twentieth Century Fox. Suddenly I saw myself in 1956 at home in the Hollywood Hills getting a call from some executive at the studio after I had finished this, my first major dubbing job.

"If anyone ever finds out that you did any part of any of the singing for Deborah Kerr, we'll see to it that you never work again in this town."

And here I was forty-eight years later being honored! The only one being interviewed. The survivor. What a difference a lifetime can make. How ironic to now be the center of attention. And a little bit satisfying, too.

We spoke for so long there wasn't even time for a "Question and Answer" segment. And when it was all over I was mobbed by well-wishers, fans, friends, and two of the original cast members of the film who had come out to see it: Patrick Adiarte, who played Prince Chulalongkorn, and Jocelyn Lew, who, like me, was uncredited on the screen, but had portrayed the tiny Princess Ying Yaawolak, who begged Anna to stay when she threatened to leave. How wonderful to see them after all these years.

Knowing I had to get up at the crack of dawn, I realized I would have to forgo any celebration after the event. After saying good-bye to my kids and their friends, I was happy to get back to the home of my dear friend, and the agent who negotiated my original deal for my work on *The King and I* (another circle completed), Hal Gefsky.

For years, whenever I would come back to L.A., Hal would insist I stay in his wonderful Frank Lloyd Wright house (which used to be owned by movie stars John Hodiak and Wright's granddaughter, Anne Baxter) on Pinetree Place. With this day full of personal ghosts drawing to a close, it's interesting to note that this house in which I was to sleep that night is said to be haunted by the ghost of John Hodiak. In fact, several houseguests have seen him hovering outside a second story window and walking ten feet off the ground in the backyard. Hal had even told me he has gotten phone calls from the ghost, though he has heard only a faint hello. But looking out my window from my room over the garage, the only ghosts I saw were now memories of this amazing day.

Before I drifted off to sleep, one more of these memories came to call. This was the one I had pushed away earlier when the limo drove by the Fox Studio. Now it crept back into my consciousness.

I was five years old and going to school for the first time.

Even before I started kindergarten I had frequently accompanied my sisters as they walked to the 54th Street Elementary School, which was not far from our home on Chesley Avenue. Now that I was going to be going to school myself, my mother purposefully took me by the hand and showed me the way in a kind of practice walk I would take by myself to get home.

My mother felt strongly that all her children had to be very independent. And I was independent if nothing else! Mother always gave me responsibilities, which I welcomed. From an early age I always wanted to do things myself, perhaps because my mother was very forceful and I was a born rebel.

So after several practice walks, the big day came when I was to walk home from school by myself without her help. But on the way home I turned left on what I thought was my street, and it turned out to be another street I had never been on before. I felt a panic rush through my five-year-old body. I didn't know where I was. It was the first time I was aware of the feeling of vulnerability. Before that moment I thought I could do anything. Now I felt totally helpless.

And betrayed.

As I remembered these emotions I was also reliving them. Betrayed. But by whom? By my mother?

I remember having the feeling (and feeling it to this day) that I was too young to make these decisions about how to get home. I remember feeling she expected too much of me. I felt I just couldn't be everything that she wanted me to be.

I looked around and saw a big, green lawn that stretched up to a house on the hillside, and out of desperation I just laid down on that lawn and cried and cried for what seemed like an eternity. I was terrified, but beyond the tears was the feeling that I was just giving up; that I was lost. As I remembered and watched the ghost of little Marni, I realized that feeling that way must have been what it's like to die. Yes, that was the feeling. The awful and yet inevitable feeling when all the energy drains out of you.

Of course my mother eventually showed up. She had been worried when I didn't come home on time. She walked to the school and found that all the children had left. When she saw me weeping on the lawn she said, "Marni, what are you doing here? You turned the wrong way. I told you to turn up the other street." She was not unkind, but she was practical in her Germanic way. Still, I felt it was her fault. How could I be expected to know, to remember, to be perfect? Even then I knew that was what my mother expected: perfection.

The memory faded as I began to fall asleep. But my mother was in my dreams that night, too. In my dream she was not kindly, but angry. My subconscious had changed the reality of my mother into the way she had made me feel.

"That's not what we do," she yelled at me as the five-year-old Marni cried in my dream. "These are not the 'rules.' You don't goof. And you should have listened! Either you're perfect, Marni, or you're nothing!"

I woke up early the next morning and flew back to New York. Although the plane was late, I determinedly pulled my rolling suitcase behind me and walked into the auditorium just in time to see my students perform. As I willed them on to success and watched them striving for perfection, I thought back to my mother in the dream.

"Either you're perfect, Marni, or you're nothing!"

Perhaps some ghosts are not so quickly put to rest and some circles not so easily completed.

Chapter One

CALIFORNIA, HERE THEY COME!

"Every family has its own script that was written before you were born. If you could somehow manage to nudge this script forward a little here and there you'll be lucky."

MARGARET WITTKE MCEATHRON, 1985

SOUTHERN CALIFORNIA IN THE LATE 1920S was America's "promised land." Open spaces, combined with eternal sunshine, the smell of orange groves, and endless opportunities, made it seem like a utopia. Despite Prohibition, or perhaps because of it, America's economy was booming and, to many adventuresome visionaries, this golden coast represented their dream of tomorrow.

Once the big Gold Rush of the 1850s petered out, many of the prospectors moved on. For some, it was to silver mining in Nevada. For others, it was a move downstate to what were then considered the "cow counties" of Southern California.

The merciless sun baked the Southern California land hard, and many wondered if anything could grow under these conditions. Some of the new settlers speculated that orange trees might, perhaps, thrive in this environment and some were imported from North Africa. Dynamite was then used to blast holes in the ground for planting, and once it was figured out how to plunder water from the Colorado River and wherever else it could be found, the settlers learned they were right: oranges *could* be grown there (and have been ever since). All sorts of plant life were then imported from Africa, Brazil, and Argentina, and an artificial beauty quickly morphed the land into a kind of paradise. A real estate boom was the result.

It was inevitable that the fledgling film industry would leave the harsh East Coast winters and set up shop in California as well. Soon the small towns surrounding Hollywoodland (as it was called in those early years of the twentieth century) were filling new homes with families as quickly as the last shingle could be put on a roof.

It seems that ever since Horace Greeley said, "Go west, young man," whole populations took him to heart. In 1927, my parents, Charles Nixon

McEathron and Margaret Elsa Wittke McEathron joined the movement westward, driving everything they owned in a beat-up old Buick from Neenah, Wisconsin all the way to Altadena, California, stopping every once in a while to scrape the mud off the car. In the backseat of the Buick was my four-year-old sister, Donyll, and in the front, on Mother's lap, was two-year-old Adair.

In 1962, when Donyll saw the film version of the Broadway musical *Gypsy*, she recognized something of Mother in the pushy leading character of Rose. In Arthur Laurents' Broadway script, Rose is described as "a pioneer woman without a frontier." I'm sure that is exactly what Mother looked like in that Buick as the road stretched before her.

Mother (she was always Mother, never Mom, Mommy, or Ma to me) was born in Oconto, Wisconsin, on November 17, 1899. She used to say that she was always one year ahead of the century and proud of it. Born to German immigrants, Pauline Grashorn and Robert Wittke, and the youngest of five daughters (most of whom would have daughters of their own) and one son, Mother grew up in a matriarchal bilingual society. Most everyone in Mayville, Wisconsin (where her family eventually settled) spoke both English and German and, as Mother noted later, the women in her family were "talkers"! Mother grew up listening and learning from those strict Germanic Grashorn and Wittke women, and as she did, she gained the confidence and developed the need to control everything and everyone in sight.

As for my father, if I were casting the movie of my life, he would be played by Spencer Tracy. Daddy, who came from a long line of Nixons and McEathrons, was a strong, sturdy-bodied, straight-talking man with bushy auburn eyebrows that emphasized the Scottish twinkle in his eyes. The family name was originally spelled McEachern, but when his Scottish ancestors emigrated to Canada and founded the town of Perth, Ontario, the name on the land grant was misspelled McEathron. It remains that way to this day. Collectively, the Nixons and McEathrons were storytellers, performers, musicians, ministers, preachers, and farmers.

When my father's parents moved to Mayville from Ontario they encountered what must have seemed like a German enclave to them. The Scots were very much in the minority, although they soon acclimated themselves.

My parents met when Daddy was three and Mother was two. They quickly became each other's best friends. Mother always delighted in telling the story of how, when Daddy went to school for the first time at five years of age, she was so lonely without him that she followed him to the one-room schoolhouse and waited on the steps until he came out. After doing this day after day, the teacher (who was probably related to her . . . almost all of the women in her family were teachers) finally decided to let her in and she began school a year early. As they grew older, it was clear to everyone in the small midwestern town that Margaret and Charlie would eventually fall in love with each other and marry. Since that's exactly what happened, I'm sure my mother planned it precisely that way.

Mother loved Daddy for many things, but she always said that his greatest charm as a boy and young man was his beautiful voice. She could play the piano, but she envied Daddy's natural ability to sing. Although Daddy took his talent for granted, Mother was in love with anything musical. So when, in 1918, while my parents were still courting, Daddy's Uncle George Nixon enlisted two other singers and my second tenor of a father, and formed the Nixon Quartet, Mother was ecstatic. The Quartet sang all over the state, making very little money, but giving joy to all. After the Quartet broke up, Daddy's voice got him a job in a men's concert trio. Now Mother was really encouraged.

"At last," she said, "he has come into his own and can make a living at what he does so well!" She pictured him as a rising opera star. She pictured herself reveling in the reflected glory of it all.

Stardom was not to be, however. Daddy hated the one-night stands and the rushing from town to town. After a few weeks he was back in Wisconsin to look for what he called "a real job." My father felt that his business was business and Mother resigned herself to this being the way it was going to be. My older sister Donyll once remarked that she thought Mother would have been willing to starve in a garret if only Daddy would have tried for a singing career. After that, the only singing Daddy did was at church on Sundays, and he didn't much like that either. Nonetheless, music was to become the centerpiece of our family.

After they married in 1923 my parents moved to the nearby town of Neenah, Wisconsin and began to raise a family. Donyll was born in 1924 and Adair in 1926. In 1927, Daddy started scouting around for a new job and before long he had several offers to choose from. He had graduated college as an electrical engineer, but always loved cars. So when one of his several employment opportunities came from General Motors in L.A., Mother's eyes lit up. She had somehow always known that Neenah was too small and provincial to contain her dreams. For those she needed space and air and light. Like those prospectors of yore, she needed Southern California.

As it turned out, Mother and Southern California were made for each other.

After a long and exhausting car trip (this was before the big highways were built), the dusty, tired family finally arrived in Altadena. They moved their belongings into a rented Spanish-style house with two bedrooms and a big porch on Maiden Lane, which was actually the only paved road in the area and was cut into a large lemon grove.

Although Mother's relatives were Lutheran (as were most Germans of their class) and she and Daddy went to the Mayville Methodist Sunday School, where my grandfather, Fred McEathron, was a deacon, she spent her whole life searching for other, less-conventional, spiritual answers. In later years she would embrace anything remotely "New Age," including but not limited to extrasensory perception, extraterrestrials, reincarnation, and several Eastern philosophies. She came by this naturally, as her mother had encouraged all her children to think for themselves and choose their own beliefs.

In 1925, after my sister Donyll experienced a dramatic and, by all accounts, instantaneous healing from scarlet fever, Mother chose Christian Science (CS). Later, when I was growing up, Mother told us that CS stood for Common Sense, but in these earlier years, she truly believed and practiced what she preached. Christian Science teaches that we are all spiritual entities, and that the material body we carry around with us in this material world is just temporary. It is a reflection of how we think. In other words, if we get sick, it's just a problem with our "way of thinking," which we can correct with our minds. It took me a long time to realize that the guilt I felt every time I got sick stemmed from this philosophy, as I took each illness to be my fault.

Over the years, Mother not only told me the story of my birth, but also of my conception. She told these tales to me so many times and with so little variation that I began to feel as though I actually remembered the experiences myself. Not surprisingly, both my conception and birth involved Christian Science.

In 1929, Daddy's work in the Parts and Service Department of Chevrolet (a division of the parent company General Motors) sometimes sent him traveling to the towns outside of the Altadena area, and since his hotel and other expenses were part of the deal, Mother and my two sisters would sometimes tag along. It was during one of these trips to Santa Barbara that Mother and her friend May, an ardent believer in CS, discussed whether or not she and Daddy should have the son they both wanted now or wait. The two women evidently decided, as Mother later wrote, that this was "a good time and that my soul was waiting for a ripe, ready, and propitious vehicle for my advent." They were so right. Even if I didn't choose to be male!

So, in the last week of May 1929 in a hotel in Santa Barbara, California, thanks to the advice of my mother's Christian Science friend, I was conceived. Thank you, Mary Baker Eddy. Oh, yes—Daddy was in the room, too.

My mother's sister, Aunt Nell, had also embraced CS, and it was through her that Mother met Amy Young, an elderly practitioner whom Mother engaged to help her through her pregnancy and my birth. She, in turn, recommended a CS nurse who would be on call when the time came. Mother was determined never again to give birth in a hospital. In 1930, this decision was considered wild and dangerous.

As part of her training for my "advent," Mother was required to come to Amy's studio and study with her at least once a week for the last four months of her term. She would have poems and articles to read, passages to study, and ideas to discuss. It was during this time that Mother became obsessed with taking voice lessons. Although my father thought it nuts and the family really didn't have the extra money, he could never deny my mother anything. So she sang. Years later it was scientifically proven that the fetus acquires the mental and emotional knowledge and atmosphere the womb lives in. Mother must have known this instinctually, and later firmly believed that the richness of the environment surrounding me prior to my birth contributed to the person I wound up becoming. As I think about it, I wonder whether it's possible for the strong desires of the fetus to influence the parent, as well as the other way around. With my innate independence and strong will of my own, did I know I was going to be a singer when I was still in the womb? Probably.

As 1929 turned to 1930, the country and the world were steeped in an economic depression that began when the stock market crashed in late 1929. *Variety*, the show business "bible," proclaimed: "Wall Street Lays an Egg!" Banks were failing and jobs became scarce. No one really knew where it would all lead. Luckily for my family, Daddy still had his job with Chevrolet (and would keep it throughout the Depression) as my impending birth approached.

On Washington's Birthday in late February (in those days, still a legal holiday), my father was off at a meeting at the Ambassador Hotel in L.A. Since it was a day off from school and Mother wanted to rest (knowing I was due any day now), my sisters were sent to my Aunt Nell's for the afternoon. About 3:00 P.M. Mother woke up from a nap in the empty house way back in the lemon grove with a whopping labor pain, and before she could scream her water broke.

She immediately called the nurse, whose husband told Mother she was out on a shopping trip. Getting a little nervous now, she called my father's secretary, who promised to get a message to Daddy as soon as possible. Lastly, she called Amy, her saintly but ancient practitioner, who called the doctor whom Mother had never even met. After making the calls, Mother calmly tidied up the house and went back to bed. It was a rainy day and she felt cozy and warm under the covers, thinking that it might be hours before I made my debut. By 4:00 P.M., with no one yet in sight, as Mother put it:

"You wanted *out*! And *now*!"

Mother kept concentrating and hoping I would hang in there, but apparently I had other ideas. Just as my head started to appear, Mother sighted an umbrella bobbing by the open window. "Hurry, hurry," she screamed to whoever it was. It was Amy, who, on a hunch, had walked the two miles (all uphill . . . she was seventy-one!) after she got Mother's phone call. Throwing her umbrella down at the door, and without removing her raincoat, she grabbed me and pulled me out. "It's okay," soothed Amy as my mother drew a big sigh of relief. "It's okay, George Washington," she said to the baby. Then she took another look at me and realized I wasn't the long-expected boy. "I mean Martha Washington!"

Soon after, the nurse burst in followed by my frantic father, who had driven as fast as he could to get there before my birth. Ten minutes later the doctor arrived to find my mother calmly holding newborn, red-haired, wet-headed me in her arms. The time was 4:45 P.M. The doctor washed his hands, examined both of us, and signed the birth certificate, leaving mother and daughter to take a well-earned nap. My mother had never seen the doctor before and, after getting his bill for $40, she never saw him again. She wasn't married to a Scotsman for nothing.

———

Mother said she knew I would be an especially gifted child even before I was born but that it was not until I was eighteen months old that she truly got a glimpse into my future.

It was around this time in 1932 that Chevrolet promoted Daddy to district manager and transferred him to San Bernardino. Although today L.A. County seems to be one big city, in those pre-freeway days it was made up of many smaller towns. People lived where they worked, and as a district manager Daddy was needed to help out in other local divisions.

Our new rented home at 1250 F Street had a large screened-in sleeping porch, common to homes in that area of California in those pre–air conditioner days. My parents slept out there with me tucked happily in my crib next to them. My sisters shared a bedroom in the house.

Although I have no memory of it, my parents and both my sisters remember a strange incident that took place at this time. Every night, sometime between 1:00 and 3:00 A.M., I would stand up in my crib, grasp the high rail, and sway and sing at the top of my lungs. After three to five minutes I would apparently lie down and go soundly to sleep. Mother said this happened every night, like clockwork. The first time she heard it, she said, she awoke with goose bumps crawling up her arms. She had never heard anything quite like it. After a while, she and my father would just lie awake and listen to me "sing" until I went back to sleep. They decided I would either become a great opera star or another Aimee Semple McPherson, the popular evangelist of the day who preached in downtown L.A. This went on for six weeks and then stopped as suddenly as it had started, never to occur again. Years later, when I would ask my mother whether I may have just been crying, she would say, "No, it was *singing*—loud, clear, and melodic!"

The fading pictures of me as a toddler show a happy, chubby, round, freckled, curly-headed little girl wearing the little strapped shorts known as sunsuits. A bonnet to protect my fair skin from the harsh rays of the sun covers the

About a year old. "Doesn't anyone hear me?" (From the author's collection)

curly hair. In one particular picture there is a handwritten sandwich board plopped on my shoulders and over the sunsuit. The sign reads: PLEASE DON'T FEED ME.

According to my family, in those innocent suburban California days I was allowed to roam alone through the neighborhood. There were very few cars and the neighbors kept watch on me. Everyone on the block adored me, and since I was so friendly and cute they constantly gave me delicious sweets to eat, mostly cookies and candy. Mother, of course, being a woman ahead of her time, believed only in healthy food for her family. She heartily disapproved of our eating any of these unhealthy treats. Later on we even chewed bones (actually bone meal). Mother said, "If it's good for a dog's teeth, why not yours?" (To this day my sisters and I have our own teeth.) We also ate alfalfa, which we'd pick ourselves in the empty lots around our house. In those unenlightened days, people would say, "You're eating that cow food? Are you nuts?"

So when Mother would see three-year-old Marni returning home time after time with a big all-day sucker or a candy cane in her hand, she would be livid. She finally got the smart idea to make me wear the "PLEASE DON'T FEED ME" sign to discourage the cookie and cake givers. Despite her best efforts, though, I still managed to return with the occasional forbidden lollipop.

By now I had someone to share my candy with as well: a new little sister named Ariel Lea (Mother did have a way with names!), whom we always called Midge. Midge arrived in 1932, exactly two years and three months after I was born. This, Mother later pointed out, was the same interval of time between my two older sisters. Was she planning and controlling this as well? In any case, we were now a family of five females . . . and Daddy.

Every West Coast child can tell you about his or her first earthquake. Mine occurred on March 10, 1933 at 5:54 in the evening. The epicenter of the shock was about three and a half miles southwest of Newport Beach and extended along the Inglewood fault. Four deaths occurred in Orange County. In Santa Ana, a man and his wife raced out of the Rossmore Hotel and were crushed under an avalanche of bricks and mortar. Another man, walking in front of the Richelieu Hotel, was struck by a piece of falling cornice and instantly killed. In Garden Grove, a thirteen-year-old girl was planning a freshman party with her friends when the earthquake hit. She was sitting on the steps of a local high school and was crushed by a falling wall.

In our little house in San Bernardino, our housekeeper, Phyla, was bathing my baby sister, Midge, and Adair was reading to Mother, who was washing the dishes. Donyll and I were listening to *Little Orphan Annie* on our big RCA radio. On top of the radio we had a goldfish in a bowl. Suddenly, just before Orphan Annie could say her last "Leapin' lizards," the room began to violently shake. The quaking was so severe that the water slopped out of the bowl onto the floor, taking with it our precious goldfish. Mother yelled for us all to get out of the house and Phyla immediately wrapped Midge up in a towel and ran. I can remember Donyll grabbing the goldfish off the floor and dumping it back into its bowl before we all fled. I was so traumatized by this that I slept with Donyll for the next year. That night Daddy put two big beds together and slept in the middle, holding out his hand to each of us on either side.

In 1934, Daddy got transferred again and this time we wound up at 5141 Chesley Avenue in L.A. proper. This was to be our home for the next four years.

Amazingly, while we were in the depths of the Depression my father kept getting promoted. Unfortunately, due to economic conditions, as he rose up the corporate ladder his salary kept going down in 10 percent increments. At this time, as Franklin Delano Roosevelt was telling us that we had "nothing to fear but fear itself," Daddy was making $230 a month. This may seem like very little today, but in those desperate times, when many people were living on nothing, with makeshift boxes or tents as shelter and apples and pencils to sell to survive, $230 went a long way.

I never felt deprived and I grew up knowing very little about the Great Depression I had lived through, except that I still exercise the frugality I learned in those days. Looking back, though, I can see that the desperation of these times hit closer to home when Mother's sister Alma and her husband Tom Taylor came to live with us in 1936.

When Uncle Tom got ill and lost his job my parents went into action. Before you could shake a stick, Daddy (who was also a trained carpenter) was fixing up the garage and the entire Taylor family, two adults and four daughters, were living with us. My four cousins lived in the garage and my Uncle and Aunt took Donyll's room, while she slept in a trailer in the backyard. Our cousins were then in their teens and used to not worrying about money. This had to have been a rude awakening for them. For us, it was nothing but fun. Mother and Daddy made everyone feel at home and created a "more-the-merrier" atmosphere, despite eight children and four adults sharing a bathroom and a half! Uncle Tom and his family lived with us for about a year. Later, after Uncle Tom died, Aunt Alma refused to take any more charity and moved her family to what was called Tin Can Beach, the California equivalent of New York's Hoovervilles. Tin Can Beach was a place along the water and the beach where homeless families could pitch a tent. Looking back at this now, I realize how incredibly fortunate we were.

The rented house on Chesley Avenue was owned by a woman whose niece, Virginia Ellis, was the child prodigy of the area. She was about seven or eight years old and already a gifted violinist and the soloist with the newly formed Karl Moldrem's Hollywood Baby Orchestra.

Moldrem had been working with orchestras for many years. In the 1920s, he was one of the founders of the Olympia Symphony in Olympia, Washington, and he would go on to teach violin to such illustrious students as future conductor Lorin Maazel.

One Sunday afternoon in 1934, Mrs. Ellis invited my whole family to see the Baby Orchestra perform at Memorial Park in downtown L.A. As I listened, I was filled with awe. The climax for me came when I saw young Virginia Ellis rise from her chair and play a violin solo. I stood up on my chair in the audience and shouted, "I want that! I can do that!" Mother knew me well enough to know that when I said I could do something, I could do it. Hadn't I screamed and yelled when I was told I was too young to ice skate? And when small enough skates were found, didn't I concentrate hard, watch how it was done, and actually skate? Mother knew I was not kidding.

Before long I was taking lessons on a quarter-size violin (which I still own) from Karl Moldrem himself and after only four lessons I was a member of the Baby Orchestra. It was early on that Mr. Moldrem found that I had perfect pitch. He would use me as a tuning fork, saying, "Marni, sing A" or "Marni, sing G."

I was four and a half years old.

Although she was older, Virginia and I became friends and she began to teach me violin. Mother was very active in the PTA and we would play for them. Then Mother and three other "club women" interested in culture formed what was called the 4 Arts Club. All of these "culture vultures" would meet and plan artistic and cultural activities that would involve their kids. Of course I played the violin for all of their functions.

At five years old I had my first official recital.

The hall was large and filled with family and friends. Virginia Ellis was there. My older sisters were there. My parents stood in the back of the auditorium with my baby sister, Midge. I was very confident. I had practiced and knew what to do. I had also become very used to everyone ooh-ing and aah-ing over my musical abilities. It felt good and I craved the approval. When I was announced, I went out onto the stage carrying my little violin. As I entered I looked down and in the front row was a little boy, no older than ten. He looked up at me expectantly, with eyes that seemed to pop right out of his head. He had the weirdest look I had ever seen. His eyes transfixed me and I couldn't focus on what I was supposed to do. The light hit me and I knew I should begin playing, but I couldn't move. The little boy had me under some kind of spell. In retrospect I know he was innocently looking up at me, but in my five-year-old mind he was like some kind of monster. I had the sense to put the violin to my chin, but after that I had no idea what to do. I was catatonic. I was sure he was giving me the evil eye and willing me to fail. I could feel the audience getting uncomfortable. There was that expectant sound of silence.

From the back of the house, breaking the silence, came my mother's voice forcefully whispering, "Play, Marni! Marni, play!" But I couldn't play. I couldn't even move. Others joined in the whispering chorus: "What is she doing?" "What's the matter with her?" "Why doesn't she play?" All I could see were that little boy's eyes bugging out at me. After what seemed like a million years, I ran off the stage. My mother was there backstage to greet me. "What's the matter, Marni?" she asked. But I had no response. I had no way to tell her what I myself didn't understand. This was my first taste of stage fright. It would not be my last. Although Mother seemed to be sympathetic, I knew she was disappointed in me. It was beginning to become apparent to me, even at that young age, that I would be loved only if I achieved.

Most of the time, I *did* achieve. Just after entering school, I was invited to be in the City Schools Youth Orchestra. My two elder sisters were already members. Donyll was on clarinet (which she loathed, but played to appease Mother, although there would come a time when she threw the clarinet on the floor and broke it on purpose) and Adair played the xylophone. I was the youngest member of the group at five and a half years of age and was lucky to have my sisters around to show me the way. There are numerous pictures of

The McEathron sisters pose for our annual Christmas card in 1936
[l to r: Donyll Mern, Ariel Lea (aka Midge), me, Paulouise Adair (aka Adair)].
(From the author's collection)

us, playing instruments, singing together, and just plain having fun. The photos remind me of what we used to look like, and whenever I look at them, my sisters' personalities jump right out at me.

My eldest sister Donyll had red hair like mine and looked like the movie actress Bonita Granville: tall and gangly. With six years between us, she sometimes felt like a second mother to me. She was the type who would have lain down her life for you and, being the eldest, she was our protector.

Adair, who is four years older than me, looked like our German ancestors: blonde, wiry, and thin. She was disciplined, wry, and funny, and she got me into all sorts of mischief. Adair always had a great vocabulary, which I envied. She was the one I most wanted to be with.

My younger sister, Midge, was adorable, smart, and witty. She wore her long blonde hair in pigtails. When she was young, Midge wanted to do everything that I did. Like me, she was devoted to music, especially her cello. Being the youngest, Midge suffered the most from the negative side of Mother. When Midge was a teenager and the rest of the sisters were off doing our own things, she was left alone with Mother, who, at that time, was probably the most controlling she'd ever been.

Life in our household was strict. Mother ruled the roost with her Germanic perfectionism and our achievement was glorified. We had stringent rules and our behavior was regulated. With specific times for chores, practicing, homework, lessons, and playtime (oh yes, we played and we played hard!), everything was run on schedule. It didn't leave much room for warmth. Daddy tempered all this with his quiet humor, masculine coolness, and cuddliness. When he would come home, we would sometimes crawl into his lap and complain about Mother. He would always wink and say, "Well, you know how she is." It was clear to us that he adored her but since he was away at work most of the time, Daddy let her run the house and raise the children. Just let anyone try to stop her!

Now that I was old enough to join my older sisters at the 54th Street Elementary School, our morning routines had to run like clockwork. All three of us had long hair that had to be tended. On school days, we would stand in line and each comb the other's hair. Mother carefully combed Donyll's, Donyll sweetly combed Adair's, and Adair haphazardly and viciously pushed a comb through mine, ignoring any knots, tangles, or screams of pain. I'm lucky I have a scalp left.

Is it any wonder that some of my most precious memories are of the summers when we would go camping in the nearby Sequoia Mountains? It was during those carefree months that we had our hair cut so short we were often mistaken for boys (which we loved!) and never had to endure putting a comb through a strand of it.

We also got to run around in our bare, calloused feet, gather firewood and cook our suppers around the campfire that we built, bike, boat, and sleep under the stars. It was during these idyllic summers that I learned about nature and escaped from the everyday rigors of practicing, studying, rehearsing, and household chores. Since my parents rented our house out while we went camping, those wonderful seasons in the sun were not only joyous, but profitable as well. As Mother might have said, "We killed two birds with one camping trip."

1937 was a banner year both for the U.S. and for me. F.D.R. was inaugurated for his second of four terms. His New Deal was helping the country begin to recover from the Depression, and he implemented Social Security, heavier taxes on the wealthy, new controls over banks and public utilities, and an enormous work relief program (WPA) for the unemployed. As for me, violin lessons and school filled my days and I continued to play with the Baby Orchestra.

One day, Mr. Moldrem, my teacher and conductor, got a call from Republic Pictures, a grade B movie studio specializing in quickie Westerns starring Roy Rogers and Dale Evans and cheapo musicals starring ice skater Vera Hruba Ralston. They were looking for a red-haired little girl who could play the violin. He said he knew just the girl and soon Mother received a call from Central Casting, a Hollywood agency all the studios used to find the people for the bit parts and extras (there was a difference—players with bits got paid more and were usually part of the scene; extras were paid to fade into the background as atmosphere) that were needed every day on one of the many movies being made at that time. Before long I was on the Republic lot making my first film.

Walking on that movie set was magical. I can remember the vast sound stages filled with activity and noise that, with the sound of a clapboard clapping, could be silenced in an instant. I can remember going to the costume department for a fitting and coming out in new and different clothes that fit my new and different character. I can remember the huge klieg lights used to light the set. I remember the other extras and bit players standing around waiting for their instructions, as well as the stars in their trailers awaiting their next scene.

The only thing I can't remember is the name of the movie!

My mother always remembered the twenty-dollar check I got for a half-hour's work. She nearly swooned. In those days that was a lot of money. She immediately registered me, and eventually my sister Midge, at Central Casting and awaited the calls, which began to pour in.

Over the next ten years, I appeared in the background of over fifty movies, including several with my idol, soprano Deanna Durbin. I can be seen as atmosphere in *The Great Waltz* (1938) with Luise Rainer, *The Grapes of Wrath* (1940) with Henry Fonda, *The Big Store* (1941) with the Marx Brothers, *Babes on Broadway* (1942) with Judy Garland and Mickey Rooney, *Song of Russia* (1943) with Robert Taylor, *Song to Remember* (1945) with Cornel Wilde, *The Bachelor and*

As Angelica Abernathy in The Bashful Bachelor *(1942), one of several Lum and Abner movies I appeared in. Making movies was how we paid for my voice lessons. Note Oscar-winner Constance Purdy to my right. (From the author's collection)*

the Bobby-Soxer (1947) with Cary Grant and Shirley Temple, *The Emperor Waltz* (1948) with Bing Crosby, and *In the Good Old Summertime* (1949) with Judy Garland and Van Johnson.

Stuck in between these blockbusters were B movies like *Sing, Dance, Plenty Hot* (aka *Mania for Melody*) (1940). This Republic musical starring Billy Gilbert was special because a photo survives of my sister Midge and myself playing one huge bass fiddle. One of us was bowing and the other was on a ladder doing the fingering. We were quite a sight.

In the early 1940s I got to play a recurring speaking role in a series of films featuring the radio characters Lum and Abner. Chet Lauck and Norris Goff had created these characters of two old-time Arkansas philosophers with the names Lum Edwards and Abner Peabody in 1931, and they continued to delight radio audiences for the next twenty-five years. I played Angelica Abernathy, a country bumpkin with freckles, pigtails, huge glasses, and a loud voice in at least three of them. After Mother and I saw a sneak preview of the first of these, I overheard her bragging to one of her friends, "Wait till you see the movie! Marni talks!"

The law, which was enforced by the Board of Education, compelled all children to have three hours of tutoring per day if they were "on the lot." I remember having to take my homework with me, and if the job lasted more than a few hours a studio-appointed tutor would arrive on the scene to supervise my homework.

After chaperoning me on my first few films, my mother got bored sitting around and waiting with the other "stage mothers." Since an adult chaperone was required, she sometimes asked other mothers to spell her while she went home to take care of the house and her other children. On those days, she would drop me off at the studio and come to pick me up later. One day I called her to pick me up after only three hours. When she arrived, I handed her the check, which was for a whole day's work ($26!). When she asked me how I had earned the whole amount for so little work, I answered, rather impatiently according to her, "Mother, I figured it out. They tell you what they want, and if you concentrate and do it *exactly* the way they say *the first time*, you don't have to do it over."

Later on she enlisted the aid of my sister Donyll and my cousin Nelda to become my chaperone when needed. Mother recruited anyone in the family who could help ensure that those checks kept coming in. As for where the money went, years later, when I asked her how she paid for all my lessons, she looked at me and answered, "I didn't pay for them! You did! All the money you made went right to all your lessons."

One night in 1937 I felt my mother shaking me awake. She told me that I should get up and get dressed. We were going downtown to the Baptist Church Auditorium to hear the Los Angeles Philharmonic Orchestra. As excited as I was, I knew that we didn't have enough money for tickets and wondered how we would get in.

When we arrived we were met at the stage door by a friend of my mother's who took us back past the doorman and the dressing rooms to an archway covered with green velvet curtains. When she pushed the curtains aside, we were right in the auditorium looking up at the stage. Before I even could focus my eyes on the stage, cutting through the rapt silence of the audience was a sound I had never heard before.

The music was so Viennese and so *gemütlich* ("like home"), as my mother would call it. I immediately recognized Fritz Kreisler's "Leibesleid" (also known as "Sorrow of Love"), but it took me a moment to realize that the rather ordinary looking man caressing the strings on the stage was one of the most distinguished and best-loved violinists of all time, Fritz Kreisler himself. The Austrian-born Kreisler was not only a violinist, but also a composer of renown, with the scores of several operettas to his credit, including the Broadway hit *Apple Blossoms* in 1919. He made his first huge splash in 1899 with the Berlin Philharmonic and then toured to great acclaim in the U.S. from 1901 to 1903. Like many Europeans in the wake of World War II, he eventually settled in the U.S. and became a citizen, dying in New York City in 1962.

That night in 1937 the combination of the music and Fritz Kreisler's play-ing brought tears to my eyes. I had loved the violin before, but had never heard it played like this. Along with the tears, I had the feeling of not being able to catch my breath. I looked around the audience and saw I was not alone; every-one was totally enraptured. Looking over at my mother's friend, she, too, had tears streaming down her cheeks. But the surprise weeper was my mother. I had never thought of my mother as being that vulnerable. I should have known better. This was the woman who would do anything to make sure that I ful-filled my destiny. This was a woman in love with talent. I pinched myself so that I would never forget that moment.

Mother decided to use my adoration of Fritz Kreisler in one of a series of monologues (there were at least six of these and, in each, I played the violin) she wrote for me to perform at benefits and other local functions. In *Kreisler and the Bootblack* I was dressed as a little ragamuffin street performer who was madly enamored of the great Kreisler and longed to play the violin just like he did.

A couple of years later, on January 24, 1940, I got to perform another one of these skits at Station KHJ on one of the first experimental color television shows ever tried on the West Coast. This monologue was called *Schumann-Heink and the Urchin*. Needless to say, I played the urchin. Mother based the monologue on an incident that had really happened when I met and talked to the great contralto, Madame Ernestine Schumann-Heink. My image was pro-jected all of a block away from the studio, but I was told that my red hair came out an orangish brown, my white blouse looked like it was about to burst into flame, and my black velvet costume appeared as a kind of rust color. It wasn't called experimental color for nothing!

We moved once again in 1938, but not far. Although we were staying in the same neighborhood, this time we were moving into the very first house that we actu-ally owned and built to our specifications. Having qualified for one of the first Federal Housing Administration housing loans in the U.S., Mother and Daddy made sure our new home at 4119 Charlene Drive would reflect our family's un-conventional lifestyle. Mother designed the two-story house that overlooked the 54th Street Elementary School to have a sunroom with a wall of windows that opened onto the backyard, giving us a sense of wide-open spaces even when we were indoors. We would soon eat all our meals in this room.

Because lima bean fields had been cut down to build the houses, there was an unobstructed view from my grammar school window. Day after day I would sit there in school and watch across the used-to-be field as our new home pro-gressed from a foundation to a real house. The house, like many others in the area, was built on a hill and we terraced our land, planting fruit trees all the way down to a ravine. In our last home, we had chicken coops and rabbit hutches (as well as the usual dogs and cats). We kept those and added a duck pond to our menagerie.

Now that Mother was completely and happily surrounded by musical talent, she felt we should have a platform (literally) on which to perform, so we built a raised area in the living room that became our stage. There were twenty-two musical instruments (five of them violins, including the one I played at the time) in a closet off the raised platform, which also held costumes and stage props. As corny as it may sound, it was inevitable that we formed a family orchestra, Mother on piano, Daddy on his coronet, Adair on bells and drums, little Midge on her huge cello, Donyll on her dreaded clarinet, and me on violin. On Sundays we would invite our neighbors to our musical salons. We had the stock arrangements and the extra instruments in the closet if anyone wanted to join in and play along. If you happened to be driving by, you might have heard our group jamming on "Tea for Two" or "Jealousy" or "Honeysuckle Rose." And if you were really lucky you might have heard my sisters and I singing, for it was about this time we started harmonizing using our voices as well.

In 1939, when I was nine years old, my mother decided to take me out of school for a term. She felt I was too young for my peers and decided that a semester at home would give me more time to practice the violin. I adored being home and having my mother's undivided attention. By Mother's estimation I practiced four to six hours daily. It was during this time that I became involved in the Peter Meremblum California Junior Symphony.

Ever since it was founded in 1936, this training orchestra, which is dedicated to the musical education of youth ages eight to eighteen, has been an important part of L.A.'s cultural life. Peter Meremblum conducted the Junior Symphony and his assistant Joseph Oroop headed the Pioneer Orchestra, which utilized the talents of the younger players. Oroop also taught violin and took me on as a special pupil, teaching me a college course in harmony in conjunction with my regular lessons. He believed in me. I can remember him saying in his thick-as-borscht Russian accent, "Marrrrni, Marrrni (I can hear those Rs rolling still), you could be the biggest violinist in the whole vorld." He would make these proclamations with a cigar hanging down from his mouth. That cigar was present during every lesson, and often its ashes would drop down and burn the varnish on the violin. To this day, the violin I used then smells of his cigar smoke.

In time I graduated from the Pioneer Orchestra to the Junior Symphony and, before long, my sister Midge and my friend Virginia Ellis also became part of the group. Our concerts were well attended by Hollywood's elite, many of whom were on the Board of Directors. When noted conductor and composer André Previn first came to America in 1939, he played with our orchestra. He was a year or so older than me, and along with many of the other girls I developed a crush on this very continental young man. Hadn't I heard from his uncle Charles Previn (who assisted every Saturday) that he had lived in both Berlin *and* Paris? What could be more romantic? André was not only brilliant, but cute as well! He went on to work at MGM (and eventually became the head of the music department), and years later I would run into him when I was a messenger girl and he was already making his mark as an arranger and orchestrator on the lot. I still thought he was cute!

By this time I was not only doing bits and extra jobs in movies, and performing with the Meremblum Junior Symphony, but also playing child roles in a repertory theater company called the Gateway Playhouse. It was fun to be acting and leave music at home for those rehearsal and performance hours. I had gotten my feet wet as an actress doing Mother's monologues, but it was more fun to be part of a group of actors and learn how to time and play a laugh to audiences of paying customers.

In 1940, my mother got involved with a group called United Races of America. This organization was formed for the high-minded purpose of bringing dignitaries, ambassadors, and other foreign luminaries together socially to promote the interchange of cultures. Although she was passionate about artistic matters, affairs of the world also affected Mother. The world was becoming a frightening and complex place. With Hitler and Stalin signing a nonaggression pact in August of 1939, it was no surprise when England and France declared war in September of the same year. Although the U.S. remained neutral for the moment, the storm clouds over Europe and in the South Pacific were never far from everyone's mind. In this divided world, Mother was obviously looking for ways of bringing diverse peoples together. Interestingly, these new affiliations also brought about new links in my chain of life.

There among the Austrian countess, the Bahai teacher, and the missionaries who had converted Chiang Kai-shek to Christianity, were Sarah and Eugene Page, an African-American couple of French and East Indian blood, who wrote music and theater pieces to promote world unity and brotherhood. Living close to each other, our family and theirs immediately became friends. They had four children, Olivia, Eugene, Jr., Sarah Jean, and Billy, who all sang and performed, too. Later, all the Page children wound up working in musical capacities at the fledgling Motown Records.

I adored going to their house, which was the antithesis of mine. Not only was everyone warm and open, but there was always the smell of something incredibly delicious and unique cooking on the stove. Something not necessarily "healthy."

And the music was always flowing. The Pages all sang by ear and harmonized without having to look at music. In my home, we each had our assignments and we did everything methodically. At the Pages', there was freedom to

The family orchestra: Dad on the trumpet, Donyll on her dreaded clarinet, Adair on bells, Midge on the cello, me with my violin, and Mother on the piano. We built the stage in our living room especially for these events. (Photo A.R. Hromatka)

express oneself in a personal, jazzy, and earthy way, which I secretly craved. At our house we were forbidden to listen to popular music (which Mother thought was beneath us). My sisters and I were used to having Mother's love doled out when we achieved something, but at the Pages I discovered that there were mothers who loved their kids unconditionally.

Sarah and Eugene had written a show called *Overture to Freedom*, which was going to be produced in the fall of 1941, first in L.A. and then, if all went well, New York. Because everyone was always singing and playing instruments in both of our houses, when the role of child singer or musical performer came up, Eugene and Sarah asked me to sing for them and for their production manager Elliot Fischer. I had been practicing a bit with my sister Adair accompanying me, but the Pages and Fischer were astounded that an eleven-year-old child could possess a soprano voice capable of singing coloratura (that is, the trills, arpeggios, etc., or "florid ornamentation," of music). Fischer immediately took me under his wing and started to coach me. He would throw all kinds of music at me and I would learn them instantly and sing them back for him. I was a musical sponge. He helped to open up a whole new world for me that summer of 1941. And, yes . . . I got the part.

The autumn of 1941 was a bustling one. I was matriculated to Audubon Jr. High School, and when I wasn't busy with homework, violin lessons, and chores, I was rehearsing for *Overture to Freedom*, which would be opening in late October. I had some lines (according to later reviews, rather comic) in one scene and was to sing "The Blue Danube Waltz." I practiced at home with my sister Adair and, of course, was coached by Elliot Fischer. "The Blue Danube Waltz" was to figure in one of the great turning points of my life.

Sometimes careers can turn on a dime. Sometimes it's the combination of many small events that lead up to a moment of truth. I used to think that my decision to become a singer was based on fate or chance. Now, as I look at it, I can see that it was always in my script, as my mother would say. And it was my turn to help nudge it forward.

The tattered, yellowing clipping from the *Los Angeles Times* says that I was ten years old, but I was really eleven. It goes on to state that on September 28, 1941, little Marni Nixon (I was already dropping my last name of McEathron. It was too hard to pronounce and kids at school called me Mac-Earthworm!), was one of eight winners at the L.A. County Fair at Pomona. For winning the vocal competition, I received $100 (a fortune in those days!) and a nationwide broadcast of my song.

I remember nothing of the actual competition, except that I sang "The Blue Danube Waltz," accompanied by my sister Adair. What I *do* remember is the fifty-mile car ride back to L.A. and the strangely euphoric feeling that I had found my niche. It had been gradually dawning on me for months now that singing was far more personal than playing the violin. Using my voice was more satisfying and made me feel closer to the music that I so loved. So, on that car trip from Pomona to L.A., I made a decision to stop studying the violin and actively pursue a singing career. Just like that.

I can still hear my violin teacher, Mr. Oroop, who believed in my future as a violinist. "Marrrni, Marrrni," he wailed, as he mangled the English language, "for vhy you vant to sing?" "I don't know," the little girl named Marni passionately replied, "I just *do!*"

On such small words, whole lives can change.

Chapter Two

SINGING MY OWN SONG

*"Those who are blessed with a talent have a responsibility
that they must carry out to the world."*

MARGARET WITTKE MCEATHRON, 1941

I T WAS THE MORNING THAT THE WORLD CHANGED FOREVER. The day was
blindingly beautiful. The robin's egg blue of the sky was dotted with an occasional fluffy, white cloud drifting lazily by. I was home, sick with a high fever,
and was dozing when the music on the radio was preempted by a news flash.
Our country had been suddenly and viciously attacked, without warning or
provocation. I was alone and frightened. Frightened to realize suddenly that a
foreign force could come and attack us just like that, and destroy so many innocent lives. I knew at that moment that the world as we knew it would never
be the same.

The date was December 7, 1941.

The Sunday that the Japanese Imperial Fleet attacked Pearl Harbor in
Hawaii was the first time America's complacency and security were threatened
on her home turf. America was scared and we were moved to immediate action.

I can remember sitting on my mother's bed all day, surrounded by my sisters
and parents listening to the radio for more news, wondering what, if anything,
we could do. Later that evening President Roosevelt came on the air to an-
nounce on this "day that will live in infamy" that we would no longer remain neutral and were embarking on what would quickly become known as World War II.

Less than two and a half months prior to that day I had made my own life-
changing decision to switch from violin to voice. I had taken great delight in
making the decision on my own. Even though I always played the obedient
child, the secret juvenile delinquent in me felt that by switching to singing I
was rebelling against all the constant discipline and practicing I had to endure
playing the violin. Now that I was a singer I would do it *my* way and not have to
practice at all. Boy, was I wrong about that! My singing teachers all made sure
I practiced as much or more than I had ever done before.

Overture to Freedom opened on October 23, 1941 at the Musart Theatre in
L.A. and I received my first set of reviews as a singer. After praising the production, the *Los Angeles Daily News* said, ". . . let it be added that Miss Nixon

should be noted by Hollywood producers at once. The youngster has natural comedy ability, charm, a nice singing voice and she's so easy in performance."

The *Los Angeles Examiner* wrote that I "delivered intricate florid measure with accuracy and aplomb that were astonishing in a little girl who is apparently not more than nine or ten." I was eleven, but what woman would deny being younger?

The *Los Angeles Evening Herald* proclaimed, "She displays wonderful stage presence for one so young, in fact much more than other members of the cast. A truly amazing soprano."

The producer of the show was ecstatic and tried to sign me to a personal management contract. Of course, since I was only eleven years old, my parents were responsible for any legal decisions and, although Mother had high hopes for the show and anticipated it would be moving to Broadway, she didn't feel that I should tie myself down with a contract at this time. Her decision proved to be a wise one as the run of the show and the dreams of the authors and producers were cut short by the start of the war. The show and I were not going to Broadway after all.

From then on everything we did was for the war effort. My elder sisters went to work at Lockheed, a defense plant in Burbank that made P-38 fighters and B-17 bombers for the armed forces. Even my mother got a part-time job at Douglas Aircraft in El Segundo, where they were manufacturing the DC-5 for the Navy.

Within days of December 7, a top-secret device called RADAR began picking up signals thought to be those of enemy aircraft up and down the West Coast of North America. Blackouts were ordered, effectively shutting down coastal cities from San Francisco to San Diego. We had to have black screens installed on our windows to totally block out the light and every night after nine o'clock the streets were totally dark. I was doing a lot of babysitting to make extra money and after the kids were asleep and the parents returned home, I would have to walk home all alone through those blacked-out streets with just my flashlight to illuminate the way. Sometimes, as I walked, I would hear the closing theme of a scary radio show called *The Whistler* coming from neighboring windows. As the final whistling theme filled the blacked-out night, I did my best not to be too scared by whistling my own more cheerful tune in counterpoint to the eerie one coming from the radio.

Rationing became the order of the day and we were all issued ration books to buy our food and staples. Americans had to manage on less. Lord knows frugality was in my family's Scottish blood, and whatever wasn't hereditary I learned from Mother's innate practicality. We had been economizing since I was born, so rationing came easily to us. But there were exceptions. In those early war days, the margarine we bought in the market had no color and was completely white, looking a little like lard. It was very unappetizing and my mother would have none of it for her family. So, she figured out how to make it look more natural by using a bit of food coloring. On those rare occasions when the family went out to dinner, Mother would bring along her own private jar of colored margarine in her purse, putting it out on the table of the restaurant and spreading it on our bread. I was embarrassed to think that anyone might see her doing that.

The war brought other changes to our lives. In addition to rationing, we all had to save things like tinfoil, paper, rubber, and string to recycle or to donate to the war effort. Many items, like the thread that my mother would use to sew, were impossible to buy. These deprivations had a long-term effect on me. To this day, I am a pack rat, saving everything, knowing that there will someday be a use for those discarded paper clips, rubber bands, and plastic containers.

The war was reflected in the movies and music as well as in our daily lives. The songs that were sung on the radio by the Andrews Sisters and recorded by such big bands as Benny Goodman and Tommy Dorsey sang of the boys overseas and of the girls who waited patiently at home for their return. It was during this time that Mother began to loosen up on some of her restrictions and actually let us listen to popular music, which used to be forbidden. In truth, I had been sneaking listens to Glenn Miller for some time now. Maybe Mother was mellowing or maybe it was a sign of the times. Even the fairgrounds in Pomona, which had been, and would be, so influential in my changing life, reflected the shift since the war.

From May until August of 1942, the fairground was used to process ethnic Japanese, who, in one of America's most shameful acts, were taken from their homes and sent to camps in Heart Mountain, Wyoming. On September 4, 1942, the Army's Ordnance Motor Transport Agency became known as the Pomona Ordnance Depot. For most of the war, the depot had a prisoner of war camp holding about 1,150 POWs who worked at the depot. This was a far cry from the fairground where a little girl had won a singing contest just a few months before.

Although I gave up violin lessons to sing, I did not give up the violin. I continued to perform with the Meremblum Junior Symphony, except that, during concerts, instead of just playing in the string section, I occasionally would get up, put my instrument down, and sing an aria. This display of versatility, which Meremblum took great pride in displaying, made me stand out from the other players and I began to get noticed by the Hollywood bigwigs who attended the concerts.

The Board of Directors of the Junior Symphony consisted of such people as film actress Beulah Bondi, conductor Charles Previn, and Ida R. Koverman. When people speak of the power behind the throne, they might be speaking of Mrs. Koverman. She had been executive secretary to President Herbert Hoover, and when Hoover left the White House, he recommended her to the most powerful man in Hollywood, L.B. Mayer, head of MGM Studios. Mrs. Koverman quickly became a political force within the MGM ranks and, although she was by all appearances a motherly figure, she was the only woman whose advice was respected by the male stars and by Mayer himself. After hearing me sing with the orchestra, Ida Koverman started to take an interest in my career and watched my growth carefully over the next few years. She would later play an instrumental role in my future.

On a personal level, singing with a full orchestra was tremendously exciting. I found that it was so much easier to sing with all these players backing me up than with just a piano accompaniment. All that resonance and vibration surrounding me lifted my voice to new heights, and the feeling that the conductor and I were equals and that he was taking his cues from *me* was intoxicating and gave me a taste for more. It was about this time I began taking voice lessons in earnest with the world-renowned soprano Vera Schwarz.

Vera Schwarz was born in 1888 in Zagreb, Croatia, but gained her fame in 1921 at the Viennese State Opera, where she sang both opera and operetta. She was often partnered with Austrian tenor Richard Tauber, and the two made many recordings together. She came to the U.S. in 1938 and began teaching me in about 1942.

Walking into Vera Schwarz's studio at the Sunset Plaza Apartments, on the Sunset Strip, was like stepping back into a time when operetta reigned supreme, when "Student Princes" sang to barmaids and expressed their ardor in three-quarter time. The first thing I noticed when I entered her apartment was the smell of expensive perfume and the yapping of her pampered little French poodle. There among the elegant European furnishings was an endless parade of memorabilia from her long and distinguished career. Posters announcing long-ago appearances adorned the walls. Ornately framed pictures of the people in her life were set up on the piano, which was covered with an expensive red velvet brocaded shawl. The photos showed Vera with Richard Tauber, Vera surrounded by the orchestra and chorus of Vienna's famed Volksoper, and Vera with composer Franz Lehár, who wrote many of the operettas in which she starred.

Vera Schwarz always had an accompanist at our lessons (quite an extravagance; usually the voice teacher plays herself) and we always vocalized first, but what I remember most was Vera teaching me wonderful old Viennese songs. Although I never heard her sing professionally I marveled at her style and flair when she demonstrated the songs for me in her home. Her tone was centered, rich, and dark, and yet it had brilliance to it. There was an emotional opulence to every phrase she sang. Although my voice was childishly pure and bright, I secretly hoped some of Vera's sophistication and theatricality would rub off on me. Sixty years later, I drew on the theatricality and opulence of Vera Schwarz to play the role of the former operetta star, Heidi Schiller, in the Broadway revival of Stephen Sondheim and James Goldman's *Follies*. It was Heidi who said, "Facts never interest me. What matters is the song."

But facts *did* interest Vera Schwarz. Especially facts like money. Voice lessons with such an accomplished teacher did not come cheaply and, although all the money I made doing bits in movies (plus my babysitting money) was going to my lessons, my parents had to supplement the rest. There came a time when we got behind in our payments and Vera refused to give me any more lessons unless something could be done to clear up my bill. Mother to the rescue! She quickly decided to pawn her diamond engagement ring to pay for the arrears. Vera was happy, I was happy, but Mother got a shock when the pawnshop owner examined her ring, found a flaw in the diamond, and told her that it was not worth nearly as much as she had always thought it was. To a woman who prized perfection, this was quite a blow and, later in life, when she was upset or disappointed with Daddy, she used the symbolism of "the flaw" in the ring as an analogy to what she perceived as her flawed marriage.

Later on Vera moved to New York and I moved on to other voice teachers. One claimed to have a revolutionary way of teaching voice. She had a large instrument that she would stick down a student's throat to lower the larynx, thus deepening the quality of his or her voice. When I saw the device I was terrified and wouldn't let her use it on me. I felt that it was invasive and unnatural. The students that did submit to her methods tended to have very deep and rich tones, but it also seemed to me that their voices developed a wobble early on.

That was one teacher I didn't study with for long.

In grammar school I had been a big fish in a little pond, but when I moved on to a much larger junior high school in 1942 I found myself lost in the shuffle. Although I sang for a few assemblies, I didn't feel a part of any crowd of friends or join any clubs or groups. These were my awkward years. I wanted to be just like everyone else, but deep down inside I knew I wasn't.

While other kids were out playing or just hanging out, I was the girl who always had to take her lessons, do her chores, audition, rehearse, learn new songs, and make the occasional movie. I knew I was different and part of me was proud of this fact, but the other part desperately wanted to be one of the gang. After all, I was twelve years old. All in all I felt like a total outsider among my peers. Perhaps this was also due to the fact that I was less physically mature than my classmates. Many of the girls my age were already developing breasts and showing other physical signs of womanhood. Later, in high school, when my body finally started to change and I got my first period, my mother reminded me that the women in our family were all late bloomers, but that only meant we would look younger when we were old. Small consolation when you are twelve going on thirteen but your body is going on ten. Besides telling me about my period and how to deal with it, like most parents in those days neither my mother nor father ever told me anything about sex, and it was the "big secret" I longed to know about. I asked everyone—my sister, my parents—but no one would tell me. I was met with embarrassed smiles and the subject wasn't discussed. This left me frustrated, a little naïve, and sometimes unprepared for the adult world I was living in.

In the fall of 1944, I was cast in a production of the comedy *Junior Miss* at the famed Pasadena Playhouse and thrust once again into a grown-up professional atmosphere. The Playhouse was founded in 1917 and, during its first four decades, produced hundreds of plays, presented 477 world premieres, and was the first American theater to present all thirty-seven of Shakespeare's plays. Over the years the Playhouse has launched the careers of countless actors such as William Holden, Dustin Hoffman, and Gene Hackman. Now, I hoped, it was about to launch mine.

Junior Miss was a coming-of-age comedy by Jerome Chodorov and Joseph Fields, which opened on Broadway in late 1941 and ran until July of 1943. This is the kind of play that was a big wartime hit yet, although there was a film version and even a TV musical in the 1950s, seldom gets revived today. The leading characters were girls my age and, when I auditioned for Howard (Happy) Graham, the director, I had no trouble getting the second lead of "Fuffy" Adams. Rehearsals were a lark and a learning experience as Graham and Founder and Artistic Director Gilmor Brown taught me the finer points of comedy, which I gobbled up like a hot lunch.

The best part of going back and forth from my home in L.A. to the theater in Pasadena was that I was now driving my own car! On my fourteenth birthday my parents presented me with a blue secondhand Chevy that I named "My Blue Heaven," after the popular song of the day. It may seem odd today, but during the war, the city of L.A. granted special junior licenses for kids my age. Daddy, that "Master Driver of Cars," as my mother called him, patiently taught me how to drive, but before I even took my first spin, I fixed the car up with curtains and a leather steering wheel cover that had a little twisty driving knob for turning corners and a spotlight outside of the driver's window. The spotlight made it easier to see those pesky L.A. street signs, especially in the dark and dangerous Hollywood Hills.

Off I would zoom in my little blue car on the newly built freeway between L.A. and Pasadena, frequently picking up hitchhiking sailors. This might sound risky today, but in 1944 sailors were always hitchhiking along the side of the road and it seemed like my patriotic duty to give the poor gobs a ride, even though my father had warned me never to pick up anyone. What would be the harm, I thought? And you know what? In those innocent days, there wasn't any! Of course there was that one time that a very nice sailor I picked up told me a very dirty joke. I must admit I didn't get it, but since the sailor laughed loudly, I made sure to remember it word for word. The next night I told the joke to my family at the dinner table. When my father turned white as a sheet and asked me where I'd heard the profane joke, I knew I had made a mistake in telling it but, having been born on Washington's birthday, I couldn't tell a lie. I obediently told him that I learned the joke from a sailor I picked up on the freeway and, well, let's just say, I had a lot of groveling to do to get my father to allow me to use my little blue car again!

Someone important must have caught my performance during the run of *Junior Miss*, because one day my mother received a call from Twentieth Century Fox asking if I would come in and do a screen test for the role I had played on the stage. Would I? I forgave them for not asking me to test for the lead because that role was going to child film star Peggy Ann Garner, who was under contract to Fox. By this time I was a "veteran" of twenty-nine films, but none of them featured me in a substantial role like this might. I felt something new inside of me, something I hadn't felt before: raw ambition. I wanted that part. I wanted to prove my prowess on the screen and be noticed.

Arriving on the Fox set that day in 1945 was a little nerve-racking, because, unlike all my other times on film sets, I wasn't one of a crowd of extras supporting the star. This time I was the star. At least for the screen test. I knew the role backward and forward and I was to do a scene just the way I did it onstage, except that the set was different and none of the staging or blocking was the same. Oops! As the cameras rolled, everything suddenly seemed confining and confusing. Still, I was a pro and I did what they told me to do and when it was all over, I thought I had done a fine job. It was a few days later that I heard they were testing Barbara Whiting, sister of singer Margaret Whiting (with whom I would costar years later in a show called *Taking My Turn*) and daughter of the late Richard Whiting, who was kind of Hollywood royalty. He had been the composer of such hit songs as "Beyond the Blue Horizon," "On the Good Ship Lollipop," "Too Marvelous for Words," and many others.

Well, you guessed it! Barbara Whiting got the role and became a contract player at Fox. But, was I jealous? You bet I was! I was "Little Miss Hot Shot" and used to always getting everything I ever set my mind to. Mother had instilled in me a wonderful kind of blind confidence. Now that I had lost a role, my footing was a bit more unsure. This was a first for me. I never saw the screen test (if anyone has it, I would still like to!) or the actual film.

My consolation prize for not getting the film was winning another role in another comedy at the Pasadena Playhouse. *For Keeps* by F. Hugh Herbert was a comedy that ran only twenty-nine performances during the 1944 Broadway season, but attracted a big Pasadena audience in 1946 because they had loved his hit play *Kiss and Tell* the season before.

Actress Nancy Robinson and I both played roles of similar size and under-studied each other, meaning we knew each other's lines. For some unknown reason, the director, Lenore Shanewise (Associate Director of the Playhouse and an actress who appeared in many TV shows in the 1950s and 1960s), decided to have us switch roles during the run of the play. The play went along just fine until I went on automatic pilot and said one of my original lines, which was now supposed to be Nancy's. She compensated by saying what should have been my line and then tried to correct it by going back to the lines she should have been saying. The light poured down on us as we spouted right lines, wrong lines, and every variation thereof, until we both "went up" on all of our lines completely, leaving a huge silence begging to be filled. We filled it all right . . . with our own laughter. After a while, we had no idea where we were in the scene at all. It took the stage manager shouting out a line from off-stage to get us back on track. What that audience thought is lost to the ages, but one thing is certain, we never switched roles again.

With the war officially over in September of 1945, America became a nation of winners. We had done it! We saved the world! My generation may have been too young to fight in the war, but we were now coming of age as a giving and caring group of young people looking to the future. Dorsey High School was where I began to come of age as a young woman and found a group of friends who were smart and wanted to do things for others. My personal life started to keep pace with my professional one, but as I became more at home in my own skin, I got the feeling there were two Marnis: the one that was finally fitting in at school and the other who reveled in her "otherness" and knew that being different wasn't so bad.

Marni #1 was thrilled to be part of the "in" crowd and to have a best friend like Carol Jenkins. We played tennis together and spent all of our spare time trying to attract the right kind of boys (they needed to be either on the football team or elected officers of the student body) in the hope of getting "pinned," which meant the boy of our dreams would give us his Dorsey High pin, and that meant we would be going steady. If the boy was really serious you might get his "letterman sweater." That would be enough to make you swoon.

Marni #2 didn't have as much time as the other kids to goof off because she was "gifted," and as Mother said, "Those who are blessed with a talent have a responsibility that they must carry out to the world." With this responsibility came the sense that perhaps my peers didn't quite admire me for the accolades I was achieving in the adult world.

Happily, both Marnis merged when I was with one particular boy. Although we never officially dated, he was the only one among my friends to have some

The entire McEathron family in 1944 in our house on Charlene Drive in L.A.
(From the author's collection)

perspective on my artistic life. He took my singing and acting seriously and we would talk about the future. I was so at ease with him, both when we talked and when we danced at a party or prom. He was a wonderful dancer. I knew he liked me and yet there was no sexual tension, as there was no sexual attraction. Was this what made it so easy? As it turned out, my friend was gay but all I knew at the time was how comfortable and happy I felt around him. Our friendship was like a peaceful port in the turbulent storm called "being a teenager."

My singing became even more important to me at this time and, besides performing whenever the school had a function (I would sing the "Bell Song" from the opera *Lakmé* at the drop of hat!), I also entered every contest I could in the hopes of making more money to pay for my ever-more-expensive lessons. One of these contests led to the L.A. school district awarding me a scholarship of $100 in 1945 and the opportunity to serenade Mayor Bowron of L.A. on his birthday.

It was yet another one of these contests that led me to Roger Wagner. Roger Wagner was born in Le Puy, France, and, since his father was an organist in

Dijon, he was immersed in music from his earliest years. The family emigrated to the U.S. in 1921, and Roger began his professional music career as a church choral director at age twelve. Roger returned to France for undergraduate studies, served in the French army, and was a member of the French decathlon team in the 1936 Olympics. He returned to L.A. in 1937, where he joined the MGM chorus and subsequently became organist and choirmaster at St. Joseph's, where he established an outstanding choir of men and boys. In 1945, Roger Wagner became the supervisor of Youth Choruses for the Los Angeles Bureau of Music.

This is where I came in.

In the early 1940s the Los Angeles Bureau of Music was created as a reaction to the cross-cultural (read: Latino) swing scene (that is, popular music and dance performances that resulted in the Zoot Suit craze) permeating the L.A. area. The Bureau of Music was formed by local politicians and municipal arts administrators in order to encourage patriotic citizenship, prevent juvenile delinquency, and bring "proper" music to the people. To this end in 1946, the Los Angeles Bureau of Music sponsored a singing contest and I made it to the finals. I was especially hoping to win because two of my screen idols, Nelson Eddy and Jeanette MacDonald, were the donors of two $500 prizes to be given (in person I prayed) to the two winners, male and female. On May 4 at 2:30 P.M. the finalists convened in the conference room at the Mayor's office in City Hall. There was to be no audience. We were to sing only for the judges and their assistants. One of those judges was Roger Wagner.

Despite my dreams of being presented with a check from Nelson and Jeanette, I only won second prize. We received the awards on May 12 at the Hollywood Bowl in a special evening hosted by film star Cornel Wilde. Metropolitan Opera star Lauritz Melchior sang two popular songs, "The House I Live In" and "Because," and I was presented with a voucher for $250 to be used to pay for my voice lessons. The biggest prize of all, however, turned out to be my invitation from Roger Wagner to be one of the twelve founding members of his newly formed Concert Youth Chorus. As Roger might have said while doing his brilliant Maurice Chevalier impersonation, "Zees was ze start of a beautiful frand-sheep."

We were originally a madrigal group singing pre-Baroque Monteverdi and Palestrina madrigals and Brahms folk songs, but we quickly blossomed into a chorale thirty-two voices strong. Eventually taking its name from its founder and conductor, the Roger Wagner Chorale was America's premier vocal ensemble and the possessor of an enviable international reputation. Following our debut in December 1946, the demands for our services were so many that in 1947 we became a professional group.

Roger had a kind of horsey face that occasionally sported a little continental mustache under his large nose. The mustache may have come and gone but one thing that always remained was his animal magnetism. All the girl singers fell for Roger, who had retained the athletic body that had served him well in the Olympics. Roger loved the feminine attention, but what he wanted most in the world was for his singers to sound like angels, with a purity of tone and with unfailing musicianship. I can still hear him in rehearsals saying, "You've been taking voice lessons again! Stop it!" He never wanted us to stand out in a choral situation and felt that a solo tone containing a rich deep vibrato would ruin his blend. With my perfect pitch and sweet high soprano, I quickly became one of Roger's favorites, but he never tired of teasing me about what he perceived as my "purity and virginal qualities." Even after I'd had my first child!

Later on Roger wrote about his techniques, "I never let them force. I always demanded a forward sound, a yawny sound, and when the sopranos got high I didn't let them shriek. I respected the fact that they were young."

When we became a professional group and began to get many paying gigs, the singers all decided that they would have to join the American Guild of Musical Artists (AGMA), the union that governed and protected musical artists. Roger was furious. He would call each of us late at night, berating and threatening us that if we joined the union, there would be trouble. It was of no concern to him that the Chorale was now raking in the dough; he didn't want us to "lose the purity of singing." Ha! He didn't want to share the money! Roger had that lovely way of being able to steal from one hand while kissing the other. Years later, he hired my husband, Ernest, to write many arrangements that he would then claim were his own, refusing to pay for them. From Ernest I learned the Yiddish word to describe Roger Wagner's dealings: chutzpah.

Still, I knew I was lucky to be one of Roger's "special singers." He always hired me and gave me the most solos of anyone. It seems I was special to Roger in another way, too. I was one of the only singers he *didn't* make a pass at! When I became aware that he had gone down the line and seduced every other girl singer in the group (and flaunted it in front of his poor wife) but me, I was . . . well, disappointed. Disappointed that I never even had the chance to turn him down!

When the group expanded we were joined by such future luminaries as Harve Presnell, a big strapping baritone who became famous in the stage and screen productions of *The Unsinkable Molly Brown* and more recently in character roles in movies like *Fargo*; Carol Neblett, who became a star at the Met; and Bruce Yarnell, another tall, handsome baritone who played opposite Ethel Merman in the revival of *Annie Get Your Gun* and died tragically young in a plane crash.

Then there was Jackie, one of the original twelve members.

Jackie (she was nicknamed by her brother at birth) was (and is) the great opera star Marilyn Horne. She was twelve years old when she joined the Chorale, and although I was few years older we immediately hit it off. We had

*That colorful
Frenchman
Roger Wagner
and me at a
concert in 1981.
(Photo Jasmine)*

a lot in common. Each of us was dedicated to our music and we both later ghosted for other artists on the screen. Our real connection, however, was that Jackie's father and my mother were both similar in giving us the gift of a strong work ethic and the drive to succeed.

In 1947, the Roger Wagner Chorale was engaged to sing on the soundtrack of the feature film *Joan of Arc* starring Ingrid Bergman. This was my first Screen Actors Guild (SAG) contract. Although I had been in dozens of films, they were under the Screen Extras Guild (SEG, which eventually merged with SAG); this was definitely a step up. In *Joan of Arc* the Chorale represented the voices that Joan/Ingrid heard in her head, which eventually led to her being burned at the stake.

The recordings were done at the RKO Studio sound stages. During a rehearsal before a take, Jackie and I were sitting together on the risers watching a heated exchange between Hugo Friedhofer, the composer; Jerome Moross, the orchestrator; and Roger. Roger continued conducting our rehearsal while keeping up his end of the animated discussion. As he conducted and argued, Jackie and I looked at each other and suddenly found it all hilarious. Our giggles blossomed into guffaws until Roger could stand it no more and crashed down his baton, stopping the rehearsal. He asked us to leave the recording studio until we could pull ourselves together enough to not break into continuous spurts of giggling fits while singing. We returned to the hall several minutes later, chastened and almost serious. Roger separated us, like little children, so we would not feed into each other's senses of humor.

Jackie and I were kindred spirits and loved to poke fun at authority. Roger was very intense and sometimes cruel. He felt that he could get the best results from his singers by insulting them. If someone made a mistake he would shout, "You stupid idiot! Why did you do that?" We grew used to it and most of the time his name-calling would just roll off our backs. One time Roger, who depended on me to keep the whole Chorale on pitch, heard me sing a wrong note. Piercing the air with his finger, he vehemently shouted, "Why did you make that mistake?" I calmly replied, "Because I'm stupid!" Well, that sent us all off into gales of laughter and it shut Roger up. For a while, anyway. Virginal little Marni was learning to stand up for herself.

In the long run we didn't care if he yelled at us or seemed not to know the music at first (he was notorious for learning material at the same time he was teaching it to us); he was able to get the absolute best out of us and I was always impressed with his dynamism and emotional flair. The experience that I garnered by singing with the Chorale could never be measured. To be able to perform the best chamber music and most glorious oratorio with a group of the top talents in California was invaluable and something I can never forget or repay.

Of course, there was that time when Roger's notorious temper almost got the best of him.

Once in a while Roger would hire some of us to be part of his choir at St. Joseph's Cathedral in L.A. We "ringers" (hired pros) would make the choir sound better and I, with my perfect pitch, was essential to make sure everyone was in the right key. Roger played the organ, which was in the balcony, and we were all were on risers in the balcony at the back of the church. On this particular Sunday, there was a whole flock of visiting nuns in the house, but since it was standing room only at St. Joseph's, the nuns were spread out against the back wall of the balcony. The piece we were to sing was to begin in open fifth harmonies. We had rehearsed with Roger at the piano, but here at St. Joseph's we would be singing with Roger at the organ. I listened for my pitch, but because of the organ's overtones and echo, I somehow heard the melody as one fifth higher than it really was. With my usual self-confidence I sang out clear and loud. Since everyone was so used to listening to me for their pitch, they followed and all sang one fifth higher than it should have been. Roger heard how off we were, but just kept playing the organ louder and louder trying to get us on key. The singers didn't quite know what was wrong, and since Roger's hands could not leave the keys, he could only signal us by jerking his now very sweaty head. As the organ rose in volume, we kept singing louder as well. The harmonies splintered into cacophony until Roger stopped playing altogether and screamed directly at me, his keeper of the pitch, "You goddamned Anglo-Saxon virgin, you!" You could hear a pin drop at St. Joseph's. The visiting nuns let out a gasp of horror at Roger taking the Lord's name in vain. We all thought that he would surely lose his job. Somehow he used his Gallic charm to retain his position and I'm sure he must have blamed Marni, "that goddamned Anglo-Saxon virgin!"

As the Chorale reaped the rewards of its reputation, I collected experiences I would never have found anywhere else. I mean, where else would I get to be spit on by a great Swedish opera star?

In those days, the San Francisco Opera would visit L.A. and play a season at the enormous Shrine Auditorium. During the 1947 season the Roger Wagner Chorale was hired to sing the roles of the bakers in Wagner's *Die Meistersinger von Nürnberg*. Famed Swedish tenor Set Svanholm was starring. Like most Wagner operas, this one was long and we were not to appear until the fourth act. During the first act of the first performance, we learned our parts in the rehearsal room (we had partially memorized it before we arrived), during the second act we were fitted for our costumes, and during the third act we rehearsed the blocking (where we would stand or sit while we were singing). Then we were finally ushered up to the huge stage and made our entrance as little baker boys. Now, Svanholm may have been a huge opera star, but he was only 5'5" and was placed on a box so that he appeared taller. We had been directed to enter and sit in a semicircle facing him with our backs to the audience. We just had to look adoringly up at him during his aria and not move a hair.

As the group entered and sat I just happened to wind up dead center stage right in front of Svanholm, who began singing. He had an amazing voice with incredible volume for a man of such short stature, and as his volume increased, so did the amount of saliva that flew from his mouth. The spit that Svanhold spewed forth with each note glistened in the spotlight that was aimed at his face. That spotlight may have been aimed at *his* face, but unfortunately, Svanholm's spit was inadvertently aimed at *mine*. It's a matter of physics that what comes out must go down and, since I was the closest target, what came out of his mouth landed all over my face and eyes and dripped down my cheeks. Good little trouper that I was, I looked right up at him as if I were enraptured and didn't move a muscle. For years I had been dreaming about performing in the opera, fantasizing about how glamorous it all would be. Well, glamour was the last thing on my mind as I sat there covered with Svanholm's saliva during this wet night at the opera.

As the years went by, the Roger Wagner Chorale morphed into the Los Angeles Master Chorale, which still frequently performs at the Dorothy Chandler Pavilion. In the autumn of 2000 Marilyn Horne, Harve Presnell, and I got together and gave our services to the Master Chorale to commemorate the retirement of Paul Salamunovich, its conductor (one of the original members of the Chorale). Several members of the original group were still singing with it and the reunion was very emotional for all of us. From musty old trunks, we dug out our old arrangements and were gratified to find that fifty years later we could still sing them in the same keys. Here we were, three soloists who had made our way in the world, blending our voices the way Roger had taught us to. Another circle of my life was completed. As the final chords of the concert rang out we all were awash in tears. I looked at Marilyn, Harve, and all the other singers and I silently said a little prayer of thanks to that enigmatic, frustrating, and very musical Frenchman, Roger Wagner.

Stephen Sondheim once wrote a song called "Multitudes of Amys" and, as I look back at 1947, it seems the song might have been written about me. I was everywhere at once trying to be everything to everyone. The two original Marnis (the "average teen" Marni and the "professional" Marni) seemed to multiply from day to day. The average teen Marni competed with the professional Marni who one day was an opera singer, the next a fledgling movie starlet delivering mail at MGM, and the day after that a classical artist singing oratorios.

I was also the good daughter who didn't make a fuss when she was accepted at Bennington College in Vermont, but was not allowed to attend.

Mother always said that we were too poor to pay for me to go and too rich for me to qualify for a scholarship, but the truth is that she didn't think I was sophisticated enough to leave home yet. Perhaps the fact that I would be away from her and out of her control was also a factor in her decision. In any case, in the fall of 1947 I was to go to City College in L.A. and live at home.

During the winter and spring of 1947 I kept winning singing contests and, because my reputation as a soloist was beginning to grow, I got to work with some of the top musicians of my era. This is the Marni who made her Hollywood Bowl debut with Leopold Stokowski, considered one of the greatest conductors of all time.

Stokowski always cloaked himself in mystery. When asked about his age, he would give 1887 as his year of birth instead of the real date of 1882, and throughout his whole life he spoke with a strange pseudo–East European accent, which was odd for a man born in London. It was as a musical innovator, though, that Stokowski was unparalleled. In 1912, he transformed The Philadelphia Orchestra with what later became known as the "Philadelphia Sound." Stokowski allowed the strings "free bowing," meaning the string players were free to move their bows up and down as they pleased, rather than in unison. This produced a very warm, silky, and vivid sound, which had never been heard before. Stokowski also made several changes to the orchestra's seating arrangement to improve the transparency and clarity of the sound. What made him truly popular, however, was his showmanship. He sometimes produced his concerts like a stage play by placing light spots on him or his always-batonless conducting hands, by making speeches to the audience, and by even once hiding the orchestra behind a curtain.

When he conducted me in "Carmina Burana" it seemed as though he had a magic beam that drew me into his interpretation of the music. He was so deeply into the music that you could *not* help but outsing yourself and be drawn into his magic orbit. I felt a mystical connection. His conducting motions were brilliant. He resembled a great magician when his hands molded the air as if they were a pair of dancers.

That same year, 1947, I sang Mozart's "Requiem" with the L.A. Philharmonic under the baton of Alfred Wallenstein. This was my first brush with Mozart and it led to my lifelong love affair with his music. This concert was notable for another reason: I got to sing at the Baptist Church Auditorium where, ten years before, I had been so entranced by the playing of Fritz Kreisler. Even in my early life, circles and ghosts figured prominently.

The "classical" Marni gave way to the "musical comedy" Marni when I won the title role in *Oh, Susanna*, a new musical playing at the Pasadena Playhouse in May of 1947. These two aspects of myself were always to be part of my split life. "What is she," my future critics would ask, "a musical comedy singer or a serious artiste?" This was the beginning of the lifelong battle I would have with small minds that longed to pigeonhole me. The classicists who looked down on me when I sang Lerner and Loewe instead of Stravinsky would plague me for years. When I was seventeen, it seemed natural to flit from one persona and style to the other, and I merrily accepted whatever opportunity came along without question. In the summer of 1947, I accepted a very unique job that gave me a glimpse into my future.

Over the years, L.B. Mayer's right-hand woman Ida Koverman had kept tabs on my career and stayed in touch with my mother. From my mother she found out the cost of my singing lessons was becoming prohibitive for the family finances. In response, Mrs. Koverman, who thought I had real talent, offered me a position as a "messenger girl" at MGM. The job consisted of delivering mail around the lot and occasionally giving guided tours of the studio and back lot to visiting dignitaries. One of the fringe benefits was free singing lessons from the same teacher who taught teen film star Jane Powell. Mrs. Koverman saw me as a possible replacement for Powell, should she give the studio any trouble. However, times being what they were in Hollywood, she was unable to actually offer me one of those famous seven-year contracts that might have made me choose a road that I was never to travel: the road to movie stardom. To understand why the timing was wrong for me to become a contract player, one has to understand the turmoil that was going on within Hollywood, and especially at MGM.

The late 1940s were tough times for the big movie studios, including MGM. Television was rearing its one-eyed head, and instead of going to the movies, many postwar Americans were staying home in front of the newfangled tube watching wrestling or Uncle Miltie. As a result, MGM's gross revenues dropped 75 percent from 1946 to 1948. In addition, the Supreme Court ruled that the major movie studios, which all owned their own chains of theaters and booked their own product into those theaters, were guilty of monopolization of the industry. The court ruling forced the studios to divest themselves of their theater chains. By 1949, MGM had to sell off their Loews' movie houses, meaning much less revenue and an industrywide tightening of belts. It was also during 1947 that the all-powerful L.B. Mayer was forced to bring in another head of the studio to "help" him climb out of the red. This would eventually lead to Mayer's being ousted from the studio altogether. It was into this atmosphere that I was plunged that summer of 1947.

Although I had walked through the MGM gates in Culver City many times as an extra, driving up every day as a steady employee and knowing I was an integral part of the studio system was exhilarating. I would sling that golden leather mailbag over one shoulder and either walk or take the tram from sound stage to bungalow to executive office and sometimes even to the dressing rooms of the stars. On the way I marveled at the enormity and opulence of the permanent sets that I had seen in all the movies. The "New York Street" that was used in every New York picture was right next to what were once the fairgrounds in *Meet Me in St. Louis*. Down the road was the Olympic-sized pool the studio built specially for Esther Williams to dive into. Every once in a while I could sneak onto a sound stage and watch a scene being filmed.

One day in July 1947, I was asked to deliver mail to Judy Garland's private bungalow. I was excited to meet her, as she was one of the biggest stars at MGM and I had seen all of her movies. I had even been an extra in a few of them. At the time she was filming *The Pirate* with her costar Gene Kelly and was being directed by her husband Vincente Minnelli. When I knocked on the door, there was no answer. I was disappointed that she wasn't there, but I had

My first lead in a musical: the title role in Oh, Susanna *at the Pasadena Playhouse in 1947. (Photo Ellen Bailey, Courtesy of Pasadena Playhouse)*

been told that if the star wasn't in, I should try the door, walk in, lay the envelope on the nearest table and leave immediately. I had done this dozens of times before, but this time was to be different. When I entered the bungalow I was surprised to see that Garland *was* there after all. I smiled and began to say hello, but when she saw me she screamed as if I had attacked her and came at me with such venom in her voice that I threw the envelope down on the table, muttered "I'm sorry," and fled as quickly as I could. It wasn't until years later when her drug problems became common knowledge that I realized what I had walked in on. Garland's pill intake had escalated to such a degree during the filming of *The Pirate* that it was not uncommon for the wardrobe people to find pills sewn into the seams of her costumes.

It was after finishing *The Pirate* that Garland was admitted first to a California sanatorium, and then to the Austen Riggs Center in Massachusetts, a hospital known for treating drug and alcohol problems, the Betty Ford Clinic of its day.

It is amazing how sometimes a question answered the right way can be a signpost that will take you on a road you never dreamed you would travel, a road that would define how you were perceived in the future. It was during a routine mail run on the MGM lot that an intensely bespectacled man walked up to me and challenged me in his Polish accent.

"Hey Nixon! You think you're so smart? Can you sing in Hindu?"

The man asking the question was Bronislaw Kaper, one of MGM's most prominent composers. He knew me from my Meremblum days and took great delight in needling me about my singing abilities. Broni, as he was known to his friends, was a Polish immigrant who wrote the scores for many Hollywood films from the mid 1930s through the late 1960s. His hit songs include "San Francisco," "Hi Lili, Hi Lo," "Cosi Cosa," and "All God's Chillin' Got Rhythm." At the time, Broni was working on the music for the film version of the classic Victorian novel *The Secret Garden*, starring child star Margaret O'Brien. O'Brien began her career doing a bit in *Babes on Broadway* (a film I had also worked on), but made her first hit in *Journey for Margaret*. She went on to win an Academy Award for her tearstained performance in *Meet Me in St. Louis* (opposite Judy Garland) and now she was going to play another heartrending little girl in *The Secret Garden*.

In this film, she was to sing a little Hindu lullaby to her doll and, although little Margaret could pull a tear from a stone, she couldn't sing to save her life.

Margaret O'Brien and me at the opening of 70, Girls, 70. Margaret was the first person I ever dubbed, way back in 1947. (Photo Ed Krieger)

So when Broni saw me that fateful afternoon and challenged me to sing in Hindu, even though I had never done it before (I had never let that stop me before), of course I said yes.

The small recording studio was darkened and quiet. I think it was kept dark so that you would concentrate only on the sound of your voice, undisturbed by visual stimuli. MGM spared no expense on their films and they hired a real Eastern Indian Swami to coach me on the dialect for the song I was to sing. I was suitably impressed when I entered the recording studio and saw him there in his billowing white robes and headdress.

The song was to be recorded "wild," meaning that I was not trying to synchronize my voice to O'Brien's lips, but rather she would have to "lip-synch" later when they played back my recording. O'Brien's speaking and singing voice came out of the large speakers over and over again so that I could listen to it and attempt to match her sound. With the music in front of me, and using a childlike voice (O'Brien was ten years old at the time and I was seventeen), I began to give examples of how I thought O'Brien might sing the song, if she could. I imitated O'Brien's vocal quality and the Swami coached me on the diction. Although I hadn't seen the scene, it was described to me and I kept it in my head along with a mental image of O'Brien in other films in which I'd seen her. Just like that I became a ten-year-old girl singing a lullaby to her doll. Simple, clear, and direct. I had to make sure that my voice would have the same emotions that O'Brien's face would, all without ever seeing the scene or meeting her.

The session went smoothly and didn't last very long and, although I enjoyed it, I had no idea at the time that I was beginning a new career. There were no crashing cymbals and no exploding fireworks—just the glimmer of a thought telling me this might be another door opening that would allow me to use my voice to make a living.

Unwittingly, Mrs. Koverman set me on this new road. It was a road that didn't lead to me becoming MGM's latest starlet as she had hoped, but a road that eventually was to bring me a very different kind of fame. A road paved with ghosts.

shoulder when he threw me a cue. Besides doing my first Mozart opera under his baton, it was in Dr. Strelitzer's class that I was introduced to German lieder and early sixteenth- and seventeenth-century French and Italian art songs. He also introduced me to my piano teacher, Leonard Stein.

In later years, when it became apparent I was never going to be a piano virtuoso, Leonard Stein joked that I was never to tell anyone I studied piano with him. I agreed to keep silent if he would never tell anyone he kicked me out of his solfeggio class for refusing to learn my "do re mis"!

The solfeggio technique of sight singing substituted syllables (do re mi and so forth) for the notes of the scale. Since I could sight-read most music that was put in front of me, without the syllables, and wend my way through most languages, why, I naïvely wondered, should I need to learn how to use the solfeggio technique? This was typical Marni.

Ever since I was a child, I was always too facile and quick for my own good. I could usually pick and choose what I thought I needed to focus on, saying to myself, "I'm going to cut corners and make my own rules." My innate ability to pick up things quickly was both a blessing and a curse, and now when faced with having to practice the piano as I had done the violin, I just wanted to sing and thus didn't spend quality time on this instrument. So Leonard kicked me out of his solfeggio class at the same time as I quietly left his piano class. Now when my students and I anguish that I'm not a better pianist, I could kick myself for being so foolhardy and arrogant. I should have taken the time to learn to play well. If nothing else, I could have had a ball entertaining myself with all that music. Ah, the folly of youth! Still, despite my pigheadedness, Leonard Stein saw something in me as a singer and *he* became a key player (pun intended) in my future.

Born in L.A. in 1916, Stein attended City College, where he studied piano. When Arnold Schoenberg, the great Viennese composer and musical innovator (he created the twelve-tone method of composition, immediately taken up by other modern composers), fled the Nazis and started teaching at the University of Southern California and then later at the University of California, Los Angeles, Leonard Stein was one of his first students. Stein soon became Schoenberg's teaching assistant and then his private assistant, eventually becoming the director of the Arnold Schoenberg Institute at USC. Until his recent death Leonard was a man devoted to Schoenberg and modern music, although he believed "all music is modern music." He was an integral part of L.A.'s musical world and my life.

I had quickly become an active part of City College's musical life, singing in a concert featuring the university's seventy-five-piece orchestra just two months after matriculating. Along with my high school friend, future film composer Jerry Goldsmith (he was one of my big crushes, and years later I was instrumental in getting him his first movie job), I was beginning to get noticed on campus. One day in late February of 1948, Leonard Stein walked into one of Dr. Strelitzer's classes and heard me sing. Knowing that I could sight-read anything, he asked if I might be interested in learning and performing a difficult modern piece by Viennese émigré composer Ernst Krenek, another music instructor at our school.

Born in 1900, Krenek became well known in 1926 in Germany as the composer of *Jonny Spielt Auf*, a jazz opera that had an international success and remains his best-known work. He emigrated to the U.S. in 1937, and in 1948 he was the first of the "exiles in paradise," as Southern California's émigré musicians were called, that I came to know.

The music scene in Southern California at this time was filled with Europe's most innovative and brilliant expatriates. When Hitler came to power in Germany in the early 1930s, the cultural life of L.A. reaped the benefits of his reign of terror by playing host to the cream of Europe's artistic castaways. The Nazis abhorred what they called "entarte musik" or "degenerate music." They equated anything artistically experimental or new with the Jews, homosexuals, and mentally ill they wanted expelled from the Fatherland. The fortunate and wise left their homeland for greener pastures. The greenest pasture for many of them turned out to be L.A.

In 1933 composer Arnold Schoenberg came to a realization that typified his fellow émigrés. He said, "I have at last learned the lesson that has been forced upon me during this year, and I shall not ever forget it. It is that I am not a German, not a European, indeed perhaps scarcely a human being (at least the Europeans prefer the worst of their race to me), but I am a Jew." That year he settled in L.A.

As the thirties and forties rolled on, Schoenberg was joined by poet/playwright Berthold Brecht, authors Thomas and Heinrich Mann, Franz Werfel and his wife Alma Mahler, conductors Bruno Walter and Otto Klemperer, and composers Ernst Toch, Erich Korngold, Hanns Eisler, Ernst Krenek, Igor Stravinsky, and many others. They congregated in Southern California for many reasons, not the least of which was the climate itself, and, of course, L.A. offered the lure of Hollywood and the prospect of lucrative employment. What also can't be discounted is that after a while they congregated to be with others of their kind. Many émigrés were forced to downgrade their vocations in their new country. A joke went around at this time about two dachshunds walking on the Santa Monica beach. One assures the other, "Here, it's true, I'm a dachshund; but in the old country I was a Saint Bernard!"

The émigré musicians, however, flourished and, because of them, L.A. in the late 1940s and early 1950s became a rich cultural paradise—and I became one of the beneficiaries of those riches. Singing the émigrés' new American music and meeting them was a fortuitous stop on my train ride through life.

I had been exposed to many kinds of music, but modern esoteric material like Krenek's was something new to me at the time. Most of the vocal music I had performed required some kind of emotional interpretation and connection, but this music was more abstract and extremely complicated rhythmically and melodically and had to be executed purely and cleanly. I was also becoming aware that if the piece were well written, the humanity in the text and the music would come bursting through without needing too much embroidery from me. It was because I could sight-read this very difficult music that my classmates gave me the flattering nickname of "the brain." Of course this nickname only applied to music!

Krenek was a cuddly teddy-bearish man and was warm and totally supportive when I sang his piece for him. He put his stamp of approval on it and was the first one on his feet on March 16, 1948, when Leonard Stein and I performed it at the 1948 Chamber Music Series. After the performance Leonard was very pleased.

"Well, I think you should come with me to *Evenings on the Roof*," he rather offhandedly remarked, "and meet all the composers that come there every Monday night."

That invitation opened up a whole new world for me.

In 1938, Peter Yates, a self-proclaimed amateur musician, and his concert pianist wife, Frances Mullen, were frustrated not only by the lack of performances of chamber music in L.A., but by Southern California's ignorance of modern music in general. L.A. meant Hollywood and Hollywood meant the movies. In this studio town, if you weren't doing movies, you were nothing. André Previn once told me an anecdote about running into MGM studio chief L.B. Mayer and mentioning that he saw the great Jascha Heifetz at the Hollywood Bowl the night before. Mayer said, "You know why he'll never be a success? Because he's not in pictures!"

To remedy this situation, Yates and Mullen (and later Lawrence Morton, a renowned music critic turned entrepreneur) inaugurated a weekly chamber music concert series that took place in a specially built studio on the roof of their home in the Silver Lake district of L.A. The Yateses sought to create an audience for "that class of music which is always contemporary, whether written by sixteenth-century composers or by Hindemith and Ives," as Yates later wrote. In the end the concerts were an ingenious mix of old and new, established and experimental, taking in everyone from Monteverdi to Webern. At first only the musical intelligencia were invited for the purpose of reading through new music. It was deemed a privilege and honor to wangle an invitation. The space was small but the talent gathered every Monday night was enormous. The Yateses named their event *Evenings on the Roof*. Taking advantage of the influx of European émigrés, their cozy Monday nights on the roof soon became so successful that they had to move off the roof and into Plummer Park and eventually to the Wilshire Ebell Auditorium. The changes of venue necessitated a change in name to *Monday Evening Concerts*. The City of Los Angeles Bureau of Music called the *Evenings on the Roof* audiences "among the most musically sophisticated in the nation."

When I first entered this hallowed rooftop in 1948 it was to meet and observe, but by 1949 Leonard and I were called upon to perform. At the beginning I was given the material by various modern composers and then I'd work on the music at home and come back the next Monday and read it though. As time went on I began to realize how important this seemingly informal recital was and I wanted to get into each piece with as much depth as possible. Leonard understood this very cerebral music, but I sometimes felt that I was barely hanging on by the seat of my pants trying to survive. It was only after I sang it that I began to understand what I had sung.

After an informal evening when I read through over fifty of the great American composer Charles Ives' songs, I made my official *Evenings on the Roof* debut in a concert that celebrated Ives' seventy-fifth birthday. Also making his "rooftop" debut that night was pianist André Previn. The evening was magical and was taped for broadcast on the radio.

My next *Evenings on the Roof* concert was as part of the Roger Wagner Chorale. Leonard Stein played one of four pianos in the first L.A. performance of Stravinsky's *Les Noces*. Although we had met before when he came to hear me as one of Roger's "ringers" in the choir at St. Joseph's Cathedral, it was during the rehearsal time for *Les Noces* that I got to know and really work with the legendary Igor Stravinsky.

Born in Russia in 1882, Stravinsky was best known for his two ballet scores "The Rite of Spring" and "The Firebird." He came to the U.S. in 1939 and in the postwar years he turned from a style of eclectic neoclassicism to composing in the twelve-note technique propounded by Schoenberg. A versatile composer, inventive in changing styles, he was, I always felt, the musical counterpart of the painter Picasso. His oeuvre included everything from symphonies to piano miniatures.

In the late 1950s Mrs. Igor Stravinsky, known to us all as Vera (she was the one who would coach me on my Russian pronounciation), would stand out on her lawn on Wetherly Drive just off Sunset Boulevard and wait for the tour buses to come by. A metallic voice would squawk over a loudspeaker, "And on your left is the house where Shirley Temple lived when she was making all those wonderful movies we all adored. Next door is the house where Lana Turner's young daughters shot her mother's lover." Vera would laugh as the tourists craned their necks out of the windows hoping for a glimpse of someone famous. Not once did any of the tour guides mention that Stravinsky lived

Igor Stravinsky gives me a few pointers before conducting me in his Nightingale *at UCLA. (Photo by Alexander Courage, through Don Christlieb)*

there. This, however, was the house where I first worked with Stravinsky and where we rehearsed his pieces both old and new.

Stravinsky was short with little sharp eyes, a balding head, and a tight, intense body that was pitched forward, giving me the impression that he was going to pounce at any moment. He had a wonderful, dry sense of humor that complemented his Russian sophistication. If one worked with Stravinsky, one also worked with Robert Craft, who was Stravinsky's right-hand man: coach, conductor, interpreter, and ghostwriter.

Since meeting in 1948, Craft and Stravinsky were inseparable. It was Craft who was instrumental in persuading Stravinsky to adopt the twelve-tone method of composition, a momentous turn in Stravinsky's creative path. He collaborated with Stravinsky on six books and was the one who taught, coached, and conducted us in anything Stravinsky wrote. At the time I knew him, Craft lived in a bungalow on Stravinsky's property and their relationship sometimes seemed to border on odd. I can remember Stravinsky listening to Craft coach us and suddenly jumping up to make a correction. Before he could even get the words out, Craft turned on him and said, "Oh, be quiet!" He then turned to us, not caring if Stravinsky heard him or not and commented, "What does that old man know?" Maybe it was his sense of humor, but we were astonished. Interestingly, Stravinsky *did* shut up.

In the studio recording Schoenberg's Quartet under the leadership of Stravinsky's right-hand man, Robert Craft (1950). (l to r: Craft, James Van Dusen, Richard Robinson, Catherine Gayer, me) (Photo Alexander Courage)

Sometimes our morning rehearsal sessions at Stravinsky's home stretched into all-day marathons. On those days we were invited to have lunch with the Stravinskys. We were always offered wine with our meal, which to little Marni was amazing. In my home, you had a glass of milk with lunch. Stravinsky loved his wines and talked about them as if they were people.

"This little wine," he would tell us in his charming Russian accent, "is made by a very special kind of grape, but he doesn't travel well. We smuggled him out of France in our suitcases, he and his brothers. Luckily the family was unharmed by all the jiggling and survived to entertain our palates today."

Accompanying the wines (which I only tasted or I would never have been able to sing anymore that day!) were exotic delicacies that had never crossed my mother's table or my lips: shrimp and blintzes and borscht. And lox. I had never seen or tasted this smoked pink fish before. It was a revelatory taste sensation.

I rehearsed at Stravinsky's house (and indulged in culinary delicacies) many times over the years for both concerts and the many recordings I did of his work, including *Les Noces*, *Nightingale*, his opera *Mavra*, and the premiere of his 1952 *Cantata*. Bob Craft was always there and I came to feel that through all of the work he and Stravinsky had become my friends.

Sometime in the mid 1950s I was engaged to record the solo part in Cantata #78 by Bach: "The Trauerode." Bob Craft was conducting the orchestra and they were also recording a chamber version of Stravinsky's "The Rite of Spring" at the same session. The session was scheduled for Monday but on the previous

Saturday, while driving my car from my home in the Hollywood Hills, I had a head-on collision. I was thrust forward onto the steering wheel with such force and banged my left eye so badly that I was immediately rushed in an ambulance to a hospital where they operated to save the eye. I was given thirty-two stitches along my eyelid and told that although my eye would be all right, I would never grow eyelashes again. They wrapped my upper face in bandages and when I got to my room and looked in the mirror I resembled a mummy. I was dizzy and nauseous and all the doctors and nurses told me to rest.

"But I have a recording session with Stravinsky and Bob Craft on Monday," I cried to their blank stares. They had no idea who these people were. "I have to be there! My voice is okay. You've got to let me out of the hospital."

Although the doctors kept advising against it, my iron will prevailed and on Monday morning they discharged me. I went straight to the recording session. When I got there, I realized that the doctors had been right in trying to deter me. Every time I tried to make a sound my head ached so sharply I felt as if I had had a concussion. The dizziness wouldn't quit and I had to hold on to anything solid to stay upright. Still I was determined to sing, but as I began recording, to my horror, I heard Bob Craft shouting at me, "Get on pitch, goddamn it!" The really odd thing was I didn't know I was *off* pitch!

By now it should be clear that consistently being on pitch was my hallmark, so this was a catastrophe in the making. I couldn't figure out what to do. Finally, in desperation, even though I could hardly stand up, I decided the only way to get the right notes out was to transpose the music in my head and imagine the notes on the page as if they were written out in a higher key. I found if I did this I could somehow land exactly on the pitches I needed to sing and make music out of it. This was an enormous mental exercise, but little by little it began to work, but not quickly enough for the exasperated Bob Craft.

After a few takes I went out of the studio into the recording booth to listen to the results. Stravinsky was in the booth with me, having just finished conducting "The Rite of Spring" a short while ago. He was sweaty and exhausted and imbibing a little of his customary "postconducting" scotch. Bob Craft remained in the recording studio with the orchestra. The orchestra was made up of the top musicians in L.A. and by now I had performed with all of them and many were friends. They knew me and sympathized with my plight. They all understood that it was totally unlike me to be unreliable musically, so they were rooting for me to get it right.

We all listened to the playback, but the engineer failed to turn off the mikes in the recording studio so, although I was in the booth, I could hear what Bob Craft was saying. He, on the other hand, had no idea the mikes were live. As he listened, he blurted out, "If we could get this goddamn soprano to sing on pitch it might be fine."

By this time I had had it with Craft and was feeling even more nauseous as a result of my mental exertion. Here I was, barely able to stand, my head wrapped up like a mummy, and Mr. Craft hadn't an ounce of sympathy for me. This was the final straw.

I asked John McClure, the engineer, to please turn on a talkback mike in the booth and with great difficulty, but enormous dignity, stood up and said, "Bob Craft, you can go fuck yourself!"

The musicians, who were all pretty sick of the insensitivity of Craft, the taskmaster, fell on the floor in laughing hysterics. Sweet, virginal Marni had never sworn before! Certainly not for God and all of Columbia Records to hear. And by God, I mean Stravinsky!

In the middle of the hilarity out in the recording studio, Stravinsky, sitting next to me in the booth, stood up, put his large tumbler of scotch down, turned to me and fixed me with an evil Russian glare that would have brought the Czar to his knees. As he opened his mouth to speak, he seemed dizzy, wobbled on his feet (how much had he been drinking?), sat down, and fell immediately to sleep. The tension was broken and I went back into the studio and finished recording the piece to everyone's satisfaction (even my own!). Stravinsky had recently named me as one of his favorite singers and now I wondered if he was going to retract the statement. Oh, Igor, what were you going to say that day?

The late 1940s were a whirlwind of professional activity for me. Famed Hollywood gossip columnist Hedda Hopper wrote about my performance at the Meremblum Junior Symphony Orchestra's tenth-anniversary concert. As I had been doing since I was eleven years old, I sometimes stood up from the violin section and sang an aria. Hopper was entranced and reported that there were "many dimmed eyes when a little girl put down her violin and sang. She's our future coloratura soloist." I tried to live up to that very kind notice.

Besides going to school and participating in the Opera Workshop, I seemed to be working all the time. One night I was being conducted by famed film composer Franz Waxman (*Rebecca*, *Suspicion*, *Sayonara*, and *Sunset Boulevard*) in a staged oratorio of Honegger's *Joan of Arc at the Stake* and the next Alfred Wallenstein was putting the Roger Wagner Chorale through our paces in a concert commemorating the bicentennial of Bach's death. The Hollywood Bowl was becoming a second home to me as I sang solos under the batons of Sir William Walton, Bruno Walter, Otto Klemperer, and Leopold Stokowski.

On the popular music front, I made my network radio debut on a CBS show called *Tomorrow Calling* singing a medley of Jerome Kern songs. After singing I told the radio audience, "I wanted to sing opera in English and bring serious music to a public who might not normally hear it." During this period I *was* singing opera. About this time I made my professional debut as the third hand-maiden in Richard Strauss' *Elektra* in April of 1948. Not exactly the lead, but one has to start somewhere!

The only thing lacking in my busy life was romance, but in the fall of 1949, that void was about to be filled.

Romance! Love! Vienna! At nineteen years old these three items blended into one fantasy for me. For years I had a constant stream of crushes. I had crushes on my schoolteachers, my voice teachers, my directors—mostly older, more experienced men. Looking back I realize that what most of these men had in common were their accents. Polish, German, Russian, and need I say it? Viennese. Wholesome American me with the freckles and red hair was enraptured with what I perceived as their dark, swarthy continental sophistication. It helped if they were also musical. As my crushes multiplied it appeared this late bloomer was ripe for the picking. Gershon Kingsley was not the one to do the picking, but he led me right to that night in Vienna I so badly craved.

Kingsley certainly fit the bill for one of my "Marni crushes." He spoke with an odd accent that mixed German, Israeli, and sloppy English in equal parts, and he was a brilliant, clever, and volatile musician who later became a well-known musical director in the theater and was instrumental in popularizing the Moog synthesizer, for which he wrote several pieces that he recorded. These resulted in hit albums. In 1949, however, he played the piano for my current voice teacher, John Lombardi. Perhaps my late-blooming hormones were raging, for one day in September of that year, after one of my lessons, I eagerly looked into Kingsley's eyes and blurted out, "Gershon, would you take me out?"

"Sure I'll take you out, Marni. But my girlfriend, Evelyn, has to come along, too!"

I must have looked crestfallen because he just laughed at my artlessness and told me he had a friend who might want to meet me and that we would all be going to his house for a party.

In the Arthur Laurents play *The Time of the Cuckoo*, the leading character exclaims that when she falls in love she will hear a waltz, a schmaltzy Viennese waltz. That night in a little house in Studio City, California, all the strings in Vienna were playing for me.

Ernest Gold was nine years older than me and wore thick Coke-bottle-like eyeglasses that made his large hazel eyes seem even bigger. In fact everything about his oblong face was large: ears, nose, lips, square-cut jaw. He had a slyly demonic smile that went with his off-center sense of humor. He was not terribly tall (about 5'9"), nor particularly well built, but when he opened his mouth out came the most charming Viennese accent I had ever heard.

On the way to the party, Gershon and Evelyn had tried to fill me in on Ernest's past. They told me he was a composer who had fled the Nazis (wasn't everyone in those days?) and arrived in New York at seventeen years of age in 1938 and then moved to L.A. in the mid 1940s to compose music for films. He had already written several hit songs in New York, including "Hi Cy, What's 'a-Cookin'" and the theme from *Your Hit Parade* ("So Long for a While").

During the party, Ernest filled me in further about his work at "Repulsive Studios," as he called Republic Studios. (Although I had also worked there our paths had never crossed.) Instead of writing the whole score of a film, at "Repulsive" the composers would divide up the chores: one would write the love theme, the other the chase sequence, and still another the opening credits. This, Ernest said, was functioning as a hack, something he feared becoming. Ernest felt that composing for films was an honorable profession and longed to join the ranks of Bernard Hermann, Franz Waxman, and Max Steiner, who composed whole scores for great films. He also told me that although he was separated from his wife, they were not yet divorced.

It was apparent that Gershon had wasted no time in telling Ernest I was a singer and that I could sight-read anything, because sometime in the middle of the party I was put to the test. Truth be told, I was happy to perform as it made me less self-conscious about my naïveté and lack of dating experience. Ernest pulled out a song cycle he had just written and wanted to share. He asked if I would read through it with him and in my usual guileless way I said, "Yes, of course!" When I sang it through without a single mistake Ernest just about died. He thought my ease at sight singing was the most fantastic thing he had ever seen, and to top it off he thought I was a good singer. Later on he also told me I was pretty. Now he was getting personal and *that* made my night!

We obviously hit it off, because before I left the party Ernest invited me to go on a double date with Gershon (my crush on him was over!) and Evelyn to the Pomona State Fair. It only hit me later that this was the very same fair where I won that fateful singing contest eight years ago, and now it figured once again in determining my future.

It was over an hour's drive to Pomona and Ernest and I shared the backseat, but in fact, if you asked Gershon and Evelyn, we weren't in the same car with them at all. So enraptured with each other were we in that first-blush-of-love way that it seemed no one else existed and that the car was propelling itself. Ernest kept making up little songs and writing them down on scraps of paper describing his feelings for me. He wrote them in outrageous tessituras and demanded I sing them out loud. I was laughing and giddily giggling and floating on a cloud. I had never had so much attention paid to me or felt so utterly romantic.

When we got to the fair we went to the international art show. Although I had learned about art in school, until now no one had ever taken the time in a formal setting to point out to me what made this or that painting interesting or important. Ernest did that. He took me by the hand and showed me what he liked or didn't like about each work of art. This was seduction by intellect. I thought his erudition and knowledge were so damned sexy. For the first time in my life I was falling in love. From the way he kept putting his arms around me and holding me on the way home it was apparent that Ernest was feeling something, too.

We quickly became inseparable. We were a clichéd pair of lovebirds and Ernest even had a pet name for me: Nusch, which was short for Marnuschka. Ernest loved to cook and he was very good at making up delightful Viennese concoctions. He would have me come to his little house and it was becoming clear that before long he would also have me. Of course I could hardly wait!

I suppose it needs to be said here, I was a virgin. Ernest, however, was a man of the world and eventually my virginal status was a thing of the past. After a while I started staying at Ernest's house more and more often. By this time, in 1950, although I was still living at home, I had moved into my own room behind the garage, with a separate entrance so that I wouldn't disturb the family with my late hours due to rehearsals and such. It was also a place where I could practice singing and not get on anyone's nerves. This meant that my parents didn't quite know whether I was home or not, making my clandestine nights out at Ernest's less of a problem. What they didn't know certainly didn't hurt them, or so I thought.

About six months after I met Ernest he told me about two friends of his who were getting married. In my romantic, dizzy haze I assumed that he was trying to tell me in his complicated, creative, and roundabout way that he wanted to marry *me*. So without saying anything to him, I excitedly ran home to my mother and told her that Ernest wanted to marry me. She listened very attentively and immediately burst into tears.

"Oh, no! I knew it! I knew it from that day you came home from the Pomona State Fair. I knew you were in love, and I knew this was going to happen. I've been so worried! I don't want you to throw away your career. You've worked too long and hard. Don't do it, Marni!"

I should have known. I thought I was hiding my emotions so carefully but my mother was smarter than I thought. She probably could even tell I was not a virgin anymore but, as usual, this was never discussed. Mother told me all the pros and cons (mainly cons) of getting married so young. She did her best to dissuade me, but I got the feeling she knew the decision was mine. To my mind, she accepted the fact that I was going to get married, so I was walking on a cloud when I went back to Ernest with the good news.

"I told my mother you wanted to marry me and she said it was all right."

Ernest turned white as a sheet. In his mind he had never asked me to marry him at all. It was my own wishful projection. At first he was in shock, but as his sense of humor took over he started to laugh and began to consider it. Within a few minutes he not only accepted the fact that we were indeed getting married, he actually thought it was a good idea. Unconsciously my feminine wiles had come to the fore. I was getting exactly what I wanted: the happy ending. Now that we were in agreement I felt terrific.

We spent the next few weeks blissfully planning our wedding. How naïve we were (or I was anyway). Ernest hadn't worked for a year at this time. Oh, yes, he was composing and I was singing his music around town, but he had left "Repulsive Studios" and was living off of his dwindling savings. In our romantic stupor, we decided that we would get married on my earnings. Meanwhile, my father weighed in with his opinion of my impending nuptials.

"Are you crazy?" he began his tirade. "This man is nine years older than you. He's European. He's a gourmet! He hardly speaks English!"

"Daddy, that's not true. He's smart and he speaks English very well. He just has an acc . . ."

"He's been married before," he interrupted without hearing me. "Is his divorce even final?" Before I could even tell him that it now was, he railed on.

"And he's asking you to get married on *your* earnings? *What* earnings? What kind of man is that? He has nothing going for him but you!"

"But Daddy . . ."

"How old are you anyway? Are you sixteen yet?"

He knew I was almost twenty years old. I was devastated. I was in anguish. I was furious! I ran to my room in the back of the garage, banged on the furniture, and cried my eyes out. I was more determined than ever to marry Ernest. Daddy was right about us not having enough money, but I had a plan. I would make my talent come to our rescue.

For many years now the Atwater Kent Foundation had an annual vocal competition. The first prize was $5,000, an impressive sum even today, but a fortune back in 1950. I had entered before and come close to winning and this time I pinned my matrimonial hopes on my prospective victory. With $5,000 in my dowry, we would be starting our marriage on the right foot.

When the day of the competition came I had tonsillitis but, although terrified and upset, I nevertheless competed. Despite my infirmity, I came in second and was awarded $2,500. Under normal circumstances I would have been thrilled, but this was half of what I had planned on. It was of some solace when Johnny Green, the famous songwriter and arranger (also a friend and colleague), who was one of the judges, told me that I was on the top of his list and the top of another judge's list. "It was so close, Marni," he said, "when finally one of the judges caved in and his points went to the other singer. Don't worry, it won't hurt your career."

Of course Johnny didn't know I wasn't thinking of my career, but of my life. He had no clue why I was banking on winning the big prize and that I was devastated to have only half of what I had counted on.

Becoming Mrs. Gold in 1950. Ernest and me surrounded by friends Joan Spafford and Peter Jona Korn (and an unidentified minister!). (From the author's collection)

"Don't worry, Nusch-Nusch," (my pet name had multiplied because I was now a second-prize winner) Ernest said in his soothing Viennese tones. "We'll work it out." His way of working it out was to take my prize money and buy us a used car.

"How could he spend your money like that?"

"He's a loser!"

"He's just using you!"

"Be careful, Marni."

The chorus of voices belonged to my friends and family. The loudest and most insistent voice belonged to my mother, who feared that after all these years I would fritter away everything that I had worked so hard to achieve. She was terrified that my career as a singer would be over, as I would be forced to take any old odd jobs that came along and not concentrate on my development as an artist. Or worse, just be known as Ernest's little "house bunny."

The night before my wedding, when I suppose most mothers are giving their daughters advice on being a good wife, my mother told me about her premonition. She said she had had it the night I came home and first told her I was going to be married. Mother always claimed to be a bit psychic. Enough to know what would happen, she said, but not enough to know what to do about it. She told me that even before I revealed my wedding plans her inner voices were telling her "this isn't right." She implored me to not go through with it.

Ernest and I were married on May 22, 1950, and as we drove off in our new used car bought with my prize money, Mother tried to smile through her tears. They came around, my parents, but in the background my mother continued to have the same foreboding premonition for the next nineteen years.

Who knew it would take me that long to realize there was some truth to what she most feared?

Chapter Four

THE FABULOUS FIFTIES, PART ONE

"I have a feeling we're not in Kansas anymore."

JUDY GARLAND as Dorothy in *The Wizard of Oz* (1939)

T HE NOISE OF THE PROPELLERS WAS DEAFENING but, on that clear July morning in 1950, I found the drone and clatter on the long cross-country flight soothing. There were no onboard films in those days and a book was your best friend. I was grateful, however, for the uninterrupted time to think and sort through my mood, which was a mixture of excitement tempered with apprehension and sadness. I had just said a tearful good-bye to my husband of only six weeks, so the sadness was accounted for. I was excited because I had been chosen before we were even married to be part of the Opera Program at the famous Tanglewood Music Center just outside of Boston. As the plane wended its way east, more tears came to my eyes. It seemed like I had been crying on cue ever since saying "I do." I cried through the ceremony, the reception, and the honeymoon. At the wedding and reception they were tears of joy, but it took me years to understand why I shed so many more on my wedding night. The answer came down to two words: "Great Expectations."

From our first date I was head over heels in love with Ernest and my surrender to our desires was delicious, but now that we were married I expected the world. To sustain that initial excitement and let a relationship deepen and grow more sexually fulfilling, one must nurture it. I had no idea how to do that except to worship him more and more. I now expected our honeymoon to be so much more wonderful than our other sexual experiences had been. To paraphrase a lyric by Johnny Mercer, "I was building up to an awful letdown." I was too shy to talk about any of this or ask Ernest for what I thought I needed. The fact that he seemed perfectly satisfied and never tried to find out if there was anything wrong from my end soon began to rankle. True to my personality, though, I tucked all these feelings of disappointment away in my metaphorical box deep in the back of my imaginary closet and blissfully anticipated the adventure of being a married woman.

The plane hit some bumps and I held tightly onto the armrest and pushed my foot down on the floor as if I were in a car and could control the brake. This was the first time I had ever flown cross-country and it was a little unnerving. I tried to cover up my nerves by thinking of how lucky I was to have been chosen by Dr. Jan Popper to be part of Tanglewood's Opera Program. It was only a year before that I had met and begun to work with Dr. Popper.

In the summer of 1949, after my first semester at City College, I was seeking out other opera opportunities and I heard through the musical grapevine that Jan Popper's Opera Workshop at Stanford University was the place to be. Dr. Popper's workshop had been established in 1939 and was the first of its kind on the West Coast. The workshop had created a sensation with its very first production, Benjamin Britten's *Peter Grimes*, which was so successful that it was taken from the Stanford campus to the San Francisco Opera House. The summer of 1949 was to be the last summer that Dr. Popper would be at Stanford. Luckily for us in Southern California, he transferred to UCLA and continued his workshops there and became an integral part of the musical life of L.A. Like a good disciple, I followed him there, too, and became one of his key singers in the newly formed UCLA Opera Theater, which also included pianist Natalie Limonick, later a well-known opera and vocal coach, and Latfollah (Latvi) Mansouri, soon to become head of the San Francisco Opera Company.

At the same time I met another of my mentors: Carl Ebert. A major presence in European opera houses where he worked as an actor under the great Max Reinhart, he is perhaps most famous for co-establishing the Glyndebourne Opera Festival in England. I first became associated with Ebert when he directed me in the West Coast premiere of Benjamin's Britten's opera *Albert Herring* in December of 1949. Ebert formed the Guild Opera Company in 1950 using talent from the USC Opera Workshop. On February 22 of that year he gave me one of the best twentieth-birthday presents anyone had ever received when he welcomed me into the company by giving me the role of Blonde in Mozart's *The Abduction from the Seraglio*. As I toured up and down the West Coast with both Popper and Ebert I realized all three of us were fulfilling one of our dreams: to perform operas in English. I became good friends with both of them, and when Dr. Popper was appointed temporary director of the Opera Program of the Berkshire Music Festival, by special request of famed conductor Serge Koussevitzky (and with the approval of Boris Goldovsky, who had formed the program), he asked me to come along with him to Tanglewood.

Even way out on the West Coast we had all heard of the musical wonders of the Tanglewood Music Center back east. Located in the Berkshire Hills of western Massachusetts, Tanglewood was established as a music center in 1940 by Boston Symphony conductor Koussevitzky. Since then it has not only become the summer home of the Boston Symphony Orchestra, but provided and

Herr Carl Ebert directing me as Blonde in a rehearsal of Mozart's Abduction from the Seraglio *at USC in 1950. (l to r: Wolfgang Martin at the piano, Ebert, Hendrick deBoer, me, and Michael [then Kalem] Kermoyan) (Courtesy of the University of Southern California)*

continues to provide a unique, in-depth musical experience for emerging professional musicians of exceptional ability. I was particularly excited to be part of the program as I was to work with such internationally renowned and up-and-coming artists as Leonard Bernstein, Lukas Foss, Sarah Caldwell, and Koussevitzky himself. Thinking on the plane about all the upcoming activity made me forget Ernest for a moment, but before long I was crying once again, remembering our tearful good-bye. My only solace in leaving him was that he would be as busy as I would be. He was composing an opera in collaboration with Ebert's daughter Christine (she was writing the libretto). As the plane bumped along through turbulence I told myself not to feel so guilty about leaving my husband so early in our marriage. After all, Ernest had known about this before we were even married. I told myself that he would he be busy writing music and would have his hands full collaborating with Christine. If only I had known *how* full!

After the seemingly endless ten-hour flight, plus a stop in Chicago to refuel (this is before jet travel and nonstop trips became the norm), the plane landed in New York's Idlewild Airport (now JFK International). Although I was supposed to take a train up to Boston, the plane was late and all my connections had to be rearranged. Knowing this delay might be a distinct possibility I was armed with the phone number of Ernest's sister Gerti, who lived on Bleecker Street in Greenwich Village. After talking to her on the phone, I gathered up my luggage and took an airport shuttle bus to Grand Central Station where, according to Gerti's instructions, I was to take the subway down to the Village and find her apartment on Bleeker Street. Oh, my God!

Here I stood, the country mouse from sunny California faced with the actuality of Big Bad New York City. It was quite a shock. On the surface New York looked familiar. I had seen its famous skyline in the movies, but MGM had built the city streets on the back lot and on-screen, and although there was the same kind of hustle and bustle, everyone had seemed so friendly. I remembered Judy Garland in *The Clock* and how the whole city conspired to help her find Robert Walker and live happily ever after. Welcome to reality, Marni.

The waiting room at Grand Central Station resembled an ant farm I had growing up: everyone rushing in every direction with some unknown but seemingly important purpose. I was faced with massive waves of humanity pushing and shoving me and ignoring one another. I was unprepared and terrified. As I walked out into the city streets near Grand Central on 42nd Street I knew what Dorothy meant in *The Wizard of Oz* when she said, "I have a feeling we're not in Kansas anymore."

New Yorkers not only had their own accelerated pace, but also seemed to have their own language. When I politely asked directions to the subway, I found I couldn't understand a word of the gruff, speedy New Yorkese that was hurled my way. With luggage in hand, I trudged down into the "hole in the ground," as the song "New York, New York" had so aptly named the subway. The man in the token booth was no help at all and finally got disgusted with me and ignored my questions about what train I should take. Finally I gave up and lugged my bags right back up to the street. After several more frustrated New Yorkers failed to help me, I decided to give in, spend some of my hard-earned money, and take a taxi to Greenwich Village. Now all I had to do was figure out how to get a cab to actually stop for me.

I must have been quite the picture of the out-of-town hick standing outside of Grand Central in my now wrinkled but very proper dress with matching hat and gloves, carrying a heavy suitcase, a purse, and a briefcase full of music. As I tried to hail a cab in vain, I heard a male voice from behind me.

"Well, you look lost. Can I help you?"

I almost wept with joy! Someone was trying to help me.

"Where are you trying to go?" he gently inquired.

Relieved, I told him I was trying to get to Washington Square. "But I can't seem to get a cab," I said.

"Well, here, I'll help you."

Before I could blink, he put two fingers in his mouth, whistled, hailed a cab, and lifted my suitcases into the backseat. He held the door for me as I followed them in.

Then he got in the cab and sat next to me.

Now I was really scared! I had been warned about the evils of New York City, and here I was in a cab with a strange man taking charge and telling the cab driver where to take us. And it wasn't to Bleecker Street! My brain started clicking. "Think fast, Marni, think fast!" All I could think of was escape. When we approached the first traffic light and the cab stopped, I opened the door, grabbed my bags, and got the hell out of that taxi before the man knew what happened.

If I learned nothing else from my first day in New York City, it was how to hail my own cab!

After spending a frightening and disoriented stormy, rainy night in Gerti's sixth-floor, roach-infested walk-up (how did New Yorkers manage the climb every day?) I got back on course the next morning and took the train to Boston and Tanglewood.

Once I arrived in the beautiful bucolic setting I immediately breathed a sigh of relief. It was worth going through the hell of New York for this. Tanglewood was a magical blend of the formal and informal, of joy and hard work. It's said that no one who spends a summer at Tanglewood leaves untouched by the experience. It's true. The spectacular panoramic 210-acre landscape was an inspirational setting for all the hard work ahead.

Although I was slightly intimidated, I was also very curious when I was plunged into the company of the high-powered, well-trained East Coast singers I met there. There was so much activity all the time, however, that there was no time for any kind of trepidation or fear. When we weren't learning music or rehearsing, we could sneak in and see a symphony and instrumental rehearsals. I was enthralled. On nights when we weren't performing we could be a part of the rest of the audience who came to the 5,100-seat open-air Koussevitzky Music Shed to be thrilled by the Boston Symphony Orchestra. There everyone would spread their picnic blankets on the lawn, and lay there listening in the warm, damp Massachusetts night air.

The atmosphere was charged with artistic temperament and raw talent. Lunchtimes, in particular, were wonderful. It was during these outdoor breaks that everyone converged and convened. At the beginning I enjoyed being like a fly on the wall, listening and absorbing as I ate my tuna sandwiches. At the next table was Koussevitzky lecturing Leonard Bernstein: "Lennie, stop with all that Broadway nonsense. You're a great conductor." Behind them was Maurice Abravanel, music director of the Utah Symphony Orchestra and Kurt Weill's preferred conductor, sadly discussing Weill's untimely death a few months earlier at the age of fifty. Sitting on a bench near him was a very large, rumpled woman named Sarah Caldwell.

Sarah was only twenty-six years old at that time, but she had been chief assistant to Boris Goldovsky (older opera lovers will remember him as Mr. Texaco from his regular Saturday afternoon *Metropolitan on the Air* broadcasts) at the New England Opera Company and at Tanglewood. She was clearly someone to be reckoned with, and with Goldovsky on sabbatical, Sarah was now moving up the Tanglewood ladder. She eventually founded the Opera Company of Boston in 1957 and headed it until its demise in 1991. In 1976, she became the first woman to conduct at the Metropolitan Opera House in New York. It was clear to us all in the summer of 1950 that Sarah was a comer. She also was already exhibiting the idiosyncrasies and foibles that made her the colorful character she is today. Despite her hefty girth and unconventional personal hygiene habits, what I remember about Sarah was her command of the magic, her down-to-earth humor, and her mastery of the literature. During the course of the summer Sarah translated, directed, and conducted *La Finta Giardiniera* by Mozart as well as several programs of scenes from operas.

Sarah, having been Goldovsky's assistant, was privy to Goldovsky's theories and put them to practice that summer and later in her career. For example, Goldovsky believed in using a very deep orchestra pit. The theory was that if we could not see the orchestra and conductor we would not rely on them. We would all be part of the great ensemble of players. We were supposed to know the music and the score so well that we wouldn't need cueing at all. We needed to be very aware of where we were at all times, both musically and physically. We needed to breathe together. Sarah's staging was always quite complicated but very in tune with the music and theatrics of each piece.

There was a great divide that summer. On one side were Jan Popper and the West Coast contingent, of which I was ostensibly a part, and on the other, the East Coasters, also known as the "Goldovskyites," since they were disciples of Goldovsky. Because I was a coloratura who always could depend on her high Fs I was extremely useful to both groups of singers. Thus I alone spanned the great divide between the East and West. I was like a bridge, if not over troubled water, then at least across the Berlin Wall. They all needed my high notes and musicianship and so, lucky me, I got to learn twice the amount of music. In July I was on the side with the East Coasters and the Caldwell/Goldovsky camp and in August I was with the West Coast group when Dr. Popper conducted us in *Le Roi D'Yvetot* by Jacque Ibert. What a thrill when Ibert showed up one balmy August evening and heartily applauded our work in his opera.

As if this weren't enough for me, I also joined Ralph Berkowitz and Paul Ulanovsky's group of musicians, who were learning and performing more avant-garde musical pieces. Berkowitz was executive assistant to Serge Koussevitzky at

Tanglewood from 1946 to 1951 and became Dean of the Berkshire Music Center in 1951, remaining in that position until his resignation in 1964. He was also a wonderful pianist who needed brave singers like me to read through new music. I enjoyed every last note of it.

All this work left little time for missing Ernest, but of course I did. We lived in communal dormitories and in those pre–cell phone days Ernest and I were lucky to speak every few days on the very expensive coast-to-coast calls I would make on the public pay phone in the hall a little ways down from my room. After inserting all those nickels and dimes into the phone ("please insert another 25 cents or your call will be interrupted") I would jabber on about all that I was doing and singing and how much I missed him and he would tell me about the progress of his opera. He would also talk about his collaboration with Christine Ebert. He talked about *her* a bit too much for my taste.

Perhaps I had inherited a bit of my mother's psychic power, or it was just plain old woman's instinct, but I soon got the distinct impression that Ernest and Christine were having an affair. I was afraid to confront Ernest myself. I guess I thought if I put it to him and told him how I felt about that he would be angry and our marriage would be over. I knew that it wasn't odd for European men to have mistresses. For me, however, it was intolerable. Instead of talking to my husband, I called Christine's father, my friend and mentor Carl Ebert, and voiced my concerns about his daughter and my husband. Ebert was shocked, appalled, and very sympathetic. None of his sympathy helped the wound in my heart that just wouldn't heal, though.

I was destroyed. It was beyond my understanding. How could it be? How could Ernest do it? Was it my fault for going away? Were my parents right after all about him? These were questions that never stopped churning in my head. My anguish and feeling of betrayal had no bounds. This was mixed with the frustration of not being able to speak to Ernest. Either I couldn't get to the phone due to work or when I finally did, Ernest wasn't home to get the call.

My greatest defense mechanism, of course, was always work, and I was lucky to be totally immersed in music that summer or I might have gone mad. Music always got me through pain and so I sang. How ironic that I had convinced Ralph Berkowitz to present an evening of Ernest's songs. There I would be, rehearsing Ernest's music by day and crying myself to sleep at night. Wherever I turned he haunted me. No one around me, however, knew my feelings or embarrassment. Alone with my pain, this was how the summer passed.

I must still have been totally preoccupied with my personal problems, because on the way back to California to salvage my marriage, I made a major professional mistake.

Stopping off in New York (this time I knew how to get around and could hail my own cab!) I auditioned for the head of New York City Opera and he offered me the role of "The Queen of the Night" in *The Magic Flute*. Do you know what I did? I turned it down. I felt that the role was totally pyrotechnic and that it only depended on the strength of my high notes. I would have taken it if they offered me a full-blown emotional role in addition. But with only "The Queen of the Night" on the table I turned them down. In retrospect I realize that if I had accepted the role it might have led to others in the company and I probably would have come to New York and based my career on the East Coast, which might have afforded me more opportunities in the opera world.

When I returned to California in the fall of 1950, whatever had been going on between Ernest and Christine was all over. Ernest was minus a librettist and had dropped his opera entirely. Nothing more was said. I assume that Ebert played some role in separating the two and I was pleased that Ernest now seemed more loving and attentive than ever. We resumed our marriage where we had left off and I pushed the hurt into that "mythical box in the back of the legendary closet" where I kept all the other disappointments and hurts. What I didn't think about wouldn't hurt me. Not then.

I immediately returned to work with the West Coast premiere of Jerome Moross and John Latouche's *Ballet Ballads*. I also received a call from Sarah Caldwell asking if I would repeat my performance in *La Finta Giardiniera* at the New England Opera Company in Boston. Since Ernest hadn't worked for a long time and our money was swiftly running out, I couldn't afford to turn down any kind of paying job, and even though I had only been back for a couple of months, in December of 1950 I found myself flying across the country again to rehearse under Sarah's leadership.

They put me up at the Copley Plaza and I put myself on a budget to save as much money as I could. When my friend and colleague Adele Addison noticed I was skipping meals, she was concerned.

"Marni, you've got to eat and eat well," she chided me. "The first rule of touring is that you do not save money on food."

But every morning, despite her admonishments, I would be too sick to eat. Was it nerves? Was I still upset about Ernest? After a while, Adele just looked me up and down and assessed my usual green morning face.

"I think you're pregnant!"

"Oh no," I responded. "We've been careful and . . . and. . . ." Of course she was right.

When I got back to California, the doctor confirmed my suspicions and my emotions flipped back and forth between total despair (after all, we had no money) and elation (I was going to be a mother!). Ernest was delighted. Despite our lack of funds, he couldn't have been happier.

"Don't worry, Nusch-Nusch," he said in his soothing voice, "we will manage."

We *did* manage, poor but happy. Every afternoon we would take very long walks and our goal would be to collect as many empty Coke bottles as we could to get the deposits back and somehow gather enough money for dinner. As my stomach grew bigger I might have walked a little slower but the scrounging for refundables continued and we somehow always had food on the table. Thankfully, it was fun!

On August 2, 1951, my water broke and Ernest rushed me to St. Joseph's Hospital in Burbank. While I waited a full eight hours for the baby to arrive, Ernest went home and promptly got sick with a fever. When they called to tell him the baby had arrived, he was shaking down a thermometer and in his excitement hit the thermometer on his glasses, shattering it and spraying tiny bits of glass and mercury balls all over the bed. After he cleaned this up, he couldn't remember the name of the hospital or how to get there.

Meanwhile back at St. Joseph's, despite my wishes, I had been given a spinal block and been totally oblivious to the birth of my son, Andrew. When I awoke and realized I had missed this long-awaited experience, I was furious. I immediately got over my anger with the hospital, however, when the nurses cheerfully tossed a tightly bound football-like object onto my bed. When I realized the object was my baby I laughed along with the nurses. They then taught me how to nurse him and the wonderful feeling of connecting with the chain of life obliterated everything negative.

St. Joseph's was a Catholic hospital and the nurses were nuns. Nuns who listened religiously to the Sunday afternoon radio show that I sang with the Roger Wagner Chorale. Roger was very well known in the Catholic Church for his liturgical music, and when the nuns found out that I was part of his group they were ecstatic and I was treated better than before.

A couple of days after Andy was born, several nuns bustled into my room with a radio.

"We've been told to listen to the radio show with you because there's going to be a special surprise today," one of the nuns excitedly told me. They tuned in the station and I heard the familiar voice of Roger Wagner.

"Ladies and gentlemen, this next song is dedicated to Marni Nixon and Ernest Gold's new baby boy."

The next thing Andy and I heard was a beautiful choral arrangement of Brahms' "Lullaby." I knew every singer's voice, but today they were dearer to me than they had ever been. I could not imagine a better welcome into the world for Andy. I cried, the nuns cried, and Andy fell asleep in my arms.

A short while later I was released from the hospital, but Andy had to stay in order to be circumcised. This separation was very hard on a new mother, but I knew I would have him home in a few days. When we came to pick him up we were told we couldn't have the baby until the hospital bill was paid. We were furious and desperate. We had been counting on a tax refund from the Internal Revenue Service, which kept being delayed and now, without any money, the hospital was holding our baby for ransom! After much fighting and arguing with the powers that be, my parents came to the rescue and lent us the money to spring Andy from his hospital prison. Mother and Daddy also did some remodeling of the kitchen in our little house and bought us a portable washing machine, which was an enormous help when dealing with cloth diapers. When the long-awaited IRS refund arrived (with interest) the Gold family settled down to a relatively normal family life and I gradually began to get back to work.

1951 and 1952 were full years career-wise. There were many concerts at *Evenings on the Roof*, a wonderful production of Humperdinck's *Hansel and Gretel* in English directed by Carl Ebert and many appearances with the Roger Wagner Chorale.

Ever since we sang on the film soundtrack of *Joan of Arc* in 1948, the Chorale was in demand for other film work and we entered what Marilyn Horne dubbed (no pun intended) our "Doo-Wah" years. Whatever the music required—liturgical, classical, romantic, or pop—the "lyrics" remained the same and consisted of "doo-wah, doo-wah, doo-wah." We doo-wahed through such late-1940s, early-1950s film blockbusters as *Les Misérables, Salome, The Happy Time, Let's Do It Again*, and *Come to the Stable*. We even doo-wahed on TV when the Chorale made its small screen debut singing all the background music on the popular sitcom *I Married Joan*, a funny rip-off of *I Love Lucy*.

My most exciting musical event of this time occurred on November 11, 1952 when Stravinsky personally chose me to sing in the world premiere of his new cantata. This was a far cry from doo-wahing on a sitcom. During this same period Ernest of course continued to write music and every so often got movie gigs orchestrating and conducting other composers' (like George Antheil's) work. Meanwhile, with three mouths to feed, I continued to take any paying job that came along.

It was during this period I did some more dubbing. I sang a tiny bit for Jeanne Crain in the 1950s nonmusical *Cheaper by the Dozen* and most amazingly mixed my wholesome tones with one of the sexiest tessituras in screen history: Marilyn Monroe. Next time you watch the film *Gentlemen Prefer Blondes* or see a clip of Monroe singing "Diamonds Are a Girl's Best Friend," listen hard when she sings: "But square cut or pear shape, these rocks don't lose their shape!" The second part of the phrase is Nixon as Monroe. Incredibly, I had been told that Twentieth Century Fox Studio wanted Marilyn's entire voice dubbed. Studio head Darryl Zanuck or someone else high up thought her voice was silly. Can you imagine? Thank goodness they let her sing her own way. That breathy, sexy sound suited her screen persona perfectly, even if she did need a little help on the high notes.

Although I was grateful for all the work in L.A., I felt that my opera career was not going to get anywhere unless I gave it a jump-start. Ernest was also growing very discontented with his lack of success writing music for better films. He was writing music for D movies and his frustration was mounting daily. For some time Ernest and I had serious discussions about our careers, and together we decided that I would do well to go abroad and try to get into one of Europe's prestigious opera companies. While I sang and hopefully made a living, Ernest would be able to get on with his serious nonfilm composing. I was armed with many letters of introduction and praise from Igor Stravinsky, Jan Popper, Carl Ebert, and others, all of whom were revered on the Continent. Ernest and I decided to take this huge leap in two steps. The first step would be New York, where we thought we could make more money and contacts before sailing across the Atlantic. In the middle of our planning I found out I was pregnant again, so we decided to wait until I had the baby before we made our next move.

My daughter Martha was born July 22, 1953 and six weeks later she, Andrew, and I were flying east. Ernest stayed behind to finish up a film-scoring job and it was my responsibility to find us an apartment. If I thought New York was daunting three years earlier, it was twice as intimidating with two small children. My sister Adair was married by now with two children of her own and living in New Jersey. Knowing how difficult finding an apartment would be with two small children in tow, she generously offered to take care of them for the time it would take me to settle into a place for us all to live. I eventually found a big apartment on Prospect Park South in Brooklyn and soon Ernest and the kids joined me. Ernest had ambitions to compose for Broadway but found that door was just as difficult to get through as the door to composing scores for major Hollywood films. He had to settle for playing rehearsal piano for dance rehearsals for Broadway shows. He was extremely frustrated. I, on the other hand, was luckier. My luck began almost as soon as I got to New York. And it began on TV, of all places.

In the early 1950s there was no bigger television star than Arthur Godfrey. Until Lucille Ball passed him in popularity, the ukulele-playing Godfrey was America's favorite redhead. Today he is remembered most for hawking Lipton Tea and for his public on-air firing of singer Julius LaRosa. Godfrey began his career in radio in the late 1930s and after more than a decade easily moved into the fledgling video arena by simply allowing his popular radio show *Arthur Godfrey's Talent Scouts* to be televised. One year after his *Talent Scouts* show debuted, *Arthur Godfrey and His Friends* joined it on the air, thus giving him two

With Arthur Godfrey during a break in one of his CBS radio shows. Late 1950s. (From the author's collection)

television outlets in addition to his regular radio slot. In 1951 he was the host of television's Number One show and until 1959 one or both of his shows were always in the Top Ten of the ratings.

Talent Scouts had a simple formula. "Scouts" presented their "discoveries," who would then perform live before a national radio and television audience. Most of these discoveries were in fact struggling professionals looking for a break, and the quality of the talent was quite high. The winner, chosen by a fabled audience applause meter, often joined Godfrey on his radio show and on *Arthur Godfrey and His Friends* for some period thereafter. In his day Godfrey significantly assisted the careers of Pat Boone, Tony Bennett, Eddie Fisher, Connie Francis, Leslie Uggams, Lenny Bruce, Steve Lawrence, Roy Clark, and Patsy Cline. And me.

In the fall of 1953 I sang my by-now ubiquitous "Bell Song" from *Lakmé* on *Talent Scouts* and won first prize. As promised, I began to appear on Godfrey's other TV show and his radio show as well. After a few appearances he gave me an open invitation to appear on his radio show anytime I was in town and I took him up on it. The conversation was always stimulating and Arthur was the best kind of host. After the shows were taped and edited the listener felt that he or she was in a living room filled with the most erudite and interesting people in town. Over the years I began to consider Arthur a friend and was flattered at first when he started to invite me out to big social events. Flattered, that is, until I was told that if I accepted an invitation from the very-married Mr. Godfrey, I might also be accepting his amorous advances. From then on I very sweetly declined his invitations and we remained, as the tabloids would say, "just good friends."

Soon after I won the *Talent Scouts* Award, I heard from my very good friend Bruce Savan. Bruce had been our rehearsal pianist at the USC Opera Workshop and was later to become a very powerful agent, but in the fall of 1953 he was stage managing and assisting the director on a new Broadway musical called *The Girl in Pink Tights.* The show had music by the late great operetta composer Sigmund Romberg (who had died in 1951 and left sketches of music that were finished and polished by the great Broadway orchestrator Don Walker), lyrics by Leo Robin (who had written *Gentlemen Prefer Blondes*), and book by Jerome Chodorov and Joseph Fields (the gentlemen responsible for *Wonderful Town*, which was still running on Broadway at the time). The star of the show was Zizi Jeanmaire, the adorable French ballerina who had won moviegoers' hearts in the Danny Kaye film *Hans Christian Andersen.* With Agnes DeMille choreographing (she had done the same job on *Oklahoma!*, *Carousel*, *One Touch of Venus*, *Bloomer Girl*, *Gentlemen Prefer Blondes*, and many other hit shows) it seemed that this musical might very well become a big hit.

Although Bruce knew I was overqualified for the chorus, he also realized it would do me good to be in a Broadway show. He talked me up to Shepard Traub, the producer-director of the piece, and I auditioned. Well, I not only got the job in the chorus but also was given a small role *and* was made understudy to dancer Dania Krupska (Me? A dancer?), who in turn was understudying the leading role, played by Jeanmaire.

We went into rehearsal in December 1953 and I very quickly learned that all my experience as a singer, both solo and choral, had not prepared me for the way things were done on Broadway. In those days of Broadway plenty there were separate singing and dancing choruses. There were twenty singers and twenty-two dancers! This was not counting all the principals.

At first the singers and the dancers were separated. We were put into one rehearsal hall to learn the music while choreographer Agnes DeMille worked on the ballets and production numbers. I was amazed that the musical learning process was so primitive. They assumed none of us read music (none was distributed) and we were taught the songs, harmonies, vocal arrangements, and all by ear. I was used to learning music in two steps: first by reading it cold and then by going home and memorizing it, thus putting it in my ear. Here we were supposed to be learning it by ear and memorizing as we went along. I would go home at night complaining to Ernest about it, wondering aloud, "Is this how they do it on Broadway? This is insane!"

Rehearsals were well organized but chaotic at the same time. Why did they have to experiment so much, I wondered. Why couldn't they just write out the show and perform it, the way we did in opera? In my naïveté about how musicals were put together I thought it should all be easier. I couldn't understand why Agnes DeMille, whom I adored and who seemed to take to me, would stage a number one day and change it the next. One song called "Up in the Elevated Railway" seemed to be altered daily. It was all new to me and ultimately fascinating. When we weren't singing and learning staging, I loved watching Zizi Jeanmaire work. She couldn't really sing, but somehow gave the impression that she could. Her role was specifically tailored for what she could do. She was an adorable and funny personality as well as a wonderful dancer. The great European actor Charles Goldner was billed over the title with her and it was an education to watch him play his scenes with Brenda Lewis. Brenda was a hoot. She was my kind of dame—bawdy, earthy, a transplant from the opera world with a huge voice and a great sense of humor. She was also a totally devoted pro. A great example of this was displayed during the blizzard of 1954.

We had been open for a few days when the New York area was dumped on by a snowstorm. No trains or buses were running, but the Broadway theaters were still open. Brenda, with her show-must-go-on attitude, strapped on some snowshoes and trudged all the way from her home in Westchester to Manhattan, walking between the railroad tracks! That was Brenda Lewis. No understudy was going to play her role!

Singer Michelle Reiner and I bonded early on in rehearsal. There was a number near the end of the show called "The Cardinal's Guard Are We" and we were supposed to wear these huge papier-mâché helmets on our heads. When Michelle and I put on our helmets we both promptly fainted. Maybe our heads were too big or the helmets were too small, but somehow they restricted our breathing and down we went. The helmets were changed after the costume department realized they were killing off the chorus girls.

In most shows the singers and dancers were separate but in *Pink Tights* we were all one big gang. I became friends with dancer and soon-to-be-choreographer Dania Krupska and her soon-to-be husband Ted Thurston, and Eva Rubenstein, who was Artur Rubenstein's daughter and an elegant dancer. One of my best California buddies was also in the chorus: Michael (then Kalem) Kermoyan.

If you're lucky in this life you have a few very special relationships that see you through, people who sometimes wind up being closer than family. Mike was one of those people. We first met as colleagues, singing opera at USC and with the Guild Opera Company, but swiftly became friends. Right off the bat Mike began playing jokes on me and since I have always been a sucker for silliness we became each other's best friend. I can still hear his loud laughter, two octaves below everyone else's. Mike had what opera people call a "Schwarze Basso" sound to his voice, meaning it was very dense, dark, and Russianlike. And low! Almost as low as his sense of humor. When I was pregnant with my first child Mike decided to bring a bucket right out on the stage when we rehearsed so that I could drop the baby when I hit one of my high Fs. Oh, how we would laugh!

You can imagine my delight when I realized that Mike would be part of *The Girl in Pink Tights* company. In fact, Mike was there even before the first rehearsal, after I found the apartment in Brooklyn, helping me wash down the walls and cooking his specialty: rice pilaf. He was a true pal.

Like most musicals in those days, *The Girl in Pink Tights* played two out-of-town tryouts, New Haven and Philadelphia. If I thought rehearsals were chaotic, New Haven and Philly took the cake. The minute a song or joke didn't land, out it went and the next day something new was in its place. The biggest change occurred when our leading man David Brooks, the star of such musicals as *Bloomer Girl* and *Brigadoon*, was fired. David had a lovely voice and we got along famously. So much so that later on he chose me to be part of a tour of two one-act operas he was directing. At the time, however, I remember Shepard Traub and Agnes DeMille were having trouble with Brooks and the way he acted and moved. They felt his gestures were stiff and had no grace. There was also a rumor that he was drinking. Whatever the case, one night David Brooks was singing "Lost in Loveliness" to Jeanmaire and the next night it was being sung by a wonderful baritone named David Atkinson. That, as they say, is show biz! Through all the changes and upheavals, one thing remained constant: my friendship with Mike Kermoyan.

Mike had been going through a breakup with his girlfriend, and after rehearsals (we rehearsed all the new material during the day and then did the show at night) or after the show, he would come up to my room and cry on my shoulder. I empathized with Mike totally. I was feeling sad, too, being apart from my kids and Ernest. We commiserated with each other and with all that warmth and comfort being shared it soon became sexual. I had heard that these things happened when people were on the road. I just never thought it would happen to "wholesome" me. Strangely, I didn't seem to feel guilty (nor did I feel I was retaliating for Ernest's indiscretions) or wicked. It all seemed so natural, sweet, warm, and easy.

The physical side of our relationship lasted the short while we were out of town and it only deepened our friendship. So, later when Mike got close to another cast member, the wonderful dancer Katia Gelesnova, I was thrilled for them.

As with many friendships, we went our separate ways, but anytime I bounced into New York for a show or a concert I would just call Mike and Katia and in a flash I would be at their house eating whatever delicious concoction Mike made that day. Mike and I would just pick up where we left off and the laughter would flow. Our great affection for each other lasted until the day he died.

The Girl in Pink Tights opened at the Mark Hellinger Theatre on March 5, 1954. Just like in the movies, we partied at Sardi's and waited for the reviews to come out. In those days, unlike today when critics are invited during several press previews, all the critics converged on opening night and had to file their reviews immediately. File them they did, and they were not what is known in the trade as "money notices."

The New York Times said the show had "a lust for mediocrity." Walter Kerr in the New York Herald-Tribune wrote, " The Girl in Pink Tights is not a show with too few jokes. It's a show with no jokes at all." Jeanmaire, on the other hand, got personal raves. Despite the pans, the producer assured us that we would run for a while.

As was the custom in those days when almost every Broadway musical was recorded, we went into Columbia Records' 30th Street recording studio on our first available day off, Sunday March 14, 1954, and recorded the whole score under the direction of producer Goddard Lieberson. Listening to the CD transfer today it's impossible to realize how dog-tired we all were from the tryout and opening. What with caring for two small children at the same time, it's a wonder I didn't drop from exhaustion in the studio. I was twenty-four years old, though, and boy, does that make a difference!

Two weeks after that, on March 28, I competed on Dumont TV's Chance of a Lifetime show and won first prize. For those who think American Idol is a new phenomenon, witness the proliferation of TV talent contests that came before it. Ted Mack's Amateur Hour begat Arthur Godfrey's Talent Scouts (which I had already won) and that, in turn, begat Chance of a Lifetime. The show's formidable prize package included, as host Dennis James announced, "a trip to New York, to stay at the glamorous Hotel Roosevelt, an opportunity with Universal International Pictures, a tryout with Columbia Records, or an engagement at the internationally famous Latin Quarter in the heart of Broadway's Great White Way." My prize was the engagement at the Latin Quarter and $1,000 cash. The money certainly came in handy because I was also learning and being coached in new operatic roles, which was very costly, in preparation for my eventual move to Europe.

With both Chance of a Lifetime and my regular Arthur Godfrey appearances, I was getting some good media exposure, which led to more singing offers of every kind. Imagine me with two small children way out in Brooklyn, having to commute into the city every day to do either Godfrey's radio or TV show, work with an opera coach, fulfill other singing or recording dates, and then do a musical six nights a week and two matinees. It was a wonder I could handle it. After a while I decided I couldn't. As other jobs presented themselves, and business began to slow down at the box office, I decided to leave The Girl in Pink Tights. There were those among my friends who thought I was nuts and should have stayed with the show out of loyalty, but I felt that I had done it and that being in the chorus of a show, although a wonderful experience, was not where I wanted my career to go. As it turned out the show didn't run much longer anyway, closing for good in June of 1954.

After I left the show, I began doing a lot more group work, including jingles and commercials. Like everything else in my career, it just kind of happened. Someone or other would need a soprano who could sight sing anything and I would be recommended. Before too long I became one of the top jingle singers in New York.

I enjoyed it, but holy cats, was it was a rat race!

Picture yourself as me in 1954 and 1955. On a typical morning, after having left the kids with either your husband or a makeshift babysitter of questionable background, you take the F train into Manhattan and rush to a recording studio where you read down and then record ten takes of a commercial jingle for a product such as Lux Soap or Pillsbury baking goods. When the session is finished you call your answering service (no answering machines or voice mail in those days). The friendly woman at your service might tell you that CBS called and they want you over at *The Ed Sullivan Show* at 1:00 P.M. to rehearse for a musical number that's going to be live on the air on Sunday, but you won't be seen. Of course, you say you will be there or else they'll just call someone else and offer her the job. So, after knocking back a quick cup of coffee and sandwich, you rush over to 53rd Street and Broadway and read down the music with Ray Bloch and the orchestra. After an hour or so you're released in time to make the rehearsal for on-camera work on *The Milton Berle Show* . . . no, this week it's *The Martha Raye Show*. They both rehearsed and shot in the same studio, so you would be safe either way. You would hope that you were not going to be on camera, because not being on camera made it easier to go from job to job. We joked that having that anonymity meant that your face wasn't overexposed on TV (oh, to have that problem!) and you would be hired more often. More work meant more money. After calling home and checking on the kids, you then grab some dinner and get to another studio in time to get into makeup and dress for a *Your Hit Parade* gig that airs live and in color at 8:00 P.M. By the end of the day you would be beat and have to go home on the seldom-running F train to Brooklyn to tuck your kids in or sit hovering over their sleeping forms debating whether to wake them up and hug them. At which time you would conk out yourself only to start the whole thing all over again tomorrow. Phew!

I would do most anything to get singing jobs in those days short of going bald. One time I almost did exactly *that*.

In those days of live TV and no reruns, the big shows all had summer replacements. *The Perry Como Show* was to be replaced in the summer of 1954 with *The Ray Anthony Show*. Anthony was a trumpeter with his own band and was famous that year for his recording of the theme from the hit TV show *Dragnet*. The chorus on his show was to be on camera and it was a weekly job with good pay. They wanted me for my high notes, but they also wanted all the girls to be blondes. They didn't want any wigs, just "natural" blondes. I decided I wanted the job enough to bleach my hair anyway. As a natural redhead I was proud of my hair's beauty and uniqueness. Everyone I spoke to was appalled that I would do anything to change it. Still, I was determined to get the job. Since I didn't have a lot of extra money or time, I wasn't able to go to a fancy colorist, but found a beauty parlor that could do it for a cheap price and when I was available. After the bleaching, I looked in the mirror and let out a scream. My hair was the color of yellow corn and the texture of hay. It was ghastly! They couldn't really get the red out of my hair and they couldn't bleach it anymore since my scalp was already developing blisters and itched like crazy! Eventually, with some finessing, it turned out white enough to pass as a blonde and I got the job, which lasted just long enough for my roots to grow out. Well, every penny counted!

Besides appearing weekly on TV, the summer of 1954 was also the summer I played Ado Annie in a summer stock production of *Oklahoma!* in Salt Lake City and made my nightclub debut at the Latin Quarter back in New York, courtesy of *Chance of a Lifetime*.

Variety reported that I "had a sweet lyrical voice and some neat head tones. With power and range, she hits a high E truly and always stays on pitch. Versatile voice can be used in club shows or opera."

"Club shows or opera."

That *Variety* revue made me think about my operatic dreams. I had come to New York to prepare for my European opera career, and although working for a living and trying to raise two small children was taking precedence, I was very much pursuing my goal. I had been getting some wonderful coaching from a variety of opera coaches, including Martin Rich, a longtime associate conductor at the Metropolitan Opera. Martin encouraged me not to get mired in the rat race of being a "working" singer and lose sight of what I really wanted. His encouragement led me to audition for and appear on the 1955 Metropolitan Opera's *Auditions of the Air*.

The Metropolitan Opera had begun sponsoring a structured auditions program for young singers in 1935 with *Auditions of the Air*, the ancestor of the present Metropolitan Opera National Council Auditions. *Auditions of the Air* was a radio program that featured exceptionally talented young American singers who were auditioning to become part of the Met's working roster. Up until 1950, when Rudoph Bing, the new general manager, changed the rules, first prize was a contract with the Metropolitan Opera. After that time, contracts were given at the discretion of the Met's artistic staff. One of the prizes, however, was a chance to be part of the Young Artist Program, which was a fantastic training course at the Met.

The radio series, which went off the air in 1958, ran from January to April, when the finalists then competed for the grand prize. I competed sometime in February, singing "Je Suis Titania" from *Mignon* by Ambroise Thomas. I did very well and became one of the finalists, meaning I would have to compete again at the end of the season if I were to have a chance of winning the big prize. But when the last show of the 1955 season aired I was not one of the contestants. Although several factors prevented my appearance on that April broadcast, the most prominent reason was that I had signed a contract before I even began the audition process and I was never one to back out of a money commitment.

Remember David Brooks, the leading man who was fired from *The Girl in Pink Tights*? He was now directing a tour of two one-act operas, *The Telephone* and *Trouble in Tahiti*, and signed me to play leading roles in both of them. The tour was to encompass six weeks of travel and singing down south and was to begin March 11, 1955, meaning I would not be in New York for the final show of the Met Radio season. Of course I was very upset over not being able to go on to the next leg of the auditions. After all, this was the Metropolitan Opera House, the ultimate dream of every opera singer in the world. When I told the powers that be at the Met about my predicament they were very kind to me and gave me carte blanche to come back and audition for them anytime I was in New York. This softened my disappointment a bit.

My life was being uprooted in other ways, too.

Although I was doing well professionally in the East, New York was becoming less and less attractive to the rest of the Gold family. Ernest's New York career had never really taken off the way he had planned. He was never cut out to be a rehearsal pianist and the days of hard playing would leave his soft fingers literally bloodied. Over the year and a half since we had moved to New York, film scoring jobs would come up for him and off he would fly to L.A. From 1953 to 1955, he wrote scores for such memorable nonblockbusters as *Jennifer*, *Man Crazy*, *The Other Woman*, *Karamoja*, and *The Naked Street*.

The result was that we were apart more than together and I began to feel like a single parent. To be truthful, the difficulty in raising kids in the city was wearing on me as well. I found that I was tired all the time, and after seeing the doctor I was diagnosed with anemia. I began to think that if it was this hard in New York, it might be twice as grueling in Europe. Choices had to be made. Andy now was four years old and would be starting school next year and I felt that he needed and we all needed some stability in our lives. I was heartsick being so busy and away from the children day in and day out when I worked. I was missing their growth. I was missing their childhood. I was missing *them* and they were missing me.

In California, I knew that, even when I worked, I could be closer by and able to supervise them more. I began to weigh my dreams of a European opera career against the needs of the family, taking into account Ernest and his career as well. We knew that Ernest needed to be in Hollywood if he was going to compose film scores. He needed to be in the loop so that he might be considered for better pictures. His music could only be as good as the movie for which it was written and he needed to press on and get better-quality jobs. I knew that I could make the same kind of living in L.A. as I had been in New York. I could continue to do jingles and keep on with concerts and opera, while having an easier, more stable time raising a family. I also rationalized that I could still go to Europe and fulfill my dreams when things eased up. It was a hard decision but after much deliberation, Ernest and I decided that after I finished my tour we would move back to L.A.

Maybe fate had its own reasons for bringing me home, because on a lovely summer day in August of 1955, just as we were settling back into the L.A. groove, the phone rang. It was Ken Darby, the vocal director at Twentieth Century Fox Studios.

"Marni, we're frantic here. Is there any chance you would be available right away to audition to dub Deborah Kerr's voice in *The King and I*?"

Chapter Five
DEBORAH AND I

"Marni was so brilliant at adapting her voice to mine I could never be entirely sure whether it was she who was helping me on the high notes or whether I myself was responsible for the sounds which came out in the completed version. Marni really deserves her recognition as a unique talent in the musical world."

DEBORAH KERR, 1956

"Ladies and gentlemen, stop that girl! The girl running up the aisle. Stop her! That's the girl whose voice you heard and loved tonight. She's the real star of the picture."

GENE KELLY as Don Lockwood in *Singin' in the Rain* (1952)

T RUE STORY ABOUT THE MOVIES. In the 1952 classic musical film *Singin' in the Rain* the plot revolves around Hollywood's transition to talking pictures. Former silent screen star Lina Lamont, played by the brilliant Jean Hagen, is starring in a musical movie but the sound of her voice could strip the paint off of cars. Enter Debbie Reynolds as Kathy Seldon, who dubs Lina's voice singing the lovely song "Would You?" When Debbie shoots the scene, however, where she (as Kathy) is dubbing Lina's voice, Debbie's voice is dubbed by singer Betty Noyes! Wait, there's more. Later, when Debbie (Kathy) is supposed to dubbing Lina's dialogue, Jean Hagen herself dubbed Debbie dubbing Lina!

At the end of the film, thinking that Don Lockwood (Gene Kelly) has consigned her to being Lina's ghost for the rest of her career (Don in fact humiliates Lina by raising the curtain to show that Kathy is really the voice behind Lina's lips), a distraught Kathy (Debbie) runs out of the movie theater in tears. Don proclaims for all the world that it was Kathy whose voice they heard and she becomes a movie star, marries Don, and lives happily ever after. And that, ladies and gentlemen, is how dubbing for a star can change your life. At least that's how it is in the movies!

Dubbing. Ghosting someone's voice. An odd concept invented by Hollywood. How did it all come to be?

When movies learned to talk in 1927 apparently they learned to sing at the same time. Al Jolson opened his mouth, out came a song, and the whole industry was revolutionized overnight. Well . . . not quite. In fact, *The Jazz Singer*, which is considered the first talkie, wasn't that at all. For several years before that time Warner Bros. had been experimenting with sound on film, but the incredible popularity of Jolson and *The Jazz Singer* (which was really a silent with partial sound) is what pushed the new technology over the edge. Ironically, when *The Jolson Story* was made in the 1940s, Jolson himself dubbed Larry Parks as Jolson!

With the switchover to sound happening in the late 1920s, Hollywood frantically imported New York actors to fill in the ranks of silent stars whose voices proved less than euphonious. Along with the actors came the musical comedy stars who had perfected their art on the stage. One by one stars such as Fanny Brice, Sophie Tucker, and others of their ilk came, shot a film or two, and went running back to New York with their tails between their legs. The public still demanded *movie* stars in their movies, and they didn't care if the voices coming out their mouths were theirs or not.

It was Douglas Shearer (film star Norma's brother) at MGM who figured out that if they could prerecord the voice and orchestra for musical films and then play them back on the set, having the singers lip-synch to their own tracks (before that time there were live musicians and live singing on the set), there would be fewer margins for error, thus the studio would save time and money. What his innovation also provided was the ability to have someone *else*'s voice emanate from the actor lip-synching on camera. Thus, movie dubbing was born.

In 1929 alone Broadway star Charles King (also the star of *Broadway Melody*) ghosted for Conrad Nagel in *The Hollywood Revue of 1929*, Eva Olivotti sang for Laura LePlante in the first partially silent version of *Show Boat*, crooner Russ Columbo dubbed for both Gary Cooper and Lewis Stone, and Diana Gaylen sang for both Norma Talmadge and Greta Garbo. The public was none the wiser as the studios seldom released any information about their trickery.

Over the next couple of decades it became a standard practice in Hollywood to dub the voice of any star not up to vocal snuff. Marjorie Lane sang for tap-dancing sensation Eleanor Powell (although Powell had already sung perfectly well on Broadway) and pre-Broadway Mary Martin dubbed for both Margaret Sullavan and Gypsy Rose Lee. The heavenly body of Rita Hayworth had singing voices that belonged to Anita Ellis, JoAnn Greer, Mercedes Ruffino, Martha Mears, Gloria Franklin, and Nan Wynn. In her many films, Cyd Charisse lip-synched to the singing voices of Carole Richards, India Adams, Eileen Wilson, Marion Doenges, and even Vicki Carr. No one, it seemed, noticed or cared as long as it looked plausible and sounded beautiful. In 1954 my friend Marilyn Horne dubbed the singing voice for Dorothy Dandridge in the film version of *Carmen Jones*. This despite the fact that Dandridge *could* sing. Just not in the keys required by Bizet.

By this time in 1955 I had also done some dubbing; nothing on a grand scale, but still enough for a publicist to dub me "The Voice of Hollywood." My voice had come out of such stars as Margaret O'Brien, Jeanne Crain, Lili Palmer, and Ida Lupino, but only in a small way. In 1955, this was about to change.

In the 1950s many of Broadway's biggest hit musicals were being transferred to the big screen. MGM had *Kiss Me Kate*, *Kismet*, *Brigadoon*, and *On the Town*. Twentieth Century Fox bid for and won the rights for the great Rodgers and Hammerstein shows: *Oklahoma!*, *Carousel*, *South Pacific*, and *The King and I*.

The King and I had been a big hit on the stage, starring Gertrude Lawrence and a newcomer named Yul Brynner. In an unusual move for Hollywood, Brynner was to repeat his role in the film version. Although Lawrence had died during the run of the show, it was unlikely that she would have been offered the role on-screen had she lived as she was never known as a box office draw in the movies. Although there had been talk of such stars as Jeanette MacDonald or Irene Dunne (who had played the role in the nonmusical film version), it was Brynner who suggested film and stage star Deborah Kerr for the role of Anna Leonowens. It went without saying that Kerr was not a singer and that she would have to be dubbed (Later Kerr admitted to the studio after hearing a test recording of her voice, "I'm sorry, I'm just not good enough!"), so it wasn't a total surprise when I got the call from Ken Darby that day in the summer of 1955.

Like everyone else who went to the movies, I adored Deborah Kerr. After a decade on the stage and in British films, Kerr was brought to the U.S. in 1946 to star opposite Clark Gable in *The Hucksters*. MGM promoted her with the legend "Deborah Kerr—Her Name Rhymes with Star!" She got her first of six Academy Award nominations, for *Edward My Son* in 1949, playing opposite Spencer Tracy. After that she was typecast as a staid, elegant English woman of refined taste in such historical films as *Quo Vadis*, *King Solomon's Mines*, *Julius Caesar*, and *Young Bess*. It was in *From Here to Eternity* that she broke out of her mold and truly entered the consciousness of the American movie-going public. In a role originally to be played by Joan Crawford, Kerr played Karen Holmes, the sexy adulterous wife living on an Army base in Hawaii, and got another Oscar nomination for her work. In 1954, she switched gears and appeared on Broadway in the play *Tea and Sympathy*. Then, in 1955 she was about to play the role for which she would be best remembered, Anna Leonowens in *The King and I*. She was perfect for the role. The only thing she lacked was a singing voice.

Deborah Kerr and me on the set of An Affair to Remember, *1956. Our hair was the same shade.*

After a nationwide search, Jean Bradley, a wonderful singer, had been signed to dub Deborah Kerr's songs. While in Milan playing the role of Laurie in *Oklahoma!*, she suddenly took ill and died, leaving Twentieth Century Fox in a bind.

"We start prerecording in September," Ken Darby said. "Do you think you can do it?"

September? That was next month!

Ken had hired me many times for group work and incidental dubbing jobs, so he was very familiar with my voice. He told me that he and Alfred Newman, the musical director of the film (with whom I also had worked), had already discussed it and felt sure I could do the job. I was totally taken aback. I *did* know the music. I mean, who didn't? The score was famous by now from all the airplay and the original cast album. I had sung many of the songs at one time or another.

Before I could really think it over, in my typical Marni way, I answered, "Yes, of course I can do it."

The studio arranged to messenger me a little black wax recording of Deborah Kerr's speaking voice, as well as her attempt to sing a couple of the songs, so that I might assess her voice and get under her musical skin, as it were. After I got off the phone with Ken, I realized how exciting this opportunity was. If the job worked out the money would be infinitely better than the many chorus and jingle jobs I accepted in order to subsidize myself. It probably also would do me good to have my name on the big screen at last.

A black limousine pulled up outside the house and out came a liveried messenger with the Fox logo on his uniform. He handed me a large white manila envelope with my name printed on the front in large black hand-printed letters. The envelope contained the Kerr recording.

With excitement and some trepidation I carefully put the recording onto my turntable and listened closely to the voice coming out of the speakers. Surprisingly it was not unmusical. The tone was breathy, straight, and pure; almost like a boy soprano. I didn't understand why at the time, but I somehow felt an immediate kinship with Deborah Kerr's voice. Perhaps it was because of all the work I did as a "ringer" in boy-soprano sections of the various Catholic cathedrals around town. It was clear to me that Deborah had a sweet sound, without the singing experience to modulate it for the many expressive and emotional loud and soft passages the songs required. It was at that time that I relaxed a bit and realized I could handle this job.

The first step, as Ken Darby pointed out on the phone, was for me to come to the studio the next day and make a demo (a demonstration recording of my voice singing one of the songs from the show—in those days they were done on disc). This was not intended for me to convince Darby and Newman. They were already sold. However, I now had to pass the Richard Rodgers litmus test. Notoriously finicky about how his music was sung, Rodgers liked to keep control of all his properties. He was someone to be nervous about.

Two famous examples of Rodgers picky ways and devastating wit:

1. In 1945, Jan Clayton, the star of *Carousel*, got nervous when hearing that Rodgers was out front. Consequently, she breathed too many times during "If I Loved You." A stern-faced Rodgers came back to see her and she immediately apologized. "I know! I know! I breathed in the middle of a phrase!" Rodgers replied without any humor, "The middle of a phrase I wouldn't mind. But between syllables?"

2. Several years later, in the early 1950s Peggy Lee recorded a very up-tempo version of Rodgers and Hart's standard waltz "Lover." She ran into Rodgers at a party and sweetly asked if he'd heard the record. "Yes," he responded with ice cubes in his voice. "It's a waltz you know!"
   Any wonder I was nervous?

I arrived at the Twentieth Century Fox studio early the next day to work with Ken Darby on the demo. Having been there many times before, my car seemed to know the way by heart. I had been contemplating my task ever since I got off the phone with Ken. The previous evening, as I lay awake in bed, I began to realize how much of a challenge it really would be. I would not only have to imitate Kerr's exact sound, but also serve the dramatic thrust of each musical scene. Every note I would be singing would have to reflect the character of Anna Leonowens, as portrayed by Deborah Kerr. It would have to be Deborah Kerr's dramatic intent I was serving. Not mine, but hers. Of course, without having met her yet, I was just going to be guessing what these intents might be for the demo. For this sample recording, I would have to imagine and give examples of what I thought the character should sound like.

In addition to my other responsibilities, I had to mimic her accent. Even though she was born in Scotland, Kerr had a beautiful mild English accent. In the trade it was known as "mid-Atlantic," and it meant she was British, but not too "veddy, veddy" aristocratic and snobbish. She had just enough lilt in her voice to let the public know she was of a certain upper class. I also had to color my own sound to match the basic timbre of her speaking voice in order for my singing to sound like her extended musicalized speaking tone. I had fallen asleep that night with all these things whirling in my brain.

As I entered the large sound stage that morning, it was already set up with an isolation booth in which I was to sing. Very few of us were there that day: associate musical director Ken Darby, pianist Harper MacKay, the engineer in the booth, and me. Our task was to lay down piano and vocal tracks of "Hello, Young Lovers" and "Getting to Know You." These two songs would show both sides of Anna's voice and character. One was wistful, nostalgic, and romantically lush and the other playful, fun, and light as air. I sang through them a few times, with Ken's insightful coaching and guidance. After he was satisfied with the way I was singing them, we did several takes of each song.

After all the anticipation of nerves, I was oddly relaxed. I shouldn't have been surprised, as I always felt at home on those old sound stages. I can still remember their distinctive smell, which was a mixture of polished oak and mustiness. I loved the blackness that surrounded the area in which I was recording and the glassed-in booth housing the unseen godlike man turning all those knobs and making my voice sound as good as it could sound. Every so often an electrician would come out and move a wire or reset a mike and then disappear into the shadows. I was always in awe of the tech guys who took care of everything from that darkened booth. Rewind, playback, slate the take, time the track. Those audio technicians were the *real* stars as far as I was concerned.

As I sang about Anna's late husband Tom and that night when "the earth smelled of summer and the sky was streaked with light," I imagined the needle cutting into and creating the grooves on the shiny black wax disc. How amazing that my voice would be contained within those crevices. After several takes of both songs, Ken and I listened to all the playbacks, and when Ken approved the best ones, he congratulated me on a job well done and I went home. To wait. The recordings would be shipped off special delivery to Richard Rodgers in New York for his verdict. Time was of the essence and I was thrilled, but not surprised, when the call came telling me it was a "go." It was an extraordinary call on an ordinary summer day, and it changed my life and pushed me onto another path of my ever-changing career.

Unlike my earlier small dubbing jobs, I realized that this one was important. Important enough for me to use an agent. If there was money to be made here (and I thought there was), I might as well let a professional get as much as we could. Enter Hal Gefsky. Hal had been representing me from time to time on the West Coast in the fields of theater, personal appearances, and television. I trusted him and felt he was the right person to handle the contract on *The King and I*.

Hal went to work and negotiated a fee of $10,000 with a guarantee of at least six weeks of work. The fee included the rehearsals and the recording of the songs for the film. Later an additional payment was negotiated for the sound-track album that would be released by Capitol Records. With some editing, the same tracks were to be released on vinyl and sold in retail stores. For this I was to be paid twice the union scale: $420! This amount was based on the length of time my voice was heard on the recording. Just think, if I had sung the songs a little slower, I might have been paid a few cents more. Ah, well.

Oh yes, I also received no royalty for the recording. Twentieth Century Fox and Capitol Records made sure it was a buyout deal. This fact would come back to haunt me.

The worst part of the Fox contract (and consequently the Capitol contract), however, was the "no credit" clause. This meant that, despite singing the lead-ing role of Anna, my name would never appear in the credits at the end of the movie, nor on the jacket of the album. Before I signed the contract, Hal and I discussed this clause heatedly. I wanted to know if it was legal *not* to get credit, so I called SAG and was told that if I signed the contract with that clause in place, then it was legal. I was torn, but the studio had made the choice *very* clear: either I do the job anonymously, with no credit at all, or walk away. It was a take-it-or-leave-it situation.

Reluctantly, I told Hal that I would accept the conditions of the Fox con-tract. I wanted so much to sing this wonderful music and work with these tal-ented people that I forgot about my pride. So, I signed to sing for Deborah Kerr . . . with no credit.

We began work almost immediately. I was nervous and a little bit in awe the first time I met Deborah (she asked me to call her that right away). She was a genuine movie star and I had no idea how she might treat me. Would she play the "grande dame"? Or would we become fast friends? It soon became appar-ent that although she was very refined and ladylike, she was not at all haughty. In fact, she seemed very down-to-earth.

Deborah was sensitive enough to recognize my nervousness and immedi-ately put me at ease by commenting on the beauty of my hair and the similarity to hers in color. Her voice and demeanor reeked of British charm and were warm and welcoming. That first day we all (Deborah, Ken Darby, and I . . . with Harper dutifully at the keyboard) went over to the piano and sat on stools. I sang the songs so that she could begin to feel how I vocalized the notes. On breaks we would sit with cups of tea, chatting about our lives. She told me about her daughters and her now-estranged husband Anthony Bartley, who was a Squadron Leader for the Royal Air Force. In the course of working together, we discovered that our ancestors were from the same part of Scotland, the Isle of MacIntyre. I felt an uncanny kinship with her and was amazed to realize that it wasn't just a theatrical camaraderie, but a real tribal connection coming from her pure, clean spirit. All of this was reflected in her Presbyterian floaty voice. It was actually our esteemed musical director and conductor, Alfred Newman, who slyly confided to me that he thought Deborah had "the most Presbyterian voice" he'd ever heard! Later, when I got to know Deborah better, I told her what Newman said. She sighed and, with a twinkle in her eye, replied, "Ah, yes, Marni, Presbyterian. But with a ginny edge!"

In a very short time it was clear we had bonded.

The rehearsals were very well organized. I would be called upon to record six songs: "I Whistle a Happy Tune," "Hello, Young Lovers," "Getting to Know You," "Shall I Tell You What I Think of You?" "Song of the King," and "Shall We Dance?" Each of the six weeks was taken up by one selection. From Monday to Friday I would arrive at the studio and spend the mornings with Ken Darby and Harper MacKay perfecting and memorizing the songs. After lunch, Deborah would arrive.

The rehearsal stage was huge. Tape was laid down on the floor to outline where the set for each scene would be. Within the taped outline were the actual furniture and props that would be used in the scene during the filming. Although Deborah and I had learned the songs separately, each day we would rehearse them together at the piano. By doing this we each began to see how the other breathed and phrased the lyric. After we sang, we would put the scene and song on its feet. In other words, we would rehearse the scene physically.

Deborah would act and move about the set the way she had been blocked by the film's director (Walter Lang) and/or choreographer (Jerome Robbins), and when she got to the song part of the scene I would join her. I would follow her around like a shadow, mimicking each of her movements and copying her stance down to the angle of her head. After a while we started to look like twins. As we would both sing "Hello, Young Lovers," for example, I would picture the inside of her vocal chords and stretch my own neck and throat into that shape as we formed the words and sang together. I actually imagined myself inside her body in order to sound like her. Simultaneously, I would listen closely, trying to understand each of her acting intents so that I might absorb them into the way I was singing. The goal was to become one Anna.

Conversely, Deborah would watch me as I sang so that she might absorb my way of singing. Slowly, she was getting the feeling of my body energy and my flow. The grounding of my torso as the energy flowed through me permeated her being. She was learning how my body looked when I sang the songs so that she could incorporate the same body language, stance, and breathing techniques into her performance. All of these would visually contribute to the illusion that she was really singing in the finished film. Don't get me wrong; neither of us knew exactly what we were doing. We were improvising a way to make two people play one role without the seams showing. We were revolutionaries!

"Is this how it should sound?" I would ask.

"Yes, that's fine," Deborah would reply. "I can do that."

We mirrored each other's actions as if playing a game or doing an old Harpo Marx routine. If she lifted a teapot, I would pretend that I was also lifting one right next to her. It was as if I was *really* ghosting her. Sometimes it was downright spooky. We had no idea at the time that we were doing anything groundbreaking, but because Deborah was so willing to experiment, and because we both wanted this to be more than just another dubbing job, we were creating a new and original way for dubbing to be done. A way that would ultimately make it *seem* as if only one person acted and sang the role.

All along the way, we were being musically held together by Harper (whose wife Margery, a wonderful mezzo soprano, did the dubbing later on for Peggy Wood in the film *The Sound of Music*), and guided and supervised by Ken Darby. I can't say enough about Ken's contribution or of the contribution of the other talented men behind the scenes who made these great musicals the treasures they remain today. Walter Lang showed up every so often to check out what and how were we doing. He was an excellent and instructive director, but it was really my little team of Harper, Ken, and especially Deborah who were *my* directors.

After the rehearsal of each song would come the time to record. Deborah and I, now each other's shadows, would go to the sound stage filled with a huge orchestra made up of the best musicians in Hollywood, all under the baton of Alfred Newman.

At that time, Newman had been head of Fox's music department for some twenty years. He was a beloved man in the business (called Papa by some because he was the head of the illustrious Newman family, which included Emil and Lionel and stretches all the way to the present with Oscar-winning songwriter Randy Newman) and a consummate professional who, in his thirty-eight-year career, contributed to over 250 movies (*How Green Was My Valley*, *Song of Bernadette*, *The Razor's Edge*, *Gentleman's Agreement*, *All About Eve*, and dozens more). Alfred had a biting wit and a good heart. You couldn't put anything over on him and it seemed to me he always got his way with the studio.

The original orchestrations by Robert Russell Bennett were enlarged and augmented by orchestrators Edward B. Powell, Gus Levene, and Bernard Mayers. What twenty-four musicians on Broadway had played was now to be played by more than twice that number of players. What a glorious sound they made.

The film was going to be shot in the new Cinemascope 55 process, promising a magnificent visual experience. The aural experience was to be nothing less. By this time, incredible breakthroughs in recording technology allowed producers the opportunity to create high-fidelity stereo soundtracks of amazing audible depth. We recorded the score in six-channel stereo on magnetically coated film stock using the Westrex recording system (which would later become the industry standard for stereo albums). Later the six-channel masters would be mixed down to the four channels that were contained on the release prints of the film. Hollywood was way ahead of the record industry when it came to stereo. The first stereo LPs wouldn't be recorded and released for another year.

With the orchestra surrounding us, Deborah and I were led into the isolated soundproof booth. This temporary structure was solidly constructed within the sound stage itself and lined with dark cork and gray foam. The booth looked like a heavy paneled screen with a double window of plate glass so we could see the conductor and still have our sound isolated from that of the orchestra on the outside. The orchestra was recorded on four separate channels and we were recorded on still another channel. Later on, if a chorus was to be added to the number (as it was in "I Whistle a Happy Tune" and "Getting to Know You"), the singers would come in on the following day, listen to their orchestra track on headphones, and record their voices on multiple microphones.

So there we were, Deborah and I, in our soundproof booth on tall stools surrounded by a variety of microphones, earphones on racks, light stands with huge switches and plugs, and music stands covered with the scores of the song we would be recording that day. To make the timbre of my voice sound even more like Deborah's, sound supervisor Carl Faulkner put a modifier in the microphone in order to make my voice sound deeper. Normally, I had (and still have) a very light, bright ring to my voice. I had tried to take that lightness out as much as possible, but by using the modifier they were able to emphasize the lower partials of my voice. In 1955 this kind of modifier was very innovative and I was impressed with the result. The gods must have also been on my side by giving me a terrible cold that lasted through several recording sessions. Not being able to breathe actually helped to dull my voice, deepening it even more and making it an even better match to Deborah's.

There were several instances in which both Deborah's voice and mine would be used on one track. She talk-sang portions of the verses (the part of the song that comes before the refrain or body of the song) of both "Getting to Know You" and "Shall We Dance?" When the singing got tougher and more sustained, then I took over. The other instance of our two voices merging was more complex and resulted in the most interesting recording session of the bunch.

Late in Act I of *The King and I*, Anna is exasperated with the King's behavior and almost decides to leave Siam and her post as teacher of the royal children. Alone in her quarters she rails against the King in a brilliant soliloquy entitled "Shall I Tell You What I Think of You?" The musical number was written for Gertrude Lawrence's strengths and uses both speech and song and moves along at a very brisk clip. We knew that this track would have to be recorded in a way that had never been done before: two voices volleying back and forth and merging into one sound. For this difficult and exacting task, Deborah and I lived by my mother's edict: "Practice, practice, practice!" We rehearsed and ultimately recorded the song with what we called "the point-and-sing technique." She would begin the song and, after a few lines or bars, point to me and I would take it over. Then I would toss the ball back to her and so on and so forth until, when we finally stood side by side at our microphones and recorded the three minute and thirty-seven second song, there was no way to tell any difference at all between our vocal timbres. It was as if one voice spoke and sang the song. *Her* voice.

Unfortunately, the scene and song are lost to future generations as they were cut from the final release print and the footage has seemingly vanished. As happens many times in the movies, several of the songs that were prerecorded did not wind up in the film ("My Lord and Master" and "We Kiss in a Shadow" also wound up on the cutting room floor), but losing this number was a shame as it not only showed another side of Anna's character but also was a great testament to both Deborah and me and our ability to fuse our voices into one. I did, however, get to see the number when the film was first released. When and why it disappeared (seemingly forever) from the release prints is a mystery to me. Perhaps somewhere deep in the vaults of Twentieth Century Fox is a can of film containing this treasure. Thankfully the song remains on the original soundtrack recording, which has been reissued on CD.

As I (or we) finished recording each song, the responsibility would shift over to Deborah. Before it was finalized and totally mixed down she would have to "audition" the track by attempting to lip-synch to the playback. If she approved it we would go on to the next song. Her comfort level was very important, because she would have to work with these tracks throughout the filming.

Contrary to popular belief, the "dubbee" must follow the "dubber." In other words, it was Deborah's job during the filming to properly mouth to the approved playback. She would actually sing along, utilizing everything she had learned in our rehearsals. When you are lip-synching, there is no time to wait.

The timing and impetus must be exact, not a second before or after. A "synch" man hovered under the camera and had the ability to stop the recording (and thus filming) if the actress' lips were not in exact synchronization with the track. Deborah had to make the endings, the recoils, and the "breathing choreography" second nature in order to give a complete performance during the playback. Although there were a few instances when I had to re-record a section because something went momentarily awry during filming, because of our extensive rehearsal process, most of the time Deborah was flawless.

———

Yul Brynner was a force to be reckoned with: an actor, singer, director, and photographer. It was clear to anyone meeting him that he was really the life and soul of *The King and I*. It had been said that Brynner, who had been a TV director previously, helped direct the show on Broadway. Now he felt that the film, too, was his domain. In fact, when director Walter Lang was nominated for an Oscar for directing the film, Deborah Kerr sent a telegram to Yul congratulating *him* on the directing nomination!

Brynner claimed to be a Russian gypsy, but, in fact, he was the son of Swiss and Mongolian parents. He spoke French and a number of other languages fluently. When I went backstage to see him in a later tour of *The King and I*, he confided in me that he had only one lung. As a result, when he did the scene "Shall We Dance?" which required him to polka vigorously around the ballroom floor, and then strip to the waist to do the whipping scene with Tuptim (the runaway girl sent as a gift from Burma) right afterward, he had to go offstage into the wings immediately and breathe emergency oxygen in order to keep going. I was amazed to hear this, as he always looked as if he had superhuman strength. He was a trouper who gave his all, and he certainly put his stamp on the role of the King of Siam.

Most days when it was time for lunch, everyone split up and I wound up eating alone. One day, however, after working all morning on the rehearsal stage with Deborah, I worked up the nerve to ask her to have lunch with me in the commissary. She turned me down with a conspiratorial wink.

"Would you take a rain check, Marni? I have an important date with a very sexy person."

I thought perhaps her husband was coming to visit. Then suddenly the huge ground-to-ceiling doors of the rehearsal stage began to open. Sunlight burst through the gloom of the sound stage and I could see a spotless new Cadillac convertible, with the top down. The license plate read Y-U-L, as if one couldn't spot that now-famous bald head and know whose car this was.

The Cadillac stopped and Yul Brynner, in all his glory, emerged. He wore tight-fitting black leather pants, a black leather sleeveless jacket with no shirt, enhancing his muscular arms, and black leather boots with silver stirrups. All of which matched the black leather upholstery of his car. Around his neck was a necklace with an icon hanging from it. Two perfectly matched (and I mean every gray and black marking was identical to the other!) German shepherd dogs straining at the leash preceded him. Yul held the two strong dogs back with one hand. In the other hand was a very long professional hand-tooled leather whip. He lifted the whip high above his head and snapped it in the air. I couldn't have been more startled, but he certainly got my attention. Then, letting go of the dogs and dropping the whip, he smiled his broadest smile, stretched out his arms and in his trademark "King of Siam" voice proclaimed for everyone within earshot, "I am here!"

I dared not look at Deborah because I thought it was one of the funniest scenes I'd ever witnessed.

He bowed to her, took her arm, and off they went to lunch. Although there were rumors (on film sets there are *always* rumors) of a romance, I never found out the real nature of their lunch. Or what they did with the dogs while they ate. Feeling like a ghostly Cinderella who can't go to the ball, I went outside, sat on a rock, and ate my tuna fish sandwich.

Early on, soon after I signed my contract with the "no-credit" clause, I received an ominous phone call from someone at Twentieth Century Fox who shall remain nameless (mainly because I can't remember the name!). The rather menacing voice on the other end of the line told me that if anyone ever found out that I dubbed any part of Deborah Kerr's voice, I would never work in Hollywood again. I was in shock! Apparently, the studio wanted the critics and public to think that Deborah was not only a wonderful actress, but a great singer as well. They were afraid that if anyone knew that part of her performance was not her own, it might reduce her chances at being nominated for an Academy Award. They felt that this was a trade secret and that the public had no right to know how the behind-the-scenes movie magic really worked.

I didn't know what to say. Frankly, I was scared. Now that we had decided to move back to L.A., I certainly couldn't afford to not work in the film or television industry. I was currently the breadwinner in my household of two adults and two small children. So I muttered some kind of agreement to the person on the other end and, before I had a chance to say anything else, the line went dead. I knew they meant business and I was determined never to be the one to reveal this trade secret.

The King and I premiered to rave reviews simultaneously at Grauman's Chinese Theatre in Hollywood and the Roxy Theatre in New York on June 28, 1956. Both Brynner and Kerr received Golden Globe Awards for their performances and the film was nominated for nine Academy Awards, including Best Picture and Best Female Performer, Deborah Kerr. When the nominations were announced I must admit that I felt quite a bit of pride for having contributed something to Deborah's Oscar-nominated performance. The picture, director, cinematographer, and Deborah didn't win the Oscar that year, but *The King and I* raked in five other Academy Awards for Best Actor (Yul), Best Scoring for a Musical Film (Alfred Newman and my darling Ken Darby), Best Art Direction, Best Costume Design, and Best Sound Recording. I rooted for my people that year and, despite being a ghost, I was thrilled that I had been involved in such an artistically and commercially successful film.

The long-playing record taken from the soundtrack was issued on June 11, 1956 in stereo (a big deal then). It immediately began selling very well, debuting on the *Billboard* charts in late July and peaking at Number One. It remained on the charts for a total of 274 weeks, and was awarded a Gold Record by the Recording Industry Association of America (RIAA), signifying sales of more than 500,000 copies. Recently, *The King and I* ranked high on *Billboard*'s list of the 100 best-selling albums (it was joined there by *West Side Story* and *My Fair Lady*). Imagine! I had a top-selling Gold Record album in the stores! And I had been paid all of $420 for it!

Now, all these years later, with the reissue of the CD, and without asking for it, I am finally given full credit for the songs I sang. It does make me feel proud and happy. Some money, though, would've been, to quote one of the songs, "something wonderful."

I must have been doing something right, because, in early 1957, Twentieth Century Fox once again asked me to be Deborah's ghost. The film was *An Affair to Remember*, a remake of the classic tearjerker *Love Affair*. Deborah was playing Irene Dunne's old role and was costarring with Cary Grant. Although this wasn't a musical, in the film Deborah played a nightclub singer and there were to be four songs for her (or rather me) to sing.

After our incredibly symbiotic experience on *The King and I*, it was surprising when Deborah decided not to be part of the process.

"Oh, Marni," she said, "you know me so well by now. Just sing the songs the way you think I would sing them and I'll just do them as you lay down the tracks!"

Wow! She really did trust me. I set out to work on the songs with Ken Darby with a real sense of purpose. I had to live up to Deborah's faith.

One of the songs Deborah's character was to sing was an Irish song called "Tomorrowland." This being the days of the great studios, there were dialect coaches available at the drop of a hat, but as Ken and I worked on the song the accent seemed to come easily to me, so I declined any kind of coaching.

Before recording the song, there was to be a presentation of it for all the powers that be. There was the composer, Harry Warren; the lyricist, Harold

Adamson; and the director (and co-lyricist), Leo McCarey; as well as Ken Darby, Cary Grant, and, of course, Deborah. Everyone was expectantly sitting forward in his or her chairs, waiting to hear me sing. As I began singing I noticed Cary covering his hand over his mouth and looking sideways at Deborah, both of them obviously trying to stifle an oncoming fit of the giggles. I forged ahead and when I finally finished what I thought was a wonderful rendition in a perfect Irish accent, everyone burst out laughing. Over the laughter, Cary Grant spoke up:

"That was wonderful, Marni," he said. "A wonderful song, Harry." Suddenly everyone laughed again. "Lovely accent, Marni! But it was Scottish, not Irish!"

I blushed three shades of red. Well, I guess singing with a Scottish accent came more naturally to me than I thought. Something in those McEathron genes, I guess. Oh well, it was back to the dialect coach for me!

When musical films, such as *The King and I*, played in foreign markets, it was not unusual for the songs to either be cut out or have them redubbed in the language of the particular country in which the film was being distributed. Even today, a film such as *The Phantom of the Opera* or *Chicago* has dozens of foreign language soundtracks, all done by artists residing in the various nations.

For *An Affair to Remember*, it was decided that, since I was trained to sing in many different languages, and had recorded numerous classical recordings in various tongues, it would be *my* voice that came out of Deborah's lips in Spain, Germany, France, and Italy, not to mention the English-speaking nations of the world. The international movie Marni was born!

Although I would once again be getting no screen credit, this time I fought to get my name on the Columbia Records soundtrack that was to be issued. Once again I would be getting no royalties, but this time the record producers agreed to put my name on the cover. The *back* cover! Only Cary Grant, Deborah Kerr, and Vic Damone, who sang the title song, also known as "Our Love Affair," over the opening credits, were on the front. There, in small print on the back of the jacket, where they list participating orchestra players, it simply reads "Soprano soloist: Marni Nixon." A step up from *The King and I* perhaps, but not exactly the kind of credit I had hoped for. What did the soprano soloist do? Was she part of the orchestra? No one seemed to care as long as people thought Deborah Kerr was singing. To add insult to injury, the reissue of the CD still contains the same credit, but misspells my name M-A-R-N-I-E!

The title song was not only to be sung by Vic Damone over the opening credits, but also in a later scene by Deborah's character, nightclub singer Terry McKay. There is Deborah in a nightclub eagerly anticipating her return to New York and a reunion with Cary Grant after six months apart.

This would be the first time in my dubbing career that I was introducing a new song (*The King and I* songs had all been introduced on Broadway before I got my vocal chords around them) with a particular emotional subtext and attitude. This time around, Deborah wasn't there in rehearsals to help form the acting intent. This time, *she* would have to adopt my vocal acting and make it her own on-screen. Ken Darby and I worked on the scene and the song and together we developed the character's attitude when she was singing. I was proud that I was the "original actress" in the singing of "Our Love Affair" in the film.

By the way, I did keep my word to Twentieth Century Fox and told no one that I was responsible for singing for Deborah. Was it my fault that before *The King and I* even opened Deborah spilled the beans? I was as shocked as the next person on March 9, 1956, to pick up the *Los Angeles Times* and read syndicated columnist Earl Wilson's latest scoop, under the byline "It Happened Last Night."

"DEBORAH TELLS A SECRET," screamed the headline!

There it was in black and white for all the world and Twentieth Century Fox to see. I quote from Wilson's column:

> From lovely Deborah Kerr I've just heard how a lovely Hollywood and/or London movie actress can sing a lovely song without fully developing a—uh—lovely voice. The songs in *The King and I* taxed even the late Gertrude Lawrence when it was a Broadway hit. Now we discover beautiful Miss Kerr confusing us by knocking them off expertly in the movie, though she's never before had a singing role.
>
> "She's a wonderful woman, this Marni Nixon," said Miss Kerr with striking honesty.
>
> "But I'd heard they weren't dubbed," I retorted.
>
> "Oh, no, they weren't. You see we split it."
>
> "Split it! I see now!" It was I who was getting British.
>
> "You see, I would lead into them," explained the refreshing English beauty "and in the middle of the song, when I couldn't go any further, Marni'd take over. She was at one mike and I was at another. She's a highly respected California concert singer and we practically lived together for seven weeks. She even looks a little like me and she got so she could do a wonderful imitation of me."
>
> "But why didn't you sing the whole thing?" I asked.
>
> "I cahn't! I'm not steady enough. I do mean to try seriously now, though. I've never sung except in the days when I was in the repertory, when I did everything."
>
> Miss Kerr and Miss Nixon even have a little running joke about a contemplated opera. Miss Kerr plans to stand at the mike onstage singing like mad while Miss Nixon belts the songs from behind the curtain.
>
> "What do you say when somebody tells you how well you sang a song?" I asked fiendishly.

"I say, 'Thank you very much,' just as I do when they tell me they enjoyed me in some picture I was never in."

A young man spoke up and said, "I want to tell you, when we played your songs in a sneak preview, everybody thought you were simply terrific."

"Well, then," said Miss Kerr, "I feel very, very proud of myself!"

She drew herself up, "And Miss Nixon," she added.

A few months later, Deborah was quoted in *Photoplay* magazine as saying, "The dubbing is so perfect I almost convinced myself that I sang *all* the numbers."

Well, part of the cat was out of the bag. As Deborah later innocently told me, "How would I know what was in *your* contract, Marni? I just thought you were so talented I wanted to give you credit."

And she did. Sort of. Well, at least they spelled my name right. From now on, that name would be forever synonymous with "ghost."

Chapter Six

THE FABULOUS FIFTIES,
PART TWO

*"I've fallen in love with England. I now wear English tweeds.
I drink English imported tea. Even I think my English
pronunciation has improved."*

ERNEST GOLD, 1961

AS THE SECOND HALF OF THE 1950S ROLLED ALONG it became more ap-
parent that moving back to L.A. had been the right decision for Ernest's
career. Ernest had been orchestrating and conducting the film scores of
George Antheil, including several of the early films of Stanley Kramer. When
George took ill and decided to compose less (he eventually died in 1959),
Kramer put all his trust in Ernest as a composer. The result was that as
Kramer's career ascended, so did Ernest's. In 1958 alone Ernest went from the
ridiculous to the sublime. From *The Screaming Skull* to Stanley Kramer's *The
Defiant Ones* was quite a leap! In a quick succession came such A-list movies as
Too Much Too Soon, *The Young Philadelphians*, and *On the Beach*. As the film as-
signments improved, Ernest began to command much better money and the
Gold family became financially secure for the first time.

From where I stood, the move back to L.A. accomplished what it was supposed to. I was in closer daily proximity to my kids, who now had a more stable
environment in which to grow and flourish. My work schedule didn't dimin-
ish, but now we had enough money to hire *real* help (as opposed to the tran-
sient babysitters with whom I had had to put up) around the house and for the
children.

Who would have guessed that eventually the very help I so eagerly sought
would wind up almost destroying my marriage?

Although *The King and I* dominated the fall of 1955 (and helped fill the family coffers), my concert, recording, and opera careers did not abate in the least.
In August of 1955 alone, I was singing every night in an L.A. nightclub and
making a daily hour-and-a-half drive to Santa Barbara to rehearse for the
fiercely difficult operatic role (which I learned in ten days!) of Zerbinetta in
Madame Lotte Lehmann's production of Richard Strauss' *Ariadne auf Naxos*.

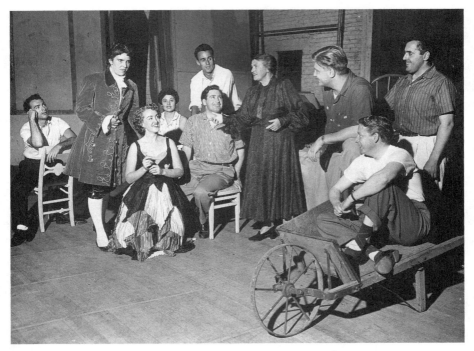

As Zerbinetta in Strauss's Ariadne auf Naxos *in Santa Barbara in 1955. (l to r: Howard Chitjian, Henny Ekstrom, me, Benita Valenti, Ronald Kirkbride behind Lincoln Clark (seated), Mme. Lotte Lehmann, Norman Mittleman, Gregory Millar behind Kelvin Service (in wheelbarrow). (Photo Hal Boucher)*

During this time I was being "looked at" for a starring role on Broadway in the new Frank Loesser musical, *The Most Happy Fella*. Loesser had just come off the incredible success of *Guys and Dolls*. I had heard he was as difficult a taskmaster as Richard Rodgers and twice as hard on sopranos. In fact, in rehearsals for *Guys and Dolls*, when soprano Isabel Bigley sang a note not to Frank's liking, he up and punched her in the nose! So, I was both flattered and a little scared when Loesser invited me to his home in Beverly Hills for a private audition. I can remember being let into the house by his wife, Lynn, with her hair pulled back in a ponytail and her oversized men's eyeglasses. It was immediately evident that not only wasn't there much warmth coming from her, but she seemed downright irritated to see me. I remember feeling uncomfortable, as Mrs. Loesser (who was coproducing *The Most Happy Fella*, so I smiled sweetly) looked me up and down to see if I was some kind of threat. After all, I was young and pretty and, in retrospect, I suppose she was seeing the writing on the wall for her marriage. After giving me "the fish eye," as Loesser himself put it in a lyric, she "allowed" me to come in and sing for Frank and some of his associates. After I sang, we all settled down for a little chat and then I left. I guess Frank was more interested in my talent than I thought, because he started showing up with more and more frequency to my nightclub gig, sometimes bringing other people with him to see how I fared in front of an audience. I was excited and hopeful. As Loesser described it, the role of Rosabella, the lovelorn waitress from San Francisco, would be perfect for me. However, as much as Loesser loved my singing, in the end he told me that I had too refined a quality for the tough and not-quite-virginal waitress role. A wonderful actress-singer named Jo Sullivan got the role and, incidentally, became the next Mrs. Frank Loesser. Now that was a gig with perks! Oh, well. At least I got to play the role (of Rosabella, not Mrs. Loesser!) several years later in a regional production.

Although much of live TV still emanated from the East Coast, the revolutionary success of *I Love Lucy*, which was shot on film instead of being transmitted live, pointed the way to the future of television. Shooting on film (videotape had yet to be invented) meant that both coasts (and the vast country in the middle) could get the same picture quality. In addition, a filmed TV show had the potential of being rebroadcast in its original form. It was actually the switch to film (and later videotape) and the possibilities of reruns that eventually killed off the summer replacement shows that permeated the airwaves in the 1950s. It also killed off the fear factor of performing live in front of millions of people and helped to keep the mistakes and bloopers on the cutting room floor. Soon the days of horrible blunders going out live on the air would be history. Which reminds me of the time I appeared on *Dupont Opera Cameos* singing the pyrotechnical aria performed by Olympia, the windup doll in an excerpt from *Tales of Hoffman*. Live! Live! Live!

There I was in my long beribboned dress with a huge hoopskirt, singing the staccati and coloratura phrases written by the great French operetta composer Jacques Offenbach. As Olympia I was to sing without any expression at all, as if I were a doll. It seemed to be going well as the huge camera followed me around the set as planned. Then I came to the one piece of furniture on the set: an ornate chair with arms on which I had been directed to sit at a certain point within the aria. While continuing to sing I was then to stand and execute some dance steps. I gracefully rose to my feet, totally unaware that the ribbons of my dress were now caught on the ornate arms of the chair. During the rest of the aria and dance my skirt was literally dragging the chair behind me. There was nothing for me to do but continue on as if nothing out of the ordinary was happening. Every so often, while still making the correct camera moves, I would improvise a movement or dance step to try to rid myself of the chair, all the while singing high Ds and Es! I never did get rid of my uninvited dance partner, and I can only hope that the director was smart enough to keep the camera tight on my face. That, ladies and gentlemen, was live TV. If something went wrong, you hid it and prayed. I kind of miss it, and in a way so does the general public, or else why would most DVDs of movies and TV shows contain countless reels of bloopers? Times sure have changed.

In 1956, though, I was about to embark on a TV venture that wouldn't be quite so dangerous because it would be shot on film. It was called *The Tennessee Ernie Ford Show*. Although not well-known today, Tennessee Ernie Ford was the first of the country-western crossover stars. He had a beautiful bass voice and a very appealing down-home charm. His recordings sold extremely well, and he had a distinct flair for comedy. NBC felt lucky to pin him down for a variety show. TV variety shows, which are all but extinct today, filled the airwaves in the 1950s and 1960s, peaking and then dying out after *The Carol Burnett Show* in the late 1970s. They were a mixture of sketch comedy (still very much around today on *Saturday Night Live* and *Mad TV*), solos, and elaborate musical numbers. Every week there would be a guest star who would perform solo as well as with the host, in this case Tennessee Ernie Ford.

I was contracted to appear on the 1956–57 season of *The Tennessee Ernie Ford Show* (which, interestingly enough, *was* sponsored by Ford Motors) as part of the Voices of Walter Schumann. Whereas the Roger Wagner Chorale (with which I still soloed on occasion) specialized more in esoteric oratorio music, the Schumann group focused on popular songs of the day. They performed on Broadway and in concert, and released many hit recordings (I was on several of them). There were twenty singers on the TV show but only eight women. Several of us, including me, were to be "featured singers," meaning we would not only sing as part of the group, but each week one of us would be the featured soloist. This was the appeal for me: to actually get my face out there in front of millions of people. The publicity department called me Ernie Ford's leading lady, but the truth was that several of us alternated in that role.

The series was directed and produced by Bud Yorkin. Yorkin entered the television world as an engineer and wound up producing and directing shows featuring Dean Martin and Jerry Lewis, Abbott and Costello, and George Gobel before joining Ernie Ford's show. In 1959 he worked on such films as *Come Blow Your Horn* and *Divorce American Style*. In 1971, he entered TV's Hall of Fame with the landmark comedy series *All in the Family*. In the days I worked with him, Bud was efficient and fun—except when he had to say no to me, but that came later.

It was a financial relief to have a steady job, although doing a half-hour weekly variety show could be grueling. We rehearsed five days a week from nine to five and shot on the sixth day. Mornings would be taken up with dance and orientation and afternoons with learning and rehearsing the material for that week. Sometimes the group was featured in sketches, but most of the time we were singing and dancing either on our own or backing up Ernie and/or the guest star of the week.

Working at NBC was a bit like my days at MGM. Whenever I wasn't busy rehearsing or was on a long break I was free to wander and peek in at other TV shows being rehearsed or shot. I can remember watching several read-throughs of *The Jack Benny Show*. Along with the rest of the country I had listened to him on radio and now watched the show on TV. And like everyone else, I always thought Benny and his costars Eddie (Rochester) Anderson, Mary Livingston, Dennis Day, Don Wilson, and Mel Blanc were hilarious. Watching them read through the script, however, was another story. Nothing seemed funny. No one seemed to be "playing" the comedy. After observing them for a while, though, I began to realize what incredible comedy technicians Benny and his writers were. They didn't have to hear material played full out to know whether it was funny or not. They all knew Benny's delivery so well that they could imagine how a joke would land. Or not. I watched and listened, the proverbial fly on the wall, as they dissected the scripts with professional expertise and mined the best from each joke or situation and tossed the dross into the wastebasket. Sometimes you would hear Jack Benny say, "Let's change that "and" to a "but." I would wonder how that would make it funnier, but sure enough when I watched the show later in the week it would be hysterical. What a learning experience that was!

I also remember watching a special (they were called "spectaculars" in those days) being rehearsed featuring the musical talents of my old crush André Previn and the great jazz and scat singer Ella Fitzgerald. They had never met before, but they somehow spoke the same musical language. I was amazed at how they improvised and managed to take some simple chord structures and weave them into spontaneous and fresh tunes that related to the originals, but propelled themselves into some musical stratosphere as yet unexplored. Sometimes on breaks their impromtu jam sessions produced some tasty musical treats that eventually wound up on the TV special. As a singer who worked specifically from the music put before me, their process seemed unique and magical.

We had many guest stars on *The Tennessee Ernie Ford Show*, including Greer Garson, Nelson Eddy, Margaret and Barbara (she who stole my role in the film *Junior Miss!*) Whiting, Rosemary Clooney, Douglas Fairbanks, Jr., Hedda Hopper, Tommy Sands, Jeannie Carson, Wally Cox, Jackie Cooper, Joseph Cotton, Caesar Romero, Carol Channing, Mickey Spillane, George Gobel, Steve Allen, Jo Stafford, Walter Brennan, and Rin Tin Tin!

But the one that sticks in my memory is that glamorous, flamboyant, and much-married Hungarian star Zsa Zsa Gabor.

I have always loved to dress well but financial realities being what they were (as well as being the frugal Scot that I am), I tried to shop economically for the best-looking clothes. The day Zsa Zsa was to appear on the set and rehearse with us I was wearing a smart and simple blue woolen dress with buttons down the side. I had bought it in a discount store and was very proud of my economical purchase. The minute Miss Gabor walked into the rehearsal studio her eyes scanned the chorus girls. I suppose she wanted to make sure no one was prettier or more alluring than she. Her eyes settled on me, as she looked me up and down. She stopped what she was doing and briskly strode over to where I was standing.

Fixing me with a stare that could melt ice, she intoned in her distinctive Hungarian accent:

"I have the original of that dress, dahling!"

With that she turned on her heels and resumed rehearsing. I presume she thought to "put me in my place," but I was just thrilled that she recognized my great taste in clothes.

The Tennessee Ernie Ford Show premiered on Thursday evening, October 4, 1956, and was broadcast every week until June of 1957 (TV shows had long seasons in those days). Virtually overnight, it cracked the Nielsen Top Ten, and before the end of its first season on the air it had become the top half-hour variety show in America. Besides having all the usual features of a good variety show, the *Ernie Ford Show* had one element that clearly separated it from all the others. Ford closed virtually every show with a hymn. Ernie Ford and our show had the distinction of almost single-handedly bringing inspirational music into the mainstream of popular entertainment.

I enjoyed appearing on the show every week, but also started to feel restricted by the tight schedule. During this period I was still maintaining our household (with some full-time help, thank goodness!) and sustaining my classical career by giving a series of orchestral concerts and recitals, making studio recordings, and singing the role of Gretel in yet another production of Humperdinck's *Hansel and Gretel*, directed by Glynn Ross and conducted by Carmen Dragon, the well-known film and TV composer, arranger, and conductor. The wonderful singing comedienne Anna Russell played the witch, and she was hilarious. Even her costume was funny. Her witch's cloak had hugely long sleeves dripping cobwebs on which were caught the most delightfully disgusting insects and other spooky objects. And she flew! This was the first time anyone had worn the famous "flying by Foy" harness in a full-blown opera and I can still hear the screams of delight from the children in the audience when Anna Russell zoomed off on her broomstick.

In early 1957, I doubled at *The Tennessee Ernie Ford Show* and at Twentieth Century Fox, where I dubbed Deborah Kerr's voice in *An Affair to Remember.*

As one of the Voices of Walter Schumann (I'm in the third row center) on NBC's Tennessee Ernie Ford Show *in 1956. Was this the dress Zsa Zsa had the original of? (Courtesy of Globe Photos Inc.)*

The producers generously let me skip morning rehearsals and warm-ups so that I could go to the Fox lot to rehearse the *Affair* songs. I would then rejoin the *Ernie Ford Show* at NBC in the afternoon. Despite some fatigue (after all, I was pushing 27!), it all seemed to work out. So when a frantic call (why are all these calls frantic?) came from Kurt Herbert Adler at the San Francisco Opera I thought everything would work out just fine.

"I've heard about you, Miss Nixon. Tell me, do you know the role of Nanetta in Verdi's *Falstaff*?"

"Of course I do," I lied.

As anyone in show business will tell you, you always say yes first and figure out the details later. Although Nanetta was a role I had studied and knew I could do, I had never actually performed it in its entirety on stage. This was just a small detail I left out when I fibbed and told him I had done the role before.

"But *where*," he pounced, "have you done the role, Miss Nixon?"

I had to think quickly and the first thing that came to my mind was Sarah Caldwell.

"I sang the role with Sarah Caldwell at the New England Opera Company," I replied with my fingers firmly crossed behind my back.

My quick thinking was canny, as it was well known that Sarah *never* answered her phone and it would be difficult for them to check my story in a timely fashion. I knew they were stuck and needed me quickly. Famed opera diva Elisabeth Schwartzkopf was singing the lead role with Albert Steinberg in the pit. This would be an auspicious debut for me. By the end of the phone call we had a potential deal. The only thing I had to do now was get the producer of the *Ernie Ford Show* to let me off for ten days (once again I had ten whole days to learn an opera!). Bud Yorkin had let me take mornings off to dub Deborah Kerr, hadn't he? I was only going to be away from the show for two episodes, wasn't I? How difficult would that be? Well, shock of shocks, he said no! He told me that if I left for two episodes, I would have to forgo my one-year contract and not return to the show at all. This was just before Ernest was beginning to make good money and I was the primary breadwinner. So I reluctantly and painfully made the decision to stay with the TV show and let go of this operatic debut. A prime opportunity had literally fallen into my lap and I had to turn it down. I cried for three weeks. Once again I was deferring my operatic dreams to keep food on the table.

Eventually I did get to sing with the San Francisco Opera (in the role of Philine in *Mignon*) but during the less prestigious spring opera season. In addition, I felt that I wasn't in as good voice as I had been when I was offered Nanetta.

Emotionally speaking, turning down Nanetta was very traumatic for me, and I realized that I had to be very careful about any long-term commitments I made in the future. With that in mind I chose not to renew my contract when the *Ernie Ford Show* was renewed for a second season, although I loved working with all the people at the show, especially the sweet Ernie Ford.

In September of 1957 I received a lovely handwritten note from him:

Dear Marni,

Since coming back from vacation and seeing all the kids again, I was sorry not to see your smiling face among the crowd. I just wanted to tell you how nice it was having you with us last year and although you won't be with us this year, I'm sure the activities you've chosen to undertake are going to keep you as busy as last year. I want to be one of the first to wish you the best of luck and lots of happiness. I'd also like to say I'd consider it an honor if you'd drop in sometime and say hello, anytime. Once again, may all good times come your way and the best of everything this season!

Very sincerely,

Ernie Ford

In late 1957 TV courted me yet again when I did several appearances on *The Lawrence Welk Show*, which was renowned for the square, middle-of-the-road arrangements of popular tunes. Who can forget "An' a one, an' a two?" I knew that Welk liked me a lot and was thinking of me as a replacement for his featured singer, known as the "Champagne Lady." This would have been a permanent job, giving me exposure to millions of viewers. At first I thought it would be ideal. Welk was very loyal to his people, and once in his employ you had a job for life. In addition there would be lots of well-paying gigs with his band out of town. Not to mention he danced a mean polka and I loved to dance. The only downside was one had to think the way Welk thought, musically speaking. You couldn't sing anything of which he didn't approve and, frankly, his tastes ran to the bland. Everything was homogenized and sweet. His music made Disney seem like rock and roll and he tried to regulate everyone's personal life as well.

After a while, I began turning down his show, even though the money was good. I knew that I just didn't fit into his tight restrictive niche. Ultimately, my good friend Norma Zimmer (with whom I had worked on jingles, TV shows, and commercials) became his Champagne Lady. She fit in well and kept the job to the very end of Welk's career. I was happy for beautiful and dear Norma, and this was one time I had no regrets.

On July 26, 1957, *Variety* reported that I was in Cedars of Lebanon Hospital after having an appendicitis attack. I had awakened a few days earlier with pains in my stomach and after a whole day in agony I put in an emergency call to my doctor who, after some prodding and poking (accompanied by my screeching in pain), had me admitted to the hospital for an immediate operation. When I came to I was told they had found a noncancerous cyst on my ovary, which had burst. Although my appendix was not the cause of my pain, they had removed it anyway. More importantly, they removed a part of my right ovary, taking the cyst along with it. I assumed that the "anemia" I had been diagnosed with back in New York had been due to the cyst. I slowly regained my old energy, and was assured that this would not affect any future childbearing. At that time I was busy enough juggling the two kids I already had and taking care of my ever-bustling career.

The concerts, chamber music recitals, operas, and recordings seemed to come all at once during this period. In 1958 I performed in an opera called *The Man in the Moon* by Joseph Haydn and directed by film and TV director Lamont Johnson, renowned for his experimental stagings of classic operas. Although it was fun, the most memorable thing about it to me was an unsolicited phone call that came during the rehearsal period.

Besides the complete works of Webern, Stravinsky, and Charles Ives, I had recently recorded an adorable children's record entitled *The Mother Magoo Suite*. At that time Mr. Magoo, the famously sight-challenged cartoon character voiced by Jim Backus, was all the rage. The cartoon shorts featuring him played not only on TV but also in the movies back when movies had double features and selected short subjects. Ernest had written the music for a couple of these cartoons in the early 1950s and now a composer named Dennis Farnon had written a suite of jazz-related songs for kids and I had the pleasure of recording them.

One day during rehearsals at the New Ivar Theatre, a young box office apprentice came running down the aisle shouting at the top of her lungs.

"Miss Nixon! Miss Nixon! There's somebody on the phone who insists on talking to you. He says he tracked you down."

I ran to the box office thinking it must be an emergency. When I picked up the phone the voice on the other end cheerfully babbled on.

"Hi, this is Mel Tormé. I just want to tell you that I just listened to your recording of this *Mother Magoo Suite* and I think you have the purest voice and are the greatest singer I ever heard. I just admire you so much and I want to tell you to just keep going. Make more records like this because they're so unusual."

Before I could respond I heard that famous velvet fog of voice singing a portion of one of the songs from the suite, "Mistress Mary Quite Contrary."

The singing cut off in mid phrase and once again he spoke.

"Well, I just wanted to say that you're the best. Bye."

I was flabbergasted and utterly flattered. I mean, Mel Tormé! He was one of the best jazz singers, songwriters, and arrangers around. I had admired him for years (and always would). I went back to rehearsal on a cloud.

Now, fast-forward thirty years later to a celebrity-laden New Year's party in Beverly Hills at the home of stage producer Herb Rogers. I was gabbing with my friend and agent Hal Gefsky and Donald O'Connor (we had costarred in a show together). Donald turned to the man next to him and introduced him to me.

"Mel, this is Marni Nixon. Marni, Mel Tormé."

"Of course I know you," Mel said as he turned around and once again proceeded to sing "Mistress Mary Quite Contrary." In its original key! He told me he played the recording all the time. Thirty years later! As you can imagine, this made my whole year!

1958 was a banner year for my opera career. Besides *The Man in the Moon*, I played the Butterfly's wife in *Solomon and Balkis*, sang under Stravinsky's baton in his opera *Mavra*, did a Los Angeles Guild Opera production of *The Bartered Bride* (with my buddy Marilyn Horne making her debut) produced and directed by my old friend and mentor Carl Ebert, and played the leading role of Rosina in Glynn Ross' production of *The Barber of Seville*.

The Barber of Seville starred the most famous Dr. Bartolo at that point in the opera world, Salvatore Baccaloni. He was renowned for his singing, acting . . . and groping! It was apparently an initiation into the world of opera to have Baccaloni's hand imprint on your breast or behind! This happened not only backstage but onstage as well. Thanks to his roaming hands I hit some of the highest notes of my career during that production!

At the end of 1958 I played the entire role of Anna Leonowens for the first time in a stage production of *The King and I*. After having contributed the musical portion of the performance in the 1956 film, I was now given the opportunity (although at twenty-eight I was still too young for the role) to let the ghost materialize and portray the whole woman. I felt that Anna was like an old friend, and her character fit me like a glove. So did her costumes.

Because of my connection with the film, the San Bernardino Civic Light Opera Association was able to borrow the incredibly beautiful Irene Sharaff gowns that Deborah Kerr wore in the movie from Twentieth Century Fox. Sharaff had designed the costumes for both the show and the film and had been honored with an Oscar (and a Tony) for her efforts. It was Sharaff who, when Yul Brynner asked her early in rehearsals for the stage production what he should do about his thin, wispy hair, told him to "shave it off!" She helped to create his image and perhaps ensured his stardom. Now I was to be wearing her magnificent creations, including the famous off-the-shoulder lavender ball gown used in the "Shall We Dance?" sequence.

The 1860s period of *The King and I* was strictly observed in these extravagant and stunning costumes and it wasn't just the dresses, but what was underneath them. First would come the pantaloons, then the hoopskirt, then the petticoat, and finally the dress itself. The custom-made hoopskirts built for the film were very special. They seemed to practically melt away when one bent down or kneeled. The rings were made of metal, not plastic as some of the later copies were. They started about a quarter inch apart and then got bigger and bigger. Sort of like an accordion that could expand and contract easily. Each of the rings was wrapped in gold brocade ribbon and each ring was linked together by a cascading grosgrain ribbon. The result was that the dress moved extremely well. The only problem was that it weighed over 100 lbs! Now, in the movie Deborah Kerr would do a take and then a dresser would remove the hoop skirt and she would rest, but onstage I had to wear the whole package for the entire scene, which contained a song and very athletic polka with the King. Plus an encore! What I found was that my waist and hips couldn't possibly hold the weight of the hoopskirt itself. Every time I walked or danced I almost fainted or fell to the ground. To solve the problem, the wardrobe department came up with the idea of suspenders to hold the weight of the metal hoops, thus transferring the weight from my hips to my shoulders, which were stronger.

Unfortunately, the bare shoulder look had to be modified. They devised some kind of tulle stole to cover up the ugly suspenders and, although I missed the sexiness of the original design, I was glad not to faint with every step I took.

Appearing in the flesh as Anna in The King and I, *with Renato Cibelli as the King, at San Bernardino Civic Light Opera, California, 1958. I wore all of Deborah Kerr's movie costumes! (Photo Neale Adair)*

In 1958 and 1959 Ernest's film career blossomed with the releases of *The Defiant Ones* and *On the Beach*. The latter garnered him his first Oscar nomination for Best Score of a Motion Picture and won him a Golden Globe. We were definitely in a new place both professionally and financially. Suddenly, I was not the primary breadwinner. We were on more equal footing and, to the outside world, we appeared to be the picture of the successful Hollywood household.

After having lived in a few rented houses, we thought it was time to build a home of our own. We found a lot in Laurel Canyon and hired an architect. This house would be the home of which we both dreamed, built to our own specifications. As the planning and building proceeded, Ernest was hired to write the score of Otto Preminger's film version of the best-selling book, *Exodus*. This project excited and stimulated him. He was to travel to Israel, research the indigenous music there, and write the score as they shot the film. More often than not, films were shot first and then the composer composed the music for it after a rough cut of the movie was assembled. Writing the score as the film was being shot was a very unusual way of working, but Preminger was an unusual director. The score was then to be recorded in London and I was to accompany Ernest on that trip as a kind of working vacation.

With all this in mind (and now that we could afford it), we hired a full-time, live-in au pair from England. With both of our insanely busy work schedules, we knew we required someone who would be able to take care of our home and, most importantly, the children. Through the recommendation of a friend, film composer Elmer Bernstein, who had recently hired similar help, Ernest got in touch with the agency specializing in British au pairs who wanted to come to the U.S. He went to their offices, looked through a book with pictures and references, and from that book he chose her. Both of us were anglophiles and we thought having someone British in the house would be terribly sophisticated and au courant.

Her name was Sally.

In a very short while she arrived from the U.K. and Ernest picked her up at the airport and brought her back to the house. When I opened the door I was stunned to see how young she looked, even younger than her age, which was twenty-one or twenty-two. Interestingly, I was not quite thirty years old, not that much older than Sally, but we were light years apart in our approaches to work and life. My first impression was of a wisp of a girl who had absolutely no experience in working or keeping house. All my life I had been a hard worker, both artistically and menially, and I expected the same from others. I found out later that Sally had been raised by a nanny and never had to learn how to keep a home clean. She had it all done for her. In fact, she was clueless when it came to which cleaning products to use on what and I found that I had to teach her everything about housekeeping (the why, when, how, and where of it all) from scratch. She didn't drive, a great liability when living in L.A., especially in the hills. She didn't swim, and we had a pool that was usually filled with children requiring strict supervision from within the water.

Despite her shortcomings, Sally seemed to be very impressed with her new surroundings: the house, the pool, the cars she couldn't drive . . . and Ernest. All of these things raised a red flag for me and before too long I started to actively question our decision to hire Sally.

Then there was her way with my children. My son Andy was nine years old at the time and beginning to get curious about the opposite sex. One day he and seven-year-old Martha asked Sally about girls and their bodies and she proceeded to give the children their lesson for the day.

"I just lifted up my dress and showed them everything!"

You can imagine how appalled I was at the blatant crassness of her answer! Ernest, however, ignored my complaints and overlooked her flaws.

"You're too demanding. She's young," he said. "She will catch on."

As it turned out, Elmer Bernstein's au pair, Eve, was Sally's best friend from England. The girls were inseparable. They were constantly gossiping on the phone, but the conversation would invariably cease when I entered the room. I heard through the Hollywood grapevine that Elmer and his au pair were having an affair. The warning signals were in the air.

I began to notice evenings after dinner, when Sally went off to her room, Ernest would seemingly retire to the living room to read. His eyes, however, would be constantly looking up over his glasses in anticipation of Sally entering the room. The whole point of finally being able to afford help was for me to have more time to be with Ernest in order to refresh our intimacy. In private. Sally, however, was being welcomed into our most intimate moments alone. There she would be, evening after evening, fawning over Ernest in an overly solicitous way, praising his work and asking him questions about the movie score he was writing. I was beginning to feel threatened and jealous.

For some time now I had been aware of tensions in the house and our inability to talk about them. With that in mind, plus the addition of the "Sally situation," I decided to start analysis to work out these feelings. For some reason, at the time it didn't seem odd at all that my psychoanalyst was the same doctor Ernest had been seeing for years. My analysis seemed to be helping me cope.

Then I had a dream.

In the dream I entered our bedroom, the one I shared with Ernest, and there was Sally dancing around in *my* lingerie, wearing *my* undergarments. She was topless and completely oblivious to my presence. She didn't seem to care at all that I was watching her. She then found a couple of pennies on the floor and stuck them on each of her bare nipples. I awoke with the terrible feeling that she was about to invade my world, to take away everything that was mine. Little did I know that the invasion was already underway!

When I told my analyst the dream he sat bolt upright in shock. He slapped his thigh and angrily muttered something sounding like "I knew it!"

When I questioned his strange response he evaded the issue and started to ask me questions about what the dream meant to me. It was incredibly clear to me what my dream meant. It meant that I felt Sally was trying to take over my family. It was obvious that she was in the market for a rich, interesting man: Ernest. I found out later that both Sally and her friend had come to the U.S. with the express purpose of finding husbands. And now she had found mine! I remember Sally's friend Eve, now the mistress of Elmer Bernstein, proudly boasting, "I'm not here to work. I'm here to meet and marry someone rich and famous." Was Sally about to follow in her friend's footsteps?

Now that I understood how much of a threat Sally was, I did . . . nothing. As usual I buried it and hoped I was just wrong. All this tucking away of the bad feeling was building up inside of me and the anger was bubbling to the surface, but with no concrete proof of infidelity, I just sat still and waited.

On reflection, I wonder why Ernest and I couldn't sit down and talk about it. Why couldn't I even broach the subject? I was so emotional and yet, for some reason, was unable to expose those emotions. Perhaps I thought if I kept them under wraps, they might just go away.

Fast-forward a couple of months. After many more sessions and complaints about Sally, "our" doctor told me why he had reacted the way he did when I first brought up the dream. It seems that he had already known about Ernest's growing affection for Sally and now questioned the advisability of having us both as patients. He admitted that Ernest was under the spell of, what he termed, "a major fascination." He assured me that it wasn't physical, but rather like the kind of letter-writing love affair playwright George Bernard Shaw enjoyed with the actress Mrs. Patrick Campbell.

"But make no mistake," he said. "This is a major inspirational thing for him. She helps his artistic flow. She is his muse."

I was appalled! I had always been an integral part of his artistic flow. I had been his muse. This was one of the reasons I had gone into analysis. I had missed our closeness and I wanted it back. Don't get me wrong. Our sex life was fine. This wasn't a case of a man not getting it at home and having to find it elsewhere. This was something far more complex.

I knew that Ernest had had flirtations and affairs over the years. Right after I gave birth to Martha he admitted to sleeping with a friend and colleague with whom I had just sung. This went on all during the latter part of my pregnancy. Rather than totally blame Ernest I blamed my friend and, as usual, felt ashamed of my own feelings and then actually blamed myself as well. In one of my rare confrontations at the time, I asked her how she could have done this. She apologized and said it would never happen again. Once again I forgave Ernest and buried the hurt where I thought I couldn't find it.

This thing with Sally, however, wasn't like the other flings. This was something deeper and ultimately more dangerous.

With all this knowledge about Ernest's "major fascination" (but no confirmation at all from Ernest) I felt I could just hold on. There was nothing physical, I reasoned. We're still a married couple. Perhaps this is just the way it is with a creative European. So off to London we blithely went to record the score of *Exodus*.

We stayed at the Mayfair Hotel and our London experience should have been the most magical and romantic time of our lives. Instead it turned into a living hell. Soon after we arrived Ernest told me that he wanted to correspond with Sally, that writing to and hearing from her was vitally important to him. Although my mother had graciously agreed to come in and temporarily supervise Sally and the children, Sally was supposed to be writing to me to keep me abreast of my kids. For some reason, though, *all* the letters were addressed only to Ernest. Each day there would be another small "par avian" letter. The delicate blue stationary that folded into its own envelope would appear and then disappear after Ernest got his hands on it. At first I said nothing, not wanting to disturb his preparation for this important, major film, but in the end I couldn't take it anymore. So, despite my usual moral feelings about reading someone's mail, when Ernest was out at Shepperton Studios rehearsing the orchestra I opened the latest missive.

My jaw dropped as I read what was clearly a passionate and juicy love letter. It was clear that they were making plans and that she was responding to his ideas for their future. In her "innocent" schoolgirl scrawl she fantasized about what it would be like to be with him when (not if!) they could finally be together.

I was in shock to say the least! In fact, I was physically ill. All my instincts had been right and my self-denial was out the window. Ernest had fallen right into Sally's trap. Her blind and worshipful adoration of Hollywood and everything that was Ernest had hooked his male ego. He didn't see her as a social-climbing, money-hungry opportunist with dirty, bad teeth. No, he saw her as his muse who looked into his eyes with unqualified admiration. He was enchanted and I was screaming into an empty room. I stood with the letter in my trembling hand for what seemed like an eternity. I began to shake and tried to stifle the involuntary wailing emanating from my soul. Suddenly, fragments of a Walt Whitman poem flooded my head.

"Captain, oh Captain! Where is my captain?"

I sank deeper and deeper into an image of myself on a small boat, absolutely rudderless, in the middle of a deep, vast, and troubled sea. Ernest was supposed to have been the captain. My captain. But he was no longer in "command." Not of himself and certainly not of me. There was no one out there in that vast watery expanse but the boat, an occasional draft of stale air, the loose flapping sails, and me. I felt myself being helplessly crushed by some invisible power. It was devastating.

When Ernest finally came home from rehearsal I calmly told him I read the letter and waited for his response. I knew this was a bad time to confront him, what with all the pressure of scoring a major motion picture, but I couldn't contain it for one more moment. After turning every shade of white possible, he told me everything.

Their relationship (God, that word!) had *not* been physical he said, but for Ernest it was very emotional. He said they were passionate . . . in their minds. I was numb. The next thing I did was call my mother, make sure that my children were all right, and tell her what had happened. Luckily Sally and the kids were down in Balboa Beach, where my parents lived and Mother was in charge. How prescient of me not to have left my children solely in the care of that girl. Mother understood my dilemma and took control. With the help of Sally's friend Eve, Mother would help Sally move out of our house and find an apartment close by. With great difficulty Ernest and I discussed what to do and what, if anything, to tell the kids. After all, they liked Sally and we didn't want to disturb their equilibrium. With this in mind, we decided to tell them nothing and to wait until we got home to figure out what to do with *our* relationship. But first Ernest had a recording session to do.

After the recording sessions were over Ernest and I went to visit his birthplace, Vienna. He had wanted to show me where he grew up. This was to be a second honeymoon, but it turned into a talk session punctuated by diffused, halting, intense days of silence, and me crying my eyes out. These were hardly the Viennese nights I had dreamed about as a girl. When we finally got home to L.A., Sally was moved out of the house (at *our* expense!) into an apartment and was about to move back to England. I had the feeling she was disappointed, to say the least. Hah! Poor baby!

I, however, had made a big decision. I told Ernest that I *wanted* him to physically be with Sally. I told him that I wanted him to go away and live with her, to finally make it real. I was so proud of myself in this decision.

"No more fantasies," I told him. "No more 'major fascinations' behind my back. Go and get it out of your goddamned system! See what she's really like. *And think of what you'll lose.*"

So he did.

We told the kids that their Daddy was away working. Ernest went to England to live with Sally. What he discovered there, away from his home, was a provincial, boring, and ignorant young country girl with no sophistication or smarts (but with nice legs). After a couple of months his fascination with his muse faded and he came home in time for the 1961 Academy Awards. *Exodus* had opened in March of 1960 and was a smash hit. When the Oscar nominations were announced in early 1961, Ernest received his second nomination for Best Music, Scoring of a Dramatic or Comedy Picture. He was up against such musical giants as Dmitri Tiomkin, our friend Alex North, my old crush André Previn, and our still-friend Elmer Bernstein (now married to Eve!).

The morning of the Academy Awards Ernest fell out of bed and broke his nose. That night he went to the Awards on painkillers and with a bandaged nose. We went together as if nothing had come between us and I was ecstatic when Sandra Dee and Bobby Darin announced the winner: Ernest Gold for *Exodus*! Our kids were at home (with a new housekeeper) watching the black-and-white Zenith. They screamed and hooted when their Daddy got up to the stage to accept the award. It was a happy time in the Gold household. But for me it wasn't to last.

Despite having gotten Sally out of his system, Ernest still felt the need to live apart from me. It was obvious to him that there was still some more sorting out to do, so after the Oscars in the spring of 1961, he moved out of the house again. Later in the summer he moved back for a while and then moved out yet again, renting a house nearby to be close to the kids. I began to feel as if we had a revolving door installed in our home and it was obviously confusing to all concerned. There was a comic element to our separations in the fact that, like a child in college, Ernest would always bring home his dirty laundry for me to do. The punch line was . . . I did it! This was not a happy time for me, to say the least.

All this time, of course, while trying to be as open and honest as we could, we attempted to keep our troubles from the children. Whether he lived with us or not, Ernest was Dad and Dad had won an Oscar, so the family was to be rewarded. He told the kids that they could either have a new color TV or a family trip to Hawaii! In the end Andy and Martha didn't have to choose. They got both.

The trip to Hawaii in late 1961 had another purpose for Ernest and me. It was during this holiday that Ernest was to make up his mind once and for all about what his part of this marriage was to be. Finally, he was to make a decision. As I waited for him to reveal to me my future, I began to realize that I, too, needed to decide. What did *I* want? What was *my* decision to be?

That night lying next to him with the surf pounding on the shore in our ears I had my answer. It was simple. I wanted a permanent part of him. Something that could never be taken away from me. And with that knowledge of what I truly wanted for myself came my strength.

We made love that night and I knew deep down in the soul of my being that I was conceiving a child. Something that could never be taken away from me.

We lived apart all during my pregnancy, but I was calm and serene in the knowledge that once he held our baby in his arms Ernest would be able to sustain our commitment to each other and come home to stay.

Our beautiful, giggly, and pure-spirited daughter Melani (pronounced as the Hawaiians do, May-LAH-nee) Christine (literally translated "daughter of sorrow") was born at Cedars of Lebanon Hospital on September 19, 1962. The next day Ernest moved back home. Everything had changed and my feminine strength had melted away all the obstacles.

For a while, anyway.

Chapter Seven

THE *WEST SIDE STORY* STORY

"Marni, we didn't hire you for your voice, we hired you for your iron nerves!"

SAUL CHAPLIN, 1961

D URING ALL THE PERSONAL DRAMA AND EMOTIONAL UPHEAVAL, both
Ernest and I somehow managed to keep our respective professional careers afloat. In fact, the more "sturm and drang" in our relationship, the better
our work seemed to be. Ironic, isn't it?

The very day after I confronted Ernest with Sally's letter back in 1960 at the
Mayfair Hotel in London we were off to Shepperton Studios to record the
score of *Exodus*. The famous English fog and Ernest's nerves (dare I say guilt?)
brought out the worst cold he had experienced in years. I was there as the du-
tiful wife to observe and support and, despite my conflicted feelings and emotional unrest, that's just what I did. The recording session reminded me that
Ernest was more than the sum of the Sally affair. He was a canny, brilliant, and
totally resourceful musician with a flair for making things come out right.

At this recording session his talents were sorely tested.

Shepperton Studios is located about an hour outside of London in Shepperton, Middlesex. The Shepperton Studios, where hundreds of British and
American films have been shot since the early 1930s, was a former manor
house dating back to the seventeenth century. Some of the most influential
British films of the 1950s and 1960s were shot there, including *The L-Shaped
Room*, *Room at the Top*, John Schlesinger's *A Kind of Loving*, *Billy Liar*, and *Darling*. Although *Exodus* was shot on location in Israel, the recording of the musical sound track and all the postdubbing work were to be done there.

I could tell during the drive to the studio that Ernest was especially skittish.
I also knew that his nerves had to do with the producer and director of *Exodus*,
Otto Preminger.

Like Ernest, Preminger was Viennese and could put on the charm when it
pleased him. He began his career in Hollywood in the early 1940s, first as an
actor, playing the usual villainous Germanic roles, and then graduating to pro-

By the pool in the Hollywood Hills in 1960 with Martha, Andy, and Susie Q and her puppies. (From the author's collection)

ducer and director of such films as *Laura, Centennial Summer, Daisy Kenyon, The Moon Is Blue, River of No Return, Carmen Jones, The Man with the Golden Arm, Porgy and Bess,* and *Anatomy of a Murder.* All during the shooting process, as soon as Ernest had written them, he would play his themes on the piano for Preminger, and Preminger adored them. So why the nerves? It was well known in the industry that Preminger could be a monster. His mistreatment of actors was legendary. He was of the school that thought you must break performers down and then rebuild them to get a good performance. Consequently, he was not exactly loved in the acting community. It was also a fact that no composer ever scored more than one Otto Preminger film. This record spoke for itself. This still didn't explain Ernest's nerves, however.

"You've told me that Otto adores the music," I told Ernest. "So why are you so nervous?"

"Because," Ernest replied, "he hasn't *really* heard it yet."

With that cryptic remark, we arrived at Shepperton Studios, where the orchestra was already tuning up. You could feel the electricity in the air. Preminger was surrounded by the usual Hollywood suspects: studio assistants,

assistants' assistants, lackeys, and lackeys' lackeys. The soundmen were in their booths, ready to record this monumentally lush score. By this time a cut of the film had been assembled and the visual for each music cue was to be projected on a huge screen behind the orchestra facing Ernest. Grafted onto the film was a line that went across the screen from left to right and, when the line ended, that was the cue for the music to begin. This is a very precise part of filmmaking, as every music cue must fit the visual with no margin for error. The music had been written for the emotions and drama of the scenes and timed with a stopwatch before the orchestra ever got to this stage. Even when the music is *rubato* (a musical instruction giving the musician or performer the license to tastefully stretch, slow, or hurry the tempo as he or she sees fit, thus imparting flexibility and emotion to the performance) and liquid, each sequence still must time out exactly to the allotted time for the visual.

As always, a rehearsal was conducted before there was an actual take. The orchestra went through the six-minute cue without the film rolling and afterward Ernest, who was also a very experienced conductor, made some corrections in the tempi and gave a few notes to some of the players. Finally the sound engineers were ready to try a take. Ernest took to the podium and lifted his baton, as the opening shot of the film loomed gigantic on the vast screen that covered the back wall of the studio. With great panache Ernest brought down his baton and began the now-famous main theme of *Exodus*.

I was in the booth listening with Otto Preminger.

At first I was taking the music in with my eyes closed, reveling in the beauty of the orchestrations I had never heard before. About halfway through the six-minute music cue, I opened my eyes and saw Preminger getting redder and redder in the face. Finally, he couldn't stand it anymore and stood and yelled at the sound engineer and anyone else unfortunate enough to be within the range of his Teutonic voice.

"Stop! Stop the orchestra! Turn on the pots!"

The pots were the microphones that would allow Ernest to hear what Preminger had to say.

"Ernest," he screamed and sputtered into the microphone with his Viennese accent sounding more Germanic than ever, "Vot you do to my picture? You ruin my picture! You ruin my picture!"

By now the orchestra had stopped dead in their tracks and it was clear to everyone in the studio that Ernest was devastated and totally nonplussed. After all, this was the same music that his "buddy," Otto, had loved just a week before when Ernest played it on the piano. When Ernest came into the booth he calmly asked Preminger what the matter was, but Preminger just continued his tirade about Ernest's music ruining his picture. I watched helplessly as "Herr Direktor" got more and more livid and Ernest grew whiter in the face by the second. Finally Ernest told the orchestra to take a break and walked out into the corridor, leaving Otto to fume in the booth to his minions. Naturally, I followed my husband.

"What was that all about?" I cautiously asked. "What are you going to do?"

"When Otto does this," he said with amazing coolness, as he coughed for the umpteenth time (the cold getting worse), "I know something is wrong. He's got very good taste, but he really doesn't *know* what's wrong. I don't think it's the music. There's something else that's bothering him, and I've got to figure out what it is."

Then Ernest started pacing the hallway, in a kind of trance, with me silently tagging along behind. I knew enough not to disturb him when he was thinking. How many times had I seen him at home like this in the middle of composing, totally unaware of his surroundings and completely inside himself searching for musical solutions? I assumed that was exactly what he was doing this time as well. Finally he turned and said to no one in particular, "Ah, I know what it is. I'm going to try something."

"What? What is it?"

"Never mind," he said, with a strategic mixture of anxiety and confidence, "you'll see."

Ernest reentered the studio with renewed vigor. In his most authoritative voice (he had that at his disposal, as well as his Old World charm) he loudly asked for everyone in the orchestra to please be ready with pencils for changes. I watched and listened in the booth as he went over and whispered something to the concertmaster, who then passed his instructions down the line to each violin stand. Then Ernest went to the leader of each section (horns, brass, percussion, harp, etc.), who in turn transferred his instructions to all of the players in each section of the orchestra. As they each got their whispered directives, they all began marking up their scores. The clock and the dollars were ticking away (time equals money in the movie business), and with an orchestra this large, this exercise took about half an hour. Finally, when everyone seemed to have made the "huge" changes in the score, Ernest was ready to go. In the booth I held my breath as Preminger, who had his face buried dismally in his hands, waited for Ernest to give the signal to begin recording once again.

Once again the film was projected and once again Ernest gave the downbeat. The music and the orchestration were exactly the same. Nothing had changed. Nothing, except the intent. This huge orchestra was now playing so softly that you could hardly hear them, but the quiet, expansive beauty of the music began to permeate my soul. As I wiped the unexpected tears from my eyes, I saw Otto Preminger's body slowly rising from its hunched-over position and I saw a broad smile widening his face.

"That boy is tcheenius! He is a tcheenius!"

I couldn't believe my ears. Forty-five minutes ago, Ernest was "ruining his picture" and now he was the savior. A "tcheenius." Dear old Otto was pleased and all was right with the world. After a few takes, Otto and Ernest listened to the playback and Otto was hugging Ernest and kissing him. It was as if a miracle had occurred. Later on after Preminger was out of the room, I asked Ernest what he had done.

"I figured out that it was just a question of dynamics," he calmly told me. "Otto always knows when something is wrong, but he flings out in passion at anything within his path . . . not really knowing *what* is wrong exactly. I knew he loved the music, so it dawned on me that perhaps it was just dynamics. But I know that in Hollywood you can't just say 'play it softer.' A man like Otto Preminger won't accept as simple a solution as that to a major problem. It has to be much, much bigger. So I put on a show and made him think that we made huge changes in the music and the orchestration and that the musicians had to make all those notes and adjustments. All that time I told them to make believe they were writing and changing the music, but the only real direction I gave was to play softer."

For the rest of the recording session, Preminger was in love with Ernest and his music. *Exodus* opened in March of 1960. Its epic story of the founding of Israel touched many hearts and minds. Having stars Paul Newman and Eva Marie Saint onboard didn't hurt the box office. The film was a huge hit for all concerned.

There is a postscript to the story.

One day early in 1961 (less than a year after the release of *Exodus*), during one of the times Ernest was living at home, we were listening to the radio. Our mouths fell open when we heard none other than Pat Boone's mellifluous voice singing lyrics to the main title of *Exodus*. The disc jockey announced that this "song" was now Number 64 on the charts and rapidly climbing. Ernest had never given Boone permission to write a lyric, let alone record the song. He immediately called Otto Preminger, who had no memory of giving Boone his consent either. Meanwhile the song was climbing the charts and other singers such as Andy Williams and even Edith Piaf were recording it. Soon such diverse artists as duo-pianists Ferrante and Teicher, jazz musician Eddie Harris, and orchestra leader Mantovani would have Top 40 hits with this song. Ernest's lawyer got into the fray, threatening to sue, but it was too late. Ernest had a hit and, as they say, the best he could do was cry all the way to the bank. We decided "If you can't beat 'em, join 'em," and on February 27, 1961, I got to sing the song at the Hollywood Bowl, under Ernest's baton, with a gorgeous new symphonic arrangement Ernest had made for me. I still use the arrangement to this day. Over the years, "Exodus" helped the Gold family live very well and I for one would like to give a grateful nod to the man in the white buckskin shoes, Pat Boone.

Just when *Exodus* was opening, I was beginning what I like to call "my Leonard Bernstein year."

I had first met Bernstein in 1950 at Tanglewood and he was already a star as a conductor and composer. His mentor, conductor Serge Koussevitzky, had encouraged Bernstein to concentrate solely on his conducting career and firmly discouraged him from writing popular and Broadway music. Consequently, after the great success of *On the Town* in 1944, Broadway was to hear no more of Lenny's music until Koussevitzky's death in 1951 freed him to spread his musical wings and encompass everything within his grasp.

The ensuing decade since I met him had only added to his luster as he wrote, among other things, the one-act opera *Trouble in Tahiti* (which I performed on the road) and the film score for *On the Waterfront*. Bernstein's music returned to Broadway in 1953 with the hit show *Wonderful Town*, the 1956 cult "flop" *Candide* (it's now considered a classic and is produced all over the world) and, in 1957, the groundbreaking *West Side Story*. In 1957 he was also appointed Musical Director of the New York Philharmonic, the first American-born and -trained conductor to be so designated. All of this, combined with his many TV appearances throughout the 1950s and his own series of "Young People's Concerts" and "Leonard Bernstein and the New York Philharmonic," made Bernstein a very famous man. So when the call came from my concert agent offering me a series of concert dates with Bernstein and the New York Philharmonic I was thrilled. I knew this would be a big feather in my cap. The first set of concerts I was to do would be the world premiere of Boulez's *Improvisation sur Mallarme #1*, written for percussion, choir, and soprano. By this time French composer and conductor Pierre Boulez had become one of the most important musical and intellectual figures of the twentieth century. As a composer, he wrote a new chapter in the history of music in the fifties, particularly with *Le Marteau sans Maître*. Premiering this new piece was to be a momentous occasion.

I flew to New York in early March to begin rehearsing for the four concerts that would take place between March 21 and April 1. Although Lenny had me to his apartment for one of his swank cocktail parties, I actually rehearsed the piece with his assistant conductor, Howard Shanet. I guess Lenny was such a big star at this time that he didn't do rehearsals! Nevertheless, I knew that these concerts were a very big deal. It was Carnegie Hall, after all! I wore my most elegant gown and had my hair done at Kenneth's, then and now one of the chicest and nicest hair salons in New York. They were kind enough to accommodate my erratic rehearsal schedule. I still go there to this day.

The Improvisation sur Mallarme #1 was a very avant-garde piece where silence was as important as the music itself. The concerts went off without a hitch and the April 1 performance was broadcast on CBS Radio. Although I had been conducted by some of the legends of music, with these Carnegie Hall concerts I felt that I had arrived. This was the East Coast, where the press one received mattered so much more to the rest of the country than the press in California, so I was thrilled when the New York *Herald-Tribune* said that the piece was "radiantly and superbly sung by Marni Nixon." As nice as the reviews were, though, acceptance from one's peers means even more. Jenny Tourel, the famed soprano and a friend of Bernstein's, attended an early performance and came backstage afterward. Bernstein introduced me and she bowed to me. A long deep bow!

"You are a great artist, Miss Nixon," she said, "and it's simply fantastic what you can do!"

Let me tell you, all the applause and the rave reviews pale when someone you admire (and who is admired by the whole world) gives you the thumbs up. There is no better boost to your self-confidence than when a fellow artist says, "Bravo." It's something you never forget.

One year later, almost to the day, Lenny, the New York Philharmonic, and I got together again to present Boulez's *Improvisation sur Mallarme #2* in program number three of a series Bernstein called "Keys to the 20th Century." We were the first part of the program and the great pianist Glenn Gould was to play a Beethoven concerto during the second half.

At the first rehearsal I had a few minutes before my part of the program to wait in the green room (a sort of waiting/receiving room) backstage. There was a small upright piano on which you could warm up if you needed to. Kind of tucked away on the floor, leaning against the wall behind the pedals of the piano, was a rickety-looking wooden chair, painted a sickening shade of green. Instead of the castors that should have been on the chair, one leg had a dangerous-looking nail sticking out of the bottom and another was wrapped in black electrical tape. I thought nothing of it at the time, except to wonder what such a pile of junk was doing at Carnegie Hall.

I sat down at the piano, played some scales, and began to warm up my voice. As I moved my foot to the pedal it touched the rickety chair, which changed position, then clattered and fell flat on the floor at my feet under the pedals of the piano. At that very moment Glenn Gould walked into the room. He witnessed the chair falling and screamed.

"How dare you kick my chair!"

I was flabbergasted. I had no idea it was his chair and I certainly hadn't touched it on purpose. Gould was livid as he raced to rescue his chair. He pulled it up from under the piano and lovingly held it to his chest. He opened it and closed it and actually seemed to be fondling it.

After a few moments (where it seemed like he might cry) someone introduced us and his mood completely flipped and he became incredibly gracious.

He told me that he was a fan of mine and that he had heard the Webern recordings that I had made with Robert Craft on Columbia Records.

I was gratified to hear this, but still totally unnerved by his outburst just a few minutes before. It seemed that everyone in the music world had stories about Gould's eccentricities (such as his fear of cold, dislike of social functions, and many addictions to prescription drugs), but up until then I had never heard about his attachment to a chair. I found out only later that his father had made that chair and Gould's insistence on sameness was the reason he was so attached to it. In fact, the chair was so closely identified with him that it is shown in a place of honor in a glass case in the National Library of Canada.

At the first performance my Boulez piece went wonderfully well and I had listened to Gould play from backstage on the internal sound system that we call the "squawk box." When Gould came into the green room, I approached him from behind and laid my hand very lightly on his shoulder and said, "Glenn, that was just so beautiful."

The moment my hand touched his shoulder, he violently turned about, wrenching my hand away. Obviously he was not to be touched. His massage therapist, who seemed to follow him everywhere, immediately began working on the shoulders and repeating that it was all right, no harm done. Once again I was totally nonplussed by Glenn Gould and vowed to stay out of his way. Later on I heard that, just a year or two earlier, a piano tuner at Carnegie Hall had patted Gould on the back and when Gould turned around, he pulled several muscles and since then was supercareful, thus the masseur and thus the fear of it happening again. In fact, Gould sued Carnegie Hall for the mishap.

During the next performance, a Friday matinee, it was not difficult to stay out of Gould's way, as he was nowhere to be found! I completed my half of the program, but when intermission came Gould was still missing. The stage managers were getting nervous. There were no cell phones in those days, so there was no way to get in touch with him. They tried his hotel, but to no avail. It was assumed he was somewhere en route, but no one knew where or how far away he was. The intermission was extended. Then it was extended even longer. Finally, with no Glenn Gould in sight, the music librarian of the New York Philharmonic came running up to me and asked if there was anything in their music library that I might know and be able to sing in case Gould didn't show up.

"For instance, can you do the fourth movement of the Mahler Tenth Symphony, *Wir Geniessen*?"

I hadn't sung it in a long time, but I knew I could get through it (especially with the music in front of me). So, the parts were pulled and distributed to the orchestra and we were all ready to go on and halt this endless intermission when Gould sauntered in, trailed as usual by his massage therapist. They had been delayed in traffic, but now that they finally arrived he went on.

I decided that I really wanted to be out front and see Gould perform. There is a special private booth that exists at Carnegie Hall, with a little window where you can see and hear a performance. It's a side view from the lip of the edge of the proscenium arch onstage, mostly hidden from the audience. I was ushered into this space so that I could experience Glenn Gould live. During the intermission a stagehand had taken away the piano bench and replaced it with that rickety, old, green wooden chair. He then sat on the eyesore, which, to me, seemed incredibly low from the keyboard.

When the Beethoven concerto began and he placed his hands on the keys, it appeared to me that the keys were almost at his eyebrow level. As he listened to the orchestra, awaiting his cue, Gould leaned back in his chair with his hands dangling at his side in a very informal position. Then he started swaying and singing and humming along with the orchestral music that preceded the first piano entrance. To all appearances, he was totally out of it or in a trance.

Then it came time for him to play.

He lifted his hands with a great effort, as if they weighed a ton, and laid his fingers on the keyboard and awaited his entrance. I was watching him carefully but before I saw any movement from his hands, I heard a most magical sound begin to blend into the fabric of the orchestral sound. To all appearances he was hardly touching the keys, but the sound coming out of the piano was like nothing I had every heard before. It was unearthly and godlike. It was obvious that all of his interesting quirks paid off. The singing and humming along (sound engineers had to carefully wipe out certain frequencies to get rid of the humming when Gould recorded), the "Don't touch me" attitude, the private masseur . . . the chair. All of it. At that moment of musical brilliance I forgave Glenn Gould all his foibles and felt doubly proud as I remembered him complimenting me after I had knocked down his beloved green chair. Watching Gould and Bernstein meld together as one unified performer that day, I felt as if I had really been welcomed into the New York musical scene by the best of the best.

It was my next encounter with Leonard Bernstein that solidified our relationship and brought us closer together as friends and colleagues.

Two weeks after the Glenn Gould concert, I was back in Carnegie Hall with Bernstein, singing in one of his fabled "Young People's Concerts." Lenny had the innovative and wonderful notion (to which I wholly subscribe) that if we exposed children to the best that music had to offer it would enrich their lives. Even with all his fame as a performer and composer, he had devoted a large part of his career to being an educator. He was brilliant at it and his Young People's Concerts are a testament to what can and should be done in this country to foster the arts in the young. The concerts were offered on Saturday mornings and televised by CBS either live or the next day.

On the morning of April 8, 1961, we gathered to do a concert entitled "Folk Music in the Concert Hall." I was to sing the songs of the Auvergne (literally meaning the Auvergne Mountains), arranged by Joseph Cantaloube. The words of these songs are in a patois that sounds like a combination of French and Spanish. The songs are sung to an orchestration that is huge, lush, and filled with the brilliance of woodwind instruments. Most importantly, though, these are folk songs and, although they have been subsequently translated, we decided to do them in their native language to give the children the real sense of history in them. Bernstein decided that I should translate the songs for the audience as well as sing them. There would be no worry about memorizing the translations, as there was a brand new teleprompter placed just under the balcony for all the things that Lenny and I would be saying that day. Lenny would frequently go off script and speak in that wonderful impromptu way he had. I, however, was happy to have the prompter for the translations.

Saturday morning came and we had a dress rehearsal at Carnegie Hall at 8:00 A.M. When I arrived at the rehearsal Lenny told me that there was a problem with the teleprompter and that *he* would be reciting all the translations for the audience.

"Like hell you will," I said.

He was visibly shocked. Sweet, little Marni Nixon standing up for what she wanted? A suspicious smile appeared on Lenny's face and, raising his eyebrows with a challenging twinkle in his eyes, he sniffed a long breath and said, "O . . . kay. We'll see about that, Marni."

And I did it. And very well, too! I guess I didn't need that teleprompter after all.

Afterward, Lenny warmly hugged and congratulated me. It was at that moment that we bonded. He reached out his hand, looked directly into my eyes, and simply said, "Friend."

I guess he recognized a fellow ham in me. From then on we were more than colleagues and he never failed to hug me, one ham to another, whenever we met.

I have no idea whether my first set of concerts in March of 1960 with Lenny had anything to do with my getting the dubbing job on the film *West Side Story*, but I like to think when they were wondering about whom they should get to possibly dub Natalie Wood as Maria, Lenny put in a good word for me.

West Side Story had originated in the mind of the gifted director and choreographer Jerome Robbins. Robbins began his career as a dancer in both ballet as well as on Broadway in the chorus. He became a choreographer and scored his first success with the ballet *Fancy Free* (music by Leonard Bernstein), which in turn inspired *On the Town*, which he also choreographed. In time Robbins became very much in demand and staged the dances for such hit shows as *High Button Shoes*, *Look Ma! I'm Dancin'*, and *The King and I*. He later expanded his horizons and became a director with *Bells Are Ringing*.

In 1949 Robbins' friend, actor and film star Montgomery Clift, asked Robbins to coach him in the role of Romeo in Shakespeare's classic tragedy *Romeo and Juliet*. Both artists were then steeped in the newly burgeoning Actors Studio (which was formed in 1947) and Robbins encouraged Clift to think of Romeo and his story in contemporary terms. The more Robbins thought about that notion, the more he was convinced that a serious musical might be created using an updated version of Shakespeare's play.

Robbins enlisted playwright Arthur Laurents (*Home of the Brave*, *The Time of the Cuckoo*, and the screenplay of Hitchcock's *Rope*) and Leonard Bernstein and they began discussions about a musical tentatively entitled *East Side Story*. The story would take place on the Lower East Side of New York City during a period of time when the Passover and Easter holidays coincide. It would involve a conflict between a Jewish Romeo and a Catholic Juliet. After mulling it over for a while, however, the director, playwright, and composer decided that their approach resembled the long-running warhorse of a play *Abie's Irish Rose*, and they each went their separate ways. Sometime in the mid-1950s Laurents ran into Bernstein at the pool at the Beverly Hills Hotel. As they talked, Laurents saw an article in the newspaper about the growing threat of gang warfare in L.A. An idea was born! Why not make the Capulets and Montagues rival gangs on New York's West Side? Both Laurents and Bernstein were so enthusiastic about this prospect that they immediately called Robbins and told him the idea. He too was excited and they all joined forces (later bringing on fledgling lyricist Stephen Sondheim) and began working on what was now to be retitled *West Side Story* (titles thought of and disposed of included *Gangway!*).

West Side Story opened at the Winter Garden Theater on Broadway on September 26, 1957 and ran for 732 performances (reopening in April of 1960 for another 249 performances). The critics and public were divided. They were both thrilled and stunned by the stark subject matter and the series of deaths, including the onstage murder of the leading man not long before the final curtain. Savvy theatergoers, though, realized that they were seeing something fresh, new, and groundbreaking. Never before had dance been such an integral part of a musical. Whole chunks of the story were told in movement alone, but it was perhaps the fusion of all the elements (song, dance, and dialogue) that was so electrifying.

Also, never before had such a young cast been called upon to do it *all*. Before *West Side Story*, actors, singers, and dancers each had their roles to play, and although they sometimes blurred into one anothers' territories, it was rare. In this show everyone had to do everything. And they did it brilliantly! The music was sometimes as demanding as opera and the choreography ran the gamut from Latin street dances to out-and-out ballet. Although the show was a success, it did not run nearly as long as such 1950s smashes as *My Fair Lady* or *The Music Man*. In fact, when the 1958 Tony Awards were announced, *The Music Man* shut out *West Side Story* in every category but Best Choreography (Jerome Robbins) and Best Scenic Design (Oliver Smith). Which is not to say the show wasn't a hit. It toured and played London's West End and brought great acclaim to Bernstein and his collaborators. However, it took the 1961 film to turn *West Side Story* into a household name and to popularize the score that onstage some critics deemed "too difficult to sing."

When it was announced that Mirisch Pictures had bought the film rights for $375,000, speculation on who would play the leads was rampant in Hollywood. As usual, the original stars (Carol Lawrence, Larry Kert, and Chita Rivera) were passed over, in this case because they looked "too mature" to play the teenaged roles. Associate producer and head of the music department Saul Chaplin theorized that even if the two leads were to be dubbed (and he was all for that), since the vocal ranges of Tony and Maria were tenor and soprano, the actors' speaking voices would have to match the timbre of the vocal doubles. This left many candidates in the dust.

Codirector Robert Wise lobbied for Elvis Presley as Tony. Audrey Hepburn was actually offered the role of Maria, but had to turn it down because she was pregnant at the time. (Would I have gotten to dub her voice twice?) Such actors as Suzanne Pleshette, Jill St. John, Elizabeth Ashley, Warren Beatty, Bobby Darin, Burt Reynolds, Richard Chamberlain, Troy Donahue, Gary Lockwood, Anna Maria Alberghetti, and Tony Perkins (of which the latter two *could* have sung their roles) were tested for the coveted roles of Tony and Maria, but none of them seemed to fill the bill. At about this time twenty-one-year-old Natalie Wood started to campaign for the role.

Natalie had been a child star who graduated from such films as *Miracle on 34th Street* to more adult teen roles in *Rebel Without a Cause* and *Marjorie Morningstar*. She had won a Golden Globe Award as Best Newcomer in 1957 and had been nominated for an Academy Award in 1956 for her performance in *Rebel*. Natalie Wood was a genuine box office name.

Natalie also liked to sing and harbored the dream of becoming a recording star. She even made a test recording of the Rodgers and Hart song "Little Girl Blue" for Capitol Records, but nothing came of it. But this did not dampen Natalie's enthusiasm for singing, and she continued to work on her voice with a coach. She felt that *West Side Story* would not only be the perfect showcase for her dramatic abilities, but would showcase her musical and dance talents as well. Wise and his associate producer Saul Chaplin had decided by this point that they didn't want stars in the lead roles, and the front-runner for the role of Maria was the little-known Broadway singer-actress Barbara Luna. Still, no final decision was made. Natalie, meanwhile, was busy filming *Splendor in the Grass* and location shooting on *West Side Story* began in New York City in August of 1960 without a Maria in place.

Unlike Robert Wise and Saul Chaplin, the money people at United Artists (who would be distributing the film) *were* very anxious for a "name" in one of the lead roles to ensure a healthy box office. They urged Wise and codirector-choreographer Jerome Robbins to screen some of Natalie's footage from *Splendor in the Grass*. Robbins, in particular, was very enthusiastic about what he saw and, later when they met, he and Natalie clicked at once, becoming fast friends. Although eager to play the role, Natalie insisted on a clause in her contract that allowed her to prerecord her own songs, then giving Robbins, Wise, and Chaplin the right to decide whether to keep her tracks or dub her later. At last, *West Side Story* had its Maria and she was a big star.

Besides coproducing, Saul Chaplin was in charge of all the musical elements of the film. It was Saul who hired Bobby Tucker, whom he knew from MGM, to be the vocal coach and Johnny Green to be the musical director. I had worked with Johnny many times in symphonic and pops concerts around the country at the Hollywood Bowl and on a few incidental MGM gigs when he had been the head of the music department. Although Green was an Oscar winner, Chaplin had to really sell him to Robert Wise, who didn't like some of Johnny's quirks, such as his joke telling and tendency to speak in dialects. Chaplin knew that Johnny was a great conductor and, despite Wise's hesitation, he prevailed. After watching one recording session and seeing Johnny in action, Wise changed his mind and was supportive of Saul Chaplin's choice.

Up to this point Saul Chaplin had had a very prestigious career in the movies. He had been a songwriter ("Bei Mir Bist Du Schoen," "Until the Real Thing Comes Along," and "The Anniversary Song") arranger, and producer since the 1930s and along the way had won two Oscars (a third would come his way for *West Side Story*) for *An American in Paris* and *Seven Brides for Seven Brothers*. He lent his musical talents to such films as *Cover Girl*, *The Jolson Story*, *On the Town*, *Kiss Me Kate*, and *High Society*.

After shooting the brilliantly choreographed and shot "Prologue" of the film on location in New York City (the playground was on 110th Street, but the street they danced on was the soon-to-be-demolished West 64th Street, the current home of Lincoln Center) the company returned to L.A. and the Samuel Goldwyn Studios in September of 1960 to record the vocal playback tracks for the film.

This is where I came in.

When I first entered the Samuel Goldwyn recording studios to work on *West Side Story* in September of 1960 I didn't have a long-term contract. In fact, throughout all my work on the film of *West Side Story* I wouldn't have any contract at all. I was working strictly by the day ($300 a day), never knowing if they would need my services the next week or if what I recorded would even be used in the final film. It would be Chaplin who would ultimately decide whose voice would be used and who would be dubbed. In the end the only leading actor who did all his own singing on the screen would be George Chakiris as Bernardo. Even Russ Tamblyn, who played Riff and had a recording contract with MGM Records, was dubbed by fellow Jet Tucker Smith in "The Jet Song."

I had been told that they might use my tracks or they might only use me to extend and enrich Natalie's longer and higher notes. Later on, I was told, I might be called upon to redo all her tracks. Everything, it seemed, was up for grabs. Little did I know then that Chaplin, who had to treat his star with kid gloves, never intended on letting Natalie sing any of her own songs on-screen.

Both Natalie and Richard Beymer, who had been cast as Tony (and was immediately told he would be dubbed by jazz singer Jim Bryant), were learning the songs and being coached by Bobby Tucker (under Chaplin's supervision). I was allowed into some, but not all, of Natalie's sessions. Determined as she was to sing the score herself, Natalie was very nervous and shy about having me in the room while she was learning, so Bobby would instead come to me after her coaching sessions and fill me in on how she would be singing the songs so that I could emulate her acting intentions and phrasing. I also had to make sure that I used the same Puerto Rican accent that Natalie used. All this without ever being in the same room! This was as different a process from *The King and I* as you could get. No working with the star and walking the set beside her this time. The Bernstein/Sondheim score was written to be sung in a disciplined, specific way, almost like opera. There were complicated rhythms and Maria's songs had a high, angular range. Bobby Tucker told me in confidence that Natalie was having some trouble mastering them.

In late September we were finally ready to start recording. Johnny Green was conducting the huge symphony-size orchestra that was, as usual, made up of the best musicians on the West Coast. Many of them were friends of mine from the L.A. Philharmonic. Some had done chamber works with me and others had played at one or more of my recording sessions. The sessions were set up so that Natalie would first record a song on her own and then I would get up and record the whole song again. I knew that this was going to be embarrassing and traumatic for her, but I was just an employee and went along with it.

Musicians, especially ones this good, are noted for their disdain of mediocrity and have no compunction about voicing their disapproval in the only way they know how. As Natalie sang, they showed their displeasure by playing poorly. They kind of sawed away at the notes instead of playing with the sensitivity of which they were more than capable. Then, when I got up to sing the identical song, the same musicians would sit up in their seats and play with renewed vigor and passion. When I finished a take they would even applaud. I was both very embarrassed and disgusted at their rudeness to poor Natalie, who was, after all, doing her best. They were making it seem as if the recording session was some kind of contest.

I'm not sure, though, that Natalie was aware of the musicians' rudeness. The entire music department, from Johnny Green to Saul Chaplin to Bobby Tucker, all kept telling Natalie how wonderful her takes were, when it was very evident they were mostly unusable. They also explained my presence by saying that they would be able to mix my high notes into her takes, which I knew at the time was in all probability—given the way we were being recorded (separately)—technically impossible.

It was very disheartening to hear them as they listened to her playbacks and extolled her vocal prowess.

"Oh, Natalie, that was just wonderful," they cooed. "Oh! Did you hear that? Wow!"

This over-the-top coddling was as damaging to her performance as the musicians' razzing her was. They were creating a monster. A monster who thought everything she sang was perfect. This did not help her to get better. I am sure, however, that they thought if they were critical of her vocals in any way that she would walk off the picture before everything was filmed. She had them hostage and they were placating her until they didn't need her anymore. Interestingly, since they said that everything she did was wonderful, when someone complimented one of my takes I began to distrust my own ears and wondered if they were just pacifying me as well. The only thing keeping me sane at that point was the knowledge that since I had no contract of any sort, if they used one iota of a song I recorded I could charge them a million dollars per note! I kept my spirits up, sang the beautiful songs, and bided my time.

In all, Maria sings six songs: "Tonight," "I Feel Pretty," "One Hand, One Heart," the "Quintet," "Somewhere," and "I Have a Love." When I did these early prerecordings I sang "Tonight" side-by-side with Jim Bryant (Richard Beymer's ghost), but most of the time I recorded separately and alone.

When the tracks were done, it was decided that during the filming Natalie would sing to her own prerecordings. This kept Natalie happy, but also built up her hopes that her voice would be retained in the final cut of the film. Natalie Wood may have been pleased to lip-synch to her own voice but, unfortunately, due to lack of experience doing musicals, most of her best takes (acting-wise) were seldom in synch with the tracks. Richard Beymer didn't have Natalie's advantage (or disadvantage); he just had to lip-synch to Jimmy Bryant's tracks.

I later became friendly with Richard and he said that although he had hoped to do his own singing, he had no choice in the matter.

"Marni," he told me, "I was so green. I didn't know what I should demand or not. They just told me what to do and I just did it." Richard was very unhappy on the set, feeling that Robert Wise wasn't giving him enough direction and, although he had nothing but love scenes with Natalie Wood, off the set Natalie was cold as ice to him. Richard felt that this was perhaps due to the fact that she had wanted her husband Robert Wagner for the role of Tony.

Although she could sing and dance, Chaplin decided that Rita Moreno's voice would be dubbed by Betty Wand. Betty was a sister ghost who had dubbed the singing voices for such stars as Shirley Temple, Esther Williams, Leslie Caron (in *Gigi*), Sophia Loren, Kay Kendall, and Pier Angeli.

When the film was finally in the can and Natalie Wood was released to go to work on her next film (which interestingly enough was another musical, *Gypsy*; she got to do her own singing in that one!), I got a call from Saul Chaplin asking me to come to the studio. They had decided to have me dub Natalie's singing voice totally.

Saul showed me the dailies of the musical numbers in which Natalie "sang" and pointed out the problems and pitfalls. I knew that I would now have to make completely new recordings to fit my voice as Maria to her lips on the screen. This was the complete opposite of how it was done in *The King and I*. In movie parlance this was called "looping," because the film is on a "loop," which allows the actor or singer multiple attempts to match the lip movements that have already been filmed. What I had to do was watch the screen; a line that proceeded from left to right would be set up, and when the line reached the right side I had to start recording my voice in time with the picture. Sometimes the crew would punch a hole in the picture, which would begin appearing in the preceding lead-in to the song in the tempo of what the song was to be upon my entrance. They kept doing this over and over until I got it just right. On long shots I would be exactly with the orchestra, but on close-ups, if Natalie's lips were a bit out of synch with the orchestra, we had to do some creative hedging to make it work. As you can imagine, this was grueling and hard work, but I was known for being a perfectionist and working until it was just right.

Natalie performed only one song to my original prerecorded track, "One Hand, One Heart," but even this one would have to be redone, as her lips didn't match the track. This song presented its own challenge. To sing it like a sixteen-year-old Puerto Rican girl, I had to keep it very, very light, and un-operatic. The only way I could really manage it was to cry as I sang. If you watch the scene and listen to the song you will find that it has a certain tone quality that lends the scene even more pathos than it already has. Singing this way, though, was taxing on my voice. Saul Chaplin had a great sense of humor and wasn't worried about this at all. He just turned to me and smiled his huge toothy grin.

"Marni," he said with a laugh, "we didn't hire you for your voice, we hired you for your iron nerves!"

There is a brilliant piece of music that comes right before the "Rumble" called the "Quintet." All of the principals and the two rival gangs join vocal forces and sing about what "Tonight" will mean to them. I learned later that before the show went into rehearsals, the song that was played during the famous balcony/fire escape scene was "One Hand, One Heart," and when it was thought that there should be something more soaring in that scene, the "Tonight" theme in the "Quintet" was extracted and expanded into what we know today as "Tonight." In any case, when I was rerecording Maria's high-soaring section of the "Quintet," Saul Chaplin turned to me once again.

"Both Betty Wand and Rita Moreno are sick with colds today. Why don't you just sing Rita's part in this too, Marni."

So when Anita is singing about "getting her kicks tonight," that's me. And when all the countermelodies of the "Quintet" come together and everyone is singing in glorious harmony, since I am singing both Maria and Anita, I'm actually singing a duet with myself. Only in the movies!

When all the singing was dubbed, there was still one small job left for me. Since Natalie was gone (off rehearsing for the film of *Gypsy*) I was asked to loop a couple of her lines at the end of the film.

It seems that when they shot the last scenes of the film when Tony has been killed and Maria points the gun at the gang members and accuses them all of "keeling heeem," the cast was so punchy and tired that Natalie (and the others) kept breaking into nervous giggles during the most dramatic and tender moments of the scene. She tried to cover up the stifled laughter by pretending to cry, but vocally it didn't quite come off. So it was Marni the "fixer upper" to the rescue. Next time when you watch the DVD of *West Side Story*, listen for my "method" looping of the lines "Don't you touch heeem!" and "Te adoro, Anton."

When my work was all done I still had no contract from the producers, the Mirisch brothers, and I was determined this time to get more than a buyout deal on the soundtrack recording. I had seen the kind of sales that *The King and I* racked up (and was still racking up; in 1994 it was listed by *Billboard* magazine as being in the Top Ten Best-Selling Soundtracks of All Time) and I felt cheated that while it was my voice on the record, still I got no royalties. Although I knew I was charting virgin territory (no voice double ever got royalties for an album), I was resolved that *West Side Story* would be different.

At the time I had a new and aggressive manager and I instructed him to go after a royalty for the soundtrack album. This, I knew, was where the real money was. The answer quickly came back that the film company had nothing to do with the recording. I knew that this was hogwash, so we went back to them again. This time they told us no royalty points were left and that the whole 100 percent of the pie had been divided between the authors and other copyright holders. Still, my bulldog of a manager persisted. I suppose the old adage is true—the squeaky wheel *does* sometimes get greased—because, after some more haggling, my manager came back and told me that Leonard Bernstein himself was giving up one quarter of a percent (not a negligible amount) of his own royalty and passing it on to me. With that incredibly generous gesture, Lennie helped to set a precedent that would assist me and other ghosts in being recognized. I might still be invisible, but the checks were solid as a rock. The soundtrack album logged an amazing fifty-four weeks in *Billboard*'s Number One position and was on the chart a total of 198 weeks. In fact, *West Side Story*'s longevity record for album logging most weeks at Number One stands to this day. It was RIAA-certified "Multiplatinum" in 1986, with sales of (at least) three million copies. Amazing!

My lack of billing, however, remained intact. Only Natalie Wood's name appeared on Columbia Records' extravagant gatefold LP cover. Still, may I say the royalty certainly helped salve any wounds?

Unfortunately, wily as my manager was, he had no provision in my contract for anything but the Long Playing Record, and when records became a thing of the past and compact discs appeared, my royalties ceased. A good lesson for anyone negotiating a recording contract today: always think of the future. And get a good lawyer!

West Side Story opened on September 21, 1961 and went on to become one of the most acclaimed musical films of all time. The soundtrack recording made the score popular for the first time (even though the original cast album sold well, the songs themselves only became widely known when the film was released) and most of the world who knew the songs now knew them through my voice. A whole generation of people grew up with the record and, despite the lack of billing, and because of some unasked-for publicity (all the critics and columnists seemed to know that I sang for Natalie and they had no problem spelling it out for their readers), many people began to find out that the voice is mine. Natalie went on to sing in *Gypsy* and *Inside Daisy Clover*. Her own natural voice was very suitable for the role of Louise in *Gypsy* and, although some of her singing was dubbed in *Daisy Clover*, she did some of her own as well. Since in both cases a low alto range was used, the voices coming out of her mouth in those later films bore no resemblance to what came out of her mouth in *West Side Story*.

Indeed, over the years, many singers and students, some of whom I have never even seen before, have approached me, saying that I was their teacher. They say that listening to me sing on the album of *West Side Story* taught them more than a year of voice lessons did. That really makes me feel good.

I heard later that Natalie Wood was very upset and felt betrayed by the powers that be. She sincerely wanted to sing her own tracks. I have to agree that it was cruel of Saul Chaplin and his musical crew to lead her on and make her believe there was a chance they would use her voice. But, in their defense, it was their job to make sure that their highly paid and very bankable star finished shooting every scene. In addition, it was their responsibility to present the brilliant and difficult Bernstein/Sondheim score in the best possible light. This they did, and did it well.

In fact, we all did our jobs well and the finished product speaks for itself: ten Academy Awards, including Best Picture; a Grammy; a Gold Record; and the undying love of generations of moviegoers.

As always, ghosting, to me, was a pleasant detour from my "real" singing and acting career. After each of these jobs, I returned to my life, a little wiser and even slightly richer. Although I wanted recognition for my work in the dubbing field, one thing I never expected from it was fame. Two years later, that's exactly what I got when I became the poster girl for every Hollywood ghost that was ever sworn to secrecy.

It was all due to a little movie musical called *My Fair Lady*.

Chapter Eight
WHICH FAIR LADY?

"I take off my hat to the marvelous people in Hollywood who twiddle all the knobs and make one voice out of two."

AUDREY HEPBURN, 1964

"Marni had this peculiar, chameleonlike quality: She could 'do' everybody. You would hand her a piece of music and say, the first four bars are cockney, then it gets French. It made no difference; she could do it."

ANDRÉ PREVIN, 1995

I N THE EARLY SPRING OF 1954, while I was appearing on Broadway in *The Girl in Pink Tights*, a rather short man with a very large head came backstage to visit one of the cast members after a performance. One of my fellow chorus singers told me that he was a composer named Frederick Loewe (she pronounced it in the old Viennese way of LOE-Veh), better known to his friends as Fritz. Later on, when I told Ernest about this backstage encounter, he remembered Fritz from the old days in Vienna. Fritz's father had been a famous tenor in operetta and now his son, the composer, had written (along with his collaborator Alan Jay Lerner) such musicals as *Brigadoon* and *Paint Your Wagon*. That night in the wings at the Mark Hellinger Theatre, however, Fritz Loewe sat down at the piano to play us something from the new musical he and Lerner were then working on. With his florid, Old World keyboard style and his thick Viennese accent he proceeded to warble a song from what he told us was a musical version of George Bernard Shaw's *Pygmalion*. The music was in 3/4 time with a very European operetta sound, and the lyric went right along with it.

"I Want to Dance All Night! I Want to Dance All Night!"

After Loewe finished playing and singing we all politely applauded and went home. I remember thinking if the rest of the show is as corny as that tune it'll close in New Haven in a week!

Two years later, Julie Andrews came out on the stage of the very same Mark Hellinger Theatre and sang what was now entitled "I Could Have Danced All Night," which had been rewritten from 3/4 time to 4/4. Needless to say, she stopped the show in, what critic Brooks Atkinson called "the musical of the century," *My Fair Lady*.

Who would have guessed on that night in 1954 that nine years later I would be at Warner Bros. Studios recording that very same song for the film version of one of the biggest hit musicals of all time?

As Fats Waller always said, "One never knows, do one?"

My Fair Lady began in the mind of Hungarian producer Gabriel Pascal. He had produced the very successful film version of Shaw's *Pygmalion* in 1938 starring Leslie Howard and Wendy Hiller, which won an Academy Award for the playwright. In the early 1950s he had the notion that a musical version of Shaw's play would be equally successful and so he, of course, approached the most successful songwriting team on Broadway. No, not Lerner and Loewe, but Rodgers and Hammerstein. For a solid year they toiled on what was essentially a brilliantly verbal drawing room comedy and never got a handle on how to present it as a big Broadway musical. Where was the chorus? How would one "open it up," as they say? Where was the essential love story? With no solution to these and other problems, Rodgers and Hammerstein gave up and the rights reverted back to Pascal, who then approached Lerner and Loewe (what a second choice!), who also found no way to get around the dilemma.

As sometimes happens with musical theater marriages, Lerner and Loewe had a fight and split up, each going on to other collaborators. Lerner toiled for a while on a musical version of *L'il Abner*, only to be frustrated by that as well. Interestingly, *Pygmalion* was never far from his mind. One day it hit him like a bolt from the blue. Why not just trust the play? Why not tell the story as Shaw did? Hadn't the film version softened the finale so that it seemed that Henry Higgins and Eliza might actually get together in the end? This at least implied romance. As for "opening it up," why not just show what happens *between* the scenes. What exactly was Eliza's father up to before he came to visit Higgins? Why not actually show Eliza at the Ascot Races and at the Embassy Ball? Suddenly it started to feel like a musical and Lerner went running excitedly back to Loewe, whom he felt was just the composer to make it sing. Loewe loved Lerner's ideas and with Herman Levin on board to produce it and Moss Hart to direct, all that they needed were the rights.

In the time it took for Lerner to figure out how to make the show work, Pascal had died and a bank that had the right to decide who would get the very valuable underlying rights to his plays was handling all of Shaw's affairs. With great self-confidence, Lerner and Loewe went ahead and began writing their show and let their lawyers handle the legalities. They figured when it was decided who was to be granted the rights, they would be so far ahead in the writing that the bank would just have to hand it over to them. Luckily, they were proven right. At the insistence of record producer Goddard Lieberson, the show was financed entirely by CBS (which owned Columbia Records), thus not only ensuring Columbia Records the recording rights to the lucrative original cast album (in fact, Columbia produced every foreign-language version and the film soundtrack as well), but bringing in millions of dollars, which Lieberson then funneled back into the classical division. *My Fair Lady* helped pay for countless classical recordings (many of which I recorded) that may never have been made.

Although he was third choice for the role of Henry Higgins (Noël Coward and Laurence Olivier were asked first and second), Rex Harrison was born to play the role. After he was cast, Lerner wrote every lyric and speech with Harrison's vocal inflections in his head. In fact, Lerner has stated that Harrison's persona haunted every character he wrote for the rest of his career, from King Arthur to Coco Chanel. Finding an Eliza Doolittle proved more daunting.

Although older actresses frequently played the role, Shaw described Eliza as eighteen years old, "certainly no more than twenty." This time around everyone was determined to honor Shaw and cast a very young girl. Of course when the forty-something Mary Martin (then a Broadway megastar) expressed interest in hearing the songs then written for the show, what could the authors do but honor her request? We will never know what the Texas-born Miss Martin might have done with the cockney-turned-posh Eliza, because after hearing several early versions of the songs she passed a message along via her husband/manager: "Those poor boys have lost their talent."

Then, in 1954, a charming little show arrived from London and took New York by storm. In the leading ingénue role of *The Boy Friend* was a fresh-faced nineteen-year-old soprano named Julie Andrews. While performing by night, Julie was auditioning for her next show by day. She was offered two very different roles for the next season. One was in Rodgers and Hammerstein's latest musical, *Pipe Dream*, and the other in what was then either titled *Pygmalion* or *Lady Liza*. (It was Harrison who put the kibosh on that. He thought it would be tasteless for the marquee and posters to proclaim "Rex Harrison *in Lady Liza*.") When Julie Andrews told Richard Rodgers that she had been offered the role of Eliza Doolittle, he advised her to take it. With his keen theater sense, Rodgers knew that playing Eliza Doolittle would make Julie Andrews a star.

On March 15, 1956, Richard Rodgers was proven right. The show got ecstatic reviews and went on to become the hottest ticket in New York and the longest-running musical of all time (at that time). Andrews, Harrison, and Stanley Holloway (one of London's great Cockney musical hall performers), who played Andrews' father, all repeated their triumphant performances at the Theatre Royal, Drury Lane in London's West End.

It was announced on February 6, 1962, that Jack Warner had outbid ($5.5 million) all the other Hollywood studios for the right to turn *My Fair Lady* into a movie. Warner wasted no time in offering the design job to Cecil Beaton, who created the original costumes, and the director's chair to Vincente Minnelli. Minnelli, who had worked with Lerner and Loewe on their Oscar-winning film *Gigi*, was anxious to do *My Fair Lady*, but demanded a percentage of the gross, which Warner was not prepared to pay. Minnelli was passed over for George Cukor.

Of course the big speculation all through the entertainment industry was, who will play the leads in what promised to be the biggest film musical of all time? Warner wanted box office names. He proposed Cary Grant, Audrey Hepburn, and James Cagney for the three leads. Supposedly, when Grant (who with that tinge of Cockney in his voice would have been absurd as the dialectician) was approached, he told Warner that not only wouldn't he accept the role, but if Rex Harrison didn't play the part he wouldn't even see the movie! Cagney turned down the role of Doolittle over some ancient haggle with his old boss, Warner, and it was offered to Stanley Holloway. This left the role of Eliza Doolittle.

Julie Andrews had practically made a career out of playing Eliza. Two years in New York and another two in London made it seem to the world that she owned the role. Returning to Broadway in 1960 as Guenevere in Lerner and Loewe's *Camelot* had solidified her Broadway stardom. The New York and London contingent was lobbying for her to repeat her triumph on-screen. Julie, herself, told Jack Warner that she was ready and interested in playing the role. He supposedly told her that she was welcome to screen test for the part, at which point she balked. She felt that Warner (and the rest of the theatergoing public) had seen her play the role and that should be enough. Meanwhile, Walt Disney offered Julie a very nice consolation prize, *Mary Poppins*. Warner didn't care. He wanted Audrey Hepburn in any case. According to inside sources, Warner had another reason to want Audrey for the role besides her box office appeal. With two Columbia Records recordings available (both with Andrews, Harrison, and Holloway), the soundtrack recording needed a fresh name on the cover to help it sell. Audrey's name. Luckily for Jack Warner, Audrey Hepburn definitely wanted to play Eliza.

At this point Audrey Hepburn was one of the goddesses of the screen. Christened Edda Van Heemstra Hepburn-Ruston, Hepburn was born in Brussels to an English businessman and a Dutch baroness. She had specialized in playing adorable gamines in such films as *Sabrina*, *Love in the Afternoon*, and *Roman Holiday*. She had even starred opposite Fred Astaire in the musical film *Funny Face*, proving that she was a lovely dancer and had a sweet, but smallish singing voice well suited to the character she played in that film. More recently she had introduced the classic Johnny Mercer-Henry Mancini song "Moon River" in *Breakfast at Tiffany's*.

Singing the exacting, high-soprano role of Eliza in *My Fair Lady*, though, would be a horse of a different color.

It's hard to imagine today, but from the moment Warner bought the film rights to *My Fair Lady*, Julie Andrews and Audrey Hepburn (and, by the way, Elizabeth Taylor was also dying to play the role) were seldom out of the press. Every day, it seemed, there was some mention of it. Hedda Hopper would rail at Warner for not giving the role to Andrews. Earl Wilson would proclaim that Audrey *could* sing it. Leonard Lyons would reveal that Audrey *would not* sing it. Articles would be written about how much money she was making ($1 million!) and how much one of her gorgeous Cecil Beaton gowns would cost. In 1962 and 1963 this was big news. All of my friends who read the publicity kept telling me that I should call my agents and tell them that I was the perfect singer to dub Audrey Hepburn's voice. After all, they said, you even kind of look like Julie Andrews. I knew it wasn't an agent who got one jobs of this kind—personal contacts did. In my experience (which by now was vast) it was the musical director or head of the music department who would decide who sang for whom. So I just bided my time.

Please don't think that I lived in a state of suspended animation waiting for my next dubbing job. Nothing could be further from the truth. During this time in the early 1960s I was quite busy keeping my family together (and Melani made three!); singing concerts, chamber works, and operas; making recordings (both for adults and children); and playing musical theater roles on the stage.

Before Melani was born I got to portray two classic musical theater characters, Nellie Forbush in *South Pacific* opposite film star Howard Keel and the elusive Rosabella in Frank Loesser's *The Most Happy Fella*.

The latter was significant for several reasons. I finally got to play the role I hadn't gotten to create on Broadway and sing that glorious Loesser music. It was also interesting because in April of 1962, as Rosabella, I went onstage each night and revealed to my friend Cleo, played by the soon-to-be movie star Dyan Cannon, that I was pregnant. What no one in the company knew was that I really *was* pregnant. I was carrying the baby Ernest and I had conceived that starry night in Hawaii. Fearing that I might lose the role or be treated like an invalid, I kept my mouth shut and hoped that the seams didn't give on my costumes as month four of my pregnancy approached.

At the time Dyan was dating (and would eventually marry) one of the dreamiest movie stars of all time, Cary Grant. Everyone was all atwitter when Grant made the trip to San Bernardino to watch his honey play her role. Of course, I was cool as a cucumber since Cary and I had met when I dubbed his costar Deborah Kerr in *An Affair to Remember*.

One night I was sitting in my dressing room and the door opened and I heard that inimitable English accent tinged with Cockney cooing, "Darling! Here I am!"

Before I could say, "What took you so long, sweetheart? Come and kiss me!" Cary noticed I wasn't the darling he had thought I was.

"Oops, wrong dressing room, darling," he apologized, and left me alone with my mouth agape.

As the door closed with Cary Grant on the other side, all I could think was, "Wow, I wish he *were* in the right dressing room!"

By 1963, my attitude toward being a closet ghost was beginning to change. The secret was seeping out slowly, and I was being interviewed about my involvement in the 1960 film of *West Side Story*. I was quoted at the time about what I felt about the lack of screen credit.

"If the role is important, the ghost singer should get screen credit. Hairdressers get credit, so why not voices?"

I was finally using *my* voice to try to change the industry's mindset about the issue. It may not have been civil rights or feminism, but I had my own little, subtle ax to grind.

It was about this time, in the middle of May 1963 (Beaton's diary pinpoints the date I auditioned as May 16, 1963) that I got a call from Warner Bros. Studios asking me to come in and audition for the singing voice of Audrey Hepburn in *My Fair Lady*. Strangely, the audition was held in costume designer Cecil Beaton's bungalow on the Warner Bros. lot. Director George Cukor was there, as was production designer Gene Allen. At the keyboard was my old friend and colleague Harper MacKay. Conspicuously absent was anyone high up from the music department. No music supervisor or musical director. I found that very odd. Still, everyone was cordial and pleasant when I sang "Wouldn't It Be Loverly?" and "I Could Have Danced All Night." They said the usual "Thank you very much" and that was that.

And then there was silence.

As with any audition, life goes on and so mine did, but I was curious as to who would get this plum dubbing assignment. A month later, in June 1963, I was singing a "Salute to France" evening with the New York Philharmonic Promenade Concerts at the then-brand-new Lincoln Center. Three conductors were on the program: Andre Kostelanetz, Morton Gould, and André Previn. It was a glorious evening, and afterward André Previn and I began to

With two Andres: André Previn on left and Andre Kostelanetz on right. Promenade Concerts, Alice Tully Hall, Lincoln Center, New York. (Courtesy of New York Philharmonic Archives)

shoot the breeze. He mentioned that he was the musical director of the *My Fair Lady* film and I told him that I had been called in to audition for Hepburn's voice double.

"You did what?!" he exclaimed in surprise. "Well, we'll just see about that."

André was obviously and rightly peeved that they had held any auditions without his input. In fact, no one had even told him about the audition.

André was highly experienced doing movie musicals and had worked with Lerner and Loewe on their Oscar-winning *Gigi*. He had dealt with dubbing a reluctant Leslie Caron (Betty Wand did the vocals) on that film and knew how important it was to get the voices right.

Knowing in my heart that I was perfect for this job, I decided to call the New York offices of Warner Bros. and let them know I was in town and available to audition, again, for the job. I was turned down in a very officiously dismissive tone by some underling at the other end of the line.

"But my dear," she cooed, "You must understand that we have to have truly native speakers. We will only be hearing authentic British and Cockney accents. We can't have any native 'Californian' to do *this* dubbing."

I reeled off some of my credits, including the fact that I "passed" as authentically British when dubbing Deborah Kerr's singing in *The King and I*, but nothing seemed to faze her. Once again I filed it away and decided to forget about it and bide my time.

I was not surprised, though, when a week or so later back in L.A. from New York, I got another call from Warner Bros. saying that now they were holding "official" auditions at the studio. Apparently, André Previn had a little talk with the powers that be and instructed them on the "correct" way to handle the tryouts.

This time the auditions were handled professionally. I was sent the actual music to learn and study beforehand (as if the whole world didn't know all the music by now!), and when I arrived I was ushered into a very private waiting room (no one in it but myself) and a little later into a dark sound booth where I could neither see the people I was singing for or, more importantly, be seen by them. Previn knew that to really find a voice double, the only thing that the people making the decisions should be concentrating on was the voice. He didn't want anyone's eye to have any part in the casting process. To that end, I was assigned a number instead of a name so that no one listening would know what I looked like or even who I was. It, of course, worked both ways. This time I had no idea (except for André) who was listening and judging my voice. Everyone who auditioned could sing and sing well; that went without saying. The most crucial criterion was for the basic timbre of the voice to not only match Audrey Hepburn's, but also be flexible enough to complement her acting style.

A few days after the audition I was told that I got the part. I learned from the sound editor, Rudy Fehr, that it wasn't the slam-dunk I thought it was. Since, like Ernest, Rudy was Viennese, he and his wife had become good friends of ours. Rudy told me that there was at least one other singer (I have no idea who) who also came close to matching Hepburn's sound. There wasn't a clear consensus among the people deciding (Cukor and Previn) and at one point Jack Warner called Rudy and said, "These guys can't come to a decision. You heard the auditions, what do you think?" To which Rudy replied, "The only one who can do this part is Marni Nixon." Warner said, "Fine, it's done! Hire her!" When I found out that Rudy was the deciding factor, Ernest and I brought a special bottle of champagne to his house in the Hollywood/Burbank Hills to thank him.

As was the case with *West Side Story*, it wasn't totally decided at first how much Audrey Hepburn would be singing and how much I would be dubbing. Audrey, of course, wanted to do it all, but realized that I might have to supplement some of the higher notes and sing some of the longer-lined, more lyrical phrases, such as those in "I Could Have Danced All Night." Audrey diligently went to the studio each day and had hours of voice lessons with Sue Seaton, a good teacher from New York City (who later taught voice to the other Hepburn, Kate). Unlike my experience with Natalie Wood, I was allowed, actually encouraged, to sit like a fly on the wall as she vocalized, exercised her voice, and eventually tackled the songs themselves. Like a sponge, I was soaking up her unusual speech patterns, the way she breathed, and the actual sound of her voice, which had a sexy, semihoarse quality, while still being soft and feminine.

In rehearsals, Audrey sometimes turned to me for singing advice, but I wasn't sure that I could have told her anything better than what Sue was telling her. It was a matter of my singing the songs with her accent, and then her imitating me. She had to have a lot of trust in me. The thrill I have is that I was able to pick up on Audrey and her style. I really felt fused with her.

In the early days of rehearsing at the studio I was picked up by Audrey's limousine. This was unheard of in Hollywood! A star sharing a ride with her ghost? Who had ever heard of such a thing? Audrey Hepburn had! We would sit together in the backseat as the long black car sped us to the Warner Bros. lot. She was absolutely charming and real, but you still had the sense of her being very aristocratic. When she spoke, it was with carefully chosen words. It seemed to me that she was always trying to understand everything that was going on, all the little nuances of people's behavior. I can remember her warmly complimenting me.

"Oh, Marni," Audrey would say, "I don't know how you do it. I do so admire how you can just hear me singing and then take over when the notes get too high for me."

As the days went by and she got more comfortable with me, our limo talks got more personal. We were both working mothers with artist husbands and had lots in common. We talked about our husbands, children, and life in general. Audrey told me about the difficulty she had with her first natural childbirth, about how large the baby was and how he almost killed her (she had a very small frame; I used to kid that she weighed 75 pounds . . . without nail polish) when he came out. Our private time together was delightful for me and proved fruitful in the end for the dubbing process. The more I know a person, the more chameleonlike I can be and the better I can serve the character being created.

I was not at all involved with Audrey's rehearsals of the scenes. How wonderful it would have been to witness Cukor, who was known as the quintessential "woman's" director, imparting his wisdom to Audrey. I am sure it would have helped in my process, but I respected the fact that some actresses need privacy in the preparation and building of a character—especially one as complex as

Eliza, who must transform herself from one woman into another in the course of three hours on-screen. Still, Audrey was never reticent about my presence and was totally self-revealing when it involved singing. I would observe, as much as possible, Audrey learning the songs and then I would work separately with Harper MacKay (as we did on *The King and I*) and glean as much information as I could from his private sessions with her.

There would be songs, such as "Just You Wait," for which it was predecided which parts Audrey would sing and when I would take over. In "Just You Wait," Audrey's Eliza began the song and when Eliza was supposedly pretending to sound posh, Marni's Eliza took over. My more polished sound (still with the Cockney accent Eliza had yet to overcome) fit the center of the song well. Then, when her highbrow fantasy of what she would do to " 'enry 'iggins" was over and she reverted back to anger, Audrey's Eliza track returned.

I can remember finally rehearsing this "compilation" number on the set at Warner's in front of "the family." This would include Cukor; Beaton; Hermes Pan, the choreographer; André; Rudi; Peter Ladefoged, an American dialect expert from UCLA ("An American who probably knows London like I know Peking," Audrey remarked); and, of course, the author and lyricist Alan Jay Lerner.

Lerner was one of the great men of the theater and *My Fair Lady* was, and would remain, the highpoint of his career. He had worked in films as well as theatre, having written the screenplay for the Oscar-winning *An American in Paris*, adapted his own *Brigadoon* and penned the multi-award-winning *Gigi*, among others. He was not only the author and lyricist of the stage play of *My Fair Lady*, but the screenwriter as well. He had power. In fact, the only place Lerner was helpless was in the casting department (he lobbied heartily, but to no avail, for Julie Andrews). Essentially, if there was a *My Fair Lady* expert, it was Alan Jay Lerner.

Like Fritz Loewe (who was not around when I was there; "I'm rich and I'm famous," he supposedly said, "I don't have to be around"), Lerner was short and in a state of perpetual tan. In later life, it was not uncommon for him to actually be mistaken for Sammy Davis, Jr.! Lerner was also a chain smoker who was constantly trying to quit. To this end, he would hold an unlit cigarette and pass it from finger to finger of the plastic-lined white cotton gloves that he wore to keep him from his chronic nail-biting habit. I can still hear the rattling, crackling, and crinkling of the plastic as he kept his hands in constant, nervous motion.

Besides these minor peccadilloes, Lerner was brilliant, erudite, nervous, flighty, and loquacious to the extreme. What would take me (and I am no shrinking violet when it comes to talking) two minutes to express would take Lerner a minimum of six or seven. He always knew exactly what he wanted to say, but if Lerner had a point to make, one had to be prepared to sit it out and listen. For a long, long time. He used a lot of hand gestures when he talked. There he would be, describing how he wanted some phrase or word to be sung, waving his rattling hands around, clenching and unclenching his bloody fingers until finally he would rip off his gloves and bite his nails. It was said that when you needed to find Alan Jay Lerner, you could just follow the trail of discarded white gloves.

Later on, it was revealed that Lerner (and many, many other celebrities, including President Kennedy) was being prescribed "vitamin" shots by the infamous "Dr. Feelgood," Max Jacobs. Unbeknown to his patients, the vitamins the doctor prescribed were actually amphetamines. Perhaps this contributed to Lerner's talkativeness, energy, and nervous habits.

There is a story about Lerner and me during one of the recording sessions that went around the lot and has been reprinted in several books. It seems that Lerner was haranguing me with a diatribe so long and involved that I finally snapped and turned to him, saying, "Mr. Lerner, I know what I am doing. After all I have dubbed the voices of Deborah Kerr, Natalie Wood, and many others." At which point, Lerner smiled at me and said, "Yes, Miss Nixon, but they all dubbed your face." Great line, Alan! Too bad it didn't happen.

Once when I was singing one of the songs on the set, Cukor stopped me and began to talk to Audrey about how Eliza felt at that point in the story. Audrey listened intently and I became the fly on the wall again. After Cukor finished his instructions to Audrey, I sang the song once more and used all of his directions. Frequently both Audrey and I would be pulled in several directions, especially when it came to the all-important question of the accent. Audrey's interesting mid-Atlantic English accent would do fine for the second part of the film when Eliza has learned to speak correctly, but like Julie Andrews before her and a whole line of actresses after, the Cockney inflections would have to be drilled and worked on. When the dialect coach would correct me, I would inform him that I was taking it from whatever Audrey was doing. When they approached Audrey, she said that she was waiting for Stanley Holloway, who was playing her father, to show up so that she could copy his accent. The only problem with that theory was that Holloway wasn't due to fly in from England until shooting began, and we had to record the songs before he arrived. Ultimately Audrey (and I) listened carefully to all the opinions, then it seemed to me she just did it her own way. Each thought she was heeding his or her advice and termed her a genius. And, of course, she was. Maybe that's precisely how good acting is perceived by others! André's wife (at the time) Dory Previn commented that Audrey had "a whim of iron."

During the prerecording sessions, I was also besieged by multitudes of conflicting opinions about how to sing this or that phrase. I found myself assessing it all and trying to be specific and truly hear what each expert was trying to impart to me. After a while, my eyes began to cross. It was brilliant André Previn who listened and assessed what everyone else was saying. Then he came over behind me, and knowing I would react like an instrumentalist, whispered in my ear, "Just sing it softer!" Shades of Ernest and Otto Preminger! I did what Previn said and everyone else thought that I had done what *they* requested. "Isn't she amazing?" they would all mutter. "She took in and did everything I said and made it her own." I guess I, too, had a "whim of iron."

Beginning on July 4, 1963, both Audrey and I initially recorded the songs in the recording studio at the Goldwyn Studios (where I also recorded *West Side Story*) rather than on the Warner Bros. sound stage. Eliza would sing: "Wouldn't It Be Loverly?," "Just You Wait," "The Rain in Spain," "I Could Have Danced All Night," "Show Me," and "Without You." These, and all the other songs, were sumptuously orchestrated by Alexander Courage, Robert Franklyn, and Al Woodbury and the vocal arrangements were by my old *West Side Story* pal, Bobby Tucker.

Cecil Beaton commented in his diaries that the recording session was "an ordeal" for Audrey. One of the first tracks she recorded was "Wouldn't It Be Loverly?" (although even on that track I sang the final high notes) and everyone was happy enough with it to let her film the number to her own voice. It was felt that the "guttersnipe" part of the role would not seem so out of place in her real slightly more raw, low-mezzo voice. I was on the sound stage for the filming of this number and saw how hard she worked and how well she lip-synched to her own vocal track. In fact, when viewing the song with her vocal track (available as a bonus on the DVD) today, it's quite charming and is filled with Audrey's personality all the way through it.

Apparently, though, Audrey was growing more and more frustrated with the situation and the fact that she couldn't seem to cut it musically. After one particular take the extras and crew applauded and Audrey took this as a vote of confidence for her voice on the track. She beamed with pride at Cukor.

"They all applauded my singing!"

"But that wasn't your track," replied Cukor. "It was Marni's."

In fact it was supposed to be mine, but the sound people made a mistake and played hers. Everyone was confused and Audrey wound up in tears.

At this point, the entire creative team was becoming perplexed. Which fair lady was going to sing? All this indecision only made Audrey more and more unhappy and uncertain. Eventually I wound up totally looping the whole track of "Wouldn't It Be Loverly?" while watching and listening to her performance. Having been fortunate enough to watch her film the number, I attempted to put as much of Audrey's accent, personality, and acting choices into my vocal track.

Matching Audrey's voice was a great challenge, much more difficult than matching that of either Deborah or Natalie. I had to be extra careful, because her essential voice was not a soprano sound. Audrey seemed to have a lower, wider-shaped hard palette than mine, which was narrower and higher in shape. These anatomic differences can affect the high partials in the resonance and the overtones in any voice. Thus, the very fabric of our tones was naturally different.

During the recording sessions when Audrey sang, she was noticeably frustrated.

"Oh I *know* I can do that better. Please let me try again." These and other apologetic phrases dotted the ends of all of her takes. Later on André Previn admitted that Audrey's voice "was perfectly adequate for the living room, but this was the movie to end all movies, with six giant surround speakers."

Interestingly, I never recorded with Rex Harrison, as Harrison had demanded that he record all of his tracks *live*. This was unheard-of in Hollywood and hadn't been attempted since the earliest days of sound in the late 1920s. Harrison rightly maintained that his brand of talk-singing ("sprechstimme," in singers' terminology) could not be prerecorded and lip-synched. To this end, the sound people wired Harrison (you could tell when he was going to sing because his tie would be stiffer and more formal to hide the small wireless microphone) and he used a tiny earphone to hear a piano track in his ear. After his songs were filmed and recorded live, the orchestra track would be added later. I was sorry not to work more closely with Rex Harrison. He was a great actor and quite a character. André Previn told me that Harrison was dead set against using him as musical director. He wanted his Broadway conductor, Franz Allers (I got to know Allers later when he conducted me and also attended my concerts in Munich). Lerner begged Harrison to try Previn during a test recording session and if he didn't like him, they would replace him with Allers. After the session Harrison called Lerner on the phone and said that André would do very well.

"So much better than that Teutonic son of a bitch I had to deal with on Broadway!"

On several songs I recorded complete tracks, and on others I supplemented Audrey's tracks with my high notes. On "The Rain in Spain" it wasn't clear at first how much would be me and how much would be her. Finally, Lerner made the decision. I got to listen to her speak the first few lines and then take over the rest of the song, speech, and song, until the very end. In the final picture I sang most of the score, except for the two large chunks of "Just You Wait." "Show Me" is now all my voice, but the original master track contained both of us. After they threw out her sections, Audrey kept begging to rerecord portions of it again. She felt that now that she heard how it *should* be done, she could actually do it. Determined as she was, her vocals were not used.

No one, it seemed, wanted to actually *tell* Audrey they would be using my tracks instead of hers. Neither Jack Warner, Alan Lerner, nor André Previn had the heart (or courage) to break the news. It finally fell to George Cukor to do the deed. When Audrey was told, she just said, "Oh," and walked off the set. The next day she returned with apologies to all for being so "wicked." Imagine! That was her idea of being wicked. She was a perfect lady.

According to several books, it's evident from the top level that there was never any question about dubbing Audrey Hepburn's voice. Rudy Fehr, who was with Warner all the time, has said that they just let her record her tracks to placate her. They never had any serious intention of using her voice. Never.

My Fair Lady opened in October 1964 to great acclaim and much controversy. Audrey did publicity, and although it had leaked out that she was dubbed, she tried to put a good face on it.

"I took singing lessons," she said, "from a New York vocal coach and prerecorded all of Eliza's songs, but the final result is a blend." Shades of Deborah Kerr!

The critics, though, wouldn't let up on her. The *London Sunday Telegraph* wrote, "Although miming to a canned voice has long been a tradition of film musicals, I still find the sight of a beautiful dummy singing someone else's head off rather less than enthralling."

An old booster of mine, syndicated columnist Hedda Hopper, wrote, "With Marni Nixon doing the singing, Audrey Hepburn gives only half a performance." Critics were actually saying that I *should* have gotten credit. The cat was out of the bag and it refused to go back in. Jack Warner tried to make light of all the adverse publicity.

"We've been doing it for years. We even dubbed Rin Tin Tin."

I had very mixed emotions at this time. Although I was very proud of my work and glad to finally be acknowledged as the voice behind Eliza, I felt terrible for Audrey, who had to take the brunt of the criticism. And then, when the Oscar nominees were announced in February 1965, *My Fair Lady's* twelve nominations did not include one for Best Actress. Audrey had been snubbed by the Academy and *Variety* was blunt about the reason.

"Hepburn did the acting, but Marni Nixon subbed for her in the singing department and that's what undoubtedly led to her erasure."

Audrey was very unhappy and I was told that she felt her snubbing was due to the dubbing. Everyone did. Cukor blamed me and so did André Previn. They thought I had blabbed too much to the press and that was why Audrey was slighted. During this time, I actually kept denying it in public, even though it seemed that everyone else already knew she was being dubbed. After a while, I began to feel it was silly to hide it, since the more I took the "Fifth Amendment" the more it became clear that I had actually done the dubbing! One thing I never wanted was to hurt Audrey, but the can was open and that was that.

The truth is that the Oscar snub was just another part of the backlash against Audrey for taking Julie Andrews' role away from her. In any case Julie benefited from it all. *She* was nominated in the Best Actress category for her performance in *Mary Poppins* and became the sentimental favorite to win. On Oscar night *My Fair Lady* came home with eight of its nominated Oscars, but Julie Andrews won Best Actress for *Mary Poppins* and had the last word, thanking Jack Warner, "who made all this possible."

Being the classy lady that she was, Audrey was on hand to present the Best Actor statuette to Rex Harrison. In his speech, he thanked both of his "fair ladies."

Poor Audrey Hepburn, who wanted so to play Eliza, was punished for not being Julie Andrews and was criticized for the very same reason Rex Harrison was praised: the inability to sing. None of this harmed the film's revenues, for the public flocked to see the musical and it grossed more than $33 million. And no one ever stopped loving Audrey Hepburn. How could they?

As for me, suddenly I was famous.

I was singing *Pierrot Lunaire*, by Arnold Schoenberg, *and* the one-woman Cocteau-Poulenc opera *La Voix Humaine* with Milton Katims and the Little Orchestra Society of Seattle, Washington when *Time* magazine called to do a story on me. It seemed the secret had officially leaked. When the magazine article came out, I was officially dubbed "the Ghostess with the Mostest." Suddenly I was beginning to be hailed by the other dubbers as their patron saint.

Because of the precedent I had set on the soundtrack album of *West Side Story*, I had less of a problem getting a royalty (still no credit!) for the Columbia Records LP of *My Fair Lady*. This time, my lawyer got me a better contract and the CD sales still bring in a little income.

Yet, with all the publicity and hoopla, it's ironic that *My Fair Lady* proved to be the last of my big ghosting jobs. What's really ironic is that, coupled with the monumental success of *The Sound of Music* the next year, *My Fair Lady* seemed to show that big movie musicals were back in style. Every studio quickly jumped on the bandwagon and made huge, road-show pictures and, one by one, they all started to flop. For every *Oliver!* and *Funny Girl*, there were ten *Paint Your Wagon*s and *Song of Norway*s. Eventually in the 1970s the movie musical format became dormant again until the incredible success of *Chicago* made everyone sit up and take notice. The truth of it was there were fewer and fewer opportunities for ghost singers in the sixties and seventies. Although Anita Gordon ghosted for Jean Seberg in *Paint Your Wagon*, even the nonsinging Vanessa Redgrave recorded her own vocals in *Camelot* (Julie Andrews created this role, too; there were rumors in 1964 that Richard Burton and Elizabeth Taylor were going to star in the film and that I was already hired to sing for Liz!).

What did it all mean? The public was wise and wasn't about to take it for granted anymore that their favorite stars *could* sing (even when they were secretly being dubbed). For me it was both a blessing and a curse. I was seemingly better known than I had ever been before, albeit as a ghost, and thought that perhaps I could use my new-found fame to further some other aspects of my career. Maybe I would even get back in front of the camera now.

In fact that's just what happened next when "the Ghostess with the Mostest" materialized on the screen for the first time in years and sang and acted in a film starring the original "Fair Lady," Julie Andrews.

That's right. Exit Marni, the ghost, and enter Marni . . . the nun.

Chapter Nine
GETTING INTO THE HABIT

*"They found out who was doing Mr. Ed's voice on that
television show; it was Marni Nixon's horse."*

THE HOLLYWOOD REPORTER, 1967

EVERYONE WAS VERY NERVOUS. I have to admit I was a little bit nervous, too. As I drove to the Twentieth Century Fox studios early in 1964, I tried to keep calm. After all, I wasn't a stranger here. I had first come through the Fox gates in 1939 and later had spent many happy days working here with Deborah Kerr on *The King and I*. There was absolutely no reason to be anxious now. Was it because, unlike my last ghostly film adventures, I was actually going to sing and be seen on the screen?

No, like everyone else in that room, I was nervous because I knew that I was about to be formally introduced to Julie Andrews.

We met in a large rehearsal room at Fox. The entire cast, crew, and creative team of the film version of *The Sound of Music* were about to meet one another for the first time. We sat in a huge circle and, one by one, we were to stand as the director, Robert Wise, introduced each of us to the star by character and name.

"Julie, this is Sister Berthe . . . Portia Nelson."

Everyone was thinking the same thing. What would she say? How would Julie feel meeting the woman who was part of one of the biggest disappointments of her life? It could have gone this way:

"Julie, this is Sister Sophia, the woman who dubbed the singing for Audrey Hepburn, who viciously stole your beloved role in *My Fair Lady* . . . Marni Nixon."

At which point Julie Andrews would storm across the room and slap my face!

But, of course, Robert Wise introduced me in a much more conventional way.

"Julie, this is Sister Sophia . . . Marni Nixon."

After a moment when everyone held their breath, Julie stood up and strode over to me, stretched out her hand, and shook mine firmly and strongly.

"Marni," she said in that delicious English accent, "I'm such a fan of yours!"

There was a collective sigh of relief throughout the room. What a Fair Lady she really was and is!

Today *The Sound of Music* is thought of as the holy grail of movie musicals, but it almost didn't get made.

Based on the semitrue story of the Trapp Family Singers, the story began life as a 1949 memoir by Maria von Trapp. Her story was then turned into a German film in 1956, which came to the attention of a director, Vincent Donahue, at Paramount Pictures when it was proposed he direct Audrey Hepburn (imagine if she had played Maria—then Julie might have gotten to play Eliza and . . . no, let's not go there!) in an American remake of the film. Donahue screened the film for his friend, musical theater star Mary Martin, whom he had just directed in a production of Thornton Wilder's classic play *The Skin of Our Teeth*. Mary and her husband/producer, Richard Halliday (the same team who turned down Eliza in *My Fair Lady*, saying that Lerner and Loewe had lost their talent; the circle tightens!), thought that the story of Maria and her seven charges would be a great stage vehicle for Mary. They envisioned a straight play with songs from the Trapp Family Singers' repertoire.

To spice it up and add some name value, Mary asked her old friends and colleagues Rodgers and Hammerstein (they wrote *South Pacific* for her) if they would write a song for the play. They mulled it over and told her that no, they wouldn't write a song, but that they would be interested in writing a whole score and turning the evening into a full-fledged musical play. Mary and the book writers, Howard Lindsay and Russel Crouse (*Life with Father, State of the Union, Call Me Madam*), were thrilled to have Rodgers and Hammerstein onboard and agreed to wait until they launched their latest show, *Flower Drum Song*, before going into production with the show. This would mark the first time that Oscar Hammerstein did not have anything to do with writing the book of one of their musicals, but he was perfectly content at this point of his life to just contribute the lyrics.

The Sound of Music opened at the Lunt-Fontanne Theatre on November 16, 1959 to mixed reviews. The *World Telegram and Sun* called it "the loveliest musical imaginable," while *The New York Times* complained that "it was disappointing to see American Musical Stage succumbing to the clichés of operetta." Walter Kerr at the *Herald-Tribune* called it "too sweet for words and almost too sweet for music." Most critics agreed that the score was top-notch Rodgers and Hammerstein. Despite the fact that New York's intelligencia seemed to think that seeing the show and Miss Martin was apt to give one sugar poisoning, the general public flocked to see the heartwarming and uplifting tale of nuns, Nazis, and children. The musical won eight Tony Awards, including Best Musical (it tied with *Fiorello!*), in a season that boasted such shows as *Once Upon a Mattress* and *Gypsy*. When Mary Martin won her award for Best Actress in a Musical, fellow nominee Ethel Merman (who chose not to attend the ceremony) was rumored to have said, "Well, you can't buck a nun!" The show ran 1,443 performances on Broadway and was even more successful in London, where it racked up 2,385 performances, making it the longest-running American musical to play the West End at the time.

Taking in the show during the second week of its run, screenwriter Ernest Lehman (who had also written the films *The King and I* and *West Side Story*, not to mention *North by Northwest*) was the first to notice the show's potential as a film. When *Variety* announced on June 13, 1960 that Twentieth Century Fox had bought the film rights for $1.25 million against 10 percent of the gross, Doris Day was the first name mentioned for the role of Maria. Like many of the other big studios in the early 1960s, Twentieth Century Fox was facing financial ruin. Studio head Darryl Zanuck had left the company he had built. This, coupled with the ridiculously overbudget production of *Cleopatra*, starring Elizabeth Taylor, brought the studio to its knees when it was finally released in 1963 and put it in a financial hole from which it was almost unable to recover. The proposed *Sound of Music* film sat on the shelf for two years, until Zanuck returned to his post at Fox and took some drastic steps. He closed down the entire studio in order to regroup. During this period of reorganization Zanuck rediscovered that the studio owned the rights to *The Sound of Music*. He sensed a potential hit.

Remembering Lehman's enthusiasm for the project, Zanuck hired him to write the screenplay. After a brief period when William Wyler was director, Zanuck approached Robert Wise to produce and direct, as he had done on *West Side Story*. Wise wisely asked the opinion of Saul Chaplin, his associate producer. After Chaplin read Lehman's script he advised Wise to take the job. With Wise and Chaplin onboard, *The Sound of Music* was put on the fast track for production. All they needed now was a star.

Having seen her on Broadway in both *My Fair Lady* and *Camelot*, both Wise and Chaplin were keen on Julie Andrews, but they wondered how she would photograph. At this point, in the fall of 1963, Julie had finished shooting her first film, *Mary Poppins*, but it had yet to be released. Disney kindly screened some of the unfinished picture for Wise and Chaplin, and before a few scenes were done Wise turned to Chaplin and said, "Let's get out of here and sign her up before anyone else gets to her first!" Negotiations began for Julie's services and, in November of 1963, while Wise and Chaplin were in Salzburg, Austria scouting locations for the film, it was announced that Julie Andrews had signed on to play Maria.

In early 1964, Saul Chaplin contacted me.

"Marni, I have this song I need you to record as a demo. But I'll have to swear you to secrecy."

Solly (as he was known to friends) told me that he had a new song by Richard Rodgers (since Oscar Hammerstein II had died in 1960, Rodgers was writing his own lyrics to the two new songs for the film, at $15,000 per song!) that he wanted me to record as a demo for Rodgers to hear. This demo recording was being made for Richard Rodgers to approve. The song was called "I Have Confidence" and I was the first person to sing it.

What I didn't know then, but found out later, was that Chaplin and Rodgers had "collaborated" on this song. "I Have Confidence" was to be a soliloquy for Maria to sing on her way from the abbey to the Von Trapp home. It would tell of her fears, qualms, and ultimate courage in taking this assignment as governess to seven children. Rodgers seemed to have trouble writing the song, and after delivering a disappointing sixteen-bar version in a minor key, finally came up with the up-tempo tune that Maria sings at the end of the number. What was lacking was the emotional progression from the abbey to the mansion. Finally, Chaplin, utilizing some of Rodgers' discarded verse from the title song of the show, wrote the song himself. He also wrote some additional lyrics to Rodgers' basic tune. With this all done, he needed the master's approval and that's when he called me to sing it. The reason for the secrecy was that Julie Andrews wasn't to know that she might be singing a song that was not quite penned by the great Richard Rodgers. Luckily, Mr. Rodgers approved of Mr. Chaplin's amendments and additions to the song and Julie learned it, sang it, and shot it. It's one of the musical highlights in a film full of them. It took two years for Saul Chaplin to summon up the courage to tell Julie the saga of "I Have Confidence." And there I was in the middle of it all.

The next time I saw Solly was at my "audition" for the role of Sister Sophia.

The potential nuns all converged in Robert Wise's bungalow on the Fox lot. Anna Lee, Portia Nelson, Doreen Tryden, Ada Beth Lee, Evadne Baker, and I would be singing together in "(How Do You Solve a Problem Like) Maria?" but on that day we didn't have to sing. We had all been recommended for the roles by the music department at Fox, and I had a special relationship with Robert Wise and Saul Chaplin from West Side Story. In addition, Robert Wise was a very cultured man who had attended some of my concerts with the L.A. Philharmonic and knew my voice well. They all knew I could sing. What we were there for was to see how we looked together as group. I guess we looked pretty good, because the next thing I knew I was being fitted for my wimple and veil and literally "getting into the habit."

Rehearsals began in February of 1964. We learned our vocals for "Maria" under the keen eye and ear of my old West Side Story buddy Bobby Tucker (and Chaplin, of course). My good-luck charm, Harper MacKay, was also on hand as rehearsal pianist. When the music was learned, we were passed onto choreographers Marc Breaux and Dee Dee Wood, who would be staging all the musical numbers (as they did on *Mary Poppins*; Julie Andrews brought them on-board from *Poppins*, along with musical director-orchestrator par excellence Irwin Kostal). Marc and Dee Dee devised all of our minimalist nun movements for the song. They made it fun and adorable, at the same time keeping the sanctity and piety of our characters' vocation in mind. It's a wonderful musical number.

During the rehearsal period I got to know my "sisters" well. Several of the other nuns were girls I had done chorus work with around L.A. There was Ada Beth Lee, who was married to singer Bill Lee (he had dubbed John Kerr's voice in *South Pacific*), who would later dub Christopher Plummer's voice in *The Sound of Music* when Plummer's tracks were deemed unusable. There was also singer-songwriter Portia Nelson, who played the sour Sister Berthe (her character was the one who was against Maria becoming a nun; in the song, she sang, "She's a clown!") and who was making her film debut. Portia and I got to really know each other better later on when I moved to New York.

Then there was Anna Lee.

Anna Lee was born in Kent, England, and had been acting in films since 1932, appearing in such classics as *The Ghost and Mrs. Muir*, *Fort Apache*, *The Horse Soldiers*, and *Whatever Happened to Baby Jane?* Anna Lee had hoped to play the Baroness (portrayed by Eleanor Parker), but was happy in the end to be portraying a nun. We became friends during the rehearsal period when she agreed to coach me on my Cockney accent for an upcoming stage production of *My Fair Lady* I was scheduled to do several weeks after the completion of the shooting of our scenes. Anna Lee was married to writer Robert Nathan, whose best-known work was the novel *Portrait of Jennie*, which was later turned into a film starring Jennifer Jones. The Nathans and we, the Golds, spent some wonderful evenings together in their house on Doheny Drive (near Stravinsky's house). Nathan loved to sing German Lieder and, every once in a while, he would hire a pianist and invite me and other singers to join in the musical fun. I can still hear the delicious echoes of Schubert, Schumann, Wolf, and Brahms coming from that house. They are both gone now and I miss them still.

The Mother Abbess was a pivotal role in the film, as it was onstage. Stage, film, and TV actress Peggy Wood (a whole generation remembered her as Mama in the TV series *I Remember Mama*) was hired for the part. Peggy had been an operetta star in her youth, creating roles in Sigmund Romberg's *May-time*, Noël Coward's *Bittersweet*, and Jerome Kern's *The Cat and the Fiddle*, among others. She had introduced such classic songs as "I'll See You Again," "Zigeuner," "She Didn't Say Yes," and "Try to Forget." The Mother Abbess was to sing in "Maria" and, of course, solo in her climactic "Climb Ev'ry Mountain." Although Peggy was known as a singer, she didn't feel confident about her voice at this point in her life, and so Margery MacKay (Harper's wife) dubbed her voice. Margery had sung at New York City Opera and we had sung many contemporary concerts together at *Monday Evening Concerts*. Peggy loved Margery's voice, saying that Margery sounded exactly like she sounded in her early days of singing.

Shooting for the film began on March 24, 1964 with the scene in Maria's bedroom that included the song "My Favorite Things." Everything had to proceed according to a strict shooting schedule as the principals were set to begin location shooting in Austria on April 23. After that bedroom scene was in the can, the nuns were next. On April 2, 1964, I took my first on-camera walk to the chapel as Sister Sophia.

Although they would be filming the exterior of the Nonnberg Abbey in Salzburg, the production had been denied permission to shoot inside of the abbey, where the real Maria von Trapp had been a postulant, so the set designers re-created the interiors on the Fox sound stage. Every brick and paving stone was identical and authentic. There would be a sequence in the film where the children come looking for Maria after she has left them and gone back to the abbey. Portia Nelson as Sister Berthe had to walk through the abbey and then greet the children at the gate. Portia walked all through the re-created set in L.A. and then with the mystery of editing wound up at the real gate of the abbey in Salzburg, Austria. Movie magic at its best.

We shot the "Maria" number April 3–8 and then proceeded with the other scenes that took place in the Abbey. On April 9 I shot my small bit where I got to carry Julie Andrews' bridal gown train right before the wedding scene (the rest of the wedding was shot in a cathedral in Salzburg).

In a later scene (shot the next day on April 10), when the Nazis come to see if the Von Trapp family is hiding in the abbey, I was to finally get a close-up! I was told by director Robert Wise to stand next to a doorway, looking a bit nervous and tight as the Nazis walked by. Since we were playing nuns, the makeup department had forbidden us to wear any mascara. As any natural redhead will tell you, the one thing we lack is color in our lashes and brows. Here I was about to have a close-up and my eyes, which I thought were two of my best features, would be washed out. I thought, "What the hell," and snuck back into the makeup room and carefully put some darker mascara on my lashes. After all, no one could tell I was a redhead with my hair covered by the wimple, could they?

I got to the set and took my place. Robert Wise, directing from behind the camera, told me what to do and we did a quick rehearsal. The lights, as usual, were very bright, maybe even brighter because this was to be a close-up. The brightness unfortunately made me blink a lot. The next thing I knew, Wise said, "No, let's not do that shot!" The lights were switched off and the crew was off to do another set up. I was crushed! Did he can the shot because of my

Getting into the habit as Sister Sophia in the 1965 film version of The Sound of Music. *Note the lack of eye makeup! (© 1957 Twentieth Century Fox. All rights reserved.)*

blinking or was it just that he had a better idea? Later on I asked Bob, but he had no memory of the event at all. Ah well. There was to be no Norma Desmond moment for Marni! I thought that perhaps I blinked so much because of the extra mascara I applied. I felt so stupid and guilty, and from that day forward I never left the makeup room without having my face totally approved by the makeup artists.

During this time I had become friendly with Peggy Wood. Her friend Jean Dalrymple, who each year produced a season of musical revivals at City Center in New York, told her they were having trouble casting Eliza in *My Fair Lady* and Peggy, who had heard me sing with the L.A. Philharmonic, recommended me. Suddenly I had an audition in New York two days after we were scheduled to finish shooting *The Sound of Music*. Although I had been studying the role (Lord knows I knew the songs!) for the upcoming Fresno production with Edward Mulhare, I was having trouble with one particular scene. I decided to go to an expert on the role of Eliza Doolittle: the woman who created her on Broadway.

I boldly knocked on Julie Andrews' trailer door and asked if she could help me with a scene.

"Of course," came her chipper reply from behind the door. "Come in, Marni."

I walked in on Julie with her arms up, and her dresser pulling off all her clothes and getting her changed into her costume for the next scene. I explained that I was to audition for the first New York revival of *My Fair Lady* since the original production (which had run for seven years) had closed. I then told her I was having trouble with one particular scene.

"I'll bet I know what scene you're having trouble with," Julie said as her dresser pulled off her dress. "It's the slipper scene, right?"

I was surprised that she guessed correctly.

"Everyone has trouble with that scene," she said.

The scene in question comes early in Act II after Eliza has triumphed at the ball and Higgins treats her poorly. Eliza is to rant and rail and throw his slippers at him. This is a very emotional and dramatic scene that is a turning point for the character and her relationship with Higgins.

Julie told me that she not only had trouble with that scene, but also with the entire role. She had been only twenty years old when she went into rehearsal for the original production in the fall of 1955 and had very little straight acting experience. In fact, she was doing so poorly that at one point Moss Hart, the director (also the renowned author of such plays as *Once in a Lifetime, You Can't Take It With You, The Man Who Came to Dinner*, and the musical play *Lady in the Dark*), dismissed everyone for the day and worked with her for two solid days. He coached, cajoled, and, as Julie told it, literally "pasted" the role of Eliza Doolittle onto her. After the two days, Julie strode into the rehearsal room with confidence. Moss Hart later commented that Julie "had the kind of British stoicism and strength that makes one wonder how they ever lost India."

All these years later, right then and there in her dressing room, a practically nude Julie Andrews (her dresser was still dressing her for the next shot) coached me on the scene, giving me the kind of inside pointers (probably straight from Moss Hart's mouth) that are invaluable to an actress. I started to feel that I understood better how to play the scene.

"So, Marni, who are you auditioning for?" she asked.

"Jean Dalrymple, the producer, and Biff Liff, the director," I responded.

Julie smiled her dazzling smile. Biff had been Moss Hart's assistant director on the original production and now he would be recreating Hart's staging.

"Okay, Marni, this is what you do," Julie told me with a twinkle. "When you feel it's the right time, either before or after you read for the role, try to give Biff a big hug. He's a teddy bear sort of person and very, very warm. It won't be difficult.

Then, at that very moment, you must quickly steal his tie clip, which he'll have on. Show him right away that you have stolen it and give it back to him and say, 'There, that's for Julie!' He'll laugh and feel good, and both of you will be at ease."

I assumed that this was something Julie used to do during the original 1955 rehearsal period of *My Fair Lady* and decided that what was good enough for Julie was good enough for me.

My role as Sister Sophia in the film of *The Sound of Music* wasn't a very large one, but I was happy to be visible on the screen for once. I finished shooting my entire role in about two weeks, and, most disappointingly, wasn't needed to go to Salzburg to film. Of the nuns, only Peggy Wood, Anna Lee, and Portia Nelson were required in Austria. But, ghost that I was, if I didn't get to go to Austria in body, I did get to go in voice. Along with a large choir, I had prerecorded all the nuns' music, including the "Preludium," "Morning Hymn," and "Alleluia" that followed Julie's title song. So while I was in the U.S., my voice (among others) was ringing out in Salzburg as they shot other "real" nuns in the abbey at their morning prayers.

The Sound of Music opened on March 2, 1965 in New York City and March 10 in L.A. Like the show before it, the reviews were not all good, but little by little word of mouth took hold and, before long, the movie was a blockbuster, breaking attendance records and challenging the grosses of that box office champ, *Gone with the Wind*.

I attended the L.A. premiere at the Fox-Wilshire Theatre and I will never forget it.

"It's her," they screamed. "It's Julie Andrews!"

Since my red hair was almost the same color as Julie's, when I arrived at the premiere and backed out of my car, everyone thought I was the star of the film. But when I turned around to see what all the screaming was about, it abruptly stopped.

"Oh, that's not Julie," several disgruntled fans moaned. "She's nobody!"

Despite being "nobody," I adored the film and felt proud to be a part of such a crowd-pleaser. When the Academy Awards were given out, *The Sound of Music* picked up five of them, including one for Best Picture (not to mention Best Director; Best Scoring of Music, Adaptation, or Treatment; Best Film Editing; and Best Sound). This marked the third time I had been involved with an Oscar-winning film.

Two days after wrapping up my scenes in the movie I was on a plane bound for New York and the *My Fair Lady* audition. I met producer Jean Dalrymple first. Jean was a very ladylike little woman who had been a press agent, an actor's agent, and a theatrical producer who had almost single-handedly created the artistic mecca that was City Center. Conceived in 1943 by Mayor Fiorello H. LaGuardia, City Center was to be New York City's cultural center and, until Lincoln Center usurped its glory, it was. New York City Opera and several ballet companies were housed there, as were many other events (today it is home to *Encores*, which revives musicals in concert format). Dalrymple handled City Center's publicity and helped shape the policy by which it was operated. She also created and directed the Drama and Light Opera companies that would take the stage on West 55th Street. Beginning with Gertrude Lawrence in the play *Susan and God* in 1943, City Center, under Jean Dalrymple's leadership, played host to a battery of revivals of plays, musicals, and operas. In the 1950s and 1960s, it became a tradition for the best of "Broadway-gone-by" to take up residence at City Center for the spring. The original sets and costumes were taken out of storage and dusted off. Frequently the original choreography and staging were re-created as well. The 1963–64 season would include *West Side Story*, *Porgy and Bess*, and *My Fair Lady*. The season before they had done *The King and I*. Looking back I realize that I had sung on the soundtracks of all of them, except for *Porgy and Bess*!

Before I auditioned for Biff Liff, the director, Miss Dalrymple put me at ease by telling me that I had come highly recommended by her dear friend Peggy Wood. Jean then proceeded to tell me that it was really she who had the idea of turning *Pygmalion* into a musical. In 1947, she had a meeting with Gabriel Pascal and George Bernard Shaw and recommended Shaw think about turning his play into a musical theater piece. Shaw became excited and began to outline ideas for how it might be laid out. Ultimately, after both Shaw and Pascal died, Dalrymple was left out of the *My Fair Lady* equation and did not become the producer of the show. She saw this, the first New York revival since the original, as her way of putting her stamp on what she perceived as her original idea.

When I met Biff Liff (he was billed as Samuel, but everyone called him Biff) I did exactly what Julie said. After the obligatory singing audition, I read for him. Then we hugged, I took his tie clip, and told him this was "for Julie." He laughed and we were immediately on good footing. He was indeed a warm teddy bear. Then he told me that he was impressed at how flexible I was in my readings. I was very able to take direction and change my interpretation accordingly. From his demeanor, I knew almost immediately that I had the job. Biff's only concern was that I was about to do another production of the show in Fresno with Edward Mulhare (who had been one of Rex Harrison's replacements in the original Broadway production and was famous for his TV portrayal of the "ghost" in the sitcom *The Ghost and Mrs. Muir*).

"I'm very worried that you're going to learn where all the laugh lines are," Biff warned me. "I am afraid that you're going to just go for the obvious and you will generalize and then everybody there is going to think it's all just wonderful. So be careful, investigate, define, deepen, and stay open to your instincts."

I returned to L.A. and opened *My Fair Lady* #1 at the College of the Sequoias Music Theatre. We ran from May 5 to 9, 1964, and I thought of it as my training ground for the City Center revival in New York. Mulhare was wonderful to work with and Al Checco, a dear friend and, incidentally, the widower of the woman whose death gave me the opportunity to dub Deborah Kerr in *The King and I*, played my father. Small world, huh?

My Fair Lady #2 was to open at City Center on May 20, 1964, which meant we only had ten days to put this mammoth show together. I had heard from Jean Dalrymple that I had been heartily approved of by the composer Fritz Loewe. This was encouraging, especially knowing how picky he was about how his music was sung. Many of the people in the ensemble had been in the original production and, since I had just done the role, I, at least, knew all my lines. I was sure we could pull it off.

The first day of rehearsal was one of the most depressing and discouraging days of my life. This was topped only by the second day of rehearsal.

It started out well. All these *My Fair Lady* mavens were brought together to re-polish this jewel of the American musical theater. The enthusiasm in the room was palpable. After one hour of rehearsal, however, I watched everyone's faces drooping and I heard small voices muttering under their breath. Somehow I knew that I was the cause of it.

I had done exactly what Biff had warned me about. I had frozen my performance in a very surfacelike state. The singing was easy for me, but I was terrible in the book scenes. I seemed to have no idea of the real organic meaning of the lines. I wasn't "there" from my own insides. I was playing it all from the outside and I was miserable. By the end of the second day of rehearsal I was in tears. I knew I wasn't good and so did everyone else. At the end of the second day, after everyone had left, I pulled Biff aside.

"I don't think I can do this, Biff," I moaned. "I think this is going to be terrible. I am not ready for this role." That dear man smiled at me and took my hand in his and spoke in a calm and reassuring tone.

"Look, Marni, I will coach you. I will have my stage manager on you all the time to go over lines and talk it over with you. And I'm available day or night to help you."

I was partially reassured. At least I didn't quit and run home to L.A. When I got to my apartment, which I had leased from my friend Gershon Kingsley (the man who had introduced me to Ernest), I did just what Biff suggested. I called him up and asked if he could possibly come over and help me, as he'd so graciously volunteered to do.

That night Biff and I went over scene after scene after scene, and he talked to me and coached me. He also told me something very interesting. He said, "You know, Marni, it's very funny. This happens to everybody who does this role. This role is not one of those little ingénue roles that you've been used to doing. This is a really intense person who develops from a guttersnipe to a lady."

Biff then told me the same story Julie had told me about how hopeless she was in rehearsal and how Moss Hart instilled confidence in her by telling her that they had hired her for her instincts. Biff now told me he had hired me for the same reason.

"We hired you for your natural instincts, Marni. You've got to use those. You have to be aware of those, because you're exactly right for the role and you can't start putting yourself down. We've got to get on with it. We've only got ten days until we go on."

He explained that, just as Rex Harrison had intimidated Julie in 1955, I was being intimidated by *my* Henry Higgins, Miles Eason. Miles was an accomplished Shakespearean actor who had worked with Noël Coward and assisted director Peter Brook on *The Visit* with the legendary Lunts. He also acted with them. Most recently he had been John Gielgud's assistant director as well. Maybe he *did* intimidate me. Biff told me that Miles had already done everything that he would be doing with his role. It was settled in and pat.

"I guarantee you," Biff said, "that his performance will be exactly the same as it is right now on opening night. I also guarantee you that every day *you* will find new things. You will take a chance, and you'll go for it. You'll realize as you go along whether your choices are right or wrong. Every day you will improve so much that you'll walk away with all the reviews. That is what I guarantee you."

Biff made me feel so much better about myself that night. His warmth and appreciation was something I desperately needed to counterbalance my sudden insecurity. As we worked during the next few days, that warmth of Biff's began spilling over into a mutual attraction. He confided in me that although he was married, he had been very involved with dancer-choreographer Carol Haney (she had danced in the stage and screen versions of *The Pajama Game* and choreographed such musicals as *Funny Girl*), who had suddenly died. In fact, her funeral had been the morning of our first rehearsal. Biff was a man in pain and, because he was married, very conflicted. I have always been very susceptible to men in need and, being sexually attracted to each other, we began a very warm little affair. At first I thought it would be one of those rehearsal "things," but Biff and I carried our warm relationship with us through the years, whether it was sexual or not.

As for my performance in *My Fair Lady*, Biff had been right. Once I got over my self-consciousness and insecurities, with his diligent and caring direction, I began to grow in the role of Eliza Doolittle. Having to really play the whole role (as opposed to just singing it) made me respect Audrey Hepburn even more (if that was possible) than I had before. The film had yet to be released and none of the backlash and Oscar hoopla had yet occurred. But now I really knew how amazingly difficult the role was.

Our wonderful musical director Anton Coppola helped me in the music department. If the name seems familiar, you are right. He was film director Francis Ford Coppola's uncle and he was a delight to work with.

Me as Eliza looking like Julie Andrews imitating Audrey Hepburn. (The Harvard Theatre Collection, The Houghton Library)

Of course as difficult as the acting of Eliza is, I made it twice as hard by insisting that I use my own very long, red hair in the show. Most stars with that many changes of costume, hat, and hairstyle wear wigs, but not me! Consequently, I had to tease my hair and backcomb it to fit under all those different hats and allow for the hairpieces that were necessary to show the complete change in Eliza's appearance to go with her new accent and manners. By the end of an eight-show week (five on the weekend alone!) I didn't even have the energy to brush it out, not to mention that it hurt to even put a comb through it. So I had perpetually ratted hair. I should have cut it off and worn a wig!

My Fair Lady opened at City Center on May 20, 1964 (according to Lerner's lyric "Eliza Doolittle Day") to rapturous reviews for the show and, most delightfully, for me.

As was the tradition in those days, Western Union delivered a multitude of telegrams with opening night wishes. From far-off Salzburg, my sister nuns wished me well:

"Success and love"—Peggy Wood

"Thinking of you know you will a smashing success"—much love, Anna Lee

"Be lovely and 'fair' tonight"—love, Portia [Nelson]

And from the original Eliza:

"Dear Marni luck and love and all my thoughts for a huge success on Eliza Doolittle day"—Julie Andrews

Biff didn't forget me either.

"For your talent I am so proud for making my belief in you come true I am so grateful and my love that you have tonight and always"—Biff

One of my most cherished compliments came in a telegram from a woman who had seen the show during a preview performance the night before. She was a friend of my friend Ray Henderson, someone I had met only once; yet her words spurred me on to give an even better performance.

"Having seen every Liza [*sic*] Doolittle from Mrs. Pat Campbell (for whom the part was written) to Marni Nixon, may I tell you that you can stand up with the best!"—Edna B. Manner

The next morning it was gratifying, after all the hard work on my acting, to read *New York Newsday* proclaim, "Glory be, she can act!" The New York *Herald-Tribune* chimed in, too.

"Miss Nixon made everything seem comfortable and homey the moment she began to sing. Her voice is lovely and shimmering."

The *New York Journal-American* was just as glowing.

"She gives a moving performance in the dramatic scenes. She would be an adornment to any Broadway show in the future."

More important than the reviews, this was the beginning of me being a better actress. Thanks to Biff and this magical show, I was going to acting school

As Eliza Doolittle singing "Show Me" to Russell Nype's Freddie in front of Oliver Smith's "in one" curtain. My Fair Lady, *New York City Center, 1964. (Photo Fred Fehl, Courtesy of Gabriel Pinski)*

every night onstage. Every performance was teaching me how to make my character richer and deeper and more real.

Ernest and the kids (two-year-old Melani was home in L.A. with my mother) came to visit during the run and we had a great time, going to see the New York World's Fair and taking the kids sightseeing in the city. As much fun as I was having, I was also conflicted at the time. I missed my precious Melani terribly, but I longed to be able to stay in New York and pursue a Broadway career. When the time came to leave I was in a constant flood of tears. I have to admit that part of it had to do with leaving Biff. The thought of not seeing or talking to him anymore was painful to the extreme. My first priority, however, was my family and my home in L.A. and, as usual, I would have to adjust and move on. But leaving New York was getting harder and harder and in my bones I knew that someday I would be back to stay.

As always, my life and career were fuller than ever. In the summer of 1964, I starred in a summer stock production of *Oklahoma!* in Milwaukee, Wisconsin, which brought out the entire McEathron clan, all embarrassingly hootin' and hollerin' every time I walked out onstage, no matter what the action.

President of the United Nations, U Thant, and me at the opening of the General Assembly of the U.N. in 1964. Note contralto Marian Anderson, pianist Emanuel Bey, and late-night host Johnny Carson in the background. (From the author's collection)

"Marni! Marni! Marni!" It was if it were a basketball game. They sounded like a bunch of hoodlums, as we used to say.

When the film version of *My Fair Lady* was released in the autumn of 1964, all the attendant publicity gave my career an interesting boost. Besides my usual complement of concerts with such prestigious orchestras as the London Philharmonic, the Los Angeles Philharmonic, the Orange County Symphony, and the San Diego Symphony (these last two conducted by Johnny Green), television began calling. I did guest appearances on *Hollywood Palace*, *The Bell Telephone Hour*, *The Danny Kaye Show* (the year before I was heard on the show when I dubbed comedienne Nancy Walker—you might remember her as Rosie on the Bounty commercials—in a very funny sketch that had her portraying a cleaning women who sang in beautiful operatic tones whenever she held her mop), and *The Ed Sullivan Show*. I also sang on a CBS TV special that emanated from the Hollywood Bowl called *Music from Hollywood*. Mel Tormé and I shared the vocal honors, and such film composing and arranging legends as Alexander Courage, Miklos Rozsa, Alex North, Alfred Newman, John (no longer Johnny!) Green, and David Raksin conducted the 100-piece orchestra.

Mary Poppins opened around the same time as the film version of *My Fair Lady* and, believe it or not, I was in that movie, too. Well, my voice was anyway! During the animated picnic in the park scene, Mary (Julie Andrews) and Bert (Dick Van Dyke) are serenaded by three geese, all of them singing with my voice! I also recorded what turned out to be a surprisingly successful album of songs from the film. Disney wisely had issued not only the original soundtrack featuring Julie and the cast, but two budget-priced children's versions (one with story and one with just songs) featuring Bill Lee (who dubbed Christopher Plummer's voice in *The Sound of Music*) and me as *Mary Poppins*. In one year the record went Gold and remained one of Disney's best sellers of all time.

With all this diversity in my career at this point I thought nothing could surprise me. Yet, if you had told me a year before that I would wind up in Las Vegas singing and dancing with Liberace and giving a series of concerts in Israel that would almost drive me 'round the bend, I'm not sure I would have believed it. Thanks to *My Fair Lady* and my blossoming fame as "the Ghostess with the Mostest," that's exactly what happened.

Chapter Ten
EXERCISING THE GHOST

"I dreamed last night that I made a date with Audrey Hepburn, but Marni Nixon showed up."

SHECKY GREEN, 1964

WHEN LIBERACE DIED ON FEBRUARY 4, 1987, the world lost one of its last great flamboyant showmen. It had been over twenty years since I had appeared with Lee, as his friends knew him, but the memories flooded in on that day.

In late 1964, thanks to all the publicity surrounding the opening of the film version of *My Fair Lady*, I was suddenly a media darling. You couldn't glance at a newspaper without some mention of Audrey Hepburn and/or Marni Nixon. My acting gig in *The Sound of Music* only added fuel to the fire. Everywhere you looked there were references to the *My Fair Lady* dubbing. Al Capp's syndicated comic strip *L'il Abner* contained a joke about a product named a "kigmy" that could be anything you wanted it to be. The strip showed Mammy Yokum saying that "Audrey Hepburn wants one, but she wants one that'll do its own singing!" Stand-up comics used me as fodder for their acts. Columnists dined out on whom I would be dubbing next. It was a first-class media circus. So it was no surprise that Liberace, "Mr. Showmanship" himself, would want to reap the rewards of my sudden celebrity. He was among the first to "exercise" the ghost.

Liberace was born Wladsziu (translated Walter) Valentino Liberace in 1919 in Wisconsin (just like my parents). His Italian father played the French horn and was a member of the Milwaukee Philharmonic Orchestra. His Polish mother played the piano and Liberace's brothers and sisters, George, Angie, and Rudy, were musically gifted as well. Lee was a child prodigy at the piano and was encouraged by the famed Polish pianist Ignace Jan Paderewski, who helped get him a scholarship to the Wisconsin College of Music. He also later advised Lee to drop his first two names and go only by the elegant stage name of Liberace.

Liberace and his trademark candelabra on the piano hit television in 1952 and, in one season, he became TV's first matinee idol. In 1953, he played to a capacity crowd at Carnegie Hall and in the same year made a record-breaking appearance before 16,000 adoring fans at Madison Square Garden (surpassing the previous record set by Paderewski). He packed an overcapacity crowd of 20,000 into the Hollywood Bowl and did it again at Chicago's Soldiers Field with an audience of 110,000. In 1955, he opened at the Las Vegas Riviera Hotel as the highest-paid entertainer in the city's history and had his first starring role in a feature film, *Sincerely Yours* (having previously appeared with Shelley Winters in a supporting role in *South Seas Sinner*).

By 1964, Liberace had become increasingly more flamboyant in his attire and presentation. Each year he presented a new live stage show to the public, and each year the pianos and candelabras grew larger and more jewel encrusted than the last and his costumes became more extravagant. His audiences ate it all up.

Lee always liked to have a girl singer in his shows as well, and took great pride in presenting the latest up-and-coming talent. In 1963, after she had appeared on Broadway in a supporting role in the musical *I Can Get It for You Wholesale*, but before she took the town by storm in *Funny Girl*, a young Barbra Streisand was Lee's opening act in Las Vegas. Lee told me that he had seen Barbra do her act at the Bon Soir nightclub in New York and then again when they were both booked on *The Ed Sullivan Show*. He was impressed with her prodigious talent. Against the wishes of his manager, Liberace booked her to be his opening act at his return, after a five-year absence, to the Riviera Hotel. Barbra, at that time, was the opposite of Liberace in every way. Her act was uncluttered and without frills: just the singer and the song. Her look, thrift shop dresses and antique shoes, was also decidedly antiglamorous. Las Vegas had never seen anything like her, but Lee was sure that his audiences would be hip enough to get how incredibly talented and unique she was.

At the first show, he was proven wrong. Those blue-haired ladies who worshiped Liberace were having none of the eccentric Miss Streisand, and the management of the room told Lee in no uncertain terms to get rid of her. Lee told the management that if she went, so did he. After some heated words, cooler heads prevailed, and Lee promised that he could fix up Barbra's act by the next show. He called a meeting in his suite.

"Here's what we're going to do," he pronounced to his minions. "I'll open the show with a fast number and then I'll introduce Barbra as my discovery. Big hit in New York and all that. Then she'll come on and they gotta like her because I'll set up what type of intense, unusual emotional experience they should expect and make sure they know that she has my seal of approval."

It worked. The management thought that Barbra had changed her act, but that was not the case at all. All she did was enter as Liberace's preapproved package, the gift he recommended. Lee knew that his audiences ate up anything he served. He had that much clout with his fans.

In 1965, it was my turn to be the dish he proffered.

I'm sure that Liberace, with his sense of who was hot at the moment, carefully read all the publicity about "Marni, the Ghost" and thought that I would be an interesting addition to his act. I can remember my audition at his home. Lee had several homes at that time, including one I auditioned at in the San Fernando Valley with a swimming pool in the shape of a piano and a living room full of antiques.

Lee accompanied me at the piano, sometimes reading from the music I had brought, and sometimes just playing by ear. It was apparent early in the process that I had the job, because he immediately started to pick and choose what I would be singing in the show. He had an innate sense of what musical numbers would not only show me off, but would also fit into his "grand scheme" of things. He also generously offered to have his musical director write my orchestrations. This was not only generous, but also unheard of in show business. Usually if one did an act or was part of a variety show, one had to bring his or her personal orchestrations, and this could run into a lot of money. So when Liberace offered to have the charts done for me, I was very impressed by his generosity. And not only did he pay for my orchestrations, but he designed my gown and had it built for me!

Now, there are gowns and there are gowns, but this one was something else. It was constructed so that it would always be in its prime at all times (wonder if they can do that with people?). It not only fit my body well, and was conceived with my particularly flattering colors in mind, but also was designed to be effective in the large auditoriums that we would be playing. The inside of the gown was solid as a rock, with boning and bra built right in. It never moved and it never wore out. The outside, on the other hand, was graceful and sylphlike. It had layers and layers of chiffon, a draped bodice, and a flowing piece that went over one shoulder. This piece could be used in several dramatic ways, draped over the other arm or hanging down the back. The feature that most appealed to me about this dress, however, was that I *never* had to iron it, even though I wore it night after night in performance.

In addition, Lee had built for me the most marvelous expandable trunk of lightweight, but very hard and durable, plastic to house my gowns. It was huge and shaped like a big, black coffin. Everything, including my orchestrations, gowns, and accessories, fit in there and traveled beautifully. Lee even taught me how to pack and roll my gowns and clothes so that nothing ever wrinkled.

Don't think that Lee stopped at the orchestrations, trunk, and the dress either. Oh no, he made sure that his own hairdresser did my hair each night. At his expense! The hairdresser was Lee's lover at the time. Of course, all during his career, Liberace was very much in the closet as far as his public was concerned, but he was nonchalant and open about his sexuality around his friends and people in his inner circle.

Our first gig was at the Phoenix Star Theatre in Arizona in early 1965. Working with Lee was always a lesson in professionalism and showmanship. His audience expected him to look outrageous, but elegant. They expected surprises, too. To this end, he would change his costumes from year to year and, during one show, he would wear at least five different outfits. He always had duplicates of each as well because he would sweat a lot when he worked. We're talking about fully sequined jackets and bejeweled capes made of heavy shiny materials and feathers.

Even after we opened, Lee was always working on making the show better. He would try to perceive the essence of "Marni" at the same time as he perceived the audiences' perception of me. With Lee, there was always room for improvement. I would sometimes stumble or reverse words in my patter or songs. He found that charming, and when he heard something that struck him, Lee would pounce when we reached the wings.

"So, do you remember exactly what you said when I said such and such?"

If I didn't remember, he would remind me. He remembered everything. He was firing on all levels when he was onstage and his wheels were always turning. If something I said was funny, which it frequently, but inadvertently, was, Lee would figure out some way to capitalize on it and multiply the laughs at the next performance. We would hone and refine what we did and said and, in this way, we developed our own little act together, while always maintaining the musical program we had devised earlier.

My part of the act featured songs in my repertoire, including Ernest's arrangement of "Exodus," and the aria "Un Bel Di (One Fine Day)" from *Madame Butterfly*. Lee and I also did a fun parody of *My Fair Lady* in which he taught me how to speak correctly and then danced with me to "I Could Have Danced All Night." It was corny, but his audiences ate it up.

Liberace's audience was primarily made up of middle-aged matrons (as the years went on, their ages increased) and the husbands they dragged along for the ride. Lee seemed to always have a pipeline to the average woman's sentimentality. He had an instinct for what his image was and the smarts to play it for the maximum theatrical effect. He was like a happy teenager who seemed to need "mama's" approval. This quality endeared him to all the potential "mamas" in the audience.

I think that when you live your entire life in front of an audience, as Lee did, you start to lose the sense of your private inner self. Lee began to become his onstage image and denied to the world at large that his private life existed. This led to Lee suing a newspaper that, in 1960, alluded to his homosexuality. He won the case, but when he died all those years later, and his true sexual identity was revealed, the paper sued Lee's estate and won!

With Liberace in 1965. Lee cried when I told him I couldn't tour with him anymore.
(Photo Thomas Buck, Courtesy of Liberace Museum and Foundation for the Performing
and Creative Arts)

Lee told me a great story that always made me think about how our theatrical selves somehow blurred the line between truth and "the act."

When he was young he accompanied the great torch singer Helen Morgan, who was famous for sitting on top of the piano and singing tear-drenched ballads in her lovely soprano voice. In 1927, she had created the role of Julie in *Show Boat* and preserved it in the 1936 film version, but her alcoholism ended her life at a tragically young age. Somewhere near the end of her career, she and Lee were appearing in a nightclub in Milwaukee. Every night she would sit atop the piano and sing her signature song.

"He's just my Bill . . . an ordinary guy."

And every night Lee would cry as he accompanied her. No one said a word to him. After a while, he started to feel embarrassed and made a vow to himself that he would hold back his emotions and tears when doing the act. Finally, one night, he was able to conquer his sentimentality and just play the piano with a poker face. Backstage, after the show, an irate Morgan stormed over to Lee and shouted, "Why did you stop crying? What are you trying to do? Ruin my act?"

I've never forgotten that, and have not been afraid of releasing my own emotionality and crying onstage ever since. It has stood me in good stead. Later on, in the 1990s, I cried real tears on cue for two years in the musical *James Joyce's The Dead*.

After playing several of the big arena theaters in the West, we were booked into Las Vegas. What can I say? It was as strange as playing on the moon.

We played the Versailles Room at the Riviera Hotel. The Riviera is still in existence after over fifty years of taking people's money at the tables and slots. These days it plays host to such production shows as *An Evening at La Cage*, *Crazy Girl*, and *Splash*. These feature half-nude (or wholly nude) girls and as many special effects as they can muster. But back then, Vegas was about stars with a capitol "S" and Liberace was one of their mainstays.

In those days, every big hotel had a top celebrity or two headlining. While we were there in the autumn of 1965, Dean Martin was at the Sands, Mel Tormé was at the Tropicana, Gordon and Sheila MacRae were at the Flamingo, and Connie Francis was at the Sahara. And these were in the main rooms! In the lounges (smaller, more intimate-sized arenas) were trumpeter and bandleader Harry James, singer Della Reese, and comics like Shecky Green. Coming attractions at the time included Tony Bennett, Donald O'Connor, Shari Lewis, Jack Carter, Vicki Carr, Kay Starr, and Allen Sherman.

This was Las Vegas in its "Golden Era"!

We did two shows a night, with a small break in between. Just as he did with Streisand, Lee would introduce me in his grandest fashion to heighten the audience's expectations.

"And now, here she is, the Ghostess with the Mostest, Miss Marni Nixon."

Frequently, after introducing me, Lee would stay onstage and warm up the crowd further. When I was doing a set from *My Fair Lady*, he would say, "Well Eliza, now tell me if you've practiced your vowels lately. Say a few of them for me now." I would improvise a few "rain in Spain"s and Lee would turn to the audience in delight and say, "I think she's got it! I think she's got it!" He would then hand the floor over, leaving me to do my set. Sometimes at the end of my set, he would return and talk to me as myself.

"Well, Marni, how do you feel singing songs and seeing your voice come out of someone else's mouth on the screen?"

I would try to answer truthfully and not employ the usual glib clichés. Sometimes I got caught up in telling too much information and Lee would deftly lead me back on track. He knew that we were entertainers first and, even though he wanted factual and direct answers, he wanted us to sparkle. The audience always loved these impromptu interview sessions. It was after these, when we were backstage, that Lee would make sure I remembered the funny and entertaining things I said, and it was during these times that we decided how to improve on our repartee for the next show. All in all, it was a blast. This improvisational attitude, mixed with figuring out what really worked, put me in good stead later on when I was working with another great entertainer, Victor Borge. It is also helpful to this day. Having the presence of mind to react to any situation onstage is what makes the best performers keep their spontaneity intact.

Between shows I would have to get out of the dressing room because the air conditioning totally dried up my throat. I was not alone in this. Singers all refer to "Vegas throat." The desert heat and the constant air conditioning are detrimental to anyone using his or her voice.

One night in Las Vegas, between shows, Lee called me into his dressing room, took me by the hand, and looked straight into my eyes. He told me that he was going to be doing a series of one-night stands in the South soon and he wanted me to be part of that tour. He told me that it would be much harder work and there wouldn't be the conveniences of Vegas or the bigger theaters we had gotten used to. But he also told me that we would have a wonderful time and that he really wanted me to be part of the show. Then he quoted a staggeringly high figure for my salary that almost knocked me on the floor! I told Lee I would have to think about it and that I had committed to appearances and recitals in various venues that were already booked.

The truth was I had already sort of made up my mind that I wouldn't be performing with Lee anymore. I didn't want to have to turn down other meaningful engagements, such as operas or symphony concerts, that a singer (especially this one) has to do to continue to grow. I also was missing my family and wanted to give them more of my time.

The next day, between shows once again, I bit the bullet and, with my heart pounding, told Lee that I couldn't go on tour with him. Lee looked at me seriously, anchored himself down into his chair, and got ready to negotiate. He wanted to know exactly what contracts I had that would keep me from working with him.

A concert with Stravinsky himself? Yes, he told me, that was wonderful, but how much would I be making?

A small recital at the Redlands Bowl in California? Didn't I realize the size of the audiences that came to see *him*?

"Marni," he cajoled and pleaded, "don't you know that you are one of the few singers I can really depend on? Don't you see how much fun we have and how good we are together onstage?"

Before I could respond, he named a higher figure for my salary!

My head was spinning with compliments and potential monetary rewards, but my aching heart was with my little, adorable, giggly Melani, my growing boy Andy, and my gentle Martha telling me about the new kitten they found and wanted to adopt. The more I said no, the more Lee raised the stakes. I told him I was a mommy first and couldn't just leave the kids for long periods anymore. Ernest was there at home to help out, but my spirits were fading here in this glitzy place. Lee smiled, said he understood, and upped my price again. After all the thrusting and parrying were done, I paused, took a deep breath, and mumbled (an unusual occurrence for me) a final "No."

Liberace sat back in his chair, wiped his brow, and took a long look at me. Then he burst into tears!

Sentimental softy that I am, I began blubbering as well. I felt terrible. Here was this man who was so generous and loving toward me and I had to turn him down. I couldn't look him in the face as he wept. He was like a little boy, used to getting his way, and I had denied him. Now that he was rebuffed, he didn't know what to do. I also wasn't used to saying no to anyone, so I understood completely. It hurt me to have to hurt him. We were like two lost souls weeping in a glamorous Las Vegas dressing room. Still, the decision had been made and the die was cast.

In the remaining few performances we did together, our onstage relationship didn't outwardly change at all, but I felt that offstage Lee was hurt and my heart ached a little, too.

After our last show, I remember seeing Lee's dresser, as usual, helping him into a beautiful smoking jacket. Then he brought out the champagne to serve to the waiting hoards of autograph seekers. As he did every other night, he sat for over two hours, signing personalized autographs for his fans and asking them how they liked the show. One little old gray-haired lady (she must have been over seventy to Lee's forty-six) came up to him and said, "Oh Mr. Liberace, I

used to love you when I was a little girl." Lee winked at me, making me feel close
to him again with that one gesture, and flashed his dazzling smile at the lady.

"Of course you did," he giggled. "Thank you so much!"

He was not only "Mr. Showmanship," he was a gentleman to the core.

Going from Liberace to Israel might seem a big leap, but both required massive amounts of patience, tons of professionalism, a hell of a lot of improvising
(in many ways), and a large dose of my famous "iron nerves."

Israel in 1965 was as exotic and remote a place as can be. I always thought
of it as a Middle Eastern "Wild West." The population in the metropolitan
areas of Tel Aviv was 882,000; in 2005 it was 2.6 million.

When the idea was broached to me about doing a one-woman concert tour
of Israel, I was immediately excited by the prospects, but I had no idea what
would lie in store.

A trip to Venus might have been better planned.

I left for my Israeli adventure on May 3, 1965. This was after a couple of my
Liberace bookings (but previous to our Las Vegas outing) and before the summer stock tryout of what I had hoped would be a brand new Broadway musical
for me to star in. The musical (*The Genius Farm*) turned out to need too much
work to ever succeed on Broadway and died quietly on the road. I liked to think
that my experience in Israel had prepared me for the out-of-town traumas of
that dying Broadway show. But I am ahead of myself. Where did it all begin?

It began in 1960 when Ernest was in Israel researching and writing indigenous
Israeli music for his score of *Exodus*. While he was there he met a Romanian impresario named John Avramesco. Well, to tell the truth, he wasn't an impresario
then (I think he was a cameraman!), but a few years later, when he read the 1964
article in *Time* magazine about me, he decided to become one. In fact, I was to be
his first production!

Avramesco sent a letter to Ernest saying that he wanted to present me in
concert in Israel. We offhandedly thought this was a wonderful idea, never realizing that Avramesco would be pulling that age-old producer's ploy: get the
go ahead from the artist (me) and then approach the orchestras and presenters
in Israel, saying that he had "the great" Marni Nixon under contract!

The "Romanian Avramesco Game" was on.

The preproduction of the tour was difficult. International phone service
then was not what it is today (not to mention the high rates and time differences, such as ten hours from California to Israel), so for the most part everything was arranged via mail and, of course, that took forever, not to mention
that the letters would frequently get lost in transit. My manager was advising
me about the monetary details, as well as trying to make sure that I got paid in

American money, and that I could take the money out of the country. Then came the question of the orchestrations. I had some orchestrations, but not enough to make up the whole program. As I mentioned earlier, getting these charts made could run into a fortune, so I was glad when, during one of our rare telephone conversations, Avramesco told me not to worry about them.

"We have orchestrators here in Israel," he boomed in his Israeli-tinged Romanian. "We can orchestrate anything."

Avramesco then engaged Tibor Cozma, a French conductor who lived in Israel, to be my musical director. It turned out that Cozma was at least thirty years behind on American music and had never even heard of *My Fair Lady*. I would send my music to Avramesco to get it orchestrated and half the time it wouldn't arrive or it would be sent back to me marked "Address unknown." I should have heeded the warning signs, but as usual I optimistically and doggedly trudged through the hard times. Then, one day in L.A., when my date of departure was drawing near, I met a writer named Dan Almagore, who was just beginning to collaborate with Ernest on the musical *I'm Solomon*.

Dan also wrote articles for the *Maariv*, the only English-language newspaper in Israel. (There were five Romanian newspapers in Israel at that time. In Israel they liked to say that the Romanians were so aggressive that they were going to take over the country!) After I told Dan I was going there to do concerts, he said, "We've *got* to talk!"

"Look," he warned me, "you've got to realize that at this point there is only one spotlight that exists in Israel."

"What!" I exclaimed. I was getting nervous now.

"The person who owns the spotlight is a man by the name of Giora Godik, and he's the producer of all the musicals in Israel. I am the translator for most of them, so I know what goes on there."

Then he asked me where I was going to do my show. At what theaters? I had no idea. I was used to just being steered in the right direction, pointed to the stage, and told to sing. As I stood there with my mouth open, Dan told me there *are* no theaters in Israel, except for movie theaters! Of course there was the Israeli Philharmonic, which had its own auditorium, but the orchestra booked that exclusively and the Jerusalem Philharmonic had certain spaces that they used. But actual theaters to house my one-woman show were as scarce in Israel as bacon!

"Where is this guy going to present you?" Dan fruitlessly asked. "At what time of day? Do you realize all the pianos have been sitting out in the desert for at least five years? They are wildly out of tune. As for instrumentalists, the good ones are playing with the Israeli Philharmonic. The rest are would-bes, has-beens, and rejects. And you must remember," he went on, " they don't necessarily all speak the same language, because they come from Morocco, Russia, Bulgaria, Romania, Germany, all over. It's a regular Tower of Babel."

By now my mouth was open wide and my eyes were glazed over from all the negative information he imparted. Dan must have seen the panic in my face, because he then offered me a lifeline.

"Listen," he sweetly offered, "I'm going to give you the translation that I made of *My Fair Lady*, and I'm going to teach you how to sing it in Hebrew, because it will be a very interesting little thing for you to do. They'll love it."

He was right, of course. So I learned both "I Could Have Danced All Night" and "Wouldn't It Be Loverly?" in Hebrew, though not without some problems. Dan had found that since there are no Hebrew dialects, there was no real way to show the progression from Cockney to High English. The only way to emphasize the dramatic difference was to choose words that were guttural for the former and use a more refined sound for the latter.

Besides the gift of the translations, Dan gave me the gift of Shraga Friedman.

At that time Shraga Friedman was the leading actor with the Habima State Theater (now Israel's National Theatre) in Tel Aviv. Dan wrote to Shraga and told him to expect to hear from me and to please look out for me once I arrived in Israel.

Armed with Shraga's phone number, my Hebrew-translated *My Fair Lady* songs, and plenty of chutzpah, I boarded the plane to "the Middle East Wild West" on May 3, 1965. Many hours and martinis later, I arrived in a jet-lagged and disoriented state at the Dan Hotel in Tel Aviv. I immediately tried to contact Shraga Friedman and, true to what I would discover about Israel's sense of time, four days later he showed up . . . unannounced! When the front desk called to tell me that someone was downstairs for me, I hurried to the lobby to find a very tall, roundish, balding, rather amusing-looking man. Shraga Friedman! He introduced himself and bowed to me, speaking in one of the most apologetic and subservient tones imaginable. Not to mention the thickest Israeli accent I had ever heard.

"Miss Nixon, please forgeev me. I deed not know who you ver. But I now read Almagore's letter. Ve are young country."

How many times would I hear that during my visit?

"Ve don't know vat ve are doing," he continued. "You are grrrrreat arrrrteeest. I'm so sorry I vas not here for you. I vill do everytheeeeng to help you!"

He could not have been sweeter and, at last, I thought my troubles were over. On the contrary, his questions and information revealed that they were just beginning. (Now that you know how he spoke, forgive me if I quote him without the accent.)

"When is your opening night?" he asked.

"Saturday night at six o'clock."

In Tel Aviv? At the Habima? He was mortified.

"Shabbat!" he exclaimed incredulously. "Theaters can't even open at six o'clock on the Sabbath! You have to wait till after sundown."

You would think I would have known that. Or that my impresario would!

"When are you going to set up the show? How are you going to do it during the Sabbath before 6:00 P.M. if your show is scheduled to begin at 6:00 P.M.?"

I had no answers to these questions. This was the producer's responsibility. Avramesco strikes again! Is it any wonder I took to calling him "Dracula"?

"You're going to have musicians? Who is this Avramesco and where is he *getting* the musicians?"

I told him, with some fear and trepidation in my voice, that I thought they had a pick-up orchestra.

"Well, how are they going to hold the music?"

This question seemed easy to answer.

"On bandstands."

"Where is he going to get bandstands?"

Now I was starting to really get the gist of this country, which was so new it didn't even have bandstands. More than that, however, I began to realize that my so-called impresario, whom I *still* hadn't met in person, didn't know what he was doing. When I finally contacted him and asked about the bandstands, he told me he would have them built. When the newly constructed, very heavy, wooden music stands arrived, we found that they had a lip measuring about a quarter of an inch. The music for the entire show was at least two inches thick, which meant that the scores would just fall off the stands. Then there was the question of how these sturdy, heavy stands were to be transported from one venue to the next, as we had appearances scheduled in many outlying towns like Haifa, Jerusalem, Ramatgan, etc.

One of my "perks" on this trip was a Sabra (meaning Israeli-born) secretary who was hired to help me, not only with secretarial duties, but also with ordering my food, arranging my travel details, and procuring my props. Unfortunately, the poor thing was overly sensitive and was very little help at all! Every time I asked her to do something for me, she would either have a headache or a full-blown nervous breakdown (and those were *my* domain!), leaving me to do everything I had asked her to. Her greatest asset was her command of several useful languages and the fact that she could put on a thick British accent and get service. The Israelis were so used to having been under British rule that they responded more quickly if they thought the orders were coming from someone from England.

So, let's recap.

In a nutshell I had a one-woman show opening on the Sabbath, without any time to rehearse in the space, with questionable musicians (who might not even show up) whose music was going to fall off their stands as I sang. Oh yes, and a Sabra secretary who cried every time anything went wrong. I was sunk. That is, until the great and glorious Shraga Friedman came to my rescue. He said that he would speak to the powers that be. He said he would talk with the rabbi and see if I could get into the space earlier. He said he would even talk to God if he had to. In Israel, Shraga said, you have to know the right people and how to scream the loudest. And in what language! Obviously, he did. Then I started to worry about the lack of publicity. After all, who knew Marni Nixon in Israel? And even if they came, how could I win them over in a language that they didn't all understand completely?

"Never mind," he soothed. "I'll fix it. I will introduce you. I will record an introduction, and before every performance they will play the recording and since everyone knows my name, and I will be speaking in Hebrew, they will then know and love you."

Wow! He thought exactly like Liberace!

Fortunately, Shraga's talks with God and the other powers-that-be proved fruitful. We actually got to rehearse and, although the musicians really didn't know how to play musical theater songs or standards, we eventually got it together. We even got the one spotlight in Israel focused on me. Even if "Dracula" himself was running it. Of course the reason Dracula was running it was that the only spotlight operator in all of Israel told us that he was only available for our rehearsals, not the performance!

Saturday night came and, thanks to Shraga, my concert was about to start. On time! Well, the newly revised but "advertised" time, anyway. Apparently this was quite a feat, as no concerts of this sort *ever* started in Israel on time. Shraga had made the promised tape and the soundman played it. His voice came over the sound system and, after introducing me, in perfect Hebrew, announced, "And now, Marni Nixon!" But instead of *my* entrance at this debut performance, to the delight and amusement of the audience, out came Shraga Friedman in his adorable hangdog comedic mode. Then this dear man described who I was, what I had done, and what I would be doing. Since he spoke in Hebrew, I never did know exactly what he said, but, if reactions are any indication, he beautifully set me up for the audience. When he was finished and I entered, it was as if I were singing to an audience of my best friends.

The opening night crowd was enthusiastic, but polite, too. Cozma, my conductor, was not. He somehow thought that whenever I was talking to the audience, setting up a brief descriptive introduction for the next number, and he wasn't waving his arms, it was a good time to give loud verbal notes and tell some jokes to the orchestra, behind my back, but in full view of the audience! It was as if we were competing for attention. This wasn't exactly kosher; neither did it make for smooth transitions, facilitate our cues, nor keep up the proper pacing of the show. Still, with all the turmoil, I got through the evening.

Well, my old *West Side Story/The Sound of Music* comrade, Saul Chaplin, always said I had iron nerves! At the end, the audience was on its feet and cheering. And there among the standing, applauding throng was Chaim Topol, whose full name means "Tree of Life."

Known today only by his last name, Topol was then the leading actor at the Chamber Theatre in Tel Aviv. This was two years before he took the West End by storm as Tevya in the original London cast of *Fiddler on the Roof*. It was also five years before he became an international star playing the same role in the hit film version of the show. He was even nominated for the Oscar for his performance. Despite his fame as Tevya, Topol was a vital young man. He just preferred to play roles much older the he actually was.

Back then, however, he was primarily an Israeli celebrity, albeit one with great influence. Wanting me to get only the best impression of his beloved land of "milk and honey," Chaim took me under his wing and, like Shraga Friedman, tried to counterbalance the trouble that he knew lay ahead for me. He took to picking me up after my concerts in his Volkswagen "bug" with the sunroof on top. We would all squeeze in: Chaim, his wife, his manager Avraham Deshe (everyone called him "Pashanel"), a reporter from the *Maariv* newspaper, and me. We would then drive to one of his friends' homes, where I would be stuffed with delicious kosher food as Chaim, with his impish toothy grin, sang Hassidim songs for me to imitate. All this was designed to get my mind off the various things that went wrong each night, such as the music falling off the stands, the bad playing, the talkative conductor who had a penchant for kissing me up and down the arm. . . .

And the strikes.

In 1965 Israel, the musicians had no union. The best of them were picked to play under Zubin Mehta with the Israeli Philharmonic or with the Jerusalem Philharmonic under Sergiu Commissiona. Needless to say, *my* musicians were the leftovers who couldn't get into the symphonies. Some were folk musicians from other countries and others were rejects from rock bands. In any case, they had very little clout and didn't make too much money. Now, however, since they were playing for a "grrrrrreat arteeeeeest" from the U.S., who was also getting some great publicity from the *Maariv* (thanks to Dan Almagore, I'm sure), they took this opportunity to go on strike! They assumed that their cause would at last be heard.

But like everything else in Israel, even the strike wasn't well organized.

My appearances on subsequent nights would begin and, after the second or third song, several musicians would just get up and walk off the stage, then some more, until there was just a skeleton band sawing and blowing away. Sometimes I would look back and see one lone pianist and the conductor waving his arms at empty chairs and talking to himself in French. As for me, I just kept right on singing. Backstage, during the intermission, the violin section would come up to me and get on their knees.

"Forgeeeve us," they would weep. "Ve are young country and you arrrre a grrrrrreat arteeeeist."

Then they would return for the second half and play as if nothing had occurred. This happened time after time. The reporter from the *Maariv* was a friend of Topol's and wrote this all up, hoping to get a union started. I hope they were finally successful.

Topol advised me that whenever the orchestra got too sparse, I should learn and sing a Hassidim song he had sung in a very popular Israeli film called *Sallah Shabatti*. It could be sung a cappella (without accompaniment) and the audience, who all knew it by heart, would sing along. So when the stage would be devoid of musicians, I would turn to the audience and tell them my nickname was "Shicksie Nixie" and I had learned this song from my pal Chaim Topol. They all knew that a "shiksa" was a non-Jewish woman and they found my nickname very amusing. Then I would start tapping out the rhythm on my hand and on the empty music stands and sing "Alla yodea huzzzz." Then I would shake my boobs and shoulders like an Arabian Bob Fosse dancer. The audience would answer in rhythm and shake their shoulders as well. We'd all start clapping and sing the rest of the song together. Afterward, they would scream and yell in delight and amazement.

Chaim, my "Tree of Life," had saved the day. Even the musicians in the wings were entranced, and I was saving my show. In fact, this addition enhanced all my future performances.

Throughout the four weeks, from Tel Aviv to Haifa to Jerusalem, every concert I gave started at least an hour late because the auditoriums were being used either as cinemas or lecture halls beforehand. The "lighting" was the simple result of whatever switch turned on a single ceiling light that lit the entire stage area and sometimes the whole auditorium. Primitive, to say the least. Traveling from place to place was an ordeal and, since my "impresario" (Dracula) didn't drive, it was left to me to navigate from the backseat of the hodgepodge of a car put together from various used parts: a Studebaker chassis mixed with Ford wheels and a GM motor. Somehow, even without knowing enough Hebrew to read the maps, I managed.

After a while, I started to understand that this *was* "a young country" and I began to relax and even enjoy the chaos. I noticed and was impressed with the warmth of the people of this young state who, like me, were totally improvising all the time. The audiences (I never quite knew where they came from. There was no publicity! Were they all Romanian relatives of Dracula?) came to be entertained, and loved whatever I did.

Although I traveled around a lot, I kept a home base at the Dan Hotel in Tel Aviv. I guess I shouldn't have been surprised at all when, one day, after two nights away, I returned to my room to find the hotel had pushed my things into one corner and rented out my room until I returned!

"Ve are young country! Forgeeeve us!"

Finally, after four weeks of this insanity, it was time for me to go home. I desperately missed my kids and, although it had been a great adventure, I was, frankly, thrilled to leave. But first I needed to be paid. And the hotel wanted *their* money, which was to be paid by the producer. Dracula strikes again! His need to suck the blood from all involved was becoming more and more apparent. This time, he just disappeared!

Off I trudged to a lawyer with the biblical name of Solomon. What I couldn't figure out was whether he was a wise man or a wise guy. Instead of helping me, Mr. Solomon decided that a naïve American woman was just the sort of easy mark he was looking for. As I tried to tell him the facts (I hadn't been paid, the hotel hadn't been paid, my costumes were missing, my music—including mountains of expensive and priceless orchestrations—was gone) Solomon was trying to put his hands all over me. Finally I gave up on him and called one of my saviors, Chaim Topol, telling him that I was having my twentieth and final nervous breakdown. I had to fly out of Israel on June 11 for a concert in London, by hook or by crook. And, if nothing else, I, at least, had to have my music and costumes.

Topol calmed me down and went into action. He called the conductor who, since he hadn't been paid either, was holding my music ransom. Topol apparently twisted the conductor's arm (or threatened him) and I got my music back (he somehow got my costumes back as well), but now I had to actually get out of the hotel, which, of course, had not been paid for! We had to escape with the huge trunk resembling a coffin that Liberace had given to me.

"Chaim, how am I going to get out of here? I have a flight to catch in an hour."

Topol was calm as a kosher cucumber. He carried my coffinlike trunk down the back stairs of the Dan Hotel and, miracle of miracles, no one questioned him. He was Chaim Topol, after all! Israel's finest actor! So out we went to his waiting Volkswagen beetle and drove off with my black Liberace coffin sticking out of the sunroof top and me crouching down, like two thieves in the night, to the airport.

"Look," Topol said as we approached the terminal, "I don't want to be seen, because everybody knows me, but I'm going to stand in a corner and make sure you're okay."

With renewed vigor, I went to the ticket counter to check in and the man at the counter went through my visa and passport.

"Oh, Miss Nixon, you stayed one day over your visa. We have to put you in jail."
Jail?!?

I was flabbergasted! I looked around for Topol, but he had hidden himself in the shadows so well, I couldn't find him. I thought, what a fitting end to a "triumphant" concert tour. Go to jail and do not collect $200! Who knew I was playing Israeli Monopoly! I visualized myself slaving away in Kibbutz-like penitentiary, never again to see my children or home. I began to cry.

Then suddenly a young man who had apparently seen my show heard my name and came rushing out of a back room to the official at the desk.

"But she is Miss Nixon," he loudly shouted at the man at the desk. "She is a grrrrreat arteeeest! Let her go!"

At which point the man behind the desk off-handedly said, "Oh, okay." Then he stamped my visa and papers and upgraded me to first class.

The Israeli rule of thumb: he who shouts loudest wins!

Before I could even say good-bye and thanks to Topol, I was on my way to London where, on June 14, 1965, I performed at Wigmore Hall. This was thanks to my good, dear, and devoted friend Gerard Schurmann (he had helped Ernest orchestrate the *Exodus* film score), who picked me up at Heathrow, scraped me into his car, and watched over me while I cried for three days straight before I could even explain what I was crying about. His devotion helped me to recover from my Israeli ordeal!

Did I ever get paid, you might ask?

Not only did I *not* get paid, but when Ernest and I contemplated traveling to Israel a couple of years later, I was informed that, according to my contract with Dracula, I, myself, was liable for the hotel charges and the salaries of the conductor and the musicians. If I stepped foot in Israel, I would *really* have been put into jail that time.

Needless to say, we vacationed elsewhere that year.

As Stephen Sondheim so aptly wrote about the joys of touring in his 1973 musical *A Little Night Music*:

"Heigh ho, the Glamorous Life!"

I returned to L.A., via New York, on June 17, 1965. My exotic "Middle Eastern Adventure" proved great fodder for anecdotes, but more than that, the hardships and mishaps steeled me for the personal upheavals that were about to accompany the rest of the turbulent decade.

America in the mid to late 1960s was a chaotic and confused place, with every day bringing news of unfathomable disaster and inevitable, but shocking change. As the war in Vietnam escalated and assassins felled our political and spiritual leaders, the country became more and more divided. In retrospect, my personal life reflected America at that time.

Everything around and within me was changing so quickly and my family, like the country, was also about to be divided.

Chapter Eleven

SONGS OF LOVE AND PARTING

"To life . . . and the only other reality, death."

INGMAR BERGMAN, *SMILES OF A SUMMER NIGHT*

IT HAD BEEN SIXTEEN YEARS since I first met Ernest's sister, Gerti (full name Gerta Goldner), in New York City. It was 1950, I had just married her brother, Ernest, and I had been on my way to my first summer at Tanglewood. Now, in the autumn of 1966, after climbing six flights of stairs and knocking incessantly on her door, she was nowhere to be found.

I had come to New York to appear as a guest on the *Today Show* and to record my voice for a fairly new invention called the Moog synthesizer.

In 1963 Robert Moog, who for ten years had built and manufactured the Theremin (a unique instrument that was the predecessor to the synthesizer; it's played by waving one's hands near two metal antennas—one for pitch and the other for volume), became interested in building an instrument capable of synthesizing sounds from other sources. To this end, in 1964 he began to manufacture electronic music synthesizers, known as Moog synthesizers. After Walter (later Wendy after a sex change operation in the late 1960s) Carlos released a hit album, *Switched on Bach*, entirely recorded using Moog synthesizers, the instrument made the leap from the avant-garde into commercial pop music. The Beatles bought one, as did Mick Jagger.

My friend Gershon Kingsley was always interested in the avant-garde and, after two years in the studio, released an album called *The In Sound from Way Out!*, using the Moog synthesizer. The album was a success and Gershon, wanting to exploit the Moog even further, asked me to contribute my pure singing voice to the cause. I agreed to come into a studio and record every pitch in my vocal range, tone by tone, one half step at a time. Later on, Gershon had an international hit song (one of the few instrumentals of the 1970s to break the Top 20 in the U.S. and elsewhere) on the Moog called "Popcorn."

After a grueling morning of singing pitches on every possible vowel, I was looking forward to being with Gerti, so I was distressed to not find her at home when we had carefully planned the day before to meet. After calling the

Hotel Salisbury, where I was staying, to find out if Gerti had called (she hadn't), I headed back to the hotel. There, to my surprise, was Gerti waiting for me in my hotel room. She grabbed my hand firmly and spoke.

"Marni," she said in her gentle Viennese way, "there's been a strange murder and I didn't do it."

I had no idea what she was talking about but, before I could speak, she went on.

"You're the only one I can trust, and I'm putting myself into your hands to help me. Everyone on the street is looking at me with an accusation in their eyes. But I swear to you I didn't do it."

I felt the hair on the back of my neck stand on end and my heart was beating a mile a minute. I knew that I had to carefully choose my words. To be able to help her at all, I had to make Gerti feel that I accepted and believed every word she said.

"Now, Gerti," I said, trying to unloosen her grip on my hands, "who was murdered? And how do you know about it? Shouldn't we just go to the police and you can explain it to them?"

"No!" she shrieked. "They would just accuse me again."

I had known that Gerti had suffered from psychiatric problems before and I was intuitive enough to realize that something was very wrong here, so I called Ernest in L.A. and had them speak to each other. When Gerti gave the phone back to me, Ernest was very concerned. He told me he thought she was in real psychological trouble and that he was going to try to reach her psychiatrist in New York. In the meantime, he gave me the name and number of another psychiatrist and told me to call the doctor and then call him back in L.A.

I needed to keep Gerti talking. We had tickets for a matinee and neither of us had had lunch yet. Oddly enough, as we chatted over lunch Gerti seemed perfectly normal, except that the stories she was telling me all seemed a little off. Gerti was a teacher, and she told me about one of her students who had been absent from class for a while.

"When she returned," Gerti calmly told me. "It was not the same girl. She was someone else."

Gerti had reported the strange body switching to the parents of the girl and to the principal, resulting in the principal putting Gerti on "leave" from her teaching position.

Sitting in the restaurant, looking at this intelligent, lonely woman, I was struck by the softness of her Mittle-European Viennese spirit and her whipped cream skin, heavy lips, and nervous hands. Although we had brought her out to L.A. to visit the kids at one point, and she seemed to have a good time, it was always clear to me that she was very lonely. Looking into her eyes as she spoke, I felt such a kinship with her, and yet we were direct opposites. Was this why I was so attracted to her angst and sorrow? Was it because my nature was so opposite? Ernest had always told me that my straightforward, spontaneous American qualities were traits he loved in me and rather depended upon. I was proud to accept that, but now I was only aware of this terrible responsibility. I had to play the role of a smart, strong, solid person. As I watched her trying to keep it together, I began to cry. She blinked sweetly and looked at me with her huge, hazel eyes, so like Ernest's.

"What's wrong, Marni? Are you all right? Did I say something to upset you?"

It was as if another person, a different Gerti who lived deep inside her, was asking me the questions.

I couldn't tell her I was worried about her, but I did suggest we should just forget about the theater tickets and go back to my hotel. I was hoping that a slow and pensive walk back to the hotel would inspire some immediate solution and I could find out what was really troubling Gerti.

When we finally got back to my hotel it was late afternoon and I still had no idea about how to deal with her. I knew that I had to call Ernest and see if he had contacted Gerti's doctor. I also knew that I should call the other psychiatrist if Ernest failed in finding Gerti's. I couldn't do any of this in front of Gerti.

I had been invited to a party at my friends Mike and Katia Kermoyan's home later that afternoon and I suddenly realized that if I could leave Gerti at the hotel for a little while I could make the phone calls at Mike's apartment and know better how to deal with her.

"You get undressed here in my safe hotel room," I carefully told Gerti, like a mother to a child. "Get yourself into a nice bubble bath and soak. Just relax away."

She wanted her typewriter and I said that I would go and get it. In the meantime, I told her to take the hotel notepaper and start to write down everything she could remember about the murder.

Gerti seemed to agree with this course of action. I then told her I would be going to my friend Mike's party to explain that I couldn't stay long because she was visiting.

"If you need me at *any* moment," I whispered as I gave her the telephone number of where she could reach me, "you call and I'll get into a cab and I'll be back in a few minutes. Don't worry, we'll get this sorted out."

This seemed to put her at ease and as I watched her undress and get into the tub, I said good-bye and raced up to the Kermoyans' apartment. I said a quick hello and asked for a quiet place to make some phone calls. As the party went on in the living room, I went into their bedroom and called Ernest in L.A. to fill him in. He told me that he was having difficulty locating Gerti's regular psychiatrist, and suggested I call the other doctor that he knew. After hanging up

Ernest's sister, Gerti Goldner.

with Ernest, I quickly phoned the psychiatrist, and after I filled him in on Gerti's odd behavior, he asked me a strange question.

"Are you afraid?"

I hadn't really thought about it, but I was upset and concerned.

"She sounds like she is having a schizophrenic-paranoia attack," he calmly told me. He told me I was handling it very well, that keeping her level-headed, talking, and engaged was just the right thing to do. He also told me that since Gerti was under the care of another doctor, he couldn't ethically take over her treatment, but that he would be there in case of a dire emergency. After we hung up, I started to realize that this might *be* a dire emergency. The doctor was right. I *was* afraid. I called Ernest back who informed me that he had yet to get in touch with Gerti's regular psychiatrist, but he had booked babysitters and was flying to New York as soon as he could get a flight out.

Putting the phone down, I started to cry. My dear friends Mike and Katia were trying to calm me down and get me to eat something. By this time, all the party guests were concerned as well. Then the phone rang. It was Gerti.

"Marni," she said in a strangely different and childlike voice, "can you come back right away? I think I've solved the mystery."

Her voice was calm. Too calm. It filled me with an unknown dread that made my heart race a mile a minute. I evenly told her that I would be there in ten minutes.

I raced from the cab into the hotel and willed the elevator to move faster. When I got to the door it was unlocked. I pushed it open and there, across the room, stood Gerti fully clothed with her raincoat on. She held her purse and gloves in her hand.

She was in front of an open window.

Gerti gazed at me sweetly, with those ancient hazel eyes, as if to make sure that it was me who entered the room.

Then, without a word, she turned and jumped out of the window.

The thud of her landing on the pavement below was the most horrible sound I had ever heard. Thud. Then silence. I ran to the window and grabbed the curtains waving there. Waving, as if they were saying good-bye. I had to fight the impulse to jump after her, to try to save her. My brain knew it was too late, but my heart wanted to follow her out of the window to somehow stop her.

As I stood there with one hand on the drapes and the other covering my mouth, somewhere, from a distant place, I could hear my own screaming. I should have been there. I should never have left her alone. I should have physically held her back. I should have. I should have. My brain was flooded with guilt, guilt, guilt. From outside of my body, I watched my shaking hands trying to muffle my sobs and wails. Somehow I managed to call the front desk and tell them what had happened. They came up with detectives who ran to the open window to look down at Gerti. It was then that I suddenly allowed myself to hope. Maybe she was alive! But no, she landed six flights down on the roof of the second floor. That dreadful thud followed by silence. I looked out the window and saw a silent figure lying there, like the letter S.

The detectives had to wake up some poor, startled lady on the second floor in order to crawl through her window and bring Gerti's body back into the building and out to a waiting ambulance. As this was happening below, I noticed that the bed was freshly made and lying there on the pillow was a torn piece of hotel stationery.

Gerti had left a note.

"Dear Marni, I cannot solve this mystery. Give me a nice grave."

I called Ernest and, thankfully, caught him before he left for the airport. He was devastated. He told me that Gerti's psychiatrist still hadn't called back. He told me to sit tight and that he would be with me in the morning. Then I called the doctor I had been talking to. Although it was too late for Gerti, somehow, through all the fog and haze, I knew it was time to deal with myself. After I blurted out what had happened, his tone changed from one of concern to a more forceful and immediate sound.

"Now, Marni, did you want to go out after her to try to save her?" He seemed to know all my feelings. "Did you feel guilty about not doing something that you thought in retrospect you should have done to save her?"

"Don't feel guilty!" he ordered. "There is nothing more you could have done. If you had gotten to her physically to save her, she would have tried to take you with her. Even if you had restrained her and had her put into a straightjacket, eventually she would have escaped and succeeded in her mission. She wanted and needed to go to another place."

Another place. No wonder she had gotten into her clothes and coat. She was going to another place.

The doctor went on talking to me. He told me that her two halves were at war with each other and that the "murder" she was speaking about was the murder of herself. One half of her had killed the other. He also said that she must have loved me very much to have entrusted herself in my care. He begged me not to be alone for a while. He knew without even seeing me that I was unraveling. He knew it before I did. What an amazing man!

By this time Mike Kermoyan had arrived, along with my publicist and good friend Gary Stevens. I didn't remember calling either of them, but I guess I must have. In my "always a professional" mode, I must have called Gary to cancel my *Today Show* appearance.

Mike asked me to come back to his apartment with him. I told him that I would be fine in the hotel and that Ernest would be arriving in the morning. Gary took charge and, echoing the doctor on the phone, told me that under no circumstance was I to be alone. I was to stay with him in his apartment where he could keep an eye on me. I spent the night in Gary's den weeping. Yet I felt safe knowing he was just a room away. How blessed I always have been to be surrounded by friends.

Ernest arrived the next day, and as soon as we saw each other we had a simultaneous urge to make passionate love. The impulse was incredibly powerful and we gave into it thoroughly. Looking back, I guess the impulse was "life and survival" taking over in our subconscious. Somewhere underneath I was feeling guilty about this ravenous desire happening at this seemingly morbid time. But it was just life expressing itself loud and clear.

As Ernest and his ex-wife, Andree Golbin, who had stayed friends with Gerti all these years, sorted through Gerti's papers, they found writings, dream material, and notes from her sessions with her doctor.

As they looked through the papers, I had only feelings of contempt for her psychiatrist, who had not responded to her cries of help. Gerti had told me she had called him and he told her it was Saturday and that he couldn't see her. Couldn't he tell she was in trouble? Had she perhaps cried wolf once too often?

As Ernest and Andree discovered more and more about Gerti's deteriorating condition, I flashed back to 1950 and the first time I met Gerti. It was the first time I had ever been in New York and I was terrified. I remembered sleeping on her couch on that first night and experiencing the terror of a New York thunderstorm in the summer. The echoing sounds of the thunder bouncing off the buildings just outside the sixth-story window kept me up all night. Six flights up. Exactly the same amount of stories from which Gerti's poor body fell.

I don't think Gerti, the daughter of an agnostic Viennese Jew and a Protestant Czech, believed in heaven. But she must have been going somewhere; all dressed up in her coat and clutching her purse and gloves. She must have been going somewhere.

In the early 1960s Ernest had written a song cycle for me entitled "Songs of Love and Parting." We performed the cycle many times, with Ernest at the piano and me singing. Little did I know the first time I sang these beautiful pieces that their umbrella title would mean more to me than I thought. The loss of Gerti signaled a change in the course of our family, some of which was natural and good and some inevitable and very sad.

The natural and good side always included my children. Whatever else was happening, there they were to indicate that the "family script" my mother always talked about was still being nudged forward.

Andy, Martha, and Melani were my "songs of love."

Every since he was a little boy, my firstborn Andy had shown signs of being a musical prodigy. He adored playing the piano and had learned by the age of six or seven to play by ear. He started taking lessons and we were amazed at how quickly he was progressing. One day, as I heard him playing a very difficult piece, I had a strange feeling. I went over to the piano and took the music away and little Andy just continued on as if it were still right there in front of him. It was then, as I realized he was playing a very complicated piece purely by ear, that I began to grasp how talented he was. As proud as I was, I was also concerned. I knew that if he could play this well without reading music, there was a good chance he would never really learn how to. The last thing Ernest

With Ernest (standing), December of 1974 in Vienna, listening to the playback of "Songs of Love and Parting." Despite having already loved and parted, our working relationship continued. (Photo by Johann Klinger)

and I wanted was for him to be musically illiterate, so we arranged for him to take formal music training. His instructor vowed to teach him theory.

But Andy did what Andy wanted to do. So we decided a little bit of deprivation might go a long way. We told him, "No more lessons until you learn to read the notes."

Andy passionately wanted to play "The Prologue" from *West Side Story.* He had heard it coming out of our stereo and thought it would be cool to actually play it on the piano. Andy's piano teacher got him his own music and put it on the piano rack, but did not play it for Andy to hear.

"Play it," the teacher said.

He sat there on the bench piled high with two telephone books for hours, his chubby little hands trying to decipher the notes and the chords. He knew how it was supposed to go and, although he didn't care about the skill of the fingering, eventually, by George, he did play it! He was that determined.

About this time, we also got him a set of used drums (much to the dismay of anyone who wanted quiet) and he practiced on those ad infinitum. I can recall him yelling at our new Danish housekeeper when he found her banging on his precious drums. They were his and his alone!

As he grew older, like many kids of the 1960s, he became more interested in playing the guitar. So, off to lessons he went. However, the same thing happened. Andy didn't want (or evidently need) the lessons. Once again, he just played by ear. Later on, he admitted that he knew more than his guitar teacher. He began to hang out wherever music was being played by bands. Soon he was sitting in with jazz and rock bands and, before long, he and a group of his friends (Richard Holland, whose father Milt was a percussionist; Peter Bernstein, who was the son of our friend Elmer, the film composer; and Clay Mantley, whose parents were in television as a director and actress, respectively) from Oakwood School were forming their own band called The Wails.

By this time Andy had been doing some studio work, thanks to my old friend Olivia Page. (Remember the Pages, the African-American family that was such an influence on my childhood? We never lost touch.) Olivia now was contracting musicians for Motown Records. By this time, Andy was also writing his own songs (he had been since he was thirteen!) for the band and, along with fellow band member Charlie Villiers, he submitted a demo recording to Polydor Records.

At sixteen years old, Andy and Charlie were signed to write and record an album. In England! Charlie, whose father was big in the English motor business (he invented the Amherst Villiers Supercharger for Bentley; this was a belt- or gear-driven automotive device that forces more air and fuel into the engine of the car to increase the horsepower), proposed that Andy come to England and live with his family for a year so that they could work on the songs and the recording. Although Ernest was delighted, I had some trepidation. But after we met the Villierses (a lovely couple), and found a good school for Andy, Ernest and I agreed to let him go.

Looking back on it now, I realize this was a radical thing to do, allowing our teenage son to leave home and forge a career in another country, but Ernest and I so believed in his talent and integrity and we knew that, under the Villiers' care, he would be fine.

So, in the summer of 1967, I watched my baby board a flight to London and he blithely hailed a fare-thee-well to his parents, not realizing that, when he would return the next summer, Ernest and I would be separated and nothing would ever be the same.

Despite several years of smooth sailing, Ernest and I had started to hit some rough patches in our relationship and the separations had begun once more. Now, with Andy off in England, Ernest told me that he needed to sort some things out. He said that he just didn't feel right about being married or connected at all and that it was affecting his creative output. He told me he was feeling stagnated.

So, once again, we agreed to a "trial separation."

I was upset, of course, but as always, forged on, hoping for the best. But what would the best be this time? Ernest returning once again? Did I even want that? Like the character of Liza Elliot I had played in a production of the musical *Lady in the Dark*, I couldn't and wouldn't make up my mind.

Martha was fourteen at the time and, when I was working, she was wonderful about helping out with five-year-old Melani, with the aid of our housekeeper Ethel. It was now a houseful of females with many questions. I had no answers, but my busy career helped me not to dwell on the uncertainty of the future.

For the rest of the 1960s my professional life continued on the same zigzagging course it had been on. For some lucky reason, with me, it was never "or" but always "and." I continued my solo career singing with such major orchestras as the L.A. Philharmonic, the London Philharmonic, the San Diego Symphony, and the New York Philharmonic.

My ghostly fame also opened many television doors and I appeared on several editions of *Hollywood Palace*, *The Pat Boone Show* (singing my version of "Exodus"!), a semi-animated musical special (with Gene Kelly) of *Jack and the Beanstalk*, *The Tonight Show* (with Johnny Carson), and many others. I also did a delightful guest shot as myself on Kaye Ballard and Eve Arden's sitcom *The Mothers-in-Law*.

I even did a club act that took me from Bimbos in San Francisco to the Sherman House in Chicago to the Maisonette at the St. Regis Hotel in New York. Sandwiched in between all this was a series of TV commercials for Biz detergent.

Of course, in the commercials only my voice really appeared. It seemed that Kaye Ballard, who had already filmed the commercials, was out of the country when they needed a few lines of singing postdubbed. They had auditioned everyone in town and then I showed up. The ad agency laughed when they saw me.

"You don't look anything like Kaye!"

Where Kaye was dark and zaftig, I was fair and slender.

"Well," I answered, "I just did a guest shot on *The Mothers-in-Law* and I know how Kaye *sounds*."

I asked them to please close their eyes. Then I sang. Just like Kaye Ballard. They were astounded. They had been casting with their eyes. I got the job, did the dubbing, and was paid full price.

Thanks to the long run of the film of *My Fair Lady*, I was still the sometime darling of the columns. The *Hollywood Reporter* quipped, "They found out who was doing Mr. Ed's voice on that television show; it was Marni Nixon's horse," and reported that I had turned down a "playmate of the month" offer saying,

"Audrey Hepburn does all my posing for me." I had learned from a publicist that any publicity is *good* publicity, if it keeps your name out there.

It was about this time, in early 1968, that my manager got a call from the people who managed Victor Borge asking if I would be interested in being part of his show.

Victor Borge was hard to pigeonhole. He was quoted as saying, "To people who take music seriously, I'm a musician. To people who don't take music seriously, I'm a comedian. To people who don't take anything seriously, I'm a clown."

Born Borge Rosenbaum in Copenhagen in 1909, he became known as "The Great Dane," the "Un-Melancholy Dane," and the "Clown Prince of Denmark." Borge had begun playing the piano at age three, was awarded a full scholarship to the Royal Danish Music Conservatory at the age of nine, and made his professional debut by the time he was thirteen. In his early twenties he was already a top entertainer in Scandinavia with his trademark blend of classical music and breaks of madcap humor. By the late 1930s, when he was touring Europe exclusively, Borge employed anti-Nazi humor in his act, getting himself on Hitler's enemy list. It was imperative that he and his wife leave what was soon to be a very dangerous continent for them. Ultimately, Borge and his wife came to the U.S. (thanks to his wife's American citizenship), settled in New York, and anglicized his name for the first time to Victor Borge. Borge (with his knowledge of three languages) took his blend of soaring classical music and comedy to nightclubs, concert halls, movies, radio, and television. His hit Broadway show *Comedy with Music* (which ran two seasons in the 1950s), along with his many *Ed Sullivan Show* appearances, established him as a solo artist who could play anywhere. By 1968, when I joined his troupe, he was already a legend.

I was being hired because Borge, unlike Liberace, who changed his program every year, always did the same show. He had a set amount of material that he had been doing for a long time and he didn't like to practice. So his managers and producers wanted somebody to spark him into reacting in a different way. They felt that, brilliant comic that he was, he would intuitively protect himself (make sure that he came out on top jokewise) and new routines would be born onstage. I was to be that catalyst.

Having played second banana (or "guest artist" as I preferred to call it!) to Liberace, I guess I was eminently suited to the kind of humor that Borge practiced and, frankly, during this period of uncertainty in my private life, I thought it would be nice to know that I had some stability on the stage, so I accepted the job.

Stability? That was exactly what I didn't get with Borge.

My friend Lee Hambro, who had frequently been Borge's dazzling piano partner in the act, had warned me about Borge.

"He will never want to rehearse and you will never get any feedback from him. He will also be very cheap."

Okay. They didn't say I had iron nerves for nothing, and the money part would be taken care of by my manager. He went on.

"Be assured, however, that whatever is happening on the stage, he will make it funny. He will always protect you and the material and he won't be evil at all."

Lee's big advice was "Just be yourself. Just *really* be yourself."

Just before I was about to go out on tour with Borge, Andy returned from his year in England. Instead of an album, a Villiers & Gold single (the label of the 45-rpm record was misprinted and read Villiers and GOD!), "Of All the Little Girls," coupled with "This East," had been recorded, released, reviewed (by one paper!), and bombed. No matter what, though, I was thrilled to see my son, even if I hardly recognized him. Andy had lost forty pounds and gained a roommate: Charlie Villiers. It seems that Charlie's mother, sadly, had succumbed to cancer and Charlie's father, without saying a word to Ernest or me, sent Charlie off to live with us.

But, of course, "us" was now *me*.

"Hi Mom, here's Charlie! He's going to live with us now!"

I was appalled. Here I was, caring for three of my own kids, without Ernest at home, virtually a single mom, working all the time, and now I was expected to watch out for another teenage boy. Charlie's father was in such a state of grief that there was no reasoning and, thinking myself superwoman I guess, I reluctantly agreed to the arrangement.

All of this coincided with my first tour with Victor Borge! Thank goodness it was still summer and before school started. The boys could entertain themselves.

The first place I played with Borge was the Melody Fair, a theater-in-the-round in Buffalo, New York. Just as my friend Lee had warned, Borge would not rehearse with me. There was a band rehearsal of some of my songs, but several of my arias were to be accompanied by Borge at the piano. Borge told me to just watch the show for one night and see what *he* did, and then the next night I was to do what I had rehearsed (or not!).

In theater-in-the-round, the aisles are numbered like the face of a clock. Borge told me that at one point in the show, he was going to be improvising some music at the piano, and since I have perfect pitch, when he was playing in the key of B minor I should just start singing the song "Summertime," while entering from the #5 aisle. So, without any rehearsal, I entered on cue and began interjecting my beginning of "Summertime" into his B minor improvised interlude. From his place at the keyboard near the center (but with his back to me) Borge looked everywhere (except at me) in the auditorium, as if to

With Victor Borge in 1968. I never quite knew what he would do next.
(From the author's collection)

find the source of this unwelcome voice that was interrupting his playing. He hadn't told me what else to do, so I just kept singing and coming up the aisle behind him. I then came onto the stage and sat on the piano bench next to him. Meanwhile, the orchestra had subtly begun accompanying me. Borge, with his impeccable timing, ignored me until I hit a particular high note. Then, as if in shock, he reeled and jumped off the bench. I don't know if he expected me to laugh and stop singing, but I didn't. This seemed to tickle the audience no end. Thus, our act was born.

Had he known what I would do? Had he planned it all in his head? I never found out. As I continued to sing, he continued to play. He acted a bit miffed but went on. Just before I was about hit another high note, Borge acted as if he saw a mosquito flying in the air. He followed it with his eyes and then visualized it landing on my shoulder. Just as I was about to hit that high note, he gave me a tremendous whack on the shoulder. Instead of screaming or stopping, I released the high note with all the finesse I could muster and kept singing. I stood up to finish the song and, as I began the long last note, which goes from a middle B natural to a high B, *pianissimo* (very softly), Borge went into his piano bench, found a banana, peeled it, and stuck into my mouth. Perhaps he thought this would finally silence me, but I just kept right on singing. This made him seemingly furious, which, of course, brought down the house.

True to form, Borge never discussed what we did onstage. He never said, "Well done, Marni!" Nor did he comment on how to do it better. We just did it. We seemed to improvise a little more each time and our "act" was hardly ever the same from night to night. This was completely opposite of the way I worked with Liberace. It was unnerving on one hand and stimulating on the other.

During this same tour, when we were appearing at Cleveland's Blossom Festival, we played a huge open-air theater with a capacity of about 20,000! A symphony orchestra was onstage with us and Borge was conducting from the piano. I had just finished singing a few arias and songs and was ready to exit when Borge announced that he and I would be singing an aria from a new opera by a German composer. He made up some phony German name that was funny, but might sound real. So, once again, without ever having rehearsed or even discussed it, Victor and I launched into an improvised duet, making up the music and the mock-German words as we went along. As I sang I gesticulated up to the general area of the source of the huge spotlight that was coming from high in the rear of the arena and pouring down its light upon me.

"Die Mothern sind geschweigen! Kommen zu mein brust, mein lieb!" I sang in a silly, mock-pidgin German.

Then, suddenly, as if on cue, a huge moth about the size of the palm of my hand emerged and flew closer and closer to me, always remaining in the spotlight. What a diva-moth, I thought! It seemed to be attracted by my glittery white sequined dress. The audience could see the moth coming toward me as I sang and they were in hysterics. Borge, singing and playing at the piano with his back to the moth-filled stream of light, was oblivious to the insect's supporting role in our "opera." Slowly he began to realize that something was going on besides our act. He started pounding the piano and shouting Germanesque expletives.

"Du geschtinkene Mägdelein! Mein Gooooott, Ach in Himmel!"

I, meanwhile, began using the moth, as if it were my long lost lover arriving from Valhalla.

"Mein brust ist geschwollen!"

By this point the moth (was this moth really a trained pro?) hurled itself onto my dress, just at about the crotch area!

Borge, who by now could stand no more of this, banged down the lid of the keyboard, stood up, and leaped over to me.

"Vat's goink on?"

At that very moment I caught the moth in the palm of my hand and innocently held it up for him to see. As I opened my palm, the moth, with the instinct of a true Wagnerian opera diva, flew right into his face and fluttered dramatically in his wet, sweaty hair, all the while attempting to fly up, up, and away to its Moth-Gott in Himmel.

The audience cheered. Unfortunately, this improvised part of our act was a little hard to recreate.

Meanwhile, back on the home front, "my two sons" began their fall school semester. It seemed that Charlie's father could not afford to send his son to the private Oakwood School and he matriculated to North Hollywood High.

To say that having Charlie live with us was a strain is putting it mildly. He was not brought up like my own kids. Right or wrong, he was just a different world unto himself. And he didn't want anything to do with our way of doing things. He quickly alienated our housekeeper, ordering her around as if she were his personal slave. Charlie went to school when it pleased him. When it didn't please him, he would drive off in Andy's car, without even asking or telling anyone where he was going. One never knew when Charlie would appear or not. Dinners would be left cold or he would show up in the middle of the night demanding a meal. As for me, I was either on tour with Borge (we were in London in September 1968 taping a special for Thames TV), or back home rehearsing for the Mexico Olympics, at which I was to sing at the end of the year. Either way, Charlie became too much for me to handle. The last straw came when his principal called to say that Charlie was suicidal and they couldn't have him in the school anymore. It was then that I picked up the phone and called his father to tell him I could no longer take care of his son.

"But he has no one else," the grief-stricken father proclaimed.

I held firm and replied that this wasn't the deal we had made and that I just couldn't handle him. Finally, Charlie Senior "remembered" an aunt who lived in the Pacific Palisades and she agreed that Charlie could come and live with her. Charlie and Andy remained friends and Charlie was still part of Andy's band. He went through many stages, finally winding up as a successful artist. He now lives in upstate New York and I was happy to run into him a few years ago and see how far he had come.

It was about this time, in early 1969, that I let another man into my life.

As our separation grew longer, Ernest continued to see the kids and even do his laundry at the house (this was a step up from *me* doing it for him), but I was slowly feeling us drifting further and further apart emotionally. When I asked him where we were headed, he said that he didn't know.

"I don't know whether we'll stay married or not," he said.

This uncertainty and indecision made me wonder about *my* future. There was no doubt that I was changing and growing stronger within myself. I was thirty-nine years old and, although I didn't know it then, it's a well-known fact today that women come into their own, sexually speaking, at forty.

So I was primed and ready for Alan Bergmann.

I met Alan (not the well-known lyricist, but an actor-director) when both of us were working at a small theater in the San Fernando Valley called Theatre West. Established in 1962 (and still going strong today), Theatre West is a democratic cooperative dedicated to the artistic growth of its members. It has been the theatrical home of such artists as Betty Garrett, Lee Meriwether, Richard Dreyfuss, Carroll O'Connor, Harold Gould, Beau Bridges, and Martin Landau. In 1969, I joined their ranks and Alan and I began to work together very closely.

Alan was a wonderful actor who had played the title roles in the national company of *Luther*, Stratford's production of *Macbeth*, and *Danton's Death* at Lincoln Center, among other shows. In the late 1960s Alan was spreading his wings and becoming a director. He found that Theatre West was the ideal place to work on his craft, and I have to admit that part of my attraction to working at Theatre West was Alan. As an actor and director, he was everything I could wish for. He helped awaken me as an actress. It also turned out that Alan brought on another awakening deep inside of me.

A new sexual awakening.

Alan was very handsome, smart, and talented, with intense, biting eyes. We clicked immediately and, before too long, we were in the midst of a very passionate and sometimes tempestuous relationship. Sexually speaking, Alan was a totally different ball game for me. I didn't know where I had been before. Don't get me wrong. Everything had been fine in the bed department at home. I had certainly enjoyed sex, but suddenly with Alan, it was as if the lights had been turned on ever so much brighter.

It was always surprising to me that I could be really turned on and experience great passion with someone I wasn't married to, even though it was all happening at home the way it was supposed to be. Despite some experience, I was learning that I *could* feel passionate about someone other than my husband and not feel guilty about it. I was brought up in a family of great disciplinarians and we were taught what was right and moral. Yet, here I was really enjoying my body and loving the sensual feelings Alan was bringing out in me. It had always been true that I needed to have intimate contact with people. This is what makes me tick. Being with Alan only emphasized these needs.

For a while, Alan and I were great together. In time, although I didn't ask him to, he even left his wife for me. At first I had tried to keep our relationship separate from the kids, but after a while he would come over and we would have dinner together and I could sense that it was fine with them. In time they grew to love him. Or so I thought.

I can remember hugging Alan once when the kids were in the room. Fifteen-year-old Martha was surprised and bemused at this show of affection.

"You realize, Mom, we've never seen you like this," she said.

They hadn't been aware of me as a romantic creature before. Underneath the approval, though, was another emotion, and today Martha remembers hating the fact that Alan seemed like a replacement for the father she so dearly loved. Still, my perception was that the kids saw him as a nice loving person who obviously liked their mother. It seemed to me at the time that he was accepted as part of the family.

However, there was a dark side to Alan, and as we grew closer, he became controlling, jealous, and possessive. Unfortunately (or fortunately) for our relationship, this coincided with my gradual discovery of my own strength and ability to stand up for my rights. I was changing and not apt to let anyone put anything over on me. As I mentioned, Alan was a wonderful actor and director and he had a way of manipulating my mind. He was a kind of Svengali. One side of me adored learning from him and the other would say, "Wait a minute, I want to discover things my own way." Frequently, the latter side would win and I would have the nerve to say what *I* wanted. That didn't always sit well with Alan. His jealousy started out small. If I was on the phone with a friend and he walked in, he would expect me to just hang up and pay attention to him. If I didn't, he would become furious.

At first, I thought that was cute, but not for long.

One of the better parts of my relationship with Alan was that we were both in the theater and could work together. Ernest and I had always been at our best when we did projects together. In September of 1969, Alan and I were cast opposite each other in a production of *The Sound of Music* in Laguna Beach. This was the first time I was doing the show on the stage (eventually, in various productions, I would play all the female leads) and I had graduated from my film role of Sister Sophia to Maria. Although he was not really a singer, Alan played the Captain.

During intermission during a matinee, I made a routine phone call to our housekeeper, Ethel, to ask her how everything was at home. Before I could even get the question out of my mouth, Ethel spoke with a controlled nonchalance that hid her terror.

"Oh, Mrs. Gold, don't worry, everything is going to be all right!"

My maternal intuition was working overtime that day.

"What do you mean? What's happened? Tell me who, what, how, when, and where?"

She finally blurted out the story. Martha, who was an accomplished horseback rider with a roomful of silver medals and trophies, had had an accident. Her horse stumbled a bit as she was taking a jump. Martha had been trained to fall off if this happened, which she did. But, during all the furor, a pole impaled the horse's rear hoof and he came thundering down on top of her (all 1,500 pounds!), burying her underneath. Of course everyone on the ranch where she was jumping came running and they were able to eventually pull the injured horse off Martha. What saved her was the metal jump hat, covered with velvet, which had come over the front of her face, so her nose was free to breath the half inch of air it provided her. Martha turned out to be lucky. She only suffered a huge gash in her knee, but it was so deep—almost to the bone—that she needed an operation. No one had been able to reach Ernest and they didn't want to bother me during a show.

There I was, in the middle of *The Sound of Music* in Laguna Beach, and my baby was being rushed to a hospital in Calabasas, about a two-hour drive away. Somehow I finished the second act and got Maria, the Captain, and the seven kids over those Alps. Still in my makeup and full of guilt and anxiety, I got there in time to watch them operate on Martha's knee. This is where my acting skills really came in handy. I was cool, calm, and collected for her, so as not to rouse her fears. I only began to shake afterward, when I was alone in the car. Thank the Lord, the operation went well and Martha recovered.

After *The Sound of Music*, Alan and I immediately embarked on a very exciting project when he directed me in a double bill of Leonard Bernstein's one-act opera *Trouble in Tahiti* (I had done a tour of this in the early 1950s, but this time I was playing the leading role) and *Kurt Weill—A Rehearsal*, a new theatrical piece comprising the great German-American composer's best songs. Artistically, things were going beautifully, but I started to get more warning signs about my personal relationship with Alan. One day in October of 1969, during the run in Pasadena, I heard from a friend that he had been to see last night's performance.

"Why didn't you come back to see me?" I asked.

I always welcome visitors after a performance and the stage doorman knew that. My friend told me that he did, indeed, start back to see me, but that Alan stopped him and said, "No one is to see Marni! She doesn't want to see anybody!"

This made me furious at Alan. After apologizing to my friend, I hung up and started to think this through. A big warning bell went off in my head. I thought, "I've got to get away from this." I started to realize that as nice as this sexual awakening was, it didn't mean that we were married. Sex isn't marriage. This was a bold, new concept for me. This thing with Alan was going too far and on the wrong path. Even if we were married I would never stand for such controlling. This was something Ernest never even *thought* of doing. Of course, I felt guilty, too. Alan had left his wife for me. Even though we never even spoke about getting married, I could tell Alan was committed to me.

During Ernest's and my separation, there were short periods of time when Ernest came home. These resulted in a few knock-down, drag-out battles that made me realize the end of the marriage was imminent. So it was a complete surprise when Ernest, who knew that Alan and I were seeing each other, walked in with his laundry and proclaimed that he had decided he was returning home for good.

"What!" I shouted. "You mean to tell me that you're unilaterally deciding you're coming back home? Without even discussing it with me?"

I was livid.

Ernest thought that he had the winning move in this game of chess.

"You can have your boyfriend," he said in a placating tone. "It's all right with me. But I miss the kids and I want to come back. You can have your boyfriend and I'll just go out the nights you want to have him over."

This made my blood boil and the words just tumbled out of my mouth.

"You mean you want to play this charade in front of the kids? That is not the way this relationship is, nor do I want that. I do not want that confusion for the kids. Even if I'm confused or you're confused, I don't want to play it out this way. I won't have that. And since you think you can just unilaterally decide what to do, so can I. You're out of here! That's it! We're getting divorced!"

With the words barely out of my mouth, I finally breathed. I told Ernest that even though this thing with Alan might not become a marriage, and that I had serious reservations, I had to play it through and see where it took me.

We began divorce proceedings the next day.

Obviously, this was a hard time emotionally for the kids. With cooler heads, Ernest and I gathered Andy, Martha, and Melani in the living room and told them that we had decided it was best for us to divorce. Martha remembers that it was a Saturday evening, because she had a horse show the next day and went off the course a few times. She was that upset and distracted.

Life with Alan went on, but it went on a downward spiral. He was more controlling and jealous than ever. The final straw came when I contradicted him about something and he got terribly angry, took my arm, and wrenched it almost out of its socket. I knew then that this wasn't right. His behavior proved that there are things more powerful than sex. I finally knew that I mustn't be ruled by my glands. We had a terrible fight about it and I broke off our relationship.

Driving home that night, up the dark, steep, winding, and treacherous hills of Laurel Canyon, all I remember was crying so hard that the car was swaying dangerously. Before I knew it, a police car was sounding its siren and I was being told to pull over. I pulled over and the officer came around and started talking before he saw me.

"Lady, do you realize that . . ."

At that moment he saw how hard I was weeping and what an emotional state I was in.

"Lady," he sympathetically said, "what's wrong? How can I help you?"

I told him I had just had a fight with my boyfriend and that my kids were home alone and I had to get back to them quickly. He was so concerned for me that he decided not only not to give me ticket, but to escort me all the way home to make sure I got there safely.

I thought Alan and I were safely broken up and I told the kids that it was over. Then, a few weeks later, he came knocking on my back door one night. The house was a two-story structure and downstairs was my bedroom with its private entrance. The kids' rooms, living room, and kitchen were upstairs, so they never heard his knocking.

"Hi," he said with the sweetest, most conciliatory voice, "I just wanna talk to you."

I let him in and it all began again. Ah, the yo-yo effect.

I knew he should leave before the kids woke up, but somehow it didn't happen. The next morning Martha, my little budding psychologist (she really is one today!), came downstairs and found me in bed with Alan. At first she just stood there, staring at us, like a wise old owl. Then she spoke, quietly and firmly.

"Mom, if you ever do this again, I'm going to disown you!"

Then she turned and walked back upstairs. Alan left and I went up to talk to Martha. My darling daughter, who was only sixteen or so, had such wisdom. She was thinking only of me. This had happened a couple of times before. I would make the big announcement that Alan and I were finished and then I would get emotional and lonesome and slip. As I looked at Martha, I thought, what am I doing? She was becoming the mother and I was the little child. I knew that I couldn't go on this way. I knew that it was time to sit down and have a meeting with my brain.

I recently found a letter that Alan had written to a mutual friend of ours late in 1969.

"Things are still up in the air with Marni," he wrote. "I love her very much and want to help her, but she's torn with fear. She needs confidence. Can you help? I'd be most grateful."

Alan was right. I *was* torn with fear: the fear of getting stuck in a relationship that wasn't right for me or for my children. But I did finally gain the confidence I needed, as well as the courage to break off a bad relationship. Once and for all.

It had been a fantastic awakening for me on so many fronts. Besides the physical aspect, Alan was responsible for helping me to become a better actor. He helped me to realize the difference between some of the superficial music theater or opera acting I had been doing and to know what was true and real. I had always been good onstage, but you don't really experience the intensity of acting until you do many straight plays or go to acting class. This is one of the reasons I originally wanted to work with Alan, because he was such an astute actor, director, and teacher. The rest was all gravy.

Songs of Love and Parting.

After nineteen years, Ernest and I, who had shared all that love, were parting. My mother's nineteen-year-old premonition had finally come true. The turbulent decade of the 1960s was ending and I was about to face some new horizons and adventures. Work was always my solace and, as usual, even under these trying emotional circumstances, it went on.

There were always surprises around the corner on that front, so it wasn't too shocking when I got a call from Mel Powell (a former Benny Goodman jazz pianist, professor at Yale, and very good composer in his own right, not to mention a charmer), asking me to meet and talk to him about an exciting project.

"Marni, I am involved in a new school just being built, called the California Institute of the Arts, and we're interested in your being the director of the vocal department."

With that sentence, my life as a teacher began. Little did I know then that it would continue for the rest of my life.

Chapter Twelve
AT THE GATES OF
THE EMERALD CITY

"It's a very ancient saying, but a true and honest thought, that when you become a teacher, by your pupils you'll be taught."

OSCAR HAMMERSTEIN II, 1951

WHEN OSCAR HAMMERSTEIN WROTE THE ABOVE LYRICS for the verse of *The King and I*'s "Getting to Know You," he actually made up this "very ancient saying." But for me, it has certainly proven to be true.

When Mel Powell asked me to lunch and started gauging my interest in helping him develop the vocal department of a new arts school, I had never taught before. Little did I know then I was opening up a door that would lead to one of the joys of my life. What I didn't realize at the time was that there was a door behind the door. That door was labeled "administrative hell"!

At first Mel simply asked me to make a list of my "druthers" pertaining to the creation of an ideal vocal department within a music school specifically focused on forming good singers. After I did this, he and I discussed our dreams and hopes for such an institution of learning. It was then that he asked me to head the vocal department for the new California Institute of the Arts, which was to be funded by Roy Disney (Walt's brother) and built just outside of L.A. in Valencia.

"But, Mel," I said, "I've never taught before, let alone been an administrator on this level."

He laughed.

"That's precisely why I want you. With all your superb taste and experience in so many disciplines of performance, you are exactly the person to begin this department. It's because you haven't had that kind of rigid rule-related university formalized training that you have had such a unique career. We *want* that. We know that you can turn out people who will sing from their own specific guts, but who will also be good musicians and complete performers."

This speech was not only flattering, but empowering. I was ready to face anything when we began putting the program together. At first I was given a batch of tapes from which to choose voice students. Then we went on a recruitment trip up and down the California coast, auditioning hopefuls along the way. Raphael Druian, who would later become the concertmaster of the New York Philharmonic, was recruiting for the orchestra. Mort Subotnick (already famous as a composer of synthesizer-enhanced music) was listening for composition students. Leonard Stein, who figured strongly in my musical life, was in charge of the piano department.

The campus was to be huge and contain all the "druthers" of the other heads of the various departments (cinema, drama, music, dance, etc.). To me, this seemed like a dream that might be difficult to attain in the short time allotted and would take a large staff of very efficient and objective thinkers. However, my youth (I was forty), my fascination for doing this job, and my "yes, of course" attitude came to the fore, pushing aside all obstacles. I was thrilled to be a part of this edified institution dedicated to higher learning.

What I soon found out was, if anyone was going to learn, it was going to be me.

We began the school at Villa Cabrini in Burbank while we waited for the big new edifice in Valencia to be completed. Even without any academic administrative experience, I could tell we'd begun in absolute chaos. At one point, Martha Scott, Mel's wonderful actress wife, popped her head into the office and, with a charmingly radiant smile, teased us by saying, "Is anything all right?"

Each department had massive space, new instruments, and state-of-the-art equipment. Each department, except mine, that is. We never seemed to get priority. I had a hard job convincing the powers that be that solid old-fashioned training was needed. I was determined that acting, movement, sight singing, reading, standard introductory piano, and harmony should be part of the curriculum. I fought every step of the way. Unfortunately I didn't always win.

The next year we moved into the wonderful new buildings, but all was not well for me. Nothing seemed to go the way I had expected. From the dance department I was assigned an inexperienced assistant's assistant to be the teacher of my movement class. My practice rooms were constantly being usurped. I quickly began to realize that I was not experienced enough in the jungle of academia and that, as usual, I didn't know how to stand up for my rights. Mel had no time or inclination at that point to consult with me about anything whatsoever. Then, later on, he just began expanding the roster by hiring new voice teachers. I started to wonder what my title "Director of the Vocal Department" meant. Whatever happened to my "druthers"?

After a couple of years of all this, I had had it! When I first began this new project, it had been the right thing for me, especially coming in the middle of my divorce from Ernest. It seemed, then, in spite of the initial chaos, that it would refresh my life. Now, it was becoming a strain. I decided to take some more out-of-town singing jobs that had been offered. One of them took me on tour to Seattle and the state of Washington, where, in 1970, while touring with the opera *Penelope*, my dear friends, Milton and Virginia Katims, threw a party for me. They, like all my friends, were constantly trying to fix me up with a new man. This time, Virginia told me, she had a "real catch" for me. The "catch" had a very interesting way of saying hello.

"So," he said, "how do you feel about masturbating?"

When I recovered from the shock of the question (we were, after all, in the middle of a party full of respectable Seattle residents!), I turned to see that the teasing, spry, manly voice addressing me belonged to Dr. Lajos Frederick Fenster, known to his friends as "Fritz" (a German diminutive for Frederick).

"Well," I gaily replied, "I suppose if you have to, you have to!"

The guests within earshot were greatly amused and hung on our conversation, wondering where it might go next. I was aware of Fritz's background. The Katims had briefed me before the party.

"He loves the arts, Marni," Virginia gushed to me beforehand. "His father was the first violinist with the San Francisco Symphony and when Fritz was a boy, Fritz Kreisler came to his house to play string quartets with his Dad. That's why he was nicknamed Fritz."

Fritz Kreisler! For those of you who are still with me from the beginning of my saga, you will remember that Fritz Kreisler had a profound effect on me when I was just a child.

Virginia told me that young Fritz was so moved by Kreisler that he began to take violin lessons, but although he loved music, it was clear to him early on that he was not fated to perform it himself.

Virginia knew that Fritz's love of music would impress me more than the fact that he was an internist/hepatologist at the Mason Clinic in the department of medicine, section of gastroenterology, and head of the subsection of hepatology (liver and biliary diseases). In layman's terms, Fritz was a music-loving liver specialist! The Katims also told me that Fritz was well known for *never* getting interested in anyone to whom they introduced him. He always found something about the woman that didn't appeal to him. Of course, every eligible female wanted to go out with him and be the one exception to the rule. With my competitive nature, I treated our encounter like a game. A game I was determined to win.

A prerequisite for being a guest of the Katims was that if you had a modicum of talent you were asked to perform. It was always "sing for your supper" time. So, of course, later in the evening, I sang.

"My God," Fritz exclaimed, as the applause died down, "she's as good a singer as I am a doctor!"

This was high praise indeed from a Scorpio who thought very highly of himself. Knowing Fritz and his biting wit, everyone hooted and laughed and the party proceeded. Fritz and I were drawn to each other and later, when the party began to disband, Milton and Virginia suggested that the four of us go out and have a nightcap somewhere. After tossing that idea around for a few minutes, Fritz came up with a better suggestion.

"It's getting so late," Fritz offered, "why don't I just drive Marni back to her hotel?"

Virginia, the matchmaker, thought this was a great idea!

"Well, all right. If you really want to," she cooed with mock innocence and bluntly winked at me.

He drove me to my hotel and it was clear that we were clicking. The laughter was easy and the conversation was flowing.

"Why don't you come up to my room," I asked, "and I'll show you a little foot reflexology?"

I was starting to understand Fritz's wicked sense of humor and I knew that doctors (at least in those days) don't usually put too much scientific stock into therapies such as massage. I figured that he could either take my invitation as a potential scientific experiment or as a come-on. Even I didn't know exactly where I was leading, but, interestingly enough, I *was* leading.

When we got to my room, Fritz took off his shoes and laid on the bed waiting for his foot message. I began working on his feet, attempting to get this oh, so scientific man to feel the nerve ends and enjoy the benefits to his body to which they corresponded. He seemed to go into a minitrance (or else he was a very good actor) and as he relaxed, he finally admitted that what I was doing felt pretty good. After a while, we decided to call it a night, leaving our first flirtation just that, a flirtation.

After Fritz left my hotel room, Virginia, who could stand it no longer, called to find out what had occurred. I told her what happened (and what didn't!) and thanked her for the introduction. She was impressed. It was obviously a very unusual thing for Fritz to be so experimental. Virginia was sure this meant he thought I was someone special.

"I'm going to get him," I announced loudly to myself.

I ignored the fact that I was living in L.A. and Fritz in Seattle. Whenever I was on tour in his neck of the woods, I would phone him. I called his office so often that his nurse got to know my name. I thought that was some kind of victory. Yet, try as I may, I just couldn't get Fritz to ask me out.

"You can't do these forward things, Marni," my roommate on the tour, Dorothy Cole, warned. "You'll scare him away."

Dorothy was only looking out for me, but I disagreed with her. I reassured myself that if I trusted my instincts and my sometimes-charm, then maybe I *could* be a little forward in this case. Fritz had told me that he played tennis at the Seattle Tennis Club. He even told me which days he played. Maybe it was a little more than forward for me to have him paged, but still I did it!

"Dr. Fenster, you are wanted in the tennis club office for a phone call."

The voice on the loudspeaker boomed out over all twenty-seven tennis courts. On one of them was Fritz. Being a doctor, naturally he thought it might be an emergency. So he interrupted his game, ran to the front office, and took the call. It was me! Fritz laughed, but was also a bit irritated. After all, it was one thing to call him in his office, but interrupting his tennis game was tantamount to treason! And now anyone who was anyone would know I was pursuing him! But he was amused, too, and so we tried to coordinate our busy schedules and make a date. For some reason our efforts were thwarted yet again.

Back out I went on tour. Up and down the state of Washington. Then a cartoon caught my eye. It was a picture of Popeye hollering out the back screen door for his baby Swee' Pea.

"Swee' Pea, Swee' Pea! Come in and get your bath. It's bedtime!"

In the next panel, there was a drawing of Swee' Pea in the backyard, having heard the call, but stubbornly not obeying. The panel after that showed Popeye coming out, grabbing the baby, taking off his clothes, and plopping Swee' Pea into the bathtub. Swee' Pea lets out a loud "Waaaah!" and Popeye has won.

"This cartoon reminds me of Fritz," I told my roommate Dorothy. "He just needs someone to show him the way to get involved. Fritz needs to be plopped into the bathtub of relationships, whether he cries or not."

So I sent the cartoon to Fritz with a note.

"This looks just like you. Love, Marni."

That really made him angry (but in a good way) and he tracked *me* down, found my phone number and, for once, *he* did the calling. This time we made a date and kept it. It was the beginning of a romance. A romance that went on the fast track.

A few months later, on July 23, 1971, we were married in L.A.

It was going to be a big move. I was selling my beloved home in L.A., which Ernest and I had built with such meticulous care, and moving to Seattle. Martha was off to UCLA. She would be all right. Talking to her today I realize that she wasn't. She felt abandoned, but kept it to herself at the time. Andy was all grown up and busy working as a sound engineer at A&M Records. Melani was only ten and, of course, would be coming with Fritz and me.

The wedding was at City Hall and Fritz forgot to bring the necessary doctor's certificate.

"But I *am* a doctor!" Fritz, feeling insulted, kept repeating to the judge.

The judge glared at him. "You are not licensed in California," he dryly replied, "and you can't sign your own certificate!"

Somehow we sorted it out and got married. The next day an upset and disruptive Melani (she had been uprooted from her school, friends, dog, brother, sister, and father), a frightened groom (wondering what he had gotten himself into), two vomiting cats (don't ask!), and I drove north on the freeway in a heat wave. We stopped in San Francisco for a reception Fritz's mother had planned, combining my invitation list of friends and relatives near the San Francisco area with her own. I had called my sister, Ariel, who lived nearby and attended, but she was the only one from my side of the family who responded. None of the friends on my list showed up. When I asked to see the invitation, I realized why. Fritz's mother had neglected to add my name to the invitation, so of course my friends didn't know who the bride marrying this Dr. Lajos Frederick Fenster was! Talk about your Freudian slips. I should have taken that as a sign.

Nonetheless, in the summer of 1971 we all settled into Fritz's house in Bellevue, Washington, and began our new life together.

Shortly after we were married, we went to see my former partner in crime, Victor Borge, at the Seattle Opera House. I had left Victor a note before the performance letting him know we would be there. Of course, he used me in his monologue that night. He mentioned that his old friend Marni had recently married a liver doctor. He then proceeded to mortify Fritz by spinning our marriage into a series of "liver and onion" jokes. I remember we had a brief snack with him after the show. No liver was served.

The move to Seattle didn't disturb what I call my "classical concert glory years." In 1972 alone, I appeared the with Syracuse Symphony singing the world premiere of a song cycle written especially for me by Gerard Schurmann, sang several contemporary music concerts with Leonard Stein in Ann Arbor, Michigan, and performed in Offenbach's *La Perichole* at the Seattle Opera, to name just a few.

In May of 1972, I sang the role of Violetta in Verdi's *La Traviata* for the first time. It was a very difficult role for me, as my voice had always been light and limpid. For this role, I had to sing *con forza* (very strong) and yet still sustain the coloratura (elaborate soprano trills) for the famous arias "Sempre Libera" and "Ah, Fors'è Lui." This was a great stretch for me and taught me a lot about singing in a more deeply connected way. The opera was being done with two casts: the "international cast," who would sing it in the original Italian, and the "national cast," who would sing it in English. I was to sing Violetta in English, while Beverly Sills was to sing it in Italian.

By this time, the Brooklyn-born Beverly Sills (known to her friends as Bubbles) was perhaps one of the best-known opera singers in America. Like me, Beverly began as a child performer. She made her operatic debut in 1947 in Bizet's *Carmen* with the Philadelphia Civic Opera. She first appeared with the

As Musetta in La Bohème, *Seattle Opera, 1972. (Photo Des Gates, Courtesy of Seattle Opera)*

New York City Opera in 1955 and won rave reviews, establishing her reputation with her appearances in Douglas Moore's *The Ballad of Baby Doe*. Sills' 1964 City Opera performance as Cleopatra in Handel's *Giulio Cesare* made her an international opera star.

When I began to work on *La Traviata*, I realized that the English translation wasn't allowing me to truly sing the role, so I took it upon myself (with the cooperation of the other singers) to change the words, going back to the original vowel and consonant sounds of the Italian and trying to make a meaningful translation that would be singable as well.

Singing the "Tipsy Waltz" in La Perichole *with the Seattle Opera, 1972.*
(Photo Des Gates, Courtesy of Seattle Opera)

Henry Holt, assistant to Glynn Ross (head of the Seattle Opera), who knew me quite well, advised me to not even think about diction, but to approach the role from a purely vocal standpoint. It turned out he was right. As I progressed, I found a much richer sound than I had ever had before and was able to let my voice soar. The kicker was that people said they understood every word I sang. Go figure, eh?

As usual in opera (and musical theater, too), I was told that there wasn't money for anything but one orchestra rehearsal. Interestingly, Beverly Sills, who had played Violetta a hundred times before, wasn't going to be there for

As Violetta in La Traviata, *Seattle Opera, 1975.*
(Photo Des Gates, Courtesy of Seattle Opera)

her orchestra rehearsal. So smart little Marni offered to sing her rehearsal for her. At no extra charge. They took me up on my offer and I was thrilled to get an extra full rehearsal with the orchestra.

At the orchestra rehearsal, Sam Kratchmalnik, the conductor, was quite impressed with my performance. After the rehearsal he asked if I had ever done the role before. When I told him I hadn't, he said that this was a wonderful role for me and that "Beverly Sills should look out!" When Beverly arrived the next day, I wickedly told her what Sam had said.

"Beverly," I teased, "Sam said that this is a great role for me and that you should look out."

With her great sense of humor, she put her hands on her hips and laughed.

"Soooo?" she said in her Brooklyn accent, "I'm lookin'! I'm lookin'!"

Bubbles could always be counted on for a laugh.

In between my gigs, and when he could get away, Fritz and I traveled together. Before we were married, we had spent a couple of weeks up in Canada at Harrison Hot Springs, a popular spa in British Columbia. This was something of a premarital "honeymoon." About a year later, in July of 1972, we went to Europe (this was what I called our real honeymoon, one year delayed), staying a few days in London, and then off to Paris, where we caught a slow train across Spain to Lisbon. I remember the train connecting us to Lisbon was late and that there was no dining car, so Fritz and I had to make do with the few crackers left in our care package. There was a man onboard who was flirting with me and offered me tickets to the bullfights when we arrived in Lisbon. He was perhaps not so pleasantly surprised when I asked if I could bring my husband. He did, however, leave the tickets for us, but I have to say that both of us found bullfighting a bit too gory for our tastes.

Then we flew to Madeira, off the coast of Portugal, where we endured a harrowing tourist bus ride around hairpin turns, looking almost straight down at the sea and the various fishing villages. On the small island of Porto Santo we were literally driven away by all the bugs that greeted us as we tried to sit on the beach. Somewhere in there we spent a few days on the Algarve, where the beaches were spectacular, with long white sands stretching from the road to the crystal blue water.

Perhaps if Fritz and I could've spent all of our time traveling, things might have been easier.

I spent 1973 settling our little family into our new home on Mercer Island, a lovely residential community that's just over five miles long and two miles wide. It sits in Lake Washington, east of the city of Seattle and west of the city of Bellevue. The move and separation from her friends, siblings, and father was very hard on Melani, and she and Fritz did not get on at all. Fritz wasn't used to having a child around and, truthfully, he didn't particularly understand her.

This put an immediate strain on all of us. I was caught in the middle. Melani was angry, not only at Fritz, but at me for forcing her into this situation.

As always, though, I tried to put a good face on it, but things were not good for Melani when she started junior high school on the island. She was in great pain and didn't get along too well with others. I talked to her teachers and they told me that she was rather standoffish. She was trying to become an independent teenager (never easy under any circumstances), but it was obviously very hard on her and her home life was not helping.

As Melani tried to adjust, perhaps I wasn't helping things by still commuting back and forth to L.A. to give master classes at the California Institute of the Arts. After a while, I realized it would be better for me to be home more and I had to let that dream go. Difficult as it was, my experience at Cal-Arts whetted my appetite for teaching. So when the Cornish Institute (now the Cornish College of the Arts) found out I was living in Seattle and asked me to teach voice and coach opera workshops there, I jumped at the opportunity.

Founded in 1914 by Nellie Cornish as the Cornish School, the Institute quickly developed into an internationally known gathering place of renowned artists, educators, and students. Dance and art were added to the music curriculum, followed by theater, design, and performance production. In 1977, the Cornish Institute became a fully accredited college offering Bachelor of Fine Arts and Bachelor of Music degrees. In 1986, the college was renamed the Cornish College of the Arts. Its students have included guitarist-singer Nancy Wilson of the rock band Heart, film star Brendan Fraser, TV journalist Chet Huntley, and dancer-choreographer Merce Cunningham. Such artists as painter Mark Tobey, musician John Cage, modern dance guru Martha Graham, and my very own Peter Meremblum (whose training orchestra was my mainstay with the violin) have taught at Cornish. In 1974 it was my turn.

Besides directing scenes for the Opera Workshop, I appeared in full productions of operas by Gluck and Bern Herbolsheimer with Melvin Strauss conducting. I also presented many recitals by my students, many of whom have gone on to wonderful careers. In addition, I was part of the formation of the Sound Expression Theatre, which then morphed into MusiComedy Theatre, with Ron Daum as its founder. The group presented musicals in Seattle, some of which I appeared in.

Seattle proved to be a hotbed of concerts for me. I sang with the Wenatchee Symphony, the Seattle Symphony, and the Olympia Symphony. Milton Katims, the man who, along with his wife, introduced me to Fritz, conducted a tour of family concerts for me. Together, we created a very successful narration for Richard Strauss' popular symphonic poem *Til Eulenspiegel's Merry Pranks*. We performed it in high schools all over the Seattle area, including the one on Mercer Island.

Although I was growing new roots in Seattle, I still sometimes shuttled back to L.A. Ernest and I had remained friendly (working together every once in a while) and, of course, still had our three children in common. Martha was in UCLA and, by now, Andy's music career was blooming and he was touring the country as musical director-arranger, and playing guitar, keyboards, and other instruments for Linda Ronstadt. On one of my trips back to L.A. I appeared in a revue produced by Erwin Jourdan called *The Happy Side of the '30s* with dancer and film star Donald O'Connor, singer-impressionist Marilyn Michaels, crooner Rudy Vallee, and Edgar Bergen and Charlie McCarthy.

I wish young people today could have witnessed the brilliance of Edgar Bergen (whose daughter is Candice Bergen). Bergen was a ventriloquist extraordinaire! Born in 1903, he displayed a talent for throwing his voice early on and created his first wooden character (we must never call Charlie a dummy) while still in college. The duo began performing in a talent show in Chicago. Over the years, Charlie became so real to audiences that he was later dubbed "the master of innuendo and snappy comebacks." Bergen and McCarthy made their radio debut on *Rudy Vallee's Royal Gelatin Hour* in 1936 and were an instant success. In 1937, they were given their own show for Chase & Sanborn. Almost immediately, *The Edgar Bergen/Charlie McCarthy Show* became one of radio's highest-rated programs, a distinction it enjoyed until it left the air in 1956. To realize how brilliant the comedy was, one must remember that Bergen was a ventriloquist on the radio. No one could see him! It didn't matter if his lips moved or not. It didn't matter if he really threw his voice. What mattered were the delightful characters he created with his voice and the comedy that emanated from them. I can still hear Charlie:

"Ambition is a poor excuse for not having sense enough to be lazy."

Or:

"Hard work never killed anybody, but why take a chance?"

Now, here I was in 1974 doing a skit with darling Edgar Bergen and irascible Charlie McCarthy. As the straight man! Heaven!

———

It's funny how some years seem to be watersheds. 1975 was one of those. Beginnings and endings all at once.

One day I got a call from Barbara Groce, a television producer for Seattle's local TV station, an affiliate of ABC-TV. She told me they were creating a children's television show for two to six year olds and were interested in my being the host. Later entitled *Boomerang*, the show was a noncommercial public affairs program, meaning they legally had to open up the audition process to everyone who applied for the job. So, even though they wanted me, I still had to audition.

Why me, you might ask? I hadn't ever been involved in children's programming before. Barbara and director Ken Schwedop informed me that they had been observing my musical career for a long time and noted that I also had a great interest in education. They decided that those were the two criteria they were looking for.

Although they were vague about what the show would be like, they requested that I put together some pertinent material and then present it on my audition tape. I leaped upon the task with great glee! I could tell this was going to be fun. Since the audition could be on any subject, I decided to use my daughter Melani's clever mind, point of view, and pristine, pure spirit. I had an idea that I should somehow use puppets, and one of my students, Binki Spahi, was a puppet maker and had a mouse in her collection. Melani and her friend Debi Lorig came up with another toy mouse of a different size that wasn't a puppet. I looked at these two mice and thought if I tied a string to the toy mouse and held Binki's puppet mouse, I could visibly operate and bring these inanimate creatures to life. Of course I knew I would sing. Melani and Debi's favorite song was "It's a Small World After All," written by my friends the Sherman Brothers (Richard and Robert, who wrote the score of *Mary Poppins*, among others). As I looked at, and played with, the small puppet and the big mouse, I realized how the song's lyric pertained to the characters to whom I was singing. I realized that it didn't matter how big or small you were, there was always someone bigger than you and someone smaller as well. The message I was going to give those two to six year olds was "You are okay no matter where you are. You are okay to be just the way you are, wherever you fit it." Eureka! I knew that I was onto something.

Out of this revelation I wrote a three-minute presentation script of these two mice having a conversation and my interacting with them. I designed the audition script to include the camera moves, meaning, ostensibly, that I was the director. I was leaving nothing to chance.

The upshot was that I was the only one with the professional expertise and guts to know what I wanted to do and to pull it off in front of the camera. After they watched the audition tape and approved of how I looked on-screen, I was in!

Now that I was part of the team, we had many production meetings to define what type of show this was going to be. Writer-puppeteer Lee Olson was brought on board along with music director Stan Keen. Ken Schwedop, the director, joined us and, after months of brainstorming, consulting with local libraries, psychological centers, children's hospitals, and school systems, we came up with the premise for the show. Stan Keen wrote and recorded the theme song and Lee Olson penned the first scripts.

I was to star in a sitcom format. It would take place in my living room and feature my adopted son, Norbert. Norbert was a puppet, of course. He had a yellow terrycloth pointed head with a tuft of red hair sticking out of the top and a striped T-shirt. Lee manipulated Norbert like a Muppet, by putting one hand in the puppet's head, which worked the mouth, while his other hand controlled Norbert's arm. Norbert would sit at various places, mostly the round table. Underneath the table or behind a counter, unseen by the camera, Lee would read his script and speak Norbert's lines. The music we used was either in the public domain or newly composed by Stan Keen.

The pressures on me to do a new show every week were tremendous. On Mondays we would have two rehearsals and then we would begin taping on Tuesday morning. I never used cue cards, as the producer thought that eye contact with the camera was different if I read them. The puppeteers (by now we had added another wonderfully talented colleague, Kathy Tolan, who operated Libby, a friend of Norbert's, as well as all the other female puppets we were to add; Lee did all the male characters), of course, read their scripts, but I had to memorize it all. I would do a scene with the puppets and then have to turn directly to the camera and explain what we had talked about in the scene, summarizing exactly what the message was, so to speak, and what we had just done or talked about. At that point they would count down, while I was speaking, to the end of the segment. If I goofed at all we had to go back and do the whole segment again. This pressure was so great that after a while it caused me to begin to stutter. I was able to control it, but it must have been more

Emmys all around for Boomerang! *(l to r: Nancy Schwedop, writer, me, and Lee Olson, puppeteer and voice of Norbert, my adopted son) (Photo John E. Walker)*

Advertising promo showing me with my favorite costars, Norbert and Libby, on Boomerang. I won four Emmys and the show ran for twenty-five years! (Courtesy KOMO-TV, Seattle)

Starring
Marni Nixon
and her friends,
Sunday through Friday
at 9 a.m.

traumatic than I thought at the time. One year after the experience, when the *Boomerang* crowd all came to see me in *I Do! I Do!*, just knowing they were there, I began to stutter on stage. I had never done that before and it was truly frightening!

Boomerang premiered on September 10, 1975, and was an instant success. We did 169 episodes (and numerous specials) and helped to bring up a whole generation of kids in the Northwest of America. The show received over thirty local Emmy Awards, the Chicago Film Festival Award, and the coveted ACT Award. Personally, I was awarded four Emmys as Best Actress in a Children's Series.

At first we had no idea how many kids were actually watching, so we decided to do some live shows and find out how big our public really was. The station advertised: "Come on Down to the Food Circus and see Marni and Norbert and friends from *Boomerang*." We didn't know what to expect, but 1,500 kids, aged two to six, showed up with their parents. We quickly learned how to entertain 1,500 short attention spans. We did sing-alongs (with the appropriate hand motions, which they all knew), told jokes from our various TV segments, and generally improvised our way through a show. The interesting thing was that the kids could now see that Lee was manipulating Norbert's arm at the end of his hand and it didn't make any difference to them. They looked at the puppet's face, ignoring Lee, and responded to Norbert as if he were real.

We did TV specials for Christmas and Easter and for the next six years the show was broadcast twice a day, six days a week! I became a celebrity to several generations of kids, as we were in reruns for the next twenty-five years!

One time I was in a supermarket and a mother with a four-year-old child said, "Look, Bruce, there's the *Boomerang* Lady!" The child was horrified and hid behind his mom's skirts.

"But she can't be the *Boomerang* Lady!"

"Why not?"

"Because the *Boomerang* Lady is only this big."

He then indicated with his fingers a span of about two inches high.

He only knew what he saw on his TV, not the giant Marni Nixon standing in the aisle in frozen foods! Kids are amazing!

Just as 1975 saw the beginning of a new career as a TV star, it also witnessed the end of my short-lived marriage. Our marriage was officially dissolved on July 31 of that year, meaning we were together for four years and one week.

What happened? Nothing and everything.

Earlier in 1975, Melani, who had been quite unhappy in Seattle, had left home and moved back to California to live with her father. She had been spending the summers with Ernest and, as she has recently told me, felt more nurtured and cared for during those times. She said that it was very difficult for her to come back in the fall to where the rules were different and where she felt lost. Melani also felt the tension at home between Fritz and me, and certainly wanted no part of that.

So one day, without consulting me, Ernest decided it would be best for Melani to live with him in L.A. and go to school there. I was very hurt at first, but rationalized that it might be what was best for everyone. Melani had made her own decision. I was devastated. Ernest had always tried to be a good father, though, and this fact made me feel a little better. Truthfully, for a while at least, this situation improved the relationship between Fritz and me. There was less tension at home, to be sure. But it wasn't to last.

Despite being alone with Fritz, I had an underlying sense of discontent that I didn't know how to voice. We went to a few group sessions using the Transactional Analysis (TA) format, best known by the best-selling book *I'm OK, You're OK* by Tom Harris, to explore our marital discord. The therapist taught

Layos Frederick (Fritz)
Fenster, MD in 1988.
We were married from
1971 to 1975. (From
the author's collection)

us to approach communication ("transactions") by analyzing what part of our personality—parent, adult, child—was being utilized at any given moment. If one of us was acting as the child and the other the parent, then a "crossed transaction" occurred. This usually resulted in arguments or hurt feelings. It was clear to me that Fritz was the "adult" who had trouble expressing his inner child. Being joyful and uninhibited was alien to his personality. One day at the dinner table, he turned to me and asked, "What is intimacy?" At first I thought he was just trying to talk about it cerebrally, but later on I realized he really didn't know how to *be* intimate. As a performer, I could easily access my "child" side, and it was obvious I was the more emotional of the two of us. Fritz's cerebral take on things sometimes clashed with my more demonstrative way of dealing with issues. As time went on, it became clear that our relationship just wasn't right.

In the end, Fritz turned to me and said, "You know I can see that in order to sustain 'us,' I will have to change a bit. But I see that I just can't. No, that's not true . . . I just won't."

In addition to being a brilliant doctor, Fritz was always a very honest and fair person. As he recently phrased it, "If there is anything like a 'no fault' divorce, this was it."

Over the years I have gathered what I like to call my "Angel Network." These are amazing people who have been there for me. People who are not my family or husbands, but friends, lovers, and sometimes-casual-acquaintances who have helped me beyond the call of duty. People who have helped me to learn and grow. Some of them I have remained friends with and some I have never encountered again. But these people appeared at times when I was spiritually and psychologically in deep trouble. Sometimes I didn't even know the extent of my own difficulties, but there they were—the angels.

After my divorce from Fritz, just when I was at my lowest ebb emotionally, an angel named Joe Scaylea descended. Joe was a passionate nature photographer who took pictures for the *Seattle Times*, among other publications. I would accompany Joe on many scenic photographic shoots and we would have a wonderful time. Often we would sit outdoors in the middle of the night waiting for a certain effect, waiting for the moon to be in just the right shadow. Waiting for the perfect picture. Although our relationship grew more and more romantic (at least to me), Joe was a lot older than I.

"Marni," he would say, "you've got to know that you have to connect up with somebody younger than I."

Joe would just appear, like a mysterious imp, whenever I really needed him. I can remember one time when I was so sad over the divorce (Joe always thought Fritz and I would get back together) that I couldn't stop crying. After hours of weeping, the phone rang. It was Joe. He somehow knew something was wrong and said he was coming over. I tried to dissuade him. I wanted to wallow in my tears, I think. But before I knew it, the doorbell rang and there was Joe in his tennis whites.

"All right. You just get into your tennis shorts and come with me."

"Oh, Joe," I wailed, "I can't."

"You're going to," Joe insisted with a twinkle in his pale green eyes. "Get your racket! We're going to go play tennis."

"Joe, I can't, I can't play tennis."

"Get into your shorts! Stop this nonsense and get dressed!"

Well, Joe won and when we got on the court he practically ordered me to return the ball. Wham! He slammed the ball to me.

"Hit the ball!" he shouted. "Hit it harder, damn it! Come on, hit the goddamned ball as hard as you can!"

Finally I listened to him. And wham! I slammed that ball with all my might. Then again! Back and forth, until we were both hysterical with laughter.

When he knew I felt better, he just disappeared again. I really loved Joe, and if he had been amenable I might have married him. But Joe had other ideas. For seven years after the divorce, and until I left Seattle, Joe was the head of my angel network.

Back in the late 1960s, Leonard Stein and I went into Herschel Gilbert's small basement recording studio in Hollywood and recorded Arnold Schoenberg's *Cabaret Songs*. These eight songs were written in 1901, when the young Schoenberg was conductor and musical advisor to the Überbrettl Cabaret in Berlin. The words were by well-known poets and dramatists of the period, such as Otto Julius Bierbaum and Frank Wedekind, the author of the novel *Spring's Awakening*.

Several years before, Schoenberg's son Larry pulled the songs out of a drawer (Schoenberg had died in 1951), handed them to me, and said that I was the only one he could think of who could do justice to them. He asked me to find some way of commercially recording them. So Leonard and I set out on our mission. After recording what amounted to a demonstration version of the songs, we submitted them to Schoenberg's German publisher to get the rights to peddle them further to a commercial record company. The publisher denied their existence.

"Schoenberg *never* wrote cabaret songs," we were informed rather imperiously by mail. "This was beneath him!"

Well, this made me see red and I decided to perform them whenever I could. We did them at the Schoenberg Institute at USC and at several other venues. I worked out my own staging of the songs, with the help of Heinz Blankenburg, a dear and crazy friend. Heinz (with whom I had gone to college) was an American baritone who was renowned in the world's opera houses, but especially in Germany, for his many operatic roles. In Germany, he was given the title of "Herr Kammersänger" (literally translated as Mr. Court Singer; it is a title given to prominent German singers), which is quite an honor. Heinz was invaluable in helping me understand and pronounce the texts of the songs correctly. He knew all the dialects and passed on his knowledge to me.

In 1975 I did a concert at Alice Tully Hall in New York, with Phillips and Renzulli, duo pianists, and sang the Schoenberg *Cabaret Songs*. I made sure we got a review and some media coverage (not an easy task), and also had pirated a live recording in the basement of Alice Tully Hall. The next day I had what I thought was an appointment with Tom Frost, the head of CBS Records' classical division. Frost, a major proponent of modern music, had known me for some time, but it turned out that somehow I had called the wrong Tom at the

Leonard Stein and I rehearsing in 1978, L.A. (Photo Frank Larkin)

wrong record company and made my appointment with Tom Shepard at RCA Records. I still don't know how I made that mistake, but fate has a way of making me do certain things.

I had rented some costume pieces for the concert and planned to return them to the costume rental company after the meeting. I also was lugging the big reel-to-reel tapes of the previous evening's concert with me, which I'd not even heard yet. So when I entered the hallowed halls of RCA, I must have looked like some kind of soprano bag lady. Tom Shepard somehow got a kick out of how silly I looked and was already giggling and teasing me a bit. A good beginning. I tried to be as cool as possible, as well as hide my confusion. I was, after all, supposed to be seeing my friend Tom Frost. Shepard was very cordial, and he asked about the concert. I started to tell him all about it when he whipped out the review that had come out that morning. John Rockwell in *The New York Times* had erroneously compared Schoenberg's *Cabaret Songs* from 1901 with the songs from the film *Cabaret*. He ended his review by saying that I was no Liza Minnelli! Tom found this very amusing. After we had a good laugh he spoke.

"Well, let's hear these tapes you made."

"I haven't even heard them yet," I stalled. "I don't even know if they came out well."

"Hand them over!"

With that he put the tapes on the machine and played the live recording of the concert. I began taking the props out and, in a reversal of my ghost singer roles, lip-synched to my own recording, performing them in his office. Tom stopped suddenly, picked up the phone, and said to someone, "Get Peter Delheim in here. I want him to hear this."

When Delheim (a major executive at RCA) came in he greeted me with his German accent and said he knew Ernest from *Exodus* times and that he admired him very much. Delheim listened to the tape, which, of course, was in German, and got very excited about the project and the fact that the songs were by Schoenberg. The two of them just loved the songs and within an hour I had a record deal. Sometimes I guess it's a good thing to be in the wrong place at the right time!

Later that year Leonard Stein and I came east and recorded the songs in RCA's wonderful New York studio. The record (they were still records then; here's hoping for a new CD release soon!) was released in 1976, and in 1977, I was nominated for a Grammy Award, which I lost to Beverly Sills.

———

The late 1970s found me unmarried, independent, and still living in Seattle. I was in my late forties and all the kids were out of the nest. One night Melani called from California to say that she left high school and wanted to get a job. I was devastated for her. I told her that without a high school education she would never go to college. I even told her that she wouldn't be able to get a passport. That's not true, of course, but I thought so at the time. Melani, however, was determined. Later on, she told me how the public school system had failed her. She said that the teachers were apathetic and the kids were all drugged out and bored to tears. Melani felt that she was wasting her time. Luckily she got a job quickly. She started out doing fashion sales and then moved on to working the box office at the Laemmle Theater in Westwood, soon becoming the manager of the theater.

Besides rehearsing and taping *Boomerang*, I kept busy doing some theater in Seattle (*I Do! I Do!*, *The Sound of Music*, *Jacques Brel*) and many concerts and recitals, such as the Schoenberg/Webern/Stein recital at Los Angeles' Schoenberg Institute in 1978. It was like Old Home Week. The whole audience consisted of friends and colleagues. It was marvelous to feel the warm welcome from these people who had practically grown up with me and were now loyal fans.

Mr. and Mrs. Stanley Kramer (he had been so instrumental in Ernest's career) at the 1978 Emmy Awards Ceremony, Seattle, Washington. (Photo John E. Walker)

In 1979 I performed the premiere of a song cycle called *Coplas*, which Mario Castelnuovo-Tedesco had orchestrated for me the year before he died. We had done these songs together with him at the piano, and premiering them with an orchestra was quite an honor. I also sang a series of concerts for the Bel-Canto series in Washington, and traveled to the L.A. County Museum in May for a tribute to Lawrence Morton, who helped found the Monday Evening Concert series that was so instrumental to my growth.

In 1980 *Boomerang* ceased production after 169 shows and some specials. The reruns would go on and on, but my commitment to the show was over. Suddenly I was free and could move wherever I wanted. I was fifty years old and decided to take stock of what I really needed and wanted. What the three of us—me, myself, and I— *really wanted*.

I had been divorced from Fritz for five years and had no lack of male companionship, but no one who sparked me. The local papers had dubbed me "Miss Glamour" and a "National Treasure," but I was getting tired of being treated by the local single men as a show-off prize on their sleeve. I wanted to relate to a man as a woman, yet also be a successful achiever in the limelight. I was a warm mother of three kids who needed emotional intimacy and friendship and understanding. I wanted to give all I had to someone else. I was lonely.

Of course, that did not mean burying and negating myself either. I wanted sovereignty over my domain, along with a man who needed what I could give.

It seemed to me that I was giving everything all the time and never getting what *I* needed, psychologically. I knew I had to learn how to center myself more and not *need* so much from the outside. Here I was, this seemingly independent person with iron nerves, and the men I'd chosen to be with were nonplussed when I needed physical and emotional help and appeared to want something from them. Did I need to just grow up and realize that it's all right if things *aren't* perfect? Or did I still need to "fix" things too much?

These were questions that needed to be answered. There were other wants as well. My professional wants. I wanted to be with other people who went to rehearsals, did shows, prepared for concerts, fought with their agents, and educated the public and themselves.

I needed a new and bigger venue. Not L.A. I needed to move forward, not back. Of course! It had been beckoning me ever since I had first gone there twenty years earlier. Marni, like Eve, was about to leave her beautiful and safe garden behind for danger and excitement. Where else?

New York City.

Chapter Thirteen
MY ANGEL NETWORK

"New York, New York, a Helluva Town!"

BETTY COMDEN and ADOLPH GREEN, 1944

(from *On the Town*)

T O THE REST OF THE COUNTRY, New York City in the 1970s and 1980s was a filthy, crime-filled, dangerous place to visit. When Shirley MacLaine opened her one-woman show at the Palace Theatre on Broadway in 1976, she dubbed New York "The Karen Ann Quinlin of cities," referring to the young woman being kept alive on life support machines. In the late 1970s, when Mayor Abe Beame asked the federal government for help, headlines blazed "President tells New York to Go to Hell!" There was no doubt about it: New York needed a better press agent. But, to me, it was always paradise! After all, wasn't it the cultural center of the world? Every time I stepped onto the island of Manhattan to work, didn't I somehow feel like I was coming home?

It was actually my daughter Melani, on one of our many long-distance phone calls, who came up with the big idea.

"You should move to New York, Mom," she told me with wisdom beyond her sixteen years. "It's time to leave Seattle and move on."

She was right. Luckily, the timing was propitious for me to sell my house in Seattle. Real estate was beginning to boom, I had residuals coming in from *Boomerang*, and the kids were all thriving in their separate worlds. It was the right time for me to make this move. On my own. A new life. A new apartment. I thought it would be a breeze. Boy, was I wrong!

In 1980, I was appearing in a wonderful nightclub revue at the King Cole Room in New York's St. Regis Hotel entitled *Thank Heaven for Lerner and Loewe* when I found an apartment on the Upper West Side. It was smaller than I had hoped, but really all I could afford at the time. I thought it would be easy to get a loan using my house on Mercer Island as collateral. I could show my increase of income over the years, and I thought that would be fine for the bank. Wrong! I was told I was a single woman without a steady job or a steady salary. Not a good risk. I was also a freelance artist working on many jobs, and the banks never want to know about such people. I had put down $20,000 for a down payment and if I didn't secure the loan, I would lose the money. I was desperate!

I had racked my brains and gone down every dead end avenue I could think of to obtain a loan when, literally one day before my deadline to secure the loan, I suddenly remembered that I had recently dated the head of one of the most powerful banks in the world, the Seattle First National Bank. Thankfully, when I called him in Seattle from New York and told him my predicament, he was moved.

"Well, Marni," he sweetly said, "I've been to your house to pick you up and I can tell what the appraisal would be. I can give you a loan so you can buy the apartment with cash and then we'll give you a second mortgage on your home in Seattle."

Hallelujah! Another addition to my angel network—in just two hours!

I bought the apartment outright and arranged to lease the house on Mercer Island. Back in Seattle, I had a giant garage sale, packed up my life—including my huge musical library and my gowns—and put them all in a moving van headed to New York, where I was to meet it.

Having lived in houses my whole life, the apartment, although large for New York, was definitely going to be something of a challenge. I knew something had to be done to make it more livable. "Look over there! There's a window in that room to the right. If you tore down this wall, you'd have this huge area and you'd walk in the room and you'd see these two windows. It would definitely look like a huge loft space."

This wonderful advice came from the baritone mouth of Steve Elmore. Steve had costarred in the Lerner and Loewe evening with me and, as soon as he told me his idea for the apartment, I knew he was right. Tear down the wall! Brilliant! Amazingly, I was able to get approval from the president of the co-op board to do it, something that wouldn't be quite so simple today.

I raced around getting estimates, hired a contractor and his crew, and began remodeling. This was the middle of summer and, of course, there was no air conditioning in the apartment yet. After all, the apartment still had to be rewired. There was so much to do.

While I supervised the proceedings and made millions of crucial choices, I was crashing at my friend actress Zoya Leporska's apartment. Then when Zoya returned from her out-of-town acting gig, I moved some of my things into one corner of my new apartment and lugged another suitcase to a crazy new friend I had just met, David Man, who had an apartment three blocks away and who subsequently became my acting teacher. With everything at my apartment in a state of flux, I would go back and forth between sleeping in David's guest room and "almost" sleeping on my little mat on the floor in the corner of my torn-up apartment. Every morning and evening, like Mother

Courage, I would trudge from place to place, pushing my little cart containing my meager belongings. Is it any wonder I became known as the "Bag Lady of West End Avenue?"

Unlike the fabled Walls of Jericho, the wall on West End Avenue did not come tumbling down easily or quickly. In fact, some of the wall still remained when the furniture finally arrived from Seattle. Now I had to figure out what to do with the furniture without the space to put it in.

To make sure that the contractor could still do his work, the movers had to pile all the furniture, including my antique mahogany piano with real ivory keys, into a corner of the room, one piece on top of another, like a jumbled jigsaw puzzle that would have to be put together later. Everything in my life was piled in a big, huge lump, taking up two thirds of one of the apartment's two rooms. This huge lump in the corner of the room was then tightly covered with plastic so that plaster dust wouldn't get into it. At least that was the plan.

And so the work continued. After the wall was *finally* torn down, resulting in floating plaster dust rivaling the eruption of Mount Saint Helens, one side of the room was then plastered and painted. When that was done, the workers painstakingly moved the entire mound to the other side of the room and began the painting and plastering process on that side. Finally, just when I thought I couldn't take another day of it, the work was done. A miracle! Now it was time to organize the furniture and storage spaces, which I had tried to create. Enter another member of my angel network.

Gene Varrone's clear, ringing tenor voice had delighted Broadway audiences for three decades, but when he walked into my chaotic apartment, he suddenly became the best interior designer in New York. Instead of a big mess, Gene saw the future!

"I love it! I just *love it!*" He operatically clenched his breast and rang out. "This is fabulous! I can see just what we're going to do!"

Right then and there he vowed to help me organize the space. We began to pull apart the puzzle that was my pile of furniture and slowly distributed it. The good news was that there was not a scratch on anything. It was like magic. The piano was even still in tune.

Little by little, though, things kept going wrong, as things will. The hardware store was out of this. That didn't fit where I hoped it would. The pipes were too old and weren't delivering hot water the way they should. These were just small annoyances that anyone used to New York City and apartment living deals with every day. I, however, was used to living in the suburbs. Consequently, every time something went wrong, I lost my legendary iron nerves and became hysterical. Gene's response was to push me down on the high wooden platform, which was to be the base of the bed, searing me with his big brown eyes and taking charge.

"What makes you think that you're not entitled to have any of these problems that we all have to go through?" he screamed at me. "Who do you think you are? This is New York. Of course you're going to have trouble like you've never had before! Now, you just shut the hell up, and stop all this feeling sorry for yourself, and let's get on with it."

I stopped my crying and we stared at each other for what seemed like a long time, but was probably a minute. Then we both broke out laughing. What else could I do? Here I was, a woman who had managed a career, built a house from scratch, been through two marriages and a couple of affairs, had fought with the world's greatest conductors, and had given birth to and raised three kids. Was I going to let a little apartment get to me? No way! Not with Gene around. Before too long everything was looking wonderful.

Of course, all during the trauma of the apartment I was auditioning for everything and anything all over town. In the past, I had always had to defer my New York dreams for the sake of the marriage, for the sake of the kids and family. But now, it was all about *me*. I was longing to become known as an East Coast dramatic actress. And what fun to be able to *walk* to an audition! You couldn't do that in L.A. It was good for the figure, too! Plus you never knew who might be looking. Romance was always around the corner in New York City, it was said.

Ever since my divorce from Fritz, I had had no shortage of romances. I had even gone so far as to become engaged back in Seattle to a very sweet man name Bill Ransdell. He was a fund-raiser for the North West Kidney Foundation and very much *not* in show biz. Looking back now, I was attracted to him because he reminded me of my parents and their midwestern ideals, and although he was also a good photographer and appreciative listener, we were more than light years apart in every way. It dawned on me at our engagement party that I might be making a mistake when I was introducing Bill to one of my friends and couldn't remember his name! I knew then that the wedding would never take place. I was definitely growing and shedding my ghostly veils when I broke it off before either of us could be hurt too much.

When I got to New York, a whole new world of men was waiting for me. One, Ned Naumburg, had been a friend for a while and had squired me around town whenever I came east. Ned was from a family of philanthropists that had, among other things, subsidized a prestigious annual vocal competition. They also dedicated their lives to presenting music free of charge in the Naumburg Band Shell in Central Park and Ned, personally, was devoted to the Naumburg Orchestral Concert series. Ned was a good deal older than I was but, at the time, he seemed the perfect escort. He was impishly elegant, collected silver and first editions of John Updike, played the violin (he had a gorgeous Stradivarius, the best violin in the world), and had an amusing wit.

Finally in the star's habit, as Maria in The Sound of Music *in a 1982 tour. (© 1957 Twentieth Century Fox. All rights reserved.)*

Perhaps thinking I was falling for him, one night Ned turned to me and twinkled at me mischievously.

"Marni," he said, "you know, I'm old and washed up, don't you?"

I just giggled. I had always taken our friendship just as it was and now that I was in a new town and feeling lonely, Ned was wonderful about filling the void between romances. His sophisticated, sweet, and knowledgeable world of genuine culture was a haven for me. Before too long, though, a *real* romance presented itself to me.

Danny Duhl and I had remodeling in common. He had just finished renovating the offices of his textile business, and that gave us something to talk about at first. We had met at a little pub on 54th Street, where I had gone by myself to see a student's nightclub act. I remember I was sitting all alone at a small table when a waiter approached me.

"Excuse me, Miss Nixon," the waiter said, "but a gentlemen who is a fan of yours wants to meet you. He also wonders if he might sit at your table, as he is alone and you're alone and there are no other tables free."

With much trepidation (and the thought of skipping out right after the show if the guy was a creep), I said yes. Happily, he turned out to be absolutely charming. It so happened that Danny lived right across the street from the pub and had a deal with the waiter to call him if anyone of "interest" showed up. That night it was me! I actually thought his little ploy was pretty clever and we laughed about it later.

Danny was wealthy, interesting, single (or so I thought at the time), and before too long we were dating. On Tuesday nights only. Danny told me very honestly that he was busy every other night of the week. I should have taken that as a warning sign. It turned out that Danny was separated from his wife and had a girl friend with whom he lived part time in Woodstock, New York. Despite not being his only girl, I fell for him. Hard. So it was shocking when I returned home one night to a message on my answering machine from his wife. She had somehow found out about me and decided to tell me some facts, the biggest of which was that she and Danny were not quite as "separated" as he had led me to believe. When I confronted Danny with this fact, he admitted that it was true. He also told me that his wife said that she would "make trouble" for him if he asked for a divorce.

The situation began to pain me. How did this happen? Little Marni was "the other woman." Not even the only other woman; I was one of two other women! Even Lana Turner in *Back Street* didn't have *that* complication.

One night I was out with Ned at a concert at Damrosch Park, the lovely outdoor concert space between the Metropolitan Opera and the New York State Theater in Lincoln Center, when I was approached by Danny's Woodstock girl friend (I was beginning to wonder how many others there might be). She was very nice and knew who I was, but it was clear that she was hurt and that I had upset their little applecart. The plot was thickening and I didn't like how it was going to play out.

That weekend, I had taken to my bed in a psychological state of catatonia because my acting teacher, David Man, had confronted me with the deepest part of myself. This started a sequence of thinking about my own deep inner self. I was furious with him for churning all this up and I was furious with Danny for not being "available." After a weekend of wailing and not eating, I came to the realization that I really *did* need to discover my own voice: my inner voice, that is. All this getting involved with men who weren't free to be involved with me was only a symptom of my grabbing at other people's support, rather than relying on myself. By the end of the weekend, it became clear that I might be alone the rest of my life, and that *that* was okay. Maybe I needed to not need a man. The turmoil began to subside. So, I decided to use my time and energy to find my own voice again, and I resolved to call a moratorium on looking for a man. On our regular Tuesday date, I blurted out all this to Danny and we parted as friends. As for myself, I felt I'd made a momentous decision about my life. I felt that I was free and clear once more. I felt empowered by my resolve. And the resolve lasted.

For a whole week.

It was a balmy June night in 1982. I arrived early and alone at Damrosch Park to represent Ned, who couldn't be there, at the latest Naumburg concert. All the tied-together white plastic chairs were sitting empty in rows. In the exact center of the vast expanse of chairs sat a lone man. I have no idea what prompted me to, but with hundreds of seats available to me, I sat right down next to him. I didn't look at him or talk to him, but just sat staring straight ahead, waiting for the concert to begin. As the sun began to set, a few people started arriving and filling the seats. From out of the small crowd came a voice I recognized.

"Marn!" she yelled for all to hear.

Michelle Reiner had been one of my best friends when we were both in the chorus of *The Girl in Pink Tights* back in 1954. We had been the two girls who fainted under the weight of our heavy helmets while rehearsing one of the Sigmund Romberg musical numbers. In the interim, Michelle had married Ned's cousin, Dr. George Naumburg, and she, too, was at the concert representing the family.

"So," Michelle bellowed, with her operatic training still apparent, "what have you been doing for the last thirty years?"

I filled her in on my thirty-year history, taking my story up to date with my recent move to New York. I told her the apartment saga and bemoaned the fact that it was very hard to meet the right kind of men in Manhattan. I confided that I had recently gotten myself out of a romantic mess. "And tennis!" I went on complaining. "I love to play tennis, but I have no idea how to find anyone to play with here."

The man next to me had obviously overheard everything. He leaned over to me, smiled, and whispered softly in my ear.

"I play tennis."

I looked at him for the first time, thinking, "Well, he's not a total reject. Actually he's kind of cute and gentlemanly."

Michelle settled back in her seat, and the man and I began to chat. He told me his name was Al Block and that he was a symphonic flutist who doubled on all the reed instruments (the saxes and clarinets). I was impressed when he told me that he had played and recorded with such jazz musicians as Charlie Parker, Miles Davis, and Benny Goodman. He also told me he played in orchestras on Broadway. In fact, he had played the original *West Side Story* and *Gypsy*. Not too shabby, thought I. We talked about music and tennis and my heart began to flutter a bit. He was so easy to talk to and so cool and nice. Our conversation just seemed inevitable. I knew a little bit about him by the end of the concert and, thanks to my babbling to Michelle, he knew *all* about the last thirty years of *my* life! As the audience filed out of their rows, Al invited me to play tennis the next day and asked if he could have my phone number. Should I give him my home number or my service number? I wondered. Throwing caution to the wind, I decided to give him my home number.

On the tennis court I could tell he had played every day for the last thirty years, for heaven's sake, while I was, well, way out of practice. He hit the ball easily to my side of the net and watched with great reserved amusement as competitive, intermediate me ran, panted, cursed, and smashed and chopped away at the ball. At least he saw I could run around every ball and my intent and energy were good! Catching my breath and sweating profusely, I wanted to sit down now and talk and laugh again. There, we were, at least, on even ground.

"You know," Al quietly said, "with a strong man you just have to tell him what you want."

Oh my God! He remembered my entire diatribe to Michelle about what I thought was wrong with the men I was meeting. I was terribly embarrassed, but also a little bit enchanted by his straightforward and simple way. It came out in conversation that we both had been divorced for seven years. A good sign! Synchronicity. He escorted me home and asked me out to dinner. I heard my heart saying yes, but I didn't want to actually utter the word. After all, hadn't I made a pact with myself last week about not starting new relationships? ("Was dinner a relationship?" my softer side asked. "Well," my newly pragmatic side replied, "it could lead to one!") So I compromised with both sides and told him that I would cook dinner for him tomorrow. As friends have told me, cooking dinner was the most intimate thing I could do on the first date. I guess they were right, because from then on Al and I were inseparable. He just kept coming over and then never left.

About a week after we had met, Al was at my place eating the dinner I had just cooked when the phone rang. It was Danny.

"Danny," I said with surprise in my voice, "what are you doing calling me tonight? This isn't Tuesday!"

Al tried to look like he wasn't listening by rolling his eyes around to find something he could concentrate on.

"Marni, I just wanted to talk to you," Danny said. "I felt something was wrong and just wanted to hear your voice and . . . I want to see you."

I could have killed him, but instead I calmly told him that I had company and would call him in the morning. When I hung up the phone there was an embarrassing silence, which Al sweetly broke.

"Look, Marni, we both didn't just fall from the sky. I am committed to you. You can just take your time. It's all right."

How many times have I yearned to hear that? This was a unique moment and I knew it.

The next morning I called Danny and told him that I had indeed met a man and that I felt I needed to experience it fully and see where it might lead. Danny said he had called because he knew something was wrong. He realized now that we were more connected than he thought we were. Sadly I told Danny that, although I did still love him in a way, he was *not* divorced and there was no guarantee of any long-term relationship. I just didn't want to get hurt that way again. It ripped me apart, but it had to be said. We sadly hung up and I realized that we would never see each other again.

I had done a very difficult thing and felt proud.

Al and I were like two bumps on a log—we sank into each other. We lived together for a little less than a year before the conversation veered toward the "M" word: marriage. Should we or shouldn't we?

One night, before Al had to go and play in the pit of *Merlin* (a musical starring magician Doug Henning and dancing legend Chita Rivera, not to mention featuring a very young Nathan Lane), the phone rang with an offer that would change my life. On the other end of the line was the social director of a cruise ship wanting to know if I would be interested in doing my act on board ship. The cruise would be leaving from the West Coast and going to the Panama Canal. I played it cool, taking down all the details, and telling him that I would call him back later with my answer. Before I could even get the receiver back on the hook Al, red in the face, eagerly pounced.

"I tell you what, if you take that cruise, let's get married on the ship!"

You could have knocked me over with a feather. My Lord, romance wasn't dead! "Why not?" I said, "Let's do it."

When we boarded the ship we were introduced to an all-purpose, generic minister-priest-rabbi with a red nose and breath that could knock a horse over. That is, if the horse liked gin! He was sloppy, unkempt, and his fly was open.

"What," he asked in his booze-soaked voice, "kind of service do you want?" There was a pause. Al, who can play it cool (after all he *is* a jazz musician), is also very opinionated and stubborn. He rolled his eyes to the heavens.

"Well," he said with great finality, "we'll let you know."

Al was not about to be married by that man. Truth be told, neither was I.

That night we went out on the deck to watch the sun set. There was not a cloud in the sky, and as the sun began to sink into the horizon we saw it: that flash of green light surrounding the orange sun that remained for several minutes until the sun just slipped into the horizon. We had heard about an unusual natural phenomenon called "the green flash" and had always longed to see it. At that very moment we saw three dolphins gracefully diving in and out of the

Making sweet music with Al at our wedding reception. The violin isn't his, but mine. Al is a reed player! (From the author's collection)

ocean, following the exact speed of the ship. It was incredible and we were the only ones on deck to see it. It was as if it happened just for us. At that moment of awe, Al turned to me and quietly spoke from his heart.

"This is for us. *This* is our wedding ceremony. This is ours and ours alone. I commit myself to you forever."

As the tears of joy streamed down my face, we just stood there together until the sky grew darker and darker, fading to black. There was not a waft of breeze to break the stillness. I searched the sky for the moon and the stars, but knew inside that I might have just found them.

When we got home, my secretary had decorated the apartment with streamers and balloons and a sign saying, "Welcome Home Newlyweds!" We felt so embarrassed that we called Al's brother and wife and asked them to join us down at City Hall where, on April 11, 1983, we indulged in the $6 wedding special.

Twenty-four years later, we're still together. No matter that our sometimes tremendous clash of opposing points of view keep us sparring, I guess our deep love somehow helps us live through the worst of our fights. And, of course, *thank God* for our sense of humor.

Married or not, I was beginning to be taken seriously in my new hometown of New York and, in June of 1983, I opened in my first off-Broadway musical, *Taking My Turn*.

Off Broadway had hardly existed when I first came to New York in the early 1950s, but ever since the successes of *The Threepenny Opera* in 1954 and the revival of *Summer and Smoke* in 1955, smaller theaters in areas such as Greenwich Village began to thrive. In 1960, a tiny musical called *The Fantasticks* opened at the Sullivan Street Playhouse in the Village and ran for thirty-six years! Off Broadway was here to stay.

In 1980, a director-writer named Robert H. Livingston, who had had a great success with the youth-oriented *The Me Nobody Knows* (1971), came up with the notion of examining the lives of older people. He brought the idea to his *Me Nobody Knows* collaborators, Will Holt and Gary William Friedman, and although they were hesitant at first (they thought old people on the stage would be depressing!), once they saw the material that Bob had gathered (letters, poems, and essays, written by the aging about aging), they became intrigued. Soon they started to formulate a musical that would deal with the problems and wonders of aging, using characters aged fifty to eighty. It would be revuelike and yet take us on an abstract journey from one spring to the next. During that period, eight characters would express their hearts and souls in a celebration of living.

They had done a workshop production in June of 1980 and, as is often the case, it took three years for them to secure the backing to move the show to a commercial venue. Edna, the role that I was asked to play, had been portrayed in the workshop by Rita Gardner, the original star of *The Fantasticks*. Actors Equity rules demanded that since she did the workshop, Rita had to either be offered her role or "bought out." I guess they decided to pay her off. I had no idea why they wanted me instead of her (she is a marvelous performer and a friend), but as I was almost fired during rehearsals, it turned out we had a lot in common.

The cast was stellar. It included vocalist Margaret Whiting, whose father, Richard Whiting, had written so many standard songs, and whose sister had played the role I screen tested for in the film version of *Junior Miss* all those years ago. Small world. Also in the cast were such Broadway mainstays as Sheila Smith (she had understudied Angela Lansbury in *Mame*, among other Broadway credits), Tiger Haynes (he was a jazz singer, and had been a big hit in *The Wiz*), Victor Griffin (he had understudied Fred Astaire on Broadway), Ted Thurston (we'd been in *The Girl in Pink Tights* together), Mace Barret (he had understudied Steve Lawrence on Broadway), and Cissy Houston (Whitney's mom and a great singer in her own right). The eight of us began rehearsals under Bob Livingston's direction. I began to have difficulties right away. The structure of the show was such that we had lots of short speeches that were not directed at any character in particular, but functioned more as audible interior monologues. I found it very hard to connect to the material and with the other characters. I was confused by the lack of contact, except in the musical numbers, and in the ever-pervasive atmosphere of sadistic hostility coming from the director.

"We've finally figured it out," he announced one day at rehearsal, "let's pretend that this is sort of like a group analysis. We've all come together as a group and, although we're not in a session, we're all friends together, and we all come from different points of view."

Very nice, but I still couldn't find out who I was and what I was supposed to play. Since this was a musical, I thought I would at least be at home in the numbers. Then the choreographer descended. There was a musical number I shared with Maggie Whiting and Cissy Houston called "Fine for the Shape I'm In," which had a country-western feel and required some foot-stomping dance steps. The choreographer (who shall remain nameless) had no assistant and so, after he taught us the combination and moved on to the next number, any questions we had about executing the steps had to be addressed to our stage manager, whose replies were either hostile stares or verbal responses littered with "Just work it out yourself" and "It's fine, you know, they'll fix it up later." "Later" never came and I grew increasingly frustrated. I am not primarily a dancer, but eventually I *do* pick up the steps. I am just used to getting help from an assistant or dance captain.

Each person in the cast was wonderful and supportive in his or her own special ways. The great Tiger Haynes had a sweetly distinctive way of trying to make me feel better. Just when everything was at its worst, he would turn to me with a twinkle in his eye.

"Hey, listen," he would croon, "have you ever eaten real Mississippi Mud Pie? I know where you can get some right here in the Village!" It was his way of saying things are going to be okay. It's only a show. Unfortunately, I couldn't think that way.

After weeks of rehearsal I felt more and more at sea until, just before the first performances were about to start, I lost it when we were staging one of my solo numbers. The director and I were at complete opposite ends of the pole about how I should be interpreting the song. I finally couldn't take it anymore. Iron nerves be damned! I walked out of the theater and onto Second Avenue, having an emotional breakdown. My frustration with the vagueness of the direction and the lack of attention from the choreographer had me banging my fists on a parked car, which, of course, set off the alarm.

"I can't figure out what he wants," I cursed to myself, as the owner of the car angrily reset his car alarm. "Why can't I do this? There's something wrong." I am sure even the regulars on Second Avenue (who were known to be a bit irregular themselves) thought I was insane. When I walked out of the rehearsal, apparently the director had halted the proceedings to wait for me. Will Holt, the lyricist and the only sane person there, it seemed to me, came running out to the street to find me and witnessed my meltdown.

"Exactly what is the problem, Marni? What's going on here?"

I filled him in on how difficult everything had been and how frustrated and mistreated I felt.

"There's nobody I can go to for help," I said.

Will understood and sympathized and tried to get me to come back into rehearsal. I refused to go back. I told him that I felt totally embarrassed and childish, and that I had never been in this position before.

"Don't worry," he said in soothing tones. "Everybody understands that these things happen. You come back and keep your head up high."

Will went in first and made sure that the atmosphere was calm and welcoming for my return. He explained to the director what I had felt was wrong. When I returned to rehearsals, time was taken on restaging the number and finally I was able to get it. Later on, after the show had closed, one of the producers, Dick Seader, confided in me.

"Remember that time that you walked out of rehearsal?"

How could I forget?

"Do you realize what happened when you went out there on Second Avenue in the street?"

I had no idea.

"The director wanted to have you fired," Dick went on. "I told him, over my dead body! If she goes, I go!"

Amazing what you don't know. It turned out that Dick wanted the quality I brought to the show and wouldn't settle for anyone else.

During the previews, I was still having some trouble with the through line of the role, so I invited my friend Martha Schlamme to see a performance. Martha was a Viennese-born singer, actress, and teacher who specialized in the songs of Kurt Weill. She had done many concerts and one-woman shows (also a series of two-person Kurt Weill shows with actor-singer Alvin Epstein), utilizing not just her voice, but her finely honed acting skills to create dramatic vignettes of great power and passion. After the show I realized I could ask *her* the questions that I was not able to ask the director.

"Fine for the Shape I'm In!": Cissy Houston, Margaret Whiting, and me in Taking My Turn. *Despair had turned to triumph! (Photo Bert Andrews)*

"So, Martha, what *is* this show? What's happening and who am I in it?"

Martha spoke carefully. "It's a show where you don't have to have a through line of what your action is, nor of what you want out of the scene. But that's all right. You don't have to know who you are as a character in this. You just have to be yourself." Myself? There it was again.

"That's why they hired you, Marni. Whatever your inner self is, even if you're not aware of it, that's what they want."

For some reason this piece of wisdom hadn't quite sunken in before. Before this, nobody would sit down with me and try to find out what my problem was.

"Be yourself." "We hired you for you, Marni."

Be yourself. In essence, method acting is about bringing what is inside of you to the external character you are creating. It is using yourself and your own experiences, no matter who you are playing on the stage. By George, I got it! Everything about my performance instantly solidified after that. I just said the words and sang the songs. It was like a completely different show for me. And guess what? I received wonderful reviews. The notoriously mean-spirited John Simon of *New York Magazine* wrote, "A superior singer best known, alas, as the singing voice of such stars as Audrey Hepburn, Natalie Wood, and Deborah Kerr, Miss Nixon has more charm than any of them and looks delightful to boot. She can deliver a song in an onrush of ravishing innocence, peer through her spectacles with bemused benignity, or just sit with turned-in toes and a look of untrammeled expectancy that breaks your heart. What a shame that heretofore she has been more audible than visible; henceforth, she must be both. I think of scores of actresses who could take lessons in charm from her, even if, as I strongly suspect, charm cannot be learned."

Well, well, well! And all I was doing was not thinking about who I was, but letting myself alone. Every one of the more than 200 performances turned out to be a wonderful learning experience. I was learning to be me, whatever that was. Theatrically speaking, I felt that I was on my way.

After the satisfying run of *Taking My Turn* (we also did an original cast recording and filmed the show for PBS), I continued my concert and recording career. Symphony dates in Baltimore and Des Moines and a recording with the Pacific Coast Symphony filled my calendar for the next couple of years. Then on March 29, 1985, I was flying across the country to sing with my old cohort Leonard Stein at the Schoenberg Institute on the campus of USC.

As the plane winged its way west, I was going over my music and became conscious of a dry, irritating cough that wouldn't go away. I also realized that when I tried to talk I couldn't quite do it. The cords would only make an intermittent sound. I found that I could forcibly drive the sound through, but I had no control over it at all. Naturally, this was very distressing and frightening. When I got to L.A., I went straight to a throat doctor, who checked my vocal folds and found nothing wrong with them, but gave me some medication (with cortisone) that he said would take effect just before the concert began. I rehearsed the material I was to sing in my head, hoping that by the time the concert was to begin, these dysphonialike symptoms would disappear. They didn't.

"I have an announcement to make," I haltingly uttered as I hit the stage at 8:00 P.M. that evening. With my speech disorder still plaguing me, and with much difficulty, I told the audience (which was filled with old friends) what was happening and that I was still hoping to sing. After all, I was known never to cancel any engagements. Even if it was hard to speak, somehow I always was able to sing.

I sampled a few vocal phrases, but the dysphasia was still evident. "Shall I go on and try to sing the concert for you?" I asked the audience.

The reply came back from the houseful of friends. "Please, Marni, stop singing!" It was really very funny to hear that loud and clear.

No one wanted me to harm my voice, least of all me, so it was decided to postpone the concert to some future date. The audience was then invited to the lobby of the theater to enjoy chocolate-covered strawberries and champagne and we had a party!

As usual, when I was in L.A., I was staying with my friend and agent, Hal Gefsky, and, when I got back from the "unsung" concert, I had a message waiting for me from Roosevelt Hospital in New York.

Right before I left for L.A. I realized that, although I had been a doctor's wife in Seattle and had been thoroughly taken care of from a medical standpoint, I hadn't had a mammogram or Pap smear ever since moving to New York four years earlier. To remedy this I had gone to a nearby clinic in New York and had the tests done. The message from the hospital said that the clinic had sent the Pap smear and mammogram results to them and that they had found some abnormalities. They wanted me to return immediately to take another mammogram. My mind immediately went into overdrive. I should have known something was wrong. My body and my voice had always been my thermometer. If I couldn't sing, then it meant something major was amiss. And there was obviously something wrong.

"Oh, my God," I thought. "I have cancer in my breast. I have it in my cervix. It must be all through my body from top to bottom."

I immediately began grieving for myself, wondering what I was going to do, how was I to manage the rest of my life. Suffice it to say, I got no sleep that night, took the earliest flight I could back to New York, and had another mammogram and Pap smear.

My worst fears were realized. Something *was* very wrong. By now, my survival instinct overcame my fear and I took action.

"The best thing is to cut the whole breast off," said the incredibly insensitive surgeon I went to see.

I was in shock. He calmly went on.

"You can always have an implant. That's the best thing, because there's a ten percent chance that these things can go bad again. The same goes for radiation."

I went home to Al and we held hands as I told him the diagnosis and prognosis. I was ready to bite the bullet and just go have the surgery, until my angel network swooped into my life. Voices and reactions to remarks I'd made had instant feedback. Like a heavenly choir, I guess, people began calling me.

"Don't you dare think that that's the only solution!"

"Are you serious? I want to talk to you right now."

"You come down to this coffee shop this instant. I want to talk to you and tell you about my cancer."

I met with a friend of a friend who had experience in this matter.

"Look," she sternly said. "I had almost the same results as you and the same prognosis. But I did the research. I went to Sloan-Kettering and I found out about alternative treatments. A radical mastectomy is not always necessary, especially at this point in time. You don't know if it's in the lymph nodes or not.

That's why they have to take a frozen section of that. Who knows? It might be totally unnecessary for you to lose the whole breast. And if you do, remember that reconstruction is another invasive process."

Other friendly angel voices echoed hers.

"You call this person." "Here's a magazine article that I wrote about this." "Listen to me!" "Read this!"

But the most persistent chorus sang about the time element.

"You've got to get the cancer *fast, fast, fast.*"

Time was definitely of the essence. I had my network investigating the latest treatments and reporting back to me as the clock ticked away. It was then that I decided to call my ex-husband Fritz. Although Fritz was a liver specialist and not an oncologist, he was a saint of a doctor, and smart and caring enough to steer me in the right direction. After I told him the results of my tests he said, "I'm going to have my best friend, who is the head of oncology here at the Mason Clinic, call you right away on the phone. You stay right where you are and keep your medical report handy so you can read what it says, and you tell him what they told you."

The treatment for cancer had not become as sophisticated as it is now, but what I found out from the oncologist was that, in my case, removing the whole breast wasn't the only way to go. It also finally began to dawn on me that this was *my* decision. It was *my* breast, for heaven's sake.

In the end, with all the facts lined up in front of me, we all chose to do a lumpectomy on my right breast. Lumpectomy is the most common form of breast cancer surgery today. The surgeon removes only the part of your breast containing the tumor (the "lump") and some of the normal tissue that surrounds it. Technically, a lumpectomy is a partial mastectomy, because part of the breast is removed. But how much of the breast is removed can vary greatly. Still, in all, it was preferable to removing the whole breast. Before the surgery, however, I signed a paper giving the surgeon permission to remove the breast if they found the cancer had spread to the lymph nodes.

When I woke up in the recovery room my gynecologist was there, stroking my cheek and whispering in my ear in the most soothing tones.

"You can go back to sleep," he said, "but I want to tell you that they did do a lumpectomy. You've still got your breast. They only took a little bit of a lump and only four lymph nodes were involved. We got it early, so you didn't lose your whole breast. Now, go to sleep, Marni. Everything's going to be fine."

This was the most tender and dear thing for a doctor to do, and I will never forget him for it.

The next six weeks were spent doing cobalt radiation at Mt. Sinai Hospital Cancer Center. At first I was required to go every day, but after a while the treatments were reduced to three times a week. The nurses who took care of me there were the latest additions to my angel network. They were colorful, fun, and fiercely devoted to their patients. These angels helped to keep our gradually diminishing spirits fresh and, although the treatment made me progressively more exhausted, the nurses always tried to make my time there bearable.

The other saving grace of this whole period was the peaceful walk to and from the hospital across Central Park. We had a beautiful spring and summer, and being able to take in the glory of nature during this difficult time most certainly helped me to recover all the faster.

Toward the end of my six-week treatment I was given the final three-day "zapping." This entailed the doctors sticking a series of cobalt wires around the total periphery of the lumpectomy scar and administering a final large zap of radiation to the appointed area in order to kill whatever cancer cells may have been stubbornly hanging on. Because I was to be continually radiated, during this course of treatment I was ensconced in a room in the most remote, dismal, and dungeonlike part of the hospital. There I was, wired and all alone. Despite a telephone, a television, and books, the boredom and loneliness were intense. Meals were delivered by anonymous hands mysteriously cracking open the door and pushing a tray just inside the room on the floor. This, of course, was done so that I wouldn't contaminate anyone with my radiation. Sometimes the zaps of radiation would be so intense that I actually glowed, making me seem like Marni the ghost. Literally!

When the treatment was finally done, the doctors (saints and angels themselves) entered the room in their huge protective aprons and gloves and ripped the wires from my flesh. This was the most painful part of the whole procedure, as the flesh had begun to grow around the wires.

Before this final treatment began, Al was playing in the pit of the hit Broadway musical *La Cage aux Folles*; in fact, he played the entire four-year run. Steady gigs like this were few on Broadway, but during this period Al was finding that playing the jaunty and optimistic Jerry Herman score difficult.

"I just can't play my show," he hovered over me with red eyes and wailed out to me one day. "I get so upset thinking about you being sick and all!"

This made me furious.

"I am *not* sick, Goddamn it!" I shouted. "Yes, there *was* disease in me, but now it's gone. And we have to make sure that all those cells *stay* gone. Don't you understand?"

Before Al could speak, I became even more agitated.

"Al, I am healing here and I need all the energy I can muster to that purpose. My mind and spirit need to concentrate on keeping the cancer cells from multiplying. It doesn't help me at all for you to sit there and feel sorry for yourself. Or for me! It drags the energy right out of me. If you can't see that, then stay away until I get better!"

Al's face turned as white as a sheet.

"You mean you're not sick?" he stammered meekly.

"I was, but now I need all my energy to get better. So bug off!"

His mouth fell open and he burst out laughing. A moment later, so did I.

"You know what?" I said, between laughs. "I think I just healed *you!*"

A great weight was taken off of Al's shoulders and, consequently, mine as well. Now I could just energize and go forward.

Even after the six-week treatment period I was still very fatigued, but I decided to accept an easy gig on the QE2 as part of a celebrity cruise. I was able to rest and, happily for my artistic psyche, I was able to do my cruise ship act. I knew if I could sing I was getting back on my professional horse, and that eventually everything was going to be all right with my health. And it was.

For the next fifteen years.

Chapter Fourteen
POSTERITY IS JUST
AROUND THE CORNER

"One of our greatest gifts is the ability to learn, grow, and change
right up to the moment we die, and after that, who knows?"

MARGARET WITTKE MCEATHRON, 1990

THE FIFTEEN YEARS AFTER MY LUMPECTOMY gleam clear and bright in my memory. In fact, they practically sparkle. When one is given a reprieve, another chance to live, it's as if the shutters have been open and the sun can come streaming in. I had my health, I had Al, and I had what always sustained me, the God-given talent and drive to go on. And go on I did. Happily, I was constantly getting work and, that magical thing that sustains all theatrical types between jobs, publicity. Sometimes it comes in the oddest ways.

Alan Jay Lerner died in June of 1986, and the lights of Broadway were lowered for one minute that night to honor his life and theatrical achievements. If he had written *My Fair Lady* alone, it would have been enough to ensure him a place in the hall of fame, but Lerner also penned *Brigadoon*, *Camelot*, *Gigi*, *An American in Paris*, *On a Clear Day*, and other great musicals and films.

I was out of town working when his memorial service was presented at the Shubert Theater, but from the press releases, it promised to be a star-studded event. When Broadway memorializes one of its own, the tributes tend to be more like well-produced shows than mere services. The biggest of stars show up to sing, dance, and tell anecdotes celebrating the deceased's life and career. Lerner's was to be no different. When it came time that afternoon to introduce Julie Andrews, who had starred not only in *My Fair Lady* but also in *Camelot*, they had decided not to introduce her by name, but to screen a film clip before her entrance. Unfortunately, they ran a clip that showed Audrey Hepburn in the film version of *My Fair Lady* mouthing to my voice. The clip ended and a light found Julie Andrews striding out onto the stage.

"Hello, everyone," Julie said in her lovely English accent, "I'm Marni Nixon!"

The house went wild with audible glee, and it made all the newscasts and syndicated columns the next day. I wrote Julie a note thanking her for the great press. She wrote me back, slightly embarrassed, saying she didn't know what came over her, but that she just couldn't resist the impulse. Good impulse, Julie!

The next time publicity knocked on my door, the real Marni was there to answer it. In fact, there were three "Marnis": the real one and a couple of imposters. The classic TV game show *To Tell the Truth* first went on the air in 1956 and lasted through the 1960s; I had the opportunity to be on the show as a contestant during its original run. When it was revived in 1990, I was asked to appear for the second time.

The show always featured a person of some notoriety (the contestant—in this case, me) and two impostors who try to match wits with a panel of four celebrities. The contestant got paid $500 for each wrong answer a celebrity gave. The impostors could lie through their teeth to convince the panel they were the "real" deal. The more celebrities you fooled, of course, the more money you made.

Before we taped the 1990 version, I conferred with and briefed the "fake" Marnis so that they could learn all about me in order to answer or fend off any questions that might be asked by the panel. Very soon after meeting them, though, I realized that my impostors were not well chosen for their tasks, as none of them could carry a tune or remember any of the lyrics to songs I had sung on-screen. In any case, when we finally played the game on the air, not one of the panelists chose any of the impostors as the "real" me. Maybe I'd been too exposed to the public by that time because, although it was great publicity, I certainly didn't make any money when they said, "Will the real Marni Nixon please stand up!"

The late 1980s and 1990s saw my career chugging steadily along, as if nothing had happened to slow it down. As in any line of business, there were triumphs and there were regrets. Munich in 1986 fell into the latter category.

For a long time I had a dream about singing American concert music all through Europe. The first step toward this dream was to be a concert encompassing such diverse material as early Purcell, Stravinsky, Rorem, Ives, Schoenberg, Gershwin, and, of course, my movie songs. The intent was variety with a capital V.

The Munich concert was to be presented by my friend Peter Jona Korn (he was an old friend of Ernest's as well, and German by birth), and his wife, Barbara, was to be my accompanist. It was only after the flights were booked and the concerts were advertised that Barbara, deciding it was too much for her to take on at the time, dropped out. To my great chagrin, my new accompanist and I had very little time to rehearse and assimilate all the different styles of music we were to present. At the same time, Peter didn't seem to be giving the

Looking oh, so glamorous as Sadie McKibben in Opal *at the Lambs Theatre in NYC, 1992. (l to r: Pipa Winslow, Judy Malloy, me, Reed Armstrong, Louisa Flaningam, Alfred Lakeman. Eliza Clark in center, Mimi Bassette kneeling next to her) (Photo Carol Rosegg)*

concert anything but perfunctory attention. Strange as it sounds, Munich was beginning to remind me of Israel!

Rehearsing under the veil of language barriers is always a challenge, but this concert was experimental and ambitious as far as the lighting and staging went, meaning that there were many more margins for error than usual. Murphy's Law reigned even in this efficient city. If it could go wrong, it did. The props were misplaced, the blackouts at the end of the song groups lasted forever, the audience was slim, there was no water backstage, and while I was onstage the superefficient German clean-up crew came into my dressing room and threw away every container that had housed all my props! Add to this that there wasn't a reviewer in sight, and the producer, my "dear friend" Peter, didn't even show up . . . the list went on and on. To add insult to injury, an agent/manager who showed interest in touring this concert left at intermission, claiming a previous engagement!

There *was* a small audience of sorts, including the great conductor Franz Allers, with whom I had worked in New York, and who conducted the original

My Fair Lady on Broadway. He tried to lead the applause, but for me the whole thing was deadly and I couldn't wait for it to end. Needless to say, nothing came of it, and my dream of turning this program into a concert tour of Europe was temporarily thwarted.

Recording has always played a big part in my career, and during the mid to late 1980s I recorded some wonderful albums: a Gershwin album, a Kern album, and a Grammy-nominated Copland album using the poems of Emily Dickinson.

The Kern album was particularly fun to put together, as I was able to spend a long weekend with Kern's biographer, Gerald Bordman, whose home in Delaware was a virtual repository of Kern manuscripts, both published and obscure. I hired a pianist and we spent long days reading through every song that might fit my temperament. We found an amazing number of obscure Kern numbers that had never been recorded, and we were all excited that the album might contain some world premieres. As fate would have it, the commercial world of recording reared its ugly head.

"Marni," the record executives said, "but you *must* sing 'All the Things You Are' and 'You Are Love' and all Kern's other standards."

Of course I did. In the end, I was able to negotiate mingling some of the obscure material with the famous pieces, and the recording, *Marni Nixon Sings Classic Kern*, now on CD, is still selling well.

Making records is a constant adventure. Having practically grown up in recording studios, it was always like a homecoming to get back in front of the microphone in an isolation booth, or in the middle of an orchestra. Yet, one of my most memorable recording experiences didn't involve my singing a note.

One day in the early 1990s I got a call from composer Carlisle Floyd.

"Marni," Floyd queried, "We're doing a recording of my opera *Susannah* at the Lyons Opera House in France and I want to hire you to be the diction coach and speech expert. Do you think you can teach an Appalachian accent in the few days we have allotted?"

By now, dear readers, you should know what my answer was.

"Yes, of course!"

As the entire opera was in English, and performed in a very specific South Carolina dialect, Floyd knew he needed someone to ensure the accents were authentic. But Marni Nixon from Southern California? Well, why not? Hadn't I sung the Welch Anna, the Cockney and posh Eliza, and the Puerto Rican Maria (not to mention that I made my living at that time doing jingles and commercials in all different accents)?

Although he had written such modern American operas as *Of Mice and Men*, *The Passion of Jonathan Wade*, and *Cold Sassy Tree*, *Susannah* remains the most performed of Floyd's work. The plot of this 1955 opera is adapted from the biblical parable "Susannah and the Elders" and set in the Deep South, specifically South Carolina. Along with George Gershwin's *Porgy and Bess* and Douglas Moore's *The Ballad of Baby Doe, Susannah* is one of the best-loved American operas. Since its premiere, it has never been out of the repertory. This, however, was to be the first complete recording.

I found out that the cast for the recording would include Samuel Ramey, Cheryl Studer, Jerry Hadley, and Ken Chester leading a cast of wonderful singers from Britain and all over Europe, with Kent Nagano conducting the Opera of Lyons Orchestra and Chorus.

As there was to be no actual live performance of the opera to act as a rehearsal, the cast was to assemble the day before the sessions and just start recording. Everyone had to sing with the same very strong regional accent (including the chorus members, who were French!), and all of this was to commence ten days hence. The opera company in France called me, worked out my fee and travel arrangements, and, "voom, voom, voom," I was on my way. But wait! Suddenly in the middle of the night I sat bolt upright in bed.

"What in the hell do I know about an Appalachian accent?" I said out loud, jolting a grumpy Al from his sleep.

Nobody had thought to ask if I could *do* an Appalachian accent. For that matter, neither had I! And I only had ten days! The next morning I got out my trusty Rolodex and found a card I always kept in case one of my students needed a dialect coach. Sam Chwat was a speech expert, specializing in accents, accent reduction, and physical remedial speech problems. I knew he would be able to help me. Luckily, he was free and enthusiastic.

"Come on over," Sam said. "I'll work until midnight!"

With the score of *Susannah* in hand, off I went to his office. We sat opposite each other at his desk and I read my score right-side up while he read it upside down. Astounding! Then he turned on his tape recorder and I read every single character into the microphone. He drilled the corrections into me, jotting down the rules for this dialect at the same time. We went back and forth and back this way for several hours. When the session was over, he handed me the tapes and notes and told me to go home and drill the accent into my head. We were to meet again the next day.

When I returned the next afternoon, we repeated the process, but this time I was reading and singing everything with the correct accent. I sounded like the hillbilly of all time. "Put the possum on the stove, Pa!" By George, like Eliza Doolittle in reverse, I got it!

"Well," he laughed, "I can see why you were so successful doing all that dubbing. I've never seen anyone catch on so quickly *and* retain it."

I was so grateful for his help, and then the guilt crept in. Shouldn't he have been the one to get this job? After all, he was the one teaching me how to teach it. When I finally admitted this to Sam, he just laughed.

"Marni, *you* have been chosen for this job because you know what you're doing and you know how to talk 'singerese,' 'actorese,' and 'musicianese.' You will be able to somehow impart your knowledge, even if they then choose to ignore it."

Ignore it?

He then warned me that although they had asked for my help, they might not want to actually take it. To illustrate, he told me a story.

"In the first movie for which I was dialogue director, we had a murderous shooting schedule. In one of the takes that was finally approved by the director, the star goofed up the accent badly. I went to the director and shouted, 'That's not the take you're going to use, is it?' The director looked at me like I was the scum of the earth and had me banned from the set. Marni, you've got to realize that you are the last one on the totem pole. I was so ashamed of the scene I thought it would be best to take my name off the credits. But the fact is, nobody else noticed, the actress got great kudos for her work, and I got paid the same as if it had been approved by me. In the end, everyone was happy."

He went on. "So, Marni, you may think that this is *your* project and that you're in charge of it, and I see how you *do* take charge, but I want you to be prepared that it just may not be so."

With Sam's advice ringing in my ears, I recorded everyone's role on individual tapes so that they could all have them to study for that one day we had before the recording began. Al and I arrived in France on Friday night, and on Saturday I tracked down the orchestra manager, who activated the project of duplicating all the tapes and got them back to me later that day. Most of the cast were staying at the same hotel as we were, so I dropped the tapes off at their doors, or left messages at the front desk for them to pick them up. Somehow I distributed all the tapes with notes saying that this was the accent "we" wished them to sing in. It told them that they could contact me anytime to go over it. I crossed my fingers and I hoped that I wasn't stepping on any operatic toes!

At the opera house the next day I found my fears were unfounded. Everyone was relieved that someone had taken the trouble to deal with the dialect. This included the engineer, Martin Sauer, with his thick German accent, who told me that he couldn't understand a word anyone was singing and begged me not to leave his side during the playbacks. After all, he would have no idea if there were mistakes or not!

The conductor, Kent Nagano (a sweetheart in his own right who knew me from my Charles Ives recordings), made a big speech to the orchestra. With great pomp and show, he introduced Carlisle Floyd and then, much to my surprise, he went on to introduce me.

"Today we have with us a speech expert, Marni Nixon, who is going to sit onstage with the singers. Marni is the only one who has the ability to wave to me and stop the recording if she doesn't approve of the dialect."

Can you imagine! I just about fell off my seat! I looked at Carlisle, the great composer, in embarrassment and he just winked and smiled at me.

"Go for it, honey," he whispered. "Go for it!"

Thus the recording began. During lunch hour (for the principals and orchestra) I went downstairs to work with the French chorus. I spoke out the words, and since they all knew the International Phonetic Alphabet symbols, I waited while they wrote the proper pronunciations into their libretti. Before long this group, who hardly spoke English, were pronouncing (and singing) the Appalachian dialect for such English words as "redemption." How amazing to hear them sing "ruhdimshon." They marked all the words and dialects correctly in their parts and never wavered. These Parisians all sounded like they had been born in Nashville and borrowed sugar from Dolly Parton. It was utterly delightful. At one point Kent came in to help and threw up his hands in mock despair.

"It's taken me five years to teach these Frenchmen how to sing with the King's English, and in fifteen minutes, you've made them all sound like they're from the Ozarks!"

My musical expertise came in handy as well during the five days we recorded. At one point Jerry Hadley, that wonderful tenor, was having problems hearing his next pitch during a complicated section of music.

"Marni," he entreated me, "you have perfect pitch. Could you just stand next to me and sing my opening note into my ear during the introduction so that I have it."

I couldn't turn him down. Floyd's music, while not atonal, is contemporary, and it can sometimes be difficult to pick out your pitch from what the orchestra is playing. When Kent saw this, instead of being upset that I was infringing on anyone's territory, he asked if I would work with Jerry and his coaches during the next break. Jerry, with his delightfully childlike attitude, chimed in.

"Oh pleeeeeeeeeease, Marni! Would you? Would you?"

Sometimes it just takes a singer (with perfect pitch) to help a singer. When we went back onstage to record, Jerry grabbed my arm and pleaded, "Don't you leave me now!" And I didn't!

All of this was great fun and very gratifying to me. It was five days of intense labor, but I never mind working hard, as long as it's appreciated and needed. I knew that we were all striving toward the same goal, the music. Listening to the opera come together was a marvelous experience. Hearing Sam Ramey's booming bass sound up close was thrilling. Ramey, the quintessential American, with his cowboy boots and his pseudo-Texas accent, is one of the most versatile of opera singers. On the one hand, he can fulfill the demands of the Handel, Mozart, Rossini, Donizetti, and Bellini repertoire with its stress on speed, flexibility, and range. On the other, he can fully meet the demands of the dramatic bass voice required by the operas of Verdi, Wagner, and Puccini. As he sang, he literally vibrated and shook the very risers we were all sitting on.

The American soprano, Cheryl Studer, who was singing the title role, however, never showed up for the recording sessions. We kept hearing she was on her way, but another day would pass and her role remained unrecorded. Each day, another excuse was given: she was sick, she was having voice problems, she had just had a baby and was in vocal transition. The rumor mill even suggested that her husband/manager was using the occasion to make her seem temperamental, thus reinforcing her "diva" role in the opera community. Whatever the real reason, she never did show up, so I decided to send her the tape I had made especially for her. I recorded a special message to accompany it.

"Cheryl, this is Marni. Jerry has already recorded his part. Now, you are playing his sister in the opera, so you have to use exactly the same accent as he! Good luck!"

Many months later, Cheryl and Carlisle Floyd went to Frankfurt and over-dubbed her role after the orchestra tracks had already been laid down in France. In fact, I helped Kent by suggesting that he record her difficult aria in several tempi, so that she could take her own time to breathe into those difficult high notes. Although I wasn't there when she recorded, I am sure she appreciated it.

When Grammy time came around, Virgin Classics' recording of *Susannah* won the 1994 Grammy Award for Best Opera Recording in the Classical Music Category. Although I didn't sing a note on it, my "voice" is all over the recording and I couldn't be prouder of the result.

Throughout the years, through marriage, divorce, remarriage, the move to New York, and remarriage again, I had always remained very close to my parents. When we didn't see each other, we were on the phone or writing letters. My father, who was two years older than the twentieth century (Mother was one year younger than he), retired at seventy-five years old as vice president and part owner of Petley, Inc, which was a division of Republic Steel.

By the 1980s my parents were living at Leisure World, a retirement community in Southern California. They had traveled all over the world and taken many cruises (frugally using only the interest from their savings and Social Security to pay for their trips), but still loved to come home to this community where there were private clubs, activities of all kinds, and dances on Saturday nights (they

Mother and Daddy in the 1960s. Their devotion never wavered. (From the author's collection)

loved to go dancing and did so even into their early eighties!). But as my father got deeper into his eighties, it became clear to my mother and all of his children that retirement didn't really agree with him. He lost his love of making jewelry and doing carpentry and seemed to grow older and more bitter. He was the antithesis of the cuddly, funny, teddy bear-like Daddy who raised me.

My mother, on the other hand, was still the energetic whirlwind of a woman she had always been. Although her health declined as she approached her late eighties, Mother always retained her zest for doing things. Even after strokes and problems with her limbs, she could be seen zipping around Leisure World on her motorized scooter. During these years, her fascination with the metaphysical expanded, encompassing extraterrestrials and past-life experiences.

But when she developed heart problems, it became more prudent for my now physically disabled Daddy to enter a skilled nursing facility, as Mother just couldn't take care of him as well as she had been. I would visit as often as I could but, when I walked into his room in February of 1991, I was a little shocked to see him propped up in his bed with extremely swollen legs. He seemed to be in pain and I could see and hear that there was something tugging on his spine. He had refused, however, to have any medical clarification as to what it might be. I suspected Daddy had cancer of the spine, and both my mother and I had a strong feeling that he knew this and wanted to die.

"Daddy," I gently said, "your legs are swollen. Aren't you in pain?"

He turned to me and gave me a stoic look that said more than words could ever convey. He wasn't concerned about the legs. He knew there was something much worse going on inside his body. I propped up his knees to relieve some of the pressure, massaging his legs at the same time. As I was leaving, I reminded him that I had taped the *Tonight Show*, which was going to air that night, and to be sure to watch. My mother, who had been sitting beside him very calmly and peacefully, said, "Of course we'll watch it." They always did. I got up, kissed my father on the cheek, and looked him in the eyes.

"Bye, Daddy."

My words seem to echo hollowly through the room. He gazed at me for what seemed like an eternity, as if searching for something to say. He gave me a small smile, and I left.

Later that night he wheeled himself into the recreation room and proudly announced to everyone, "You have to come and watch! My daughter is about to sing!" Along with his fellow patients, he contentedly watched me sing. Then he went back to bed and died. It was February 4, 1991, a couple of weeks before my sixty-first birthday.

Daddy was an uncomplicated and very loving man. How often I remember him telling us his credo: "Pay your debts, tell the truth, and learn to say no!" Whenever I think of him, I smile.

Mother, who had been so active for so long, declined when Daddy died.

"That so and so!" she railed with fierce resentment about Daddy. "We were so connected that when he went, my body started to fall apart, too."

As she had always done with the rest of her life, Mother intended to control her death. Before Daddy died, he and Mother had cooked up a plan to be able to end their lives when they wanted to and not be a burden on anyone else. Mother belonged to the Hemlock Society (now known as End-of-Life-Choices), which has been in existence since 1980, advocated suicide and euthanasia, and sent out helpful pamphlets to its 25,000 members. My parents were always against having machines or any artificial means keeping them alive. They both believed it was a big waste of money and preferred that their inheritance go to their children.

Mother always said, "Your death is a part of your own life and you should have a choice in it, if and when it becomes inevitable."

When Daddy was still alive, Mother would drill him, in front of us, so that we got the message.

"Now, supposing I fall down on the floor right now and have a heart attack. What is the next thing you're supposed to do?"

Daddy would respond, "Call 911."

"No!" Mother would scream. "You fool! I don't want you to spend any money or effort keeping me alive. I've lived a full life and it's silly to spend all that money on me. If you do, I'll be laughing at you from my grave!"

All of us knew exactly what her wishes were.

In the months after my father's death, Mother did her best to be as vital as she could be but, by now, she couldn't feed or bathe herself. As you can imagine, she absolutely hated not being in control.

In late July I received a phone call from my older sister Donyll, who had taken an apartment in Leisure World to be near Mother.

Mother was now ninety years old.

"The doctors have been here," Donyll explained, "and have told me that it's not going to be long for Nonnie." Ever since the grandchildren had come along, we sometimes called her Nonnie.

"She's not in pain," Donyll continued, "but if you could arrange your schedule, it would be a good idea to come from New York for a visit."

The next voice I heard was Mother's.

"Marni," she said, "I want to go. And you're the only one strong enough to be able to help me."

I told her that I understood and I would be there.

When I hung up the phone I became angry. Was this what I got for being strong? Did being "the strong one" mean that I got to help my mother die? Was this it? Mother and her cursed controlling of everything deciding now was the time?

When I arrived in California it seemed Mother was shifting into final gear. The second day I was there, Mother, who loved rituals, the more archetypal the better, made a decree.

"Marni, while you are here I want to have a last supper."

Donyll and I looked at each other. Mother told us that she wanted albondigas soup, a salad, apple cobbler, and ice cream.

"And I want to have a drink before I eat."

I found this particularly odd, as Mother never drank at all. But, according to Donyll, my father had told her that one could drink oneself to death if one wanted to. She told us to go to the market for the food and to the liquor store to buy her a special bottle of French brandy. Mother, the teetotaler, didn't really know much about liquor, but she knew she wanted something "fine," elegant, and high class for her parting dinner.

"Make sure it has a gold label and it's French," Mother said. "Then I'll know it's the best!"

At the liquor store we found a gold label brandy that looked kind of French (by this time Mother's eyesight was very poor anyway) and hoped that she would think it was a special brandy for the occasion.

When we returned with the food and the liquor, we found that Mother had taken a sleeping pill. She was very groggy and could hardly speak, but kept muttering the word "Halcyon." Halcyon, it turned out was a brand of sleeping pill that Mother had stashed all over the place. Evidently Daddy had also told her that if she took enough sleeping pills she could kill herself in that way. Please understand that giving her this information was all done with great love.

So there we were, Donyll and I, about to begin the ritual. We lit some candles, which Mother loved, put on her favorite Gregorian chants, and opened the doors to all the rooms. Mother had told us the doors had to be open when she died so that her spirit would be free and unrestricted. Due to her stroke only one of mother's arms was of practical use to her by this time, but she began drinking a mixture of heavy brandy and disgustingly sweet cherry-flavored Pepsi from one of her spill-proof "sippy cups." Although she had no teeth to chew with, Mother insisted on trying to eat some of the sunflower seeds she had been keeping since Halloween. Mostly they fell on her lap before making it to her mouth, which, strangely enough, amused her no end. Still, she seemed to be happy with the taste of the nuts and the foul-tasting drink.

At this point, Mother seemed in a state of euphoria, knowing that she could have anything that she wanted. My sister heated up the soup and, since I had forgotten to buy the apple cobbler, with the ingenuity Mother had bequeathed to all of us I put together a concoction using Bisquick and a can of peaches. I then smothered it with ice cream and Donyll fed it to her. While she was eating, I sneaked into the other room and phoned the doctor who was on call at Leisure World. I innocently asked him about the effects of brandy mixed with Halcyon.

"What are you trying to do," the doctor asked, "kill her?"

I quickly hung up. What *were* we trying to do? We were letting Mother take control, as usual. We were following her lead. As she attempted to drink more brandy, she muttered a word that we finally deciphered as "bowl, bowl" and we realized that she might be feeling nauseous. Nevertheless, that didn't deter her from gobbling down her desert. Content with her meal, but still anxious, Mother began wheeling herself around (she was in a wheelchair), opening up closets looking for something. She muttered "bag, bag" under her breath and we realized that she was looking for the plastic bags she and Daddy had stashed away in case they wanted to suffocate themselves at the end. My sister and I distracted her from this task, but she got agitated and started asking for Halcyon again. We got her into bed and, instead of the Halcyon, I put a few baby aspirin into her hand, thinking that in her groggy state she wouldn't know the difference. After all she could barely see, had trouble moving her limbs, and, because of the strokes, could hardly even make herself understood. She looked at the pills, sat bolt upright in bed, and with eyes as gray as steel (they were normally blue) shouted at me.

"This is not Halcyon!"

No wonder she was known as "The Witch of Leisure World"!

My sister and I began to giggle at the macabre bizarreness of the situation.

Luckily, when I turned up the volume on the Gregorian chants, Mother began to fall into a deep slumber. With a sigh of relief I turned to Donyll. Suddenly we were both filled with trepidation.

"What are we going to do when she wakes up and finds out she's not dead? She's going to be furious!"

Knowing that this might be "it," I made sure to call my children, Martha and Melani (Andrew was out of town), who both lived in the L.A. area (they still do), so that they could come and say their good-byes.

The next morning Mother woke up and didn't say a word about the ritual, "the last supper," or the fact that she was still alive. During the afternoon, however, it became apparent that Mother was not doing well, and probably wouldn't last the day. At this point Mother was in a kind of coma, so I put earphones in her ears for her to hear the Gregorian chants she loved so much. But whenever she would move or turn, the earphones would fall out, making her stiffen up. To make her feel more secure and relaxed, I decided to lie down across her body so that I could get my mouth closer to her good ear.

"Mother," I tenderly said, "if you really seriously want to go, it's *you* who has to give up to the powers that be. You, yourself, have to relax and give in, no matter how hard that might be."

I began to quietly sing my own improvised Gregorian chants into her ear and as I hummed to her, my sister sweetly told her that she was the best mother who ever lived, and that we loved her very much. She whispered in her ear that all her kids and grandkids would always be able to use her wisdom. As she spoke and I sang, we both constantly felt her pulse. Eventually it subsided and stopped. Mother was gone. Her last words were, "I tried my best." Even at the end, it was hard for her to say, "I love you." We sat there in silence for what seemed like an eternity.

At this precise moment Melani arrived. She and Nonnie had been very close and we left her alone to commune with Nonnie's spirit in this transitional state. We knew that somehow Mother would know she was there. Very soon after, Martha and her husband Dick arrived and they, too, had their own private moment with Nonnie.

The date was July 25, 1991, just slightly less than six months after Daddy died. Mother was a few months shy of ninety-one years old. She had lived a long and vital life by any standards. And, as she had found it important to do her whole life, it looked as if Mother had orchestrated her own death after all.

My parents lived rich lives, but were always frugal. They left each of their children a neat and tidy financial legacy, but in the end we were left much more than money and things. From my parents I was left values that stay with me to this day. From my mother, my sisters and I were also left a legacy of "control" issues that we continue to deal with every day of our lives.

Over the years, each time my sisters and I would get together, the subject always veered toward how to circumvent the sort of rigid control we had endured and the perfectionism that was instilled in us. Although we all eventually became focused achievers, we also took away from our upbringing the feeling that our own individualism was stifled and our intuitive, creative selves were squelched in us. My youngest sister, Midge, unfortunately, bore the brunt of Mother's unrelenting drive. She eventually had to detach herself from Mother and, indeed, from all of us, in order for her soul to survive. In her own journey to come out of it, she is now in a different place, as they say, and we are all happily a family again. But it has never been easy. In fact, as Yul Brynner said in *The King and I*, "Is a puzzlement."

I say puzzlement, because all this hurt and pain came in the person of a wonderfully experienced teacher, a forward, open thinker who was also a vigorous and caring community leader. Our mother. It has taken years for me to figure out what was behind the bad part of Mother's sometimes overcontrolling, perfectionist ways. But in 1991, all I could do was miss her. Eventually, though, I would have to come to terms with her "legacy." Stay tuned.

Teaching voice is one of the joys of my life. Ever since the early 1970s, when I was the Director of the Vocal Department at Cal Arts, I have been teaching. All during my years in Seattle I taught, and the minute I hit the isle of Manhattan in the early 1980s I set up shop in my newly renovated studio/living room.

My students have ranged from stars who need coaching for a particular role to established classical, opera, and musical theater performers. Also in the group are up-and-coming youngsters who eventually begin to get jobs and settle into their own musical lives. Sometimes they leave the nest. But often, years later, having experienced other teachers, or having finally realized how much there always is to learn, they will come back, like chickens to a roost, with a new sense of appreciation of what I've given them.

Every day, I thank my lucky stars that I began teaching, for as Hammerstein so aptly put it, "By my students I am taught." In fact, in the summer of 1997, I realized that it was time for me to take a lesson from myself and put my voice where my mouth was (to coin a phrase!).

That summer I was in a production of the musical *Cabaret*, playing the role of Fräulein Schneider, the German landlady. Lotte Lenya, the Viennese actress and singer who would forever be associated with her husband Kurt Weill's music, created the role on Broadway in 1966. Songwriters John Kander and Fred Ebb fashioned her musical numbers to take advantage of the smoky, guttural, Weimar German sound that Lenya made so famous. Although at sixty-seven years of age I was physically right for the role, my still-young and pure

With Spiro Malas and Cabaret's *famous pineapple at the Barrington Stage (1997). It was in this show that I learned how to belt. (Photo courtesy of Richard Feldman)*

soprano was decidedly wrong for this woman who had lived her life with a "So what?" attitude.

"Don't worry, Marni," composer John Kander told me. "We'll transpose the songs into any key you want."

It wasn't just a question of changing keys, however. It was a question of the sound required to make these songs exciting. It was a question of "belting" them out.

Over the years, in the course of my voice teaching, I had been studying the scientific verities in the term "belting," and how to teach it properly to my vocal students who also sang classically. Although I understood the technique, I had not actually done too much of it myself. I always knew that if a song could be pitched in a really low range, I could just use my chest voice and get away with "saying" that I was belting. Real belting is a different mode of singing, and musical theater belting is inevitably pitched higher than a chest voice. Many people don't distinguish this difference. Now it was my turn to learn how to do what I only had taught.

The Kander and Ebb songs that I was to sing continually rise and modulate, so I knew that the same mode of sound had to be used at the low end, as well as the high end, of my voice. Musical director Darren Cohen and director Julianne Boyd patiently allowed me to experiment with keys, tones, and muscular pressures on the vocal chords. They suffered me making extremely ugly (dare I say it?) "noises" while I tried on various sounds until I finally got to the point where I could "belt" out the numbers readily and easily, and more importantly, within character. It was a miracle! During the course of rehearsals, I had taught myself to belt. From that moment on, I've been able to demonstrate true "belting" technique for my students instead of just explaining how to do it. As they say, "Physician, heal thyself." I guess the same goes for voice teachers.

As former silent screen star Norma Desmond said in the film *Sunset Boulevard*, "It's not a comeback, it's a return!" At the end of the 1990s, my Hollywood past came back (or "returned") for an encore and, unlike the fictitious Miss Desmond, I was suddenly up there on the big screen again. Twice! And this time, with credit!

In 1997, my agent called to tell me I had an audition for a movie called *I Think I Do* that was going to be made in New York, and that she was faxing the sides (scripts with only your role and your cues on the page) to my apartment. When I got the sides, I was astonished to see that my appointment was only an hour away and that I would be auditioning for the role of a forty-year-old Hispanic woman! Did I have the right script, I wondered? After all, by this time I was a sixty-eight-year-old Scottish-German woman with red hair and blue eyes. Not exactly typecasting! Still, blithely off I went to the audition.

The office, on some remote street in a lost corner of lower Manhattan, was not exactly Twentieth Century Fox, but hey, it was a movie! The audition space was a room with a desk and a video camera. Sitting with his feet up on the desk was a disinterested-looking man reading *Rolling Stone* magazine. He barely noticed when I walked in for my appointment.

"Excuse me," I said, "but I was wondering if you had any special take on this character."

He looked at the script and then looked up at what was clearly not your average forty-year-old Hispanic woman. I smiled my best Marni Nixon smile.

"Well," he muttered in a disinterested voice, "why don't you just read it the way *you* feel it, and I'll put it on camera."

He focused the video camera next to him on me, put his feet back up on the desk, and continued reading his magazine.

"All right," I thought, "you don't care and I'm so tired that I don't care, so let's just have some fun."

On the spot I improvised a character with a South Carolina accent (was I channeling those characters in *Susannah*?) who just happened to mispronounce some of her words. I was amusing myself, if nothing else. I got through the scene, looked over at man with his feet on the desk, said thank you, and went back out to the waiting room. I assumed he was now going to look at my take, but after waiting for a while, my energy faded away and I just went home. At the corner of the street was a telephone booth, and I thought perhaps I should call my agent and tell her what had happened. She might be amused.

"Where are you?" she yelled. "You got the part, but you forgot to take the script with you and they start shooting tomorrow. They're sending the script to your apartment right now."

I couldn't believe it! I got the part. The very next day I was on the set making a movie!

I guess they were either so stuck at the last minute that they would have taken anyone at all, or my unusual take on the character made them change the whole concept of the role. I never did find out which it was, but the shoot was fun and the film, a screwball comedy about a gay wedding, enjoyed a minor cult run. The big lesson was, as always, just let go and use your instincts. Do I understand that now? As the film title says, *I Think I Do*. In fact, my next big-screen appearance, albeit as a voice only, drove that point home once more.

During my dubbing days in the 1960s, I had not only dubbed the three Cockney geese in *Mary Poppins*, but also recorded a full version of the Sherman Brothers' score as Miss Poppins herself. All this was done at the Disney Studios. In 1998, Disney came back into my life when its voice-over department called to see if I would be interested in dubbing the singing voice (not the acting voice) of Grandma Fa in a new animated musical feature, *The Legend of Mulan*.

They weren't actually offering me the role at that point, but merely ascertaining whether I would be interested in coming in to audition. When wasn't I interested, I thought? Disney told me that another actress had already voiced the acting portion of the role (this was becoming standard procedure in animated films; I guess they think singers can't act and vice versa), and they sent me a cassette of her voice to hear how she sounded. I suddenly flashed back to the days of receiving Deborah Kerr's recording and hearing it for the first time. How thrilling that was! When I got this cassette, though, I was far from thrilled. I called the people at Disney and told them there was no way I could match this voice. The actress obviously smoked and wasn't very musical, and the timbre of my voice would never fit hers. That was that! So I thought.

Several weeks later they called back and asked me to reconsider. Mind you, this was still for an audition, so I thought what could I lose? At the auditions were many famous actresses vying for this singing role, including June Havoc (the real Baby June of *Gypsy* fame) and screen and stage legend Lauren Bacall. Neither of these ladies, by the way, could be called "legitimate" singers. They were probably more on the money to match the actress's voice, I thought. At the same time, my strong competitive spirit came to the fore and I felt myself wanting to "win" this role.

They had given me the music (it was a song called "Honor to Us All" by Matthew Wilder and David Zippel) to look at in advance and, before I was finally called in to audition, they showed me the storyboard of the face that they were going use for Grandma Fa. This cinched it! I was enchanted. She had the funniest, cutest old lady face I had ever seen. She was Chinese, of course, but with no teeth and a twinkle in her eye. I simply fell in love with that face and said to myself, "Well, Marni, you've just got to give her a voice . . . or, in this case, an unvoice."

When I got into the room I improvised Grandma Fa's voice from scratch. I tried not to sing with a "singing voice" of any kind, but to just let Grandma make a sound as if she were "trying" to sing. I wanted to bring out the twinkle in those eyes and not forget that she had no teeth! The key was also to *not* try to match the timbre of the voice of the actress with whom I didn't feel a kinship.

It worked! The Disney people loved the voice I created and Bacall and Havoc were sent packing! I had the job. It was a simple gig, but it was wonderful to be back in Hollywood dubbing someone, even if it was an animated face. I had only thirty-two measures to sing, but I did it as professionally and artfully as if I were performing the whole score. Eventually, I was joined in this number (although we never recorded together) by Broadway veterans Beth Fowler and Lea Salonga.

Being back in the studio was wonderful. The songwriters and musical director all knew what they wanted in terms of timing. They had seen a rough cut of the film and arranged the music around that. Later on, the animators would make sure that the lips of the characters fit what we sang.

The kicker was that Disney loved the voice I gave Grandma Fa so much that they fired the previous actress and hired June Foray, one of the most famous voices in all of animation (she voiced the original Rocket J. Squirrel in *The Adventures of Rocky and Bullwinkle!*). June was wonderful and actually sounded like me, too!

When the film, which was the first full-length movie animated only at the Florida animation studio (and not so incidentally was the only Disney film score my old friend and high school crush Jerry Goldsmith composed; he got his last Oscar nomination for it, too.), was released in June of 1998, Disney flew me back and forth to the Coast to be a guest at several premieres. The West Coast premiere took place at the Hollywood Bowl and the party reached star-studded proportions that harked back to "old" Hollywood.

There were acres and acres of Chinese food, calligraphers, ethnic musicians, Chinese dragons, games for children to play with kites, candy made on a stick according to your whim and in the shape you requested, fortune-tellers, desserts, and a picnic basket with a blanket and a bottle of wine when it came time to watch the movie. The Bowl was replete with spotlights, fireworks, and press people from all over the world.

My whole family was invited, including the grandchildren. After the film was over, a chauffeur drove us to the after-party, which was to be a dance at the old Palladium Ballroom on Sunset Boulevard. There, we were all feted with various gifts, including a sumptuous hardcover book on the making of the film, picture books on the actual "Legend of Mulan," posters, balloons, and CDs. It was as if Christmas had come early and Disney was Santa.

The same thing went on when we premiered at Radio City Music Hall in New York in August of 1998. It was a great way to finish out the decade, being back in the movies. It also didn't hurt my feelings to receive my second Gold record for the soundtrack CD.

But as I watched the film for the second and third time, I began to get angry. Since they had fired the first actress because they liked my take on the role and the voice I gave Grandma Fa, why hadn't they even considered the fact that I might be the perfect "acting" voice for the role as well?

Why? Because in Hollywood, I was still pigeonholed as a "singer" (meaning they thought I couldn't act) or, even worse, a ghost singer.

For quite some time I had been interested in doing more straight acting roles for just this reason—to escape the typecasting. Now that I was older (almost seventy! When did *that* happen?), there were more roles for my age group in straight plays than in musicals. The problem I sometimes had with musical theater was that older roles required older voices. Mine was still a pure and youthful-sounding soprano.

I knew that acting, and acting on the stage, was the key to longevity in this career I was still forging. I still harbored not only the pure musical dream of re-vitalizing the classical vocal recital, but also the hope that had first lured me to New York: being on Broadway in a juicy role that would challenge my acting (and singing) abilities.

It turned out this role was waiting around the corner, and had been for a long time. In fact, it had been conceived almost 100 years ago across the sea by an Irish genius named James Joyce.

Chapter Fifteen
GIVING UP THE GHOST

"On then with the dance, no backward glance, or my heart
will break. Never look back . . . never look back."

STEPHEN SONDHEIM, 1971 (sung by Heidi in *Follies*)

T HERE WILL ALWAYS BE PEOPLE who only know me as "the ghost": the
spectral voice behind Audrey Hepburn's unbridled joy at being able to
pronounce her vowel sounds, the musical personification of Natalie Wood's
naïve romanticism, the happy tune that facilitated Deborah Kerr's cautious
optimism while facing a new life in a foreign land. My own one-woman show,
Marni Nixon: The Voice of Hollywood, has even helped to perpetuate this myth,
the myth that says "That's all there is, folks." But for thousands of Broadway
theatergoers since the millennium began, I have become known as a versatile
actress who just happens to sing. To savvy and sophisticated Broadwayites, the
past is the past, and Hollywood and its dubbing scandals are a million miles
away. These are the people who have seen me materialize, fully formed, onstage in three Broadway shows in three seasons.

In September of 1999 I was called in to audition for a new musical that was
to premiere Off-Broadway at Playwrights Horizons, a small theater on 42nd
Street, which had been doing interesting work for years. Many plays and musicals had premiered there and then moved to Broadway or extended Off-
Broadway runs. These included the Pulitzer Prize–winning *Sunday in the Park
with George* by James Lapine and Stephen Sondheim and *Falsettos* by William
Finn and James Lapine. The musical I was to audition for was officially titled
James Joyce's The Dead. It was based on the Irish author's classic story, the 1987
screen version of which had been John Huston's last film as a director. I would
be auditioning for the esteemed Broadway director Jack Hofsiss (*The Elephant
Man*) and Richard Nelson (*Some Americans Abroad, Two Shakespearean Actors*),
the author of the book and lyrics.

The character breakdown the casting director gave my agent said that the
role of Aunt Kate called for an Irish woman in her late sixties. So far, so good.
Singing was necessary, but they were primarily looking for an actress. They

*With Nanette Fabray and Monte Hall after our performance with the
Los Angeles Youth Symphony at the Dorothy Chandler Pavilion in L.A.
in 2003. (From the author's collection)*

wanted to hear a folk song, so I decided to sing a song by Carol Hall called "The
Color of Wheat," which had a folksy quality. The song was intrinsically sad, and
when I got to the climax, for some unknown reason I began to cry. I guess this
wasn't a bad thing, as the next thing I knew they asked me to read for the role of
Aunt Kate. As I read the lines of the play, once again I got tears in my eyes.

"I don't know why I'm so weepy today," I said to the director, as I wiped
away my tears.

He just laughed, smiled warmly, and said, "Never mind. I know why." He
then gave me some adjustments to do with the lines and I did them with ease.

When I was leaving, I asked the casting director if I could perhaps read for
the role of the other aunt, Aunt Julia, who seemed to have a much larger part.
I was told the role was already cast and that Sally Ann Howes would be playing
it. Sally Ann had been Julie Andrews' replacement in the original *My Fair Lady*
on Broadway, so we had Eliza Doolittle in common. Still I was peeved that I
wouldn't be able to try for the larger role.

Within an hour of my returning home I got the call saying I had the part of Aunt Kate. I was pleased, but still a bit miffed that I wasn't playing the character with more lines. When I got to rehearsals, however, I realized that I was part of an incredible cast (Blair Brown, Paddy Croft, Brian Davies, Daisy Eagan, Dashiell Eaves, John Kelly, Brooke Sunny Moriber, Alice Ripley, Emily Skinner, Stephen Spinella, and film star Christopher Walken) and that we were going to approach this show as if it were a straight play. The songs were to be performed as if we were at a party and wouldn't be "staged" book songs in the usual musical theater sense. I had a feeling I was going to be part of something really special and began to believe the old adage "There are no small roles in the theater, only small actors."

For the first three days of rehearsal we dealt solely with the music and the dances. Our composer, Shaun Davey, supervised conductor Charlie Prince (the great director-producer Hal Prince's son and the grandson of Saul Chaplin, famed musician, composer, arranger, and my beloved vocal director on the film *West Side Story* and *The Sound of Music*; Charlie is now a good friend of mine), and we had the delightful bushy eyebrowed Sean Curran choreographing our Irish jigs. The show took place at a party in Dublin in 1905, and all of the songs and dances at the party were treated realistically. It was as if the audience was sneaking a peak into a window of someone's home, so none of the characters were supposed to be professional singers or dancers.

On the fourth day we got down to reading the play and getting it on its feet. Several years earlier, Jack Hofsiss had had a terrible accident while diving into a swimming pool. His spine had been so badly injured (rather like the late Christopher Reeve) that he was confined to a wheelchair. Fortunately, this has not stopped his directing career. However, we found it difficult getting used to his way of communicating ideas, and his blocking of the scenes seemed very confusing and vague, with no clear-cut psychological reasons for where we were placed or how we moved. Consequently, I had no idea who my character was, as well as where and why she was doing the things she was doing. Still, I did my best. After a while, though, I began to feel more uneasy, and it slowly dawned on me that I was getting nothing from Jack's direction. At first, of course, I blamed myself. But as time went by, I found that the whole cast was in the same boat.

We would sometimes share lunch together in the park near the rehearsal space, and it was there that we all began comparing notes. We all were feeling shaky about what we were supposed to do and how we fit into the scheme of things. Opening night was looming and we were all more than a little bit nervous. Finally, after much discussion, we agreed that something drastic had to be done, such as speaking with the producers and letting them know that a change needed to be made. With the strength of the entire cast on our side, we did just that.

Throughout the rehearsals, Richard Nelson (also a very qualified director) was there in the back of the room, trying his best to be peaceful, receptive, and respectful to Jack. The producer must have spoken to Jack about the cast's concerns, because the day after our mutiny, Jack told us he understood we were having some problems and that he was turning this rehearsal over to Richard, who, being the author, would best be able to get us on the right track. In that one rehearsal, Richard was able to enlighten us about the concept of the show, discuss the reason for the music being conceived in the folksy way it had been, and most importantly, explain how each character needed to relate to the others. We were so inspired and excited by this single rehearsal that during our lunch break Christopher Walken, who had approved of going to the producer, but wasn't terribly vocal, decided to make a stand. He paid a call on Tim Sanford, the artistic director of Playwrights Horizon, and requested that Richard replace Jack permanently as our director.

The upshot was that Jack agreed to step down, and the next day he actually presented Richard to the cast as our new director. This kind of gentlemanly behavior, of course, was rare in the theater! I was amazed and touched by Jack's generosity of spirit. I am sure it must have been hard for him to do this, and we all felt terrible, being party to firing a director (in a wheelchair, no less!), but we were exhilarated to finally be getting on track.

Richard took over as director, with Jack coming in for a while to make sure everything was all right. Everything was more than all right. We were gleefully working our tails off and seeing—no, *feeling*—the results. Richard was an inspiring and totally accessible director. We felt that we could now make up for the valuable lost time.

At one point in the rehearsal process, I approached Richard about an acting dilemma I was having.

"I'm having a problem relating to the characters of Aunt Julia and Mary Jane. Whenever I speak to them I feel that I am saying things to them with a certain emotional intent, and they aren't reacting at all the way I think they should react to this intent. This is making me, or rather Aunt Kate, cry, because I feel so misunderstood."

Richard began to laugh.

"Marni," he said, "Don't you realize that you're just living the part? Don't you understand why we hired you? When we saw how easily the tears came to your eyes, we knew your emotional sensitivities were just right for Aunt Kate."

How amazing! Once again, I was hired for being "me." But now that I knew it, I was afraid it might ruin what I had already been doing with the role. There was a scene in the show where I would sit facing the audience dead front and weep my eyes out. No one had told me to cry at that moment, but there the tears were, coming from some deep and secret place. After talking to Richard,

I was concerned that I wouldn't be able to cry anymore, that I might dry up, now that I was conscious of it. I didn't need to worry. I cried on cue for two years. Each of us in the company had our own very effective private moments, sometimes wordless. These were often so subtle that one thought they could only be captured by a close-up lens of a movie camera. But, because of the focus of the direction, the audience always got it.

James Joyce's The Dead opened on October 22, 1999, to mixed reviews, with an emphasis on the positive. In addition, the buzz around town was that one *had* to see this miracle of an acting ensemble. Every night the small house was filled to capacity with New York's acting intelligencia. We were slated to run for only the six weeks allotted to experimental/developmental works of this sort, but in mid-November the rumor mill began buzzing about moving the show to Broadway.

"You can't walk away from a show like this without trying to extend its life," producer Gregory Mosher (along with Arielle Tepper, one of the producers shepherding the show to Broadway) was quoted in the newspapers as saying. "You'd be the dodo head of the century if you did."

Talks began with our agents, and we were told that we would all have to take union minimum and a favored nations contract, meaning no one could earn more than anyone else.

Christopher Walken and me as his Aunt Kate in James Joyce's The Dead *at the Belasco Theatre on Broadway in 2000. He was a sweet enigma. (Photo Joan Marcus)*

"Nobody involved in this project is going to get rich," Mosher said to the press. "You don't do *James Joyce's The Dead* to get rich."

He was right. We all did it for the sheer joy of making art. Broadway was just the cherry on the sundae. We moved to the Belasco Theatre on January 11, 2000 and all seemed right in the world. The feeling was not to last for long.

A few weeks after the triumphant opening night, the doctors found a lump in my left breast, and determined that it was cancerous. After 15 years of being cancer free, I have to admit I was devastated. This time a lumpectomy wasn't recommended. This time, I would have to have a mastectomy.

After picking myself up and dealing with my emotions, I realized that I would have to leave the show for a short while. I was most upset about letting down the cast, who had by now become my second family. I felt I was leaving them in the lurch.

"Marni," Richard Nelson said, with great kindness, "don't you think that you have to take care of this right away, regardless of anything else? The show will run. The sooner you take care of your health, the sooner you can return."

He was right, of course.

The operation went well. After surgery, while still in the recovery room, I called the stage manager at 7:30 P.M. (a half hour before the curtain) and told him everything was fine and that I would be back in the show soon. There were hoots of joy when he relayed the information to cast members passing in the hallway at the Belasco Theatre. I think, though, that everyone thought I was a bit crazy, assuming I would be returning in a few days. I guess they didn't know me as well as they thought.

Christopher Walken, who was funny, crazy, amazing, and very hard to fathom, had called when I was in the hospital. Although we shared a stage every night, he and I didn't have too much personal contact, so this was a pleasant surprise.

"Look Marni," he sweetly said, "don't worry. My sister just had a mastectomy and they know what they're doing nowadays. You're in the right hospital and you'll be well taken care of. We will miss you, but this is just a temporary setback."

He was right. Two weeks later I was back in the show.

Yes, my surgical wound was still draining (much to the delight of my wardrobe woman! Not!), but it never leaked. Everyone in the company thought I was incredibly brave, but I knew that doing the show was the one thing that would get me through the crisis. The cast had been told I was taking some time off to have a small growth removed, but somehow everyone knew the truth. Every single one of them was warmly supportive, way beyond the call of duty.

Blair Brown took up a collection from the company and arranged it so that her favorite catering company would hand deliver organic, healthy food in clearly marked plastic containers for myself, Al, and my daughter Melani, who had flown from California to help care for me. This thoughtful and priceless gift was greatly appreciated and helped me to recover my spiritual and physical strength.

Once a week—on Mondays, our day off—I had to do chemotherapy, which is horribly debilitating for some. It can make you nauseous and bone tired, as you are literally pumping poison into your system to kill the cancer cells. Fighting fire with fire, they say. But the fire can kill or cure. Difficult as these Mondays were, I was always there onstage at 8:00 P.M. on Tuesday night. There was, of course, the wonderful Patricia Kilgarriff (she went on to replace me in the Boston and San Francisco engagements of the show) standing by for me every night in case I didn't feel well enough, but I never missed a show. If, during the evening, one of the choreographed Irish jigs got too strenuous for me, I would just sit down and it looked like it was part of the show. After all, I was playing a woman in her late sixties at the turn of the century! She was allowed to sit one out.

The show closed on Broadway on April 11, 2000, after a run of 120 performances and 24 previews. As our producer, Gregory Mosher, had said, no one produced this show to get rich, and the artistic nature of it was perhaps not to every Broadway theatergoer's taste. But the folks who got it really got it and loved it.

Although the show was already closed, when the annual Tony nominations were announced we were thrilled to receive five nominations: Best Musical, Best Book of a Musical (Richard Nelson), Best Actor (Christopher Walken), Best Supporting Actor (Stephen Spinella), and Best Original Musical Score (Shaun Davey and Richard Nelson). In the end, Richard Nelson won the award for his book.

Being a Best Musical nominee means that the show gets to do a musical number on the nationally televised Tony Awards. This is always a great boon to the nominated shows, and one can usually see a rise in the box office receipts the day after the show hits the airwaves. For us it was different, as our show was closed on Broadway, but it was about to open in L.A. Since, for no good reason I can think of, we never got to record a cast album, we went on to do our segment with the feeling of "See what you are going to miss, Broadway!"

All this time, the chemo, as it usually does (they always warn you about it, too), was thinning out my hair to an alarming degree. After our live televised musical number was over and everyone else had exited the dressing room, I was left alone with Paul Huntley, one of the best wig designers around. As usual after a performance, he was waiting for me to give him back my wig. Boy, did he get a surprise when he pulled the wig off, only to find that all of my remaining hair, with the hairpins still pinned to it, came off in my wig cap, revealing my totally bald pate. Even the unflappable Paul, who must have seen everything, muttered, "Oh yuck!" The theater is so glamorous, n'est pas?

The show reopened for the summer season (July 19 to September 3, 2000) at the prestigious Ahmanson Theatre at the Los Angeles Music Center. I was thrilled to be bringing my performance west, and to be able to see my kids and friends on the Coast. During the Broadway run, both Blair Brown and Christopher Walken were replaced by Tony Award–winner Faith Prince (*Guys and Dolls, The King and I*) and Stephen Bogardus (*Falsettos*). Our L.A. cast consisted of many wonderful replacements for the New York actors, including Alice Cannon, Sean Cullen, Shay Duffin, Donna Lynne Champlin, Patricia Kilgarriff (my patient cover), Angela Christian, Brandon Sean Wardell, and Russell Arden Koplin.

In L.A., Al and I stayed (as usual) with my dear friend and former agent, Hal Gefsky. Of course, I continued my chemotherapy and, although I always got through the show (Thank you, Doctor Footlight!), as soon as the curtain came down, I was so exhausted that my dresser had to literally push my fanny into my dressing room. I would sit in my chair and take off my wig, revealing my now-bald head, put a scarf over it, and get escorted down to the parking lot, where I would drive myself back home. Against everyone's wishes, I insisted on driving myself. In typical style I always wanted to do everything for myself. Al would be waiting for me with some food and the right dosage of antinausea pills to get me through the night.

One Monday in L.A., as I was having my umpteenth chemo treatment, something strange occurred. Taxol, the clear fluid that is used in most breast cancer cases, was being pumped into my veins through a needle that was inserted into my right hand. I had also been given a sedative and was quite relaxed when I suddenly felt my right hand becoming numb. I looked down at my hand in my drug-induced state to discover that the needle had come out of the vein, and the Taxol was pumping directly into my skin! This unfortunate event is called an infiltration. I suddenly realized that I was alone in the room, and when I attempted to call out for someone to help me, no one was around. I heard myself trying to scream, but, due to the drugs, only unintelligible sounds came out of my mouth. Finally, someone heard me and, with great alarm and confusion, stopped the pumping. But it was too late. The Taxol had been pumped into my hand (causing a numbness that hasn't left to this day), my arm, and my whole system. In a short time my hand and arm swelled up and turned red with sores.

My first concern (after my health) was that I wouldn't be able to fit into my costume the next night. The turn-of-the-century gowns (by designer Jane Greenwood) I wore in the show had tight Elizabethan sleeves, and we were corseted "up the wazoo," as they say. The costume person came to Hal's house to assess the damage to my swollen arm, and by the next night the costume was redone so that I could once again fit into it and play Aunt Kate.

In October 2000, we took the show to the Kennedy Center in Washington, D.C. Some more of the cast had changed by then (Megan McGinnis, Laura Woyasz, and Stephanie Block were new additions), but it was still a glorious experience. After that production closed (another tour went on to Boston and Chicago), I had to be in New York for a continuous time to do radiation. The radiation and breast reconstruction were harder to deal with than the chemo, perhaps because I no longer had the show to concentrate upon.

The year I spent with James Joyce, Richard Nelson, and the magnificent company of *The Dead* helped to change my perception of myself. Besides all the health issues I was facing I was most exhilarated by the fact that I had held my own as an "actress" (not just a singer) with a cast that could read the telephone book and still be entertaining. Perhaps it was time for me to try to get rid of my insecurities.

At the beginning of the rehearsal process I thought of myself as an inexperienced actress, but I now realized that I could keep up with the best of them. What most people don't realize is that *all* actors feel insecure and exposed at some point. From the least to the most experienced; we all just deal with it from show to show. "The show must go on" isn't just an adage created to put money in the producer's pockets. To me it means I must always endeavor to satisfy my own artistic requirements of myself. My magical years with *The Dead*, cancer and all, proved to me that I was very much alive and becoming a better actress with each experience on the stage. Thankfully, there was more to come.

———

Ever since Stephen Sondheim's lyrics were first heard on Broadway in *West Side Story* in 1957, he has been in the forefront of the American Musical Theater. In 1959 he cemented his place as a top-notch lyricist with *Gypsy*, and forged a career as a composer-lyricist with the hilarious and successful *A Funny Thing Happened on the Way to the Forum* in 1962. Starting in 1970 with *Company*, Sondheim (along with producer-director Hal Prince) revolutionized the Broadway musical to such an extent that the form is still reeling from the changes. To this day, partisans sitting on either side of the fence either love or hate the kind of "thinking man's" musicals that Sondheim has helped to foster. *Company* was a modern musical about marriage and the difficulty human beings have in finding some kind of solace in being together. It was a great success and was immediately followed in 1971 by a show so grand in its themes and size that it was said it could never be reproduced.

The book of *Follies* by playwright James Goldman (*The Lion in Winter*) told an abstract, fragmented, and sometimes disjointed story of two showgirls who had been in the chorus of the last "Weismann (read: Ziegfeld) Follies" in 1941 and who are now attending a reunion (in 1971) in a theater about to be torn down to make way for a parking lot. There, they confront the ghosts of their past and try to work out what went wrong with their marriages, lives, and the entire American Dream.

The show was so big that it was directed by both Hal Prince *and* choreographer Michael Bennett. Despite some rave reviews and many awards (including the New York Drama Critics' Circle Award for Best Musical), the show was so expensive to run (a bigger-than-usual orchestra and a huge cast wearing incredibly elaborate costumes added to the costs) that even though it ran a year, it was a financial failure.

After the musical closed, it passed into legend, with many people merely remembering a few of the songs, such as "Losing My Mind" and "I'm Still Here." Producer Cameron Macintosh (*Les Misérables*, *The Phantom of the Opera*, *Cats*) brought a much-revised version of the show, with a completely new book and several new songs, to London in the 1980s and that, like the original, was an artistic success, but a financial failure.

In 2000, it was announced that the Roundabout Theatre in New York, a not-for-profit organization that has been in existence since the mid 1960s, would be staging the first Broadway revival of *Follies*. Roundabout had had great success with musicals ever since their revival of *She Loves Me* (a 1963 musical by Joe Masteroff, Jerry Bock, and Sheldon Harnick), which settled in for a nice Broadway run and even transferred to London's West End. But it was their groundbreaking revival of Kander and Ebb's *Cabaret* in 1998, which ran and ran at Studio 54 (a former 1970s disco), that cemented Roundabout's dedication to reviving edgy and interesting American musicals. *Follies* certainly qualified.

In late 2000, after having just returned from the Kennedy Center production of *The Dead*, I was called in to audition for the British director Matthew Warchus. The role I was up for was Heidi Schiller, a Viennese opera singer who had sung in the Follies many years before. In the show, Heidi gets to sing "One More Kiss," a gorgeously witty and sentimental pastiche of all the Franz Lehár/Sigmund Romberg waltzes that ever were.

After my experience with *The Dead*, I was feeling very confident about my acting chops and I gave a very good audition. Everyone present, including Stephen Sondheim, was very responsive and enthusiastic. When I spoke to my agent later that day it seemed as if they were going to offer me the role.

Up until a week before the finalization of casting, the rumor mill had me cast, even though I hadn't been officially offered any contract. When the casting announcements were finally made, it turned out that the powers that be had the brilliant notion of casting all the subsidiary roles with people who had been stars on Broadway once, but hadn't been heard of since. How ironic! Now that I had materialized and been noticed in *The Dead*, I was too "well known" in New York to fit into that category. Joan Roberts, who had played the role of Laurie in the original 1943 production of *Oklahoma!*, and hadn't been heard of much since, was cast. Ah well, I thought.

On March 8, 2001, the Roundabout revival of *Follies* opened to rather mixed reviews. Many who had remembered the splendor of Boris Aronson's original set or the sumptuousness of Florence Klotz's dazzling costumes were disappointed at the minimalist physical production. There was also a part of the critical fraternity (and the public as well) who felt the vocal elements had not been successfully realized. Still, when it was clear that the show was going to run, I began getting calls from the casting people, wanting to know if I would understudy five of the roles. Still smarting from losing the role I wanted, and not really wanting to have to learn five different parts and songs that I was really not suited for, I turned them down. A few weeks later, my agent called to tell me that Joan Roberts was unhappy doing the show and was going to turn in her notice. Was I interested in replacing her? After cursing under my breath ("Why didn't they ask me in the first place?"), I tried to be gracious and said, "Yes, of course." It was then that I first went to see the show.

I am a purist at heart and wasn't entirely sold on certain aspects of the production, but the storyline had been clarified for me. More importantly, I realized that "One More Kiss," the song I would be doing, was a little jewel all its own, and I was feeling good about the prospect of making it glitter and shine. The next day I accepted the role and waited for Joan Roberts to turn in her notice, which she did in due time.

When I went into rehearsal with Matthew Warchus, I told him that I had an idea of how I wanted to perform the song "One More Kiss." I believed that this song was the archetypal moment and centerpiece of the whole show. If the number was presented properly, it could stand out as an operettalike jewel and express the basic sentiment of what the entire musical was about. The song begins as a solo for Heidi, but suddenly becomes a duet with her younger self. As the whole show was about the ghosts (oh, that word again!) of the characters' youth, I realized that my song was the first time one of the characters in the play actually confronted the past. This happens to each of the characters very soon after. The ghosts are coming back and not allowing the characters to forget them. They need to be dealt with. At this point in my life, I understood that concept only too well.

I told Warchus that I wanted to show him, within the parameters of the existing lighting and physical blocking, how I would look when I became aware of my younger self, and the exact moment I would actually turn and sing to her. I wanted to convey what was happening inside both of us at that moment of recognition in a slightly different way than what I had seen onstage. Brooke Sunny Moriber, who was playing my younger counterpart, was all for it as well. Warchus hemmed and hawed, but finally agreed to let me try it my way in performance.

My opening night arrived. Even with an orchestra of fewer players than the original, the sounds emanating from the pit were thrilling. While thinking about Heidi, I remembered one of my first voice teachers, Vera Schwarz, who shared so much history with the fictitious Heidi. Vera really *did* have Franz Lehár write waltzes for her, as Heidi claims in the show. I was confident that I knew who this woman I was portraying really was. But more than that, I understood how important this song was to the very fabric of the show. I stepped onstage, opened my mouth, and out came the beautiful waltz.

"All things beautiful must die," I sang, harmonizing with my youthful counterpart. "So lover, give me one more kiss, and good-bye."

The applause was deafening. I realized later it wasn't me imposing myself on the song, but the import of the song and the moment coming *through* me. All I had to do was obey. Fortunately, I was on the composer's intuitive wavelength.

When I got offstage, everyone in the cast (including Polly Bergen, Treat Williams, Marge Champion, Donald Sadler, Betty Garrett, Blythe Danner, Judith Ivey, Gregory Harrison, Louis Zorich, Carol Woods, and Jane White, among others) gathered in the hallway of the Belasco Theatre (yes, I was back there again!) applauding, with tears in their eyes.

After the show, members of the cast told me how happy they were to have me among them. I thanked my lucky stars and felt empowered as we enveloped one another in great respect and love night after night.

The only downside of doing *Follies* was the fact that since I was not part of the "original" cast, the big publicity push was over, and no one really knew I was in the show. I even had to go to the mat to get management to properly replace the picture of the cast out front, so that I would be represented among them. It seems there's always more to show business than the show!

As *Follies* ran into the spring of 2001, I was booked to do a scene on the television series *Law and Order: Special Victims Unit*. The director promised me that he would get my scene in the can and get me off the set by 5:30 P.M. so that I could do the show that night. When 3:00 P.M. rolled around and they still hadn't shot my scene, I began to consider calling the stage manager and having them put my understudy on. I kept vacillating, but finally decided to gamble and not make the call. Thankfully, they shot my scene at the last minute, and I had just enough time to get out of the TV makeup, grab some takeout food, and rush to the theater. After a whole day on the set (where even sitting is tiring), I was exhausted as I made up for *Follies*.

As Heidi Schiller singing "One More Kiss" on Broadway in the 2001 revival of Follies.
(Photo Joan Marcus)

I shared my dressing room with Carol Woods, who had understudied Cissy Houston in *Taking My Turn* back in the early 1980s and was stopping the show nightly, singing "Who's That Woman?"

"Has Sondheim seen you do this role, Marni?" she gently asked.

"No," I answered, as I applied the final touches to my face, "but I'll try to invite him. I do so want him to see me."

As I made my first entrance, I thought of how exhausted I was. I just wanted to get through the show without seeming as tired as I felt. I finished the show and went back to my dressing room, happy that it was over. I opened the door to the hallway and there, with his arms outstretched, stood Stephen Sondheim. Before I could say a word, he enveloped me in a very long and warm embrace. Now you can say many things about Sondheim. He is brilliant, incisive, sharp . . . but outgoing is not usually on the list. This was a very special moment. As he released me from the embrace, he spoke about his great happiness in seeing what I was able to portray in the role. That night I was literally buoyed by praise from a revered master. Just think, I almost let my understudy go on. Once again, I thanked my lucky stars!

Just when the show was getting better and better, picking up momentum and gaining in ticket sales, the Roundabout announced that it would be closing on July 14, 2001. We were all devastated.

Fortunately, I have had the opportunity to revisit the role and the show in the summer of 2005 at Barrington Stage in Great Barrington, Massachusetts. Although this was essentially a regional theater production, it was so beautifully directed by Julianne Boyd and featured such wonderful performances (including Tony Award–winner Donna McKechnie as Carlotta singing "I'm Still Here") that everyone from New York who loved the show made a beeline to see it and, once again, I was lifted by Stephen Sondheim, whose praise made me feel so good. One of the great things I know about playing Heidi is that, no matter how old I get, if there's a voice in my body, I will still be right for the part.

Less than two months after *Follies* closed on Broadway, the world changed forever.

I am not an early riser and I was a little peeved when the phone rang at 9:00 A.M. on September 11, 2001.

"Mom," my daughter Martha screamed from L.A., "turn on the television! The World Trade Center has been hit by a plane and you're not going to be flying anywhere today."

I turned on the TV and watched in horror as the second plane flew into the second tower. Like the rest of the civilized world, I was in shock and anguish over this incredible atrocity. The flight I wouldn't be taking that Martha referred to was to have taken me to L.A., where I had been engaged for three concerts with John Mauceri and the Hollywood Bowl Symphony. Mauceri had designed the concert as a tribute to the émigré musicians and composers who spent the 1950s in L.A. I was to sing my movie songs with the huge orchestra, plus the intimate piano versions of Schoenberg's *Cabaret Songs*. Broadway and TV star Nell Carter was also to appear.

My heart was in agony, as was the whole world's, for all the victims and their families, and I longed to be with my children, so far away in California. I also needed to find out if the concerts were still going to be happening. No matter what, I had never missed a performance if I could help it. As our mayor said on the air, we couldn't let the terrorists win. Life must go on.

After trying in vain to phone the Hollywood Bowl, it turned out that e-mail was the best form of communication at this time. Obviously, my piano rehearsal on September 12 had to be canceled, but they were not going to cancel the concerts two days later. Everyone was feeling defiant and wanting to go on. I was told to take whatever flight I could get to L.A., let them know I was coming, and they would meet me.

Before I got in touch with the people at the Bowl they had called my daughter Martha to see if I was all right, and if she thought I would be able to make the concert.

"My mom is like a pit bull," Martha replied. "If she has a concert and needs to get there, she will find a plane and hang onto the wings with her teeth if need be!"

How well my children know me!

The orchestra rehearsal was still going to happen on September 13, with the dress rehearsal at the Bowl the next morning. The first concert was scheduled for the evening of the 14th. I spent all day on Tuesday the 11th alternating between watching the unfathomable news on TV and trying to book any flight I could to get to L.A. The next day I did the same thing. Of course, every time I would book something, the flight would be canceled before the transaction could even be completed.

Finally, at the end of the day on Wednesday, I got through to United Airlines and was able to book a flight that was scheduled to leave at 4:00 P.M. on Thursday. This flight was the one that might possibly get me to the rehearsal at Warner Bros. Studios on Thursday night. The three-hour time difference would be working in my favor.

Thursday morning I got up very early (I knew I might need the extra time at the airport with all that had occurred), dragged my huge suitcase into the street, and took a cab to Newark Airport in New Jersey, only to find when I got there that *my* flight was to leave from Kennedy Airport in Queens! Back downstairs and outside I went, schlepping the huge bag behind me, and hailed a cab. Before I even got in, the cab driver told me that JFK was closed down due to a passenger with a knife in his shoes!

I slammed the cab door, schlepped my way back to the ticket counter, totally obscured by the chaotic hordes of confused travelers trying to get to their destinations. When I finally got to the counter, I was told that the only flight they had from Newark left at 3:00 P.M. that day, but was sold out. It was waiting-list time. Incredibly, and perhaps inevitably, when the flight time arrived, half the passengers didn't show up and I got a seat.

It was a slightly eerie feeling knowing there were four armed military men in combat uniforms in the back of the plane. I didn't have a clue who or what they were going to shoot up there in the blue, but it was a comfort to have them anyway in those trying times. When we landed at LAX airport, chaos ruled. No one was allowed to pick up anyone at curbside, and I was told to take a shuttle bus to parking lot B and tell my party to meet me there. I was able to use a pay phone (I didn't own a cell phone yet) to reach the cell phone of the person picking me up, and then I got on the bus. Unfortunately, I was let off at a very deserted parking lot A instead of B, and, without a cell phone, I was stranded with no way to find my pickup. Thank the Lord someone with a mobile phone walked by and was kind enough to let me use it.

"Oh, don't worry," the voice on the other end of the phone promised. "I'm very close. I'll be there in a few minutes."

Forty-five minutes later (don't ask), I was whisked off to Warner Bros. (where I had recorded the soundtrack of *My Fair Lady*) and got there in the middle of the rehearsal. I had made it. It seemed that I had gotten on the *only* flight that left from the East Coast that day. Once again (and this is the story of my life), being in the wrong place at the right time somehow paid off.

Scott Dunn, my pianist, who was also coming from New York, was to accompany me on several of the Schoenberg *Cabaret Songs*. On the morning of the concert, however, Scott still hadn't shown up and no one could get in touch with him. Since he lived down by the World Trade Center in New York City, we were all afraid to say anything, but we started to fear the worst.

"Should we rehearse a substitute pianist?" I asked Mauceri. "No," he answered. "If he doesn't show up, we just won't do those songs."

The concert had been sold out (near 18,000 seats!), but many people were still in such a state of mourning and shock that they were unable to attend. For those who did attend, however, there was a feeling of urgent togetherness in the air. We were all still here and sharing our need for music together.

Before every concert at the Hollywood Bowl, the National Anthem is always sung. In the past, we all gave it a perfunctory once-over, as if by habit. I've even been known to forget the words. But on this night, as we sang with tears streaming down our faces, we were a single mass of soaring, praying souls, bewailing the loss of our own American innocence.

With still no word about Scott Dunn, the concert began. I sang some of my movie songs, and it looked like the concert would be shorter than planned. Then, suddenly, at intermission, in walked Scott! Whereas on Thursday I'd inadvertently caught the only plane that left from the East Coast, he had magically caught the only one out on Friday. By way of introducing us, Mauceri told the audience of the events of the last few days and how luck had been with us both. Then I set up the atmosphere of the Schoenberg *Cabaret Songs* I was about to perform. As I spoke, the huge audience of the Hollywood Bowl seemed to shrink down to nightclub size, so intimate was the focus. Our songs went over like wildfire and, at the end of the concert, we all symbolically joined hands while we loudly sang "God Bless America" with new vehemence. During the singing, without any provocation, the audience lit matches, cigarette lighters, and candles, as if to light our way to a better future.

"God Bless America," we sang, "my home sweet home!"

I knew then that there had been a reason I fought so hard to be there. The reason shone brightly in the light of those candles. It was this connection we all shared that night. We were one people, one heart, one nation. I felt honored to be a part of the music and the healing process. I know it is something I will never forget.

The cast of 70, Girls, 70 *at El Capitan Theatre in L.A.,* 2002. *(l to r: me, Robert Mandan, Charlotte Rae, Jane Kean, William Schallert) (Photo Ed Krieger)*

On March 23, 2003, the Roundabout Theatre Company presented yet another revival of a classic American musical entitled *Nine*. This show, with a book by playwright Arthur Kopit and a score by Maury Yeston, was based on the Fellini film *8½*. It had originally opened more than twenty years earlier under the inspired direction of Tommy Tune, who had the brilliant idea of making everyone but the leading man (Raul Julia and his young counterpart) a female character. The original production showcased some of the most dazzling female talent on Broadway (Anita Morris, Karen Akers, Liliane Montevecchi, Shelly Burch, Camille Saviola, and Kathi Moss, to name a few) and the show won a Tony Award as Best Musical.

Now it had been reimagined by a young British director named David Leveaux. The revival was designed around the bountiful talents of film star Antonio Banderas as Guido Contini, a Fellini-esque film director struggling with a mid-life crisis. Banderas possessed a surprisingly (well, not that surprising; he did star in the film version of *Evita*) mellifluous voice, and his energy won everyone's hearts.

When the show opened to rave reviews, however, I was *not* in the cast.

It was the same old story. I felt a bit like the *Follies* audition experience was coming back to haunt me. When I auditioned for the role of Guido's mother, both the director and the composer-lyricist Maury Yeston seemed to love me. Once again, my agent and I had been led to believe I had the part. And once again, just before the casting was finalized, they decided to go with the concept that all the women in the show had to be tall and leggy. Even Guido's mother! Height is something I knew I couldn't act, so the tall and leggy (and very talented) Mary Beth Peil won the role. Coincidentally, Mary Beth had also worked with Boris Goldovsky, singing opera at Tanglewood some years before, and had also been the last Anna opposite the late Yul Brynner in the Broadway revival of *The King and I*. Somehow we were connected.

The reviews were smashing and, with Banderas (plus the legendary Chita Rivera and TV and stage star Jane Krakowski) drawing the crowds, the show kept getting extended. Finally it was announced that most of the original cast would be leaving, but since the show was still going so strong (it had won the Tony Award for Best Revival), a new group of actors would be cast. This is where I came in. They hired John Stamos, most famous for his 1987–1995 TV series *Full House*, to play Guido and, now that tall and leggy wasn't a prerequisite anymore, I was cast as his mother. Hallelujah!

TV star Jenna Elfman, best known for the TV series *Dharma and Greg*, was hired to replace Jane Krakowski as Carla. Jane was a very tough act to follow. The character of Carla was the sexy Italian mistress of Guido, and she had a very funny and sensual song entitled "Call from the Vatican" to perform. In this production, the number was choreographed so that she sang the song in a sling that descended from the top of the stage. She needed to sing in an insinuatingly sexy manner, as she was lowered from the flies (the overhead space where scenery could be stored until needed) sitting in a sling. Toward the end of the song, she was pulled slowly back up to the flies, lying upside down in the

As Guido's mother on Broadway at the Eugene O'Neill Theatre in 2003, singing the title song of Nine *to nine-year-old Daniel Manche. (Photo Paul Kolnick)*

sling with her head hanging down facing the audience, all the while singing a long high C. It was a showstopping moment, and helped Krakowski win the Tony Award that year.

After the first dress rehearsal, Jenna Elfman, who had never sung in a musical before, let alone while ascending to the flies, made an announcement that she was not ready, and would not be going on when we opened. We were all shocked. The stage manager told us that Sara Gettelfinger, who had been understudying the role for months, would be playing the role, while Elfman continued "rehearsing." As fate had it, Sara did the first performance, knocked the audience dead, and a new star was born. Elfman never did return to her role in *Nine*.

My role wasn't large, but I enjoyed getting to use an Italian accent and singing the beautiful title song to the young nine-year-old version of Guido, played by Daniel Manche. Each night, I gloried in the performances of Eartha Kitt, Mary Stuart Masterson, Myra Lucretia Taylor, Rebecca Luker, and, of course, John Stamos.

I don't think John Stamos (a very sweet and generous colleague) was happy doing the show. Following Antonio Banderas couldn't have been easy, in any case. Despite the reviews and the awards, *Nine* lasted just a couple of months more, and only made me crave more Broadway experiences. I hope to be back on the Great White Way soon.

Ghosts. Who's afraid of them? I'm not! Not anymore. After all these years? For a while I may have resented being a ghost on the screen. Then I accepted it. Now I celebrate it. The more I accepted the ghost I was, the more human I became. Still, it took until very recently for me to understand the other ghost dwelling inside of me. The ghost that was holding back the healthy evolution of my family script.

In June of 2005, as the deadline for this book neared, I was in Atlanta, Georgia, participating in the Harrower Opera Workshop at Georgia State University. This is an unusual workshop that gives young opera singers exposure to professionals from all disciplines. It deals with acting, movement, and staging of opera scenes, culminating in a big gala where the students perform in various ways.

The year before, I was a visiting clinician who taught master classes and directed some opera scenes. This year my role was to be greatly expanded. I was asked to be the overall acting teacher, in addition to being assigned my usual individual coaching sessions and master classes. Unfortunately, I found out about my new duties only a week or so before I was to leave for Atlanta. I protested that there was not enough time for me to prepare a proper acting class. It's one thing to be a coach, direct a scene, and hone and refine a singer's approach to an aria or song, but quite another to prepare a class of two hours every day of the week for two weeks! Protest though I did, I realized that there was nothing for me to do but bite the bullet and obey my challenge buttons, which were being pushed. Something began to bubble inside and I found myself saying my usual "Yes, of course!" before really thinking it through.

Then the magic started.

While literally wondering what on earth I was going to do, I ran into a neighbor, Rory Pinto, who had recently been licensed as a psychotherapist. He asked if he could talk to me about the creative process. I told him I would be happy to speak with him but, due to the impending workshop, my time was limited. We made a date to chat. Right after making the date with him, I "accidentally" encountered one of my voice students, who is also an actress. I asked her if she had ever taught a full-time acting class. She had, and the next day, she brought me some of her books on acting and we discussed the idea of "theater games."

Theater games are designed to introduce and increase performance or creative skills. The best theater games have neither winners nor losers. The participants work individually or with others to accomplish the goal of the game, and if the goal or point of focus is not accomplished on the first attempt, the participants have still learned something from the experience.

In the middle of our conversation, as per our appointment, Rory Pinto rang the bell and joined us. After my student left, Rory stayed on to interview me. He told me that he, too, had used theater games in his psychology classes and intended to use them in his therapeutic practice. We talked, traded games and ideas, and the clouds began to part. From these discussions, I started to become more confident that I might be able to handle the classes I had to teach.

When I arrived in Atlanta and met the eager and talented students, my confidence expanded. I somehow knew that I could do it. Don't ask how I knew, but I did, and everything just fell into place. Incredibly, without really knowing what I was going to do, I just did it. For the first time in this kind of situation, I felt I was in a bubble of well-being. Every decision I made, even while winging it on occasion, seemed to spring from a well of deeply connected purpose.

Each class addressed various aspects of the performing arts, and each one helped the students to discover and solve their own emotional disorders and hang-ups. Together we dealt with many of the usual nerve and fright problems that plague performers.

As the week went on, it began to dawn on me that I had solved a major problem of my own. Actually, I hadn't solved it at all. *It* had solved itself.

What was the problem, you may well ask?

Control and fear. Those interrelated cousins have haunted many lives, including mine. Strangely, I lived loosely and fearlessly onstage, but it seemed that fear of the unknown had always fed into my need to control personal situations. This need to control was a gift from my mother and her mother before her.

I remembered that time when I was five years old and got lost walking home from kindergarten. I remembered the desperation and fear. I also remembered my mother's voice telling me that I shouldn't have goofed. That I should have been perfect. Perfect?

After all this time, and with all the skills I've been able to acquire, why did I still have the need to control, and why did I have the same childish fear of betrayal? I needed to be perfect. Why? Because, I learned, I had not been truly centered, and therefore could not be completely "here." All these years my colleagues have known me as skilled, precise, instinctual, and a perfectionist. I have always empowered my students to find their own centers. Ironically, in my own personhood, I had never had the nerve to know that I was already "here" myself, and available to myself. If only I had known! But I was stuck with the same old tapes of impossible expectations echoing in my head.

"That's not what we do," Mother yelled at the five-year-old Marni as she wept. "These are not the 'rules.' You don't goof. And you should have listened! Either you're perfect, Marni, or you're nothing!"

Today, psychologists might say that Mother, who was definitely a high-functioning person, had "narcissistic personality traits." This terminology can be confusing because of the word "narcissistic."

In my lay understanding, a baby—who is normally narcissistic—eventually reaches the stage where he or she begins to form an identity separate from the parent. If for some reason this does not occur, from that point on, anything that happens is perceived by the child not as circumstance driven, but as if it were caused by the child him- or herself. That means that if something is not perfect, or does not work out right, the child feels responsible; he or she does not "exist" if things are not perfect. This child then "becomes" the imperfection and unwittingly transfers this tendency to his or her children. And on and on it goes, from one generation to the next.

I have only recently begun to understand that my mother was treated in this way by her mother and, being the last in a long line of matriarchs, had to fight for her own survival. She, in turn, perpetuated this behavior in her children, and, according to my daughters, I have, in my own way, sometimes treated them just as my mother had treated me. None of this is easy. My children, of course, had been confused and hurt in those times when I acted like my mother. I thought I knew enough not to "be" my mother, but it was all too ingrained in my script and I, somehow, didn't avoid the pitfalls. This applied to my life and career, as well. The fear of betrayal and need for control sometimes took over and were detrimental to everything around me.

Teaching the acting class in Atlanta became a personal epiphany. It was magic. I left the fear and the control behind and just went with the flow. By using my intuition and trusting my subconscious, I not only helped the students along, but like a mirror, what I taught reflected back to and onto me to absorb and project yet again. The result of seeing the actor-singers respond made me understand my very attraction to becoming an actress in the first place. What keeps me getting better and better at that craft is the need to center myself and accept myself the way I am.

How many people had told me, "Just be yourself, Marni?" "We hired you because of who you are." Martha Schlamme told me. Dick Seader (one of the producers of *Taking My Turn*) told me. Victor Borge and Liberace told me. Richard Nelson told me. I heard them all, but just didn't know what they meant, I guess. Mother wanted me to be perfect; I just needed to be me.

It's so simple. "Listen to yourself, trust yourself, and accept yourself." That adds up to finding your own true voice saying, "Love yourself." Simple? Human.

How I long to walk into the past and hug that five-year-old girl crying on the vast lawn and tell her that I love her. I want her to know that it was all right to get lost. That she was only human and I wasn't really being betrayed.

I guess what I am finding out is that my whole life has been about becoming truly human, in all its vulnerable ways. The striving (with various degrees of success from the outside) has all stemmed from the desire to evolve. Even the process of writing this book has contributed to my "humanization." To finding out how my children perceived me. To finding out in what ways I was driven. To accepting how much like my mother (and my father, too, don't forget) I really am. Maybe even to starting to realize why I chose my husbands.

I feel lucky, after seventy-five years, to have the chance to clarify and work through the emotional traumas of my relationship with my kids. And I'm sure it's not over yet. Is it ever?

My daughter Melani says, "Mom, don't worry so much about the past."

I'm trying.

I guess I was more of a ghost than anyone knew, including myself. Underneath all my vitality, verve, and energy was a ghost somewhere inside all the time. A ghost of a human being.

Sometimes in bed, when it's quiet, late at night, I turn and just look at Al, my sometimes friend, my sometimes mortal enemy, and I realize that we are total opposites. Neither of us are perfect, nor is our relationship. We admittedly drive each other crazy sometimes, but we love each other and show it in our different ways. Al can judge and grunt, and growl and disapprove. But it's amazing how he can just "be there" and sniff the flowers. Although I oftentimes think that he is from Venus and I am from Mars, I also think that somewhere and somehow we do need each other. And he won't go away.

In the end, the ghosts to shed are merely the superficial veils that can cover the human experience inside of us. So my journey proceeds from here, and who knows where it will lead? Here's to curtains going up. To voices on the screen. To acting and singing on and on.

To evolving, developing, and changing. And just think about it. I don't have to come back and *be* a ghost. I've already been one! Deborah's ghost, Natalie's ghost, Audrey's ghost. Marni's ghost.

I have only one question. Just how long can this process take, for heaven's sake?

As they say in Yiddish, the "ganse mishpocha"! The entire family at Christmas 2005: Back row with tree in between: Andrew Gold (with his family all in front of him), Tim Carr. 2nd row: Emily Gold, Vanessa Gold (Andy's ex-wife), Victoria Gold, husband Al Block (that's me seated in front), Dr. Richard Carr, Martha (Gold) Carr, Alicia Carr, Robert Light, Jr. (Jan Gold's son), Dr. Howard Friedman. 1st row is Olivia Gold, me, seated next to Melani (Gold) Friedman, holding Alma Sophia Friedman, Jan Gold (Ernest's third wife and widow). (Photo Tim Carr)

Index